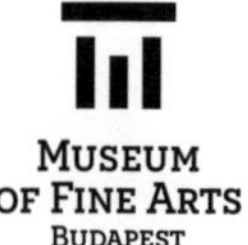

MNG HUNGARIAN NATIONAL GALLERY

MUSEUM OF FINE ARTS BUDAPEST

Systems of Logic / Logic of Systems: The Art and Mind of Agnes Denes

Museum of Fine Arts - Hungarian National Gallery, Budapest, 2024

Foreword

Sixteen years have passed since the 2008 exhibition of Hungarian-born, New York-based artist Agnes Denes, held at the Ludwig Museum in Budapest. The Museum of Fine Arts, Budapest is delighted to once again offer the public a glimpse of this fascinating and rich oeuvre with our representative exhibition. A selection of drawings, prints, and photographic documentation will attempt to survey all the major groups and periods of the oeuvre.

Agnes Denes is a major figure in international contemporary art. Born in Budapest in 1931, she moved with her family to Sweden in the 1940s and later to the United States. As a young woman, she started writing poems before turning to the visual arts, but she soon found the boundaries of traditional artforms constrictive. Denes thus began a systematic visual experimentation that drew on findings from various disciplines. She reinterpreted mathematical, philosophical, psychological and linguistic research into her art in an original and innovative way.

Agnes Denes was a trailblazer with her environmental and ecological approach to art. In the late 1960s, she coined the concept of *Eco-Logic*, which referred to the two pillars of her complex artistic thinking: ecology and logic. Many of the environmental and socially conscious art movements of our time would be unthinkable without Agnes Denes's large-scale land art projects. The exhibition includes photographic documentation of some of the artist's most emblematic ecological works, including the 1982 action *Wheatfield – A Confrontation*, in which she sowed wheat in a Manhattan landfill site and later harvested the crop.

As a message to the people of the future, the time capsule is a recurring element of Agnes Denes's projects. The motif first appeared in her 1968 performance *Rice/Tree/Burial*, in which she buried a manuscript of her haikus for the future. In later versions of the performance, the time capsule was filled with answers to a questionnaire she had formulated, recording contemporary people's ideas and feelings about the future. Over the past decades, Agnes Denes has created several time capsule installations in different parts of the world, which carry the message of today for the people who will uncover them in a thousand years. We are delighted that her next time capsule will be placed in the renewed City Park, Budapest in the spring of 2025 as a special event accompanying the exhibition.

It has been an exceptional privilege to work closely with Agnes Denes at every stage of the preparation of this exhibition. We thank her for her time and energy, her ideas and her invaluable thoughts, which helped us create the exhibition and this catalogue. The more we got to know her and her art, the more we admired her inexhaustible energy, her insights and attention to detail. For decades, Agnes Denes's art and ideas have given strength and direction to a human world that has much to learn from her as it faces an ecological crisis.

László Baán
General Director of the Museum of Fine Arts, Budapest

Manifesto

Working with a paradox

Defining the elusive

Visualizing the invisible

Communicating the incommunicable

Not accepting the limitations society has accepted

Seeing in new ways

Living for a fraction of a second and penetrating light years

Using intellect and instinct to achieve intuition

Achieving total self-consciousness and self-awareness

Being creatively obsessive

Questioning, reasoning, analyzing, dissecting and re-examining

Understanding the finitude of human existence and still striving
to create beauty and provocative reasoning

Finding new concepts, recognizing new patterns

Desiring to know the importance or insignificance of existence

Seeing reality and still being able to dream

Persisting in the eternal search

I believe that artistic vision, image and metaphor are powerful tools of communication that became expressions of human values with profound impact on our consciousness and collective destiny.

I plant forests on abused land to be kept alive for centuries and fields of grain in the heart of megacities. This work goes beyond just planting a field or a forest, or creating masterplans for large spaces. It is benign problem solving and shaping, structuring the future: an ego-less art form that calls attention to social concerns and involves people from all walks of life. It builds pride and self-esteem in people and benefits future generations with a meaningful legacy.

Some of my works deal with inner space, visualizing invisible processes such as time, mathematics. logic, thinking processes, evolution, other works are dealing with very large spaces, large by necessity in order to rebuild our environment and make a difference. As difficult as it is to realize these works, it is absolutely necessary to make them happen all over the world as examples of what needs to be done to restore landfills, or destroyed barren land where resource extraction has taken its toll, and on deforested soil to stop erosion, purify the air, protect fresh groundwater and provide homes for wildlife. And it is important to do them in the nervous tension of cities to afford people a chance to stay in touch with nature. And on the journey inward, it is equally important to give analytical propositions shape and form for better understanding.

© Agnes Denes

Art for the Third Millennium – Creating a New World View (Excerpt from a Lecture)

Agnes Denes

I started out as a poet but gave up poetry for the visual expression when I lost my language.

I realized that art had to change in a world drastically changing, when humanity was facing major decisions in order to survive on the planet while striving to maintain moral values and quality of life. I wanted to cleanse art from its elitist self-involvement, to achieve greater universal validity. I left the ivory tower of my studio and entered the world of concerns. I wrote books, spoke at global conferences and began to create large scale environmental projects I called *Philosophy in the Land*. I created *Rice/Tree/Burial*, the first large scale ecological site work in 1968 with these concerns in mind (fig. 1, cat. no. 26).

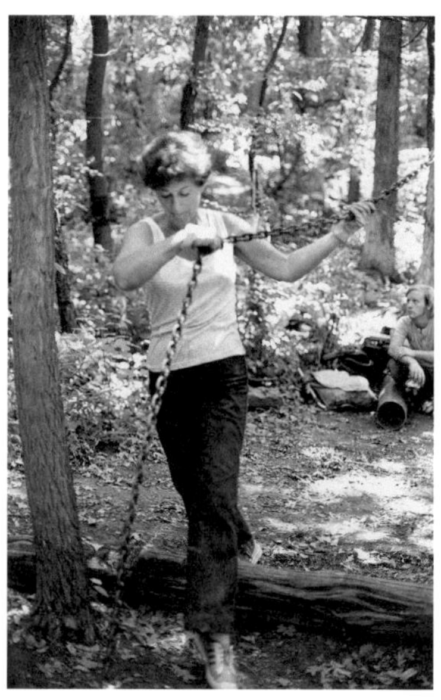

(fig. 1) Rice/Tree/Burial Project (Tree Chaining), 1977–1979/2012 [cat. no. 26]

These works probed ecological, cultural, and social issues; explored the paradoxes of human existence, and addressed global survival. I began by visualizing invisible process such as logic, thought processes, evolution, time, music (sound), and mathematics. Some of these works became the building blocks for my pyramids, expressions of social philosophy: an investigation of what it means to be human that eventually became survival structures for humanity.

The early *Philosophical Drawings* took me into the sciences, technology, dialectics, symbolic logic, theology, time & truth functions (fig. 2, cat. nos. 1–5). I was beginning to unite disciplines alienated through specialization, and came to look at art as an integrator of disciplines and the role of the artist as developing a new vision for humanity.

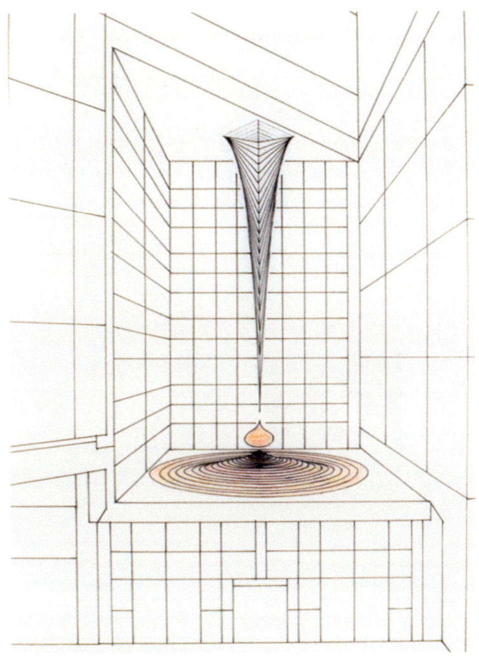

(fig. 2) <u>Systems of Logic/Logic of Systems</u>:
Teardrop Monument with Upside-down Logic
Finalist Drawing for University City Science
Center Philadelphia, 1988

I believe that the new role of the artist is to create an art that questions the status quo and the direction life has taken, the endless contradictions we accept and approve, offering intelligent alternatives.

The issues touched on in my work range between individual creation and social consciousness. They address the challenges of global survival and are often monumental in scale – by necessity. It has to be to make a statement and make a difference.

I plant forests on abused land to be kept alive for centuries and fields of grain in the heart of megacities. This work goes beyond just planting a field or a forest, or creating a masterplans for large territories in need of rebuilding. It is benign problem solving and shaping, structuring the future: an egoless art form that calls attention to social concerns and involves people from all walks of life.

They address the first species that can consciously control its own evolution and have also begun controlling nature.

The philosophy behind my work is to create meaningful and memorable works of art that build pride and self esteem in people, inspiring young minds to feel good about themselves and have the courage to achieve their dreams.

These works are intended to help the environment and benefit future generations with a meaningful legacy. They open doors to the future. My foremost concerns are the welfare of humanity and the quality of life.

This new art form goes beyond the self and the ego without being selfless. It assumes the difficult task of maintaining a delicate balance between thinking globally and acting independently, for the ego must remain intact to allow the self to act fearlessly, with the certainty and confidence necessary for true creation, while the ego must be relinquished in order to think universally and for the good of others. So it's self-esteem vs selflessness.

Designing space is complicated. We can go inward into inner space and out into the universe. The distance is about the same. For me both of these journeys are necessary. Some of my work deals with this inner space, visualizing invisible processes such as time, mathematics, logic, thinking processes, evolution, and so on. Other works are dealing with very large spaces, large by necessity in order to rebuild our environment and to make a difference.

Artistic vision, image, and metaphor are powerful tools of communication that can become expressions of human values with profound impact on our consciousness and collective destiny.

Rice/Tree/Burial, first realized in 1968, was philosophical in orientation and dealt with our relationship to the earth. I planted a rice field above the Niagara gorge at the border of the US and Canada, chained a sacred Indian forest, and buried a time capsule to be opened in 1,000 years – it included my Haiku poetry. I kept no copies. Then I went out to the edge of Niagara Falls and for eight days and nights lived a foot away from the torrent. It was a "symbolic" event that announced my commitment to environmental issues and human concerns.

In 1982 I created *Wheatfield – A Confrontation*, planting and harvesting 2 acres of wheat in Manhattan's financial district on land worth $4.5 billion (fig. 3, cat. nos. 27– 41). The work addressed greed and misplaced priorities. Wheatfield was a calling to account, it represented food, energy, commerce, world trade, economics. It referred to mismanagement, waste, world hunger, and ecological concerns.

Another project, *Tree Mountain – A Living Time Capsule – 11,000 Trees, 11,000 People, 400 Years*, 1982– 1996 (fig. 4, cat. no. 42). commissioned ten years after its design, is a 400 year project, allowing the ecosystems to rebuild itself. It is considered one of the largest reclamation sites in the world and the first to deal with creating a man-made virgin forest for our descendants. It involves the first human contract that reaches 400 years into the future.

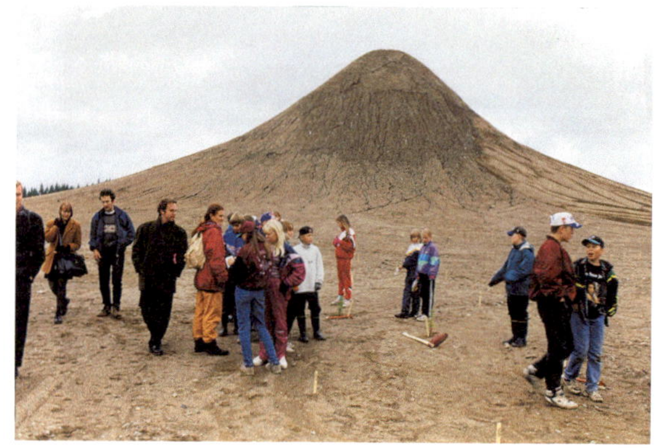

(fig. 4) <u>Tree Mountain - A Living Time Capsule</u> Finnish Children, 1992-1996

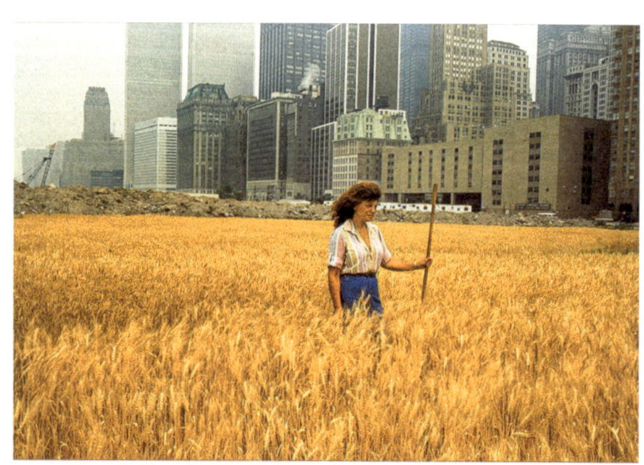

(fig. 3) <u>Wheatfield - A Confrontation: Battery Park Landfill, Downtown Manhattan - With Agnes Denes Standing in the Field</u>, 1982 Photo: John McGrail

A millennial work is a 25 year masterplan that involves 85 kilometers of the center of the Netherlands to be restructured and made environmentally conscious. To deal with the expense, I designed a full size glass fortress that stands as total opposite to the opaque fortresses of the past occupying the site. With its myriads of reflections this unique structure will enhance tourism and help defray some of the costs involved.

My forest in Australia of 6,000 trees planted in 1998 addresses endangered species and land erosion. And *Poetry Walk – Reflections: Pools of Thought*, at the University of Virginia rescues the essence of great minds from sinking into dusty memory by bringing them into fruitful use and present relevance.

These projects are difficult because there is no precedence for them. But as difficult as it is to realize these works, it is absolutely necessary to make them happen all over the world as examples of what needs to be done to restore landfills, or destroyed, barren land where resource extraction has taken its toll, and on deforested soil to stop erosion, purify the air, protect fresh ground water and provide home for wildlife. And to create them in the nervous tension of cities, to give people a chance to stay in touch with nature, allowing it to speak its own special language articulated through human intelligence (fig. 5).

Although I am foremost an artist, my large scale environmental work requires knowledge beyond the techniques of art and becomes a blend of architecture, landscaping, design, urban planning, soil science, mathematics, forestry, the social sciences and philosophy.

I look at art as the integrator of disciplines, and see the role of the artist is to develop (as developing) a new vision for humanity.

The powerful tools of artistic vision, image and metaphor become expressions of human values with profound impact on our consciousness and collective destiny. This is not just the artist being a modern day shaman, but a new breed of scientific and technological seer and sensitizer.

© Agnes Denes 1996

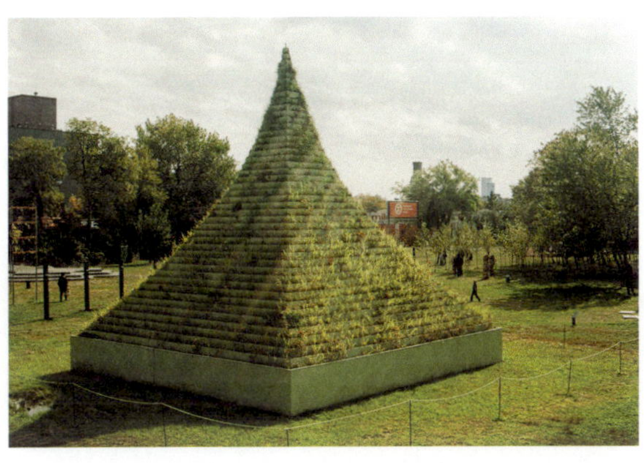

(fig. 5) <u>The Living Pyramid</u>, 2015, Socrates Sculpture Park, Long Island City, New York, USA

When I designed my future cities that foresaw global warming and weather problems 40 years ago, the project got no that attention at all. It was handled as an artist's project not a serious scientific investigation because it was beautiful. The attention it received was for beautiful drawings, not for protecting humanity from disasters.

And now, when we are facing major weather issues and global warming can no longer be ignored, my present project of designing dunes for the Rockaway shores and a barrier islands to hold back the sea, is going to be taken seriously. I will talk about this further when showing images of my work.

Systems of Logic – Logic of Systems:

The Art and Mind of Agnes Denes

Mónika Kumin

"The eternal paradox built into the universe has shaped my book. As we grow up, it slowly dawns on us that there are no ultimate conclusions, only intermediate steps in a process that never ends."[1]
Agnes Denes

In summer 1982, Agnes Denes and a group of volunteers sowed and later harvested wheat on a two-acre landfill site in lower Manhattan, New York, not far from the World Trade Center. Denes's emblematic project *Wheatfield – A Confrontation* [cat. nos. 27–41] attracted an unusual amount of media attention. The iconic photograph taken by John McGrail of the artist as a "modern-day Demeter",[2] standing staff in hand amidst the waving golden wheat, was published by the world's press. It even made its way across the Iron Curtain, appearing in the 9 February 1983 issue of socialist Hungary's trade union journal *Népszava* (fig. 6), together with a detailed description of the project.[3] The artist's Hungarian origins gave the subject added relevance. Then 52 years old, Agnes Denes had lived outside Hungary for decades. With a unique artistic output to her name, she nevertheless regarded herself as a philosopher at least as much as a fine artist. The intellectual prowess with which she addressed the global survival of humanity, her synthesis of various knowledge systems, and the related complex visuality, have led many of those familiar with her art to refer to her as a visionary or a "modern Leonardo".[4] As Emma Enderby put it, on the occasion of the artist's 2019 retrospective: "Her vision was radical and in retrospect, terrifyingly prophetic."[5]

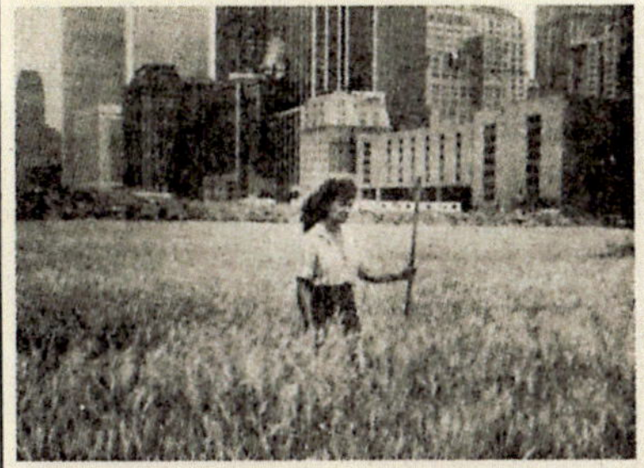

Búzaföld mint műalkotás

A képen látható búzaföld nem az, aminek látszik, hanem műalkotás. A magyar származású képzőművész, Agnes Dénes úgy gondolta, szembeállítja a túlnépesedett, elgépiesedett, kifinomult várost a vidék széles távlataival, ezért aztán New York, *Manhattan kellős közepén,* hat háztömbnyire a Munka Világközpontjának iker felhőkarcolóitól búzát ültetett. A terület eredetileg — ugyan későbbi építkezésre kijelölt — roncstelep volt, amelyet Agnes Dénes előbb munkatársaival letisztogatott, majd vidékről 500 köbméter termőföldet hozatott, és ezt öt centiméteres rétegben szétterítette a roncstelep fölött, végül a kézileg megművelt területen elvetettek hat véka acélos észak-dakotai *búzát.*

A *koncept-art* jegyében készült műalkotás természetesen keveset mond a világ művészetkedvelő millióinak, s noha húsz magánszemély meg a New York városi művészeti alap tízezer dolláros támogatása művészi célt szolgált, a munka igazi érdekessége *környezetvédelmi jelle*gű. A nagy kérdés ugyanis az volt, kibírja-e a vidék tiszta levegőjéhez szokott gabona a világ egyik *legszennyezettebb városának* esős, szmogos klímáját. Ezt a Cornell egyetem mezőgazdásza, dr. John Ameroso figyelte, és igen érdekes megfigyeléseket tett: „Amint a búza nőni kezdett, kialakította saját mikrokörnyezetét. Megjelentek az imádkozó sáskák, szöcskék, szentjánosbogarak, és itt, a város közepén, még kilométerekre is érezni lehetett a *búzaföldek illatát.*" A környezeti hatások természetesen megtették a magukét: a búzát elég korán *megtámadta a gabonaüszök,* és a vegyszeres-ónos esőktől penészbetegséget kapott. Ahogy Ameroso költőien mondotta, a búza gyorsan közeledik a végelgyengülés felé, ezért korai aratásra lesz szükség. Mindenesetre a kísérlet valamit bizonyított: bárhogy igyekszünk is, a természetet egészen még nem pusztítottuk el, az Életben még léteznek — eddig *ismeretlen* — *vésztartalékok.*

D. Á.

(fig. 6) Á. D.: "Búzaföld mint műalkotás"
[Wheatfield as artwork]
Népszava, 9 February 1983

Agnes Denes began writing poetry at a very young age, while still living in Budapest. In view of the increasingly grave war situation, she moved with her family to Sweden in the 1940s, before settling in the United States. Later, she wrote that, as a poet, "she had lost her mother tongue".[6] Visual art gave her a way out of this enforced silence. She studied painting first at the New School in New York, and then at Columbia University. In the early 1960s, she worked in the then fashionable, nonfigurative styles, and her work was even shown in exhibitions. In the early 1960s, New York, where Denes still lives, had just "stolen the idea of modern art"[7] from Paris. Clement Greenberg's essential modernism – the concept of "flatness" and the masculine heroism of the most influential artists of the period (Ellsworth Kelly, Barnett Newman, and Ad Reinhardt) – eventually felt restrictive to Denes. "It seemed like someone else's language",[8] she recalled. She moved beyond the dimensions of the easel painting, embarking on the kind of systematic visual experimentation that synthesised several academic disciplines. She was fascinated by mathematics, philosophy, psychology, biology, and linguistics, while her formal experiments were associated with conceptualism, systematic art, site-specific art, and land art. Deneswas also influenced by the information art of the 1960s. Her investigations were inspired by language and mathematics. In the late 1960s, she began an extensive series of "philosophical drawings" – pencil and ink drawings, as well as monotypes, drawn freehand on graph paper with extraordinary delicacy and elegance. Denes's goal was to visualise the "invisible processes" that probe "the essence and self-contradictions of human knowledge".[9]

In one of the early works from the series *Strength Analysis – A Dictionary of Strength*, produced between 1965 and 1971 [cat. no. 2],[10] Denes extracted from *Webster's International Dictionary* all the words signifying "strength" in one form or another. She arranged the resulting 3,000 words into a triangle (or pyramid), where they interacted with one another, while their definitions were organised into a constantly fluctuating, changing texture. "Held together by their own strength, the words created an undulating form, like a swarm of bees."[11] In Denes's methodology, her individual series are typically an integral part of profound academic research. She spent years studying the individual aspects of an issue; her written output includes volumes of scientific, philosophical, and poetic texts.[12]

One of her most important philosophical drawings is the 1968 work *Dialectic Triangulation: A Visual Philosophy,*[13] a large-scale print divided into three parts [cat. no. 1]. The upper section contains meticulously drawn two- and three-dimensional geometrical shapes, based on the figure of the triangle. The triangle – one of the most fundamental and important conceptual shapes in Denes's art – functions as a kind of "idea generator". The triangular shapes combine into various flow diagrams, while condensed into a single image they evoke the whole of cultural history. In Denes's words, *Dialectic Triangulation* endeavours "to locate and expose the center of things, the true inner core of inherent but not yet understood or disclosed meaning".[14] *The Human Argument* – which also exists as an independent work – forms a discrete unit within the composition. Taking as its starting point Whitehead and Russell's mathematical system, and presenting "claims and contradictions", it attempts to illustrate the processes of "the human argument" and deductive logic, as well as the contradictions of thought.[15]

Denes unceasingly tests the limits of "facts" and logic, experimenting with paradoxes in order to convey a more profound and intuitive understanding of reality. She is fascinated by the nature of "reality": its relativism, mutability, and illusory quality. "We must accept the possibility that there may be no language to describe ultimate reality, beyond the language of visions", she wrote.[16]

In the 1969 installation *Human Dust*[17] (fig. 7) as well as in the *Book of Dust*,[18] on which she worked continuously between 1972 and 1988, logic and science are accompanied by her unique poetics. As one of her important materials, *dust* "symbolises the elements of the ultimate, unchanging laws and dynamics that govern the fate of the universe".[19] In Denes's later ecological works, *dust* undergoes repeated transformations: it is the soil in *Rice/Tree/Burial* [cat. nos. 25–26], in which she sows grains of rice and buries a time capsule; and it is the *Wheatfield – A Confrontation* landfill, as well as the soil that yields ears of wheat. It symbolises both destruction and rebirth, "residue as well as raw material, the fabric as well as the essence".[20]

The goal of the series *Introspection* is to reveal unexplored correlations. The first part, *Introspection I – Evolution* (1968–1971), portrays the story of evolution from the first anthropoids to the beginnings of art. *Introspection II – Machines, Tools & Weapons* (1972) (figs. 9–10). explores advances in technology, from the handheld tools of prehistoric humans to the atomic bomb. The two works, which create the impression of monumental photographic negatives or X-ray images, are monotypes, each measuring over 5 metres in length, printed on pre-sensitised paper using a special technique. Both comprise sequences of horizontally composed diagrams, like something out of an old medical or engineering handbook. Through her profound exploration of visual cultural history, Denes moves beyond the traditional pictorial dimension: with their sideways progression, her image sequences, executed with painstaking realism, are simultaneously reminiscent of Egyptian wall paintings, the painted narrative cycles on medieval church walls, and academic tomes.

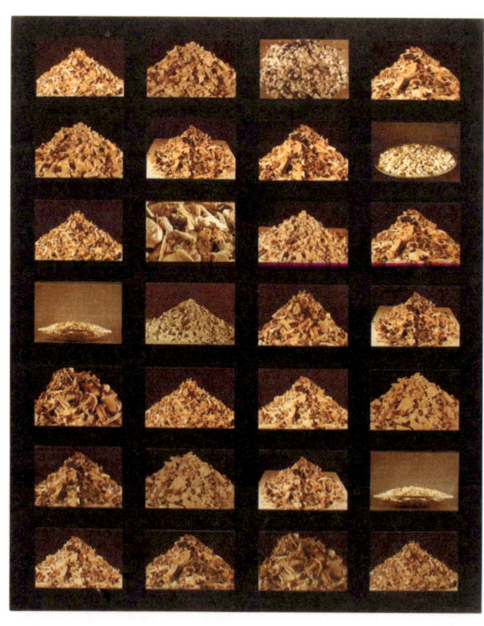

(fig. 7) <u>Human Dust</u>, 1969

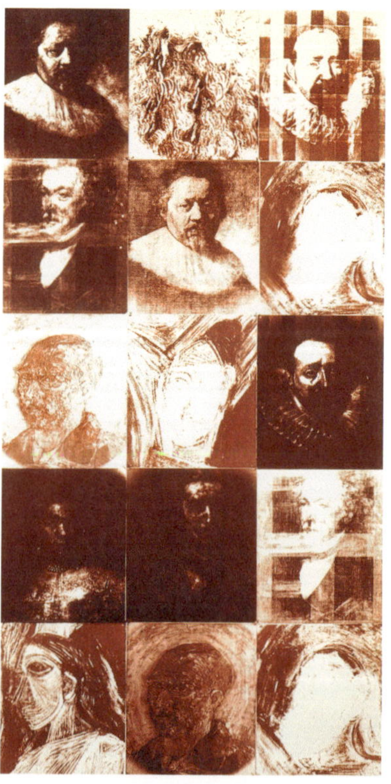

(fig. 8) <u>Introspection III – Aesthetics</u>, 1972

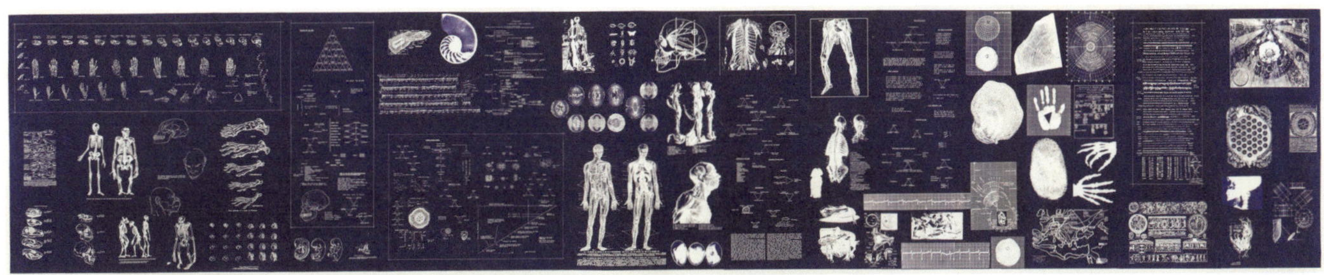

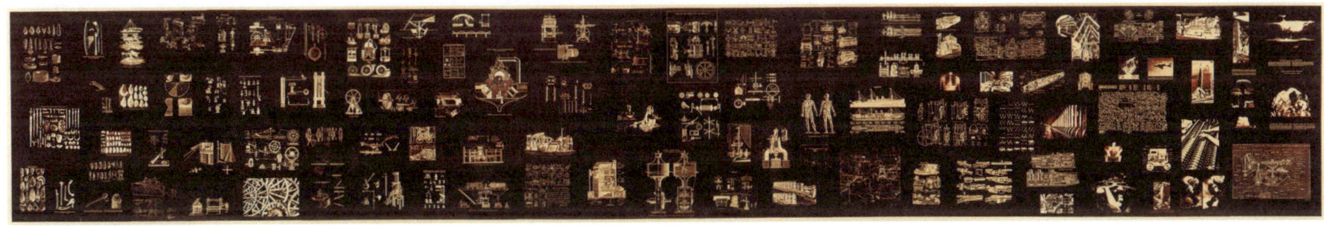

(fig. 9) <u>Introspection I - Evolution</u>, 1968-1971
(fig. 10) <u>Introspection II - Machines, Tools & Weapons</u>, 1972

Denes even uses "X-ray vision" to probe the history of painting. The third piece in the *Introspection* series (*Introspection III – Aesthetics*, 1972) comprises X-ray images of the most significant self-portraits in the history of painting (Rembrandt, Van Gogh, Picasso) (fig. 8). Using X-ray, the artist "peels back" the layers of pigment to expose the "inner life" of the paintings and the mystery of the original brushwork.[21]

The individual works in the *Kingdom Series* [cat. nos. 45–49], produced between 1971 and 1973, are also associated with the analysis of substructures. These large-scale X-ray images of plants and animals reveal "the strange beauty and exquisite anatomical structuring one may imagine but never otherwise see in these forms".[22] In *Anima/Persona – The Seed* (1978–1980) [cat. nos. 50–51], a series of micro photographs, Denes likewise worked with plants, capturing the development of sprouting seeds, movements invisible to the naked eye. The results were displayed in the form of large-scale, representative images. Denes was so intensely interested in the definition and nature of growth, that she recorded the sprouting of a seed over three days, later turning the photographs into a 360-degree hologram.[23]

Besides science, spirituality is an important aspect of Agnes Denes's art, as demonstrated in her ecological projects as well as her philosophical drawings and *Pyramid* series. In her essay *On Spirituality*, written in 2000, she defines "powerful art" as art that "lifts you out of your everyday existence" to ascend to another, spiritual location.[24] In the *Introspection* and *Kingdom* series, Denes was concerned not only with revealing the hidden correlations of micro and macro structures, but also with unravelling the mysterious and unknown that underlie reason. Anyone familiar with Hungarian modernism might instinctively associate the works in these series with the concept of bio-romanticism, coined by the Hungarian art critic Ernst Kállai, who, taking as his starting point the neo-romantic and biocentric theories popular at the turn of the 19th and 20th centuries, combined the contemporary natural-scientific worldview with the visuality of nonfigurative-surrealist art.[25] The illustrations in Kállai's 1947 volume *The Hidden Face of Nature*, and the reproductions from the *New World View* exhibition, including works by Yves Tanguy, Paul Klee, and Wassily Kandinsky, also featured "micro and X-ray images, engineering drawings, and diagrams".[26] In fact, one of the sources for Kállai's bio-romanticism was Ernst Haeckl, the German biologist and palaeontologist who is regarded as the founder of modern ecology, who illustrated his popular volumes, *Kunstformen der Natur*, published from 1899 with his own drawings. In relation to bio-romanticism, Kállai was interested not only in nature but also in irrationality, the "depths of the soul", influenced primarily by C. G. Jung.[27] Kállai was greatly inspired by his years at the Bauhaus, and by the art theory of Wassily Kandinsky, among others. Another influential art teacher at the Bauhaus school was László Moholy-Nagy, who, in his 1929 volume *From Material to Architecture*, compared natural structures with constructivist art and architecture. He later transferred the "new vision" and the practice of the Bauhaus to the "New Bauhaus", which opened in 1937 in Chicago. The teachers at the Chicago school included Moholy-Nagy's former colleague György Kepes (also a Hungarian), who, as the first director of the MIT Center for Advanced Visual Studies, advocated the intentional harmonisation of scientific disciplines, art, and ecology. In the foreword to his 1965 collection of essays *Structure in Art and Science*, he argued at length for the "marriage" of science, nature, and art, the task of modern science and art alike being to chart the structures of those forces that sustain and unite our world.[28] Denes's criteria are in many respects analogous with those of Kepes, since her goal is likewise to unite "disciplines alienated through specialisation". She too saw art as an "integrator of disciplines", its most important role being to "develop a new vision for humanity".[29]

Agnes Denes, of course, was not familiar with the works of Kállai or Kepes, she went her own way. One of the most attractive examples of micro- and macrocosmic perspectives in her oeuvre is the 1973 drawing *Point + Line + Intellect = Artist's Tool* (fig. 11), in which she schematically recorded the forms of motion of liquid crystals, galaxies, and subatomic particles, simultaneously alluding to Leonardo's studies of movement, Kandinsky's 1926 book *Point and Line to Plane*, and reproductions from Kállai's *New World View*. Denes encoded her own artistic manifesto into the morse code of the final frame: "If the mind possesses universal validity, art reveals a universal truth. I want that truth."[30]

The pyramid, which is present in many cultures (often in burial structures), is Denes's paradigmatic model for visionary art that connects past, present, and future. The *Pyramid* series [cat. nos. 6–15] that she began in 1969 became, for her, "the vehicle through which analytical propositions can be visualised".[31] Denes originally executed the works in the series freehand, on large sheets of paper, creating ethereal, needle-sharp linear structures in black or silver ink, from which she later produced lithographs. In a similar way to map projections, she deconstructed and manipulated the pyramid shape, which, for the ancient Egyptians – according to Denes – expressed both a static worldview based on dichotomy,[32] and, at the same time, a symbolic meaning linking the terrestrial sphere with the hereafter. In a more general sense, the

pyramid might also be interpreted as a representation of hierarchical power and knowledge. One of the conceptual models for her pyramids is Pascal's triangle, familiar from mathematics, which is based on the additive principle. Starting from Pascal's triangle, Denes transforms the classic pyramid shape into a bending, twisting, almost fluid configuration, depriving the pyramid of its monumentality and hierarchical structure. Her *Restless Pyramids* "slough off the rigidity associated with form and break loose from the tyranny of being built"; defying gravity, they float freely in the universe, becoming streamlined, almost breathing organisms.[33] However, these pyramids, which assume the shape of a bird, a flying fish, an egg, or a teardrop, along with her drawings for the *Future City*, are intended for future populations. They are models of self-sustaining, self-regenerating, futuristic settlements that float in space or on water, their structure resembling that of natural systems. In the lithograph *Pascal's Perfect Probability Pyramid & the People Paradox – The Predicament* (1980), Denes replaced stones and numbers with tiny individual human figures, which together build the architecture of the pyramid, ironically evoking the duality of crowd and individual.[34]

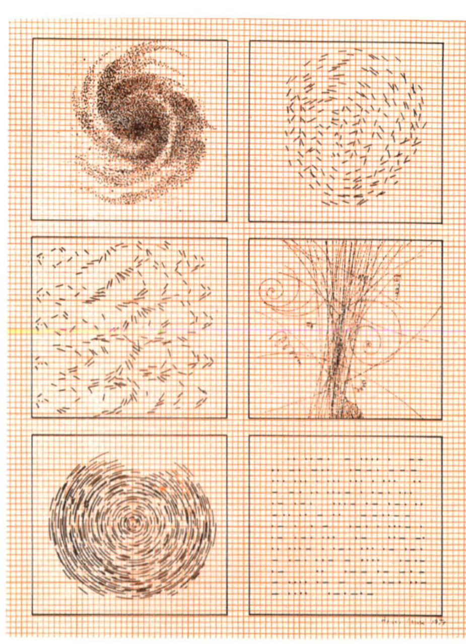

(fig. 11) <u>Point + Line + Intellect = Artist's Tool</u>, 1973

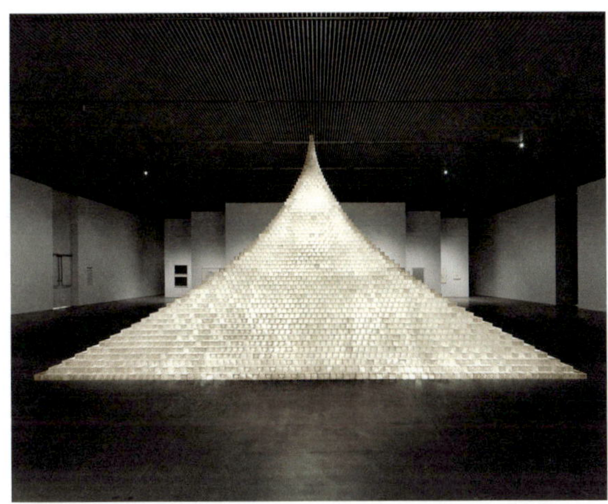

(fig. 12) <u>Model for Probability Pyramid–
Study for *Crystal Pyramid*,</u> 2019

In the 1970s, Agnes Denes began work on another remarkable series. In *Isometric Systems in Isotropic Space – Map Projections* [cat. nos. 16–24], begun in 1973, she experimented with mathematically correct visual distortions of the globe.[37] In the absence of advanced computer programs, once again she initially drew her subtly beautiful, highly accurate "maps" freehand on graph paper. She projected mathematical figures into "fluid space", transforming the planet Earth into a cube, pyramid, ovoid, helix, "hot dog", and even doughnut. However, the proportions of the manipulated forms, their longitudinal and latitudinal coordinates, and the positioning of the continents were mathematically correct topological equivalents of the original sphere. Agnes Denes liberated her maps from the consensual network of "facts": she regarded these shapes as sculptures produced in the universe, which floated paradoxically on the borderline between scientific fact and artistic invention, rationality and irrationality (fig. 13). Through her playful manipulation, she was also pointing to the relativity of scientific facts, the illusory nature of precise mapping. By retailoring the proportions and scales of Earth, Denes literally introduced new dimensions. "Seeing in new ways", "finding new concepts, recognising new patterns", as she wrote in her *Manifesto*.[38]

In her shifting pyramid shapes, Denes touched on social, cultural, and ecological themes, just as she did in her philosophical drawings. With its curved sides and pointed peak, covered entirely in plants, the 2015 work *The Living Pyramid*, created for the Socrates Sculpture Park in New York, as well as the 2017 version created for the Kassel documenta, emerged within the fabric of the cities "as a paradox planted in the ground".[35] In connection with her 2019 retrospective exhibition, organised in The Shed in New York, Denes realised one of the biggest models in her oeuvre. Executed according to designs produced in 1976, the six-metre-tall *Model for Probability Pyramid – Study for* Crystal Pyramid (2019) (fig. 12) was formed from 6,000 internally lit, biodegradable transparent bricks, made using a 3D printer. Despite its monumental size, the ethereal, apparently weightless structure, permeated with light, is the antithesis of the Egyptian pyramids, an equally paradoxical "incomprehensible temple to human civilisation".[36]

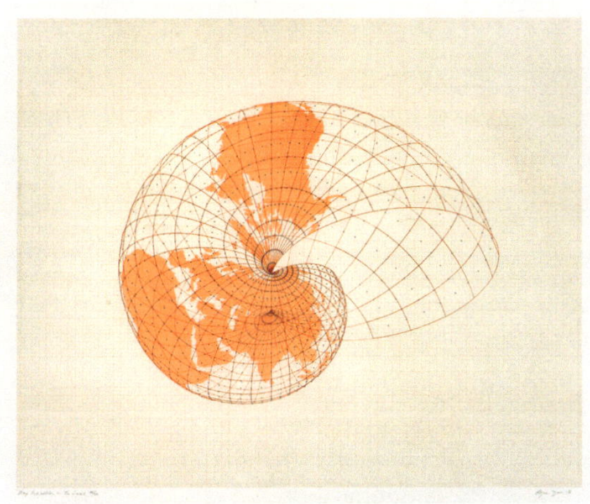

(fig. 13) <u>Isometric Systems
in Isotropic Space - Map Projections:
The Snail,</u> 1976

Even in the late 1960s, Denes already sensed that the development of information society demanded a conceptual model encompassing several disciplines. The 1970 work *Matrix of Knowledge* [cat. no. 3], which she imagined as an illustration of "an entire field, branch of science or a human life at a glance", visualised a future in which "abridgements and reductions will appear at the press of a button on a systems analyser, decoder, or computer."[39] At the time, perhaps even Denes herself could not have imagined that the future envisioned by the *Matrix of Knowledge* would be realised in her lifetime, and that advances in digital technology and software would pave the way for the age of artificial intelligence – with all its unforeseeable consequences.

In the 1960s and 1970s, with her conceptual synthesisation of science, philosophy, and poetry, and the unique aesthetic of her works, Denes was seen as following an individual path among American conceptual artists. Her visual philosophy and her pyramids nevertheless brought her into proximity with those – almost exclusively male – minimalist and conceptual artists who were also open towards land art (Sol LeWitt, Mel Bochner, Tony Smith, Robert Morris). Influenced by contemporary psychological, linguistic, and scientific innovations, and with the help of the rules of mathematics, flow charts, geometric shapes (cubes and triangles), and natural proportions (the Fibonacci sequence, the golden ratio), these artists redefined the concept of art. In contrast to the spare, anti-aesthetic conceptualism of the above artists, Denes's work was flawlessly executed, and her uniquely beautiful graphics continued to carry the connotation of "works of art". Although the intellectual and visual complexity of Denes's works frequently far exceeded that of her male colleagues, she often felt marginalised. In the traditionally masculine world of science, ecology, and information theory, Denes's complex art was difficult to interpret. "I'm a visual artist, a philosopher, a draftsman, an environmentalist, and a woman. I'm hard to fit in one box",[40] she declared, with characteristic wit.

Lucy Lippard is one of the foremost critics and curators who were quick to recognise Denes's originality. From the late 1960s, Lippard strove to break free of the frameworks of studio art and the world of galleries towards nature, to explore the interaction of the built environment and nature with the help of, among other things, land art, concept art, environment, public art, and the various

feminist theories and practices. Besides ecological awareness, the radical rethinking of the role of art and its (often contradictory) position was a permanent feature of Lippard's oeuvre and became as important a reference for present-day environmentally conscious artists and thinkers[41] as Denes's holistic perspective and ecological projects. Lippard's 1973 publication *Six Years: The Dematerialization of the Art Object from 1966 to 1972*, a summary of the conceptual art of the period, featured the work *Dialectic Triangulation: Visual Philosophy* by the then relatively unknown Denes, while the same volume also contained an early version of Denes's *Psychograph* project (1971–1972) "examining the nature of communication".[42] In the neo-avant-garde artists' leanings towards prehistorical cultures (ancient structures, systems of numbers and signs), Lippard recognised the desire to restore the social function of art; she understood that the most important element of all progressive images of the future was the restoration of a coherent connection between nature and culture.[43]

This was something Denes had already been fully aware of in the late 1960s. It was then that she came up with the notion of Eco-Logic, referencing the two fundamental pillars of her complex artistic approach – the duality of ecology and logic. Eco-Logic was also an important consequence of her visual philosophy. "Today, all my philosophical concepts seem to culminate and come to life in my ecological site works",[44] she wrote in 2007. It was in Sweden, as a teenager, that Denes first initiated an environmental work by studying the movement patterns of migrating birds on the island of Gotland, which later led to the 1979 work the *Bird Project - Visual Investigation of Moving Systems* (fig. 27). The most significant environmental project of the 1960s was the 1968 action *Rice/Tree/Burial*, during which she sowed rice "to represent life", and chained trees, indicating human intervention and death (fig. 14).[45] The burial of her haiku poetry, without keeping any copies, symbolised the human intellect and, at the same time, Denes's close relationship with the earth. The action was a kind of "private ritual", which she repeated in 1977 above Niagara Falls, in a territory originally occupied by Native Americans: she sowed rice and chained trees in what was once a Native American burial ground, while responses to a questionnaire concerning the future were placed in a time capsule and buried in the soil. Prior to that, reframing the notion of the sublime through a radical performative act, Denes

– exposing herself to the destructive forces of nature and to genuine risk – spent a week filming on a narrow ledge at the edge of Niagara Falls. The ritual performance generated a dialectic unity of thesis, antithesis, and synthesis (which she called "dialectic triangulation"[46]); her haiku and rice were a reflection on the synthesis of Eastern and Western thought; while by evoking the spirit of the Native Americans, she reflected on questions of colonisation and territorial expropriation.

At the same time, the photographs documenting her action called into play the visual tradition of the "sower" – from the parable of Christ the Sower to the heroic depictions of sowers by Jean-François Millet and Vincent van Gogh, which combine the cycles of nature with the humanitarian ideal. In the symbolic act of sowing (giving life), just as in burial or interment, it is not only the cyclical nature of earthly life that is at work, but also the desire to perpetuate ideals and the human intellect. The emphasis in Denes's photographs is not on the person of the sower (who in this case, in contrast to iconographic tradition, is a woman) but on the lifecycle of plants and the local ecological impact.

The theme of sowing (birth) and burial is not unprecedented in the context of contemporary American land art: it appears – in a more transgressive form than in Denes – in the work of Charles Simonds (*Birth*, 1970), Keith Arnatt (*Self-burial*, 1967), and, from a female perspective, Ana Mendieta (*Untitled – Grave Pyramid*, 1974).[47] Grain is also used quite frequently, featuring in the land art of Carl André (*Together*, 1968), Dennis Oppenheim (*Direct Seeding – Cancelled Crop*, 1969), and Richard Fleischner (*Hay Maze*, 1971), among others. These works, however, were expressions of the conceptual approximation of space and scale, or nature and the body, rather than of ecological perspectives. In the course of her actions, Denes was regularly confronted with soil pollution and had to contend with destructive plant diseases; at other times, she herself planted "alien" seeds (e.g., rice at Niagara Falls), anticipating present-day discourses on the exploitation of natural resources.

(fig. 14) <u>Rice/Tree/Burial Project (Rice Planting)</u>,
1977–1979/2012 [cat. no. 26]

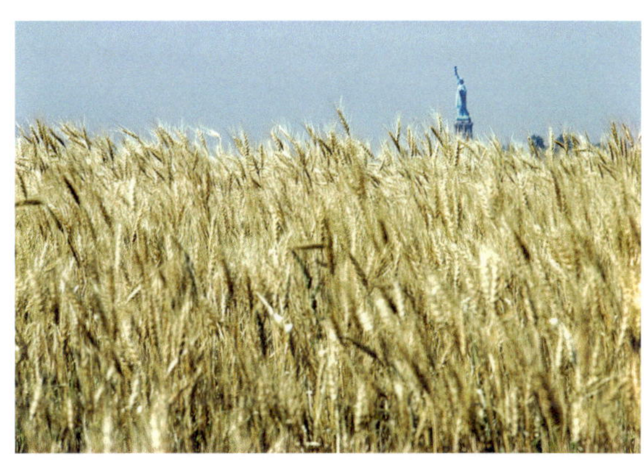

(fig. 15) <u>Wheatfield –
A Confrontation: Battery Park Landfill,
Downtown Manhattan, with Statue
of Liberty Across the Hudson</u>, 1982

The ritual act of community seed sowing was an element of the above-mentioned 1982 action *Wheatfield – A Confrontation* (fig. 15, cat. nos. 27–41), which, in Denes's own words: "referred to mismanagement, waste, world hunger, and ecological concerns."[48] The incursion of the countryside into the vicinity of the Twin Towers in New York, and the confrontation between the wildlife attracted by the agricultural land and growing wheat (ladybirds, grasshoppers, spiders, and mice) and the world of money, power, and corruption, is the most powerful paradox in Denes's oeuvre. In Caroline A. Jonas's apt phrase, the iconic photo-documentation belongs among those "anthropogenic images" that soberly connect the "Edenic fantasies" associated with *Wheatfield* to the present-day reality of overproduction, artificial fertility, and overpopulation.[49] As Jonas put it: "Denes anticipated the epoch now known as anthropocene."[50]

The first man-made virgin forest, *Tree Mountain – A Living Time Capsule* (1982–1996) was a land reclamation project created from a disused gravel pit. Eleven thousand people in Finland planted a total of eleven thousand trees, which were arranged in an elliptical pattern derived from a mathematical formula for the golden ratio [cat. nos. 42–43].[51] The objective of this multi-generational project, which was planned to run for a minimum of four hundred years, was to combine human creative power and natural processes. Denes saw *Tree Mountain* as a kind of time capsule. In the artist's own words, the trees of this "curious mathematical forest", which evoke the pyramid shapes of Pascal's triangle, "must outlive the present era and, by surviving, carry our concepts into an unknown time in the future".[52]

Denes's land-art-style works are free of the grandiose masculinity and radical, even aggressive, gestures of land expropriation typical of the emblematic output of the American earth work movement in the 1960s and 1970s (Michael Heizer, *Double Negative*, 1969; Robert Smithson, *Spiral Jetty*, 1970; Walter de Maria, *The Lightening Field*, 1977).[53] Her ecologically committed, more socially specific, poetic works are more closely aligned conceptually with the works of Joseph Beuys (*7000 Oaks*, 1982), Michael Singer (*First Gate Ritual Series*, 1979), Alan Sonfist (*Time Landscape*, 1978), and Helen and Newton Harrison (*Lagoon Cycle*, 1972–1984).[54]

"These works are intended to help the environment and benefit future generations with a meaningful legacy. They open doors to the future. My foremost concerns are the welfare of humanity and the quality of life."[55] Denes's entire oeuvre might be seen as a single time capsule or series of time capsules. They are *Messages from Another Time*, as posited by the subtitle of the 1986 work *Stelae*, which records the major scientific breakthroughs of the period on massive, hand-carved marble tablets, which are presented as finds that have been excavated in the future (fig. 30).[56]

The ship is a recurring motif in her visionary works. The design for the 1982 work *Noah's Ark – A Spaceship* (fig. 16), in keeping with Denes's typical interweaving of past and future, is a combination of "an ancient Viking sea vessel, modern ocean cruiser, barge, and spaceship". The body of the ship was to house thatched huts, "outfitted with the luxuries and doodads of a high-tech civilisation", while the structure as a whole gave the impression of confusion and futility. In Denes's own words, it is "a salute to human achievement in the face of prodigality and inefficiency".[57] One side of the earth-filled ship in the 1992 installation *Hot/Cold Earthship with Heartbeat* is icy and quiet, while the other is warm, with an infinite heartbeat audible from within.[58]

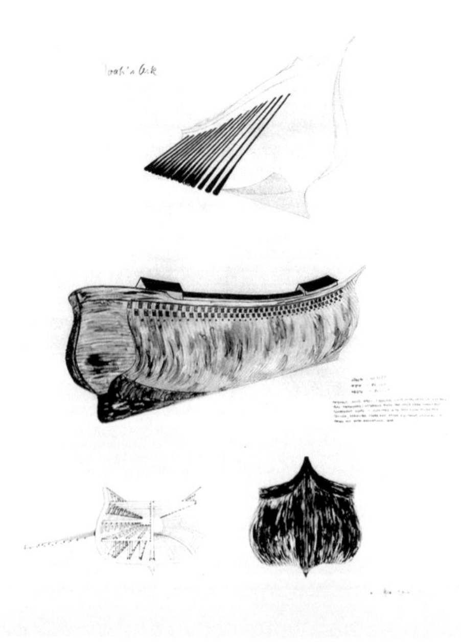

(fig. 16) <u>Noah's Ark - A Spaceship</u>, Proposal for Miami International Airport and North Waterfront Park, 1982

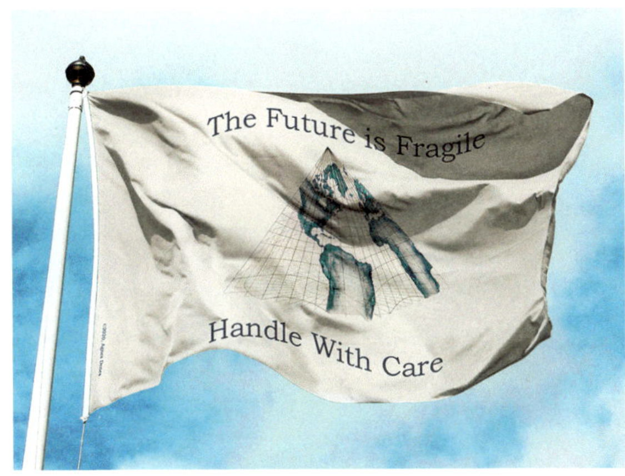

(fig. 17) <u>The Future is Fragile,
Handle With Care</u>, 2021 [cat. no. 44]

The ark built by Noah at God's command, in which he saved the human race and all the animals of the Earth from the Flood sent by God as a punishment, is one of the most iconic time capsules in Western cultural history. For the people of the Anthropocene age, faced with the threat of ecological catastrophe, Denes's "arks" are well-constructed refuges. They are places of safekeeping, metaphors for the possibilities of future inheritance, survival, and new beginning.[59] "The future is fragile, handle with care": Denes wrote this slogan on her "flag of the future", which flew boldly from both the roof of Tate Britain and in the Venetian Lagoon[60] in 2021, after the pandemic, and which now appears, in 2024, in the exhibition spaces of the Museum of Fine Arts in Budapest (fig. 17, cat. no. 44).

Denes's prophetic ecological visions predicted that the accepted conceptual structures and survival practices of our age will not necessarily be functional in the shadow of ecological catastrophe, and that, toppled from the sure foundations of the past, humankind must establish new, more sustainable economic and ecological structures in the interests of survival. Her "systems of logic" are adequate, highly original responses to world affairs. Agnes Denes's art and philosophy teach us to recognise inadequate, erroneous strategies, and they call for openness towards non-human agents, materials, and ecologies.

1 Agnes Denes, "Book of Dust. The Beginning and the End of Time and Thereafter (1972–1987)," in ibid, *The Human Argument. Writings of Agnes Denes*, ed. and foreword by Klaus Ottman (Putnam, Conn.: Spring Publications, 2008), 26.

2 On the comparison with Demeter, see Thomas McEvilley, "Philosophy in the Land: Agnes Denes," *Art in America* 92, no. 10 (2004): 160.

3 D. Á. "Búzaföld mint műalkotás" [Wheatfield as work of art], *Népszava*, 9 February 1983, 9.

4 The first retrospective exhibition of Agnes Denes's work in Hungary took place in 2008 in the Ludwig Museum, Budapest: *Agnes Denes. A harmadik évezred művészete – egy* új *világkép teremtése* [Agnes Denes. The Art of the Third Millennium – Creating a New World View]. Ludwig Museum – Museum of Contemporary Art, Budapest, 26 September – 7 December 2008. Curator: Róna Kopeczky. Cf. *Agnes Denes. A harmadik* évezred *művészete – egy* új *világkép teremtése* [Agnes Denes. The art of the third millennium – Creating a new world view], ed. Róna Kopeczky Budapest: Ludwig Muzeum – Kortárs Művészeti Múzeum, 2008.

5 Quoted in N. N., "Agnes Denes: Absolutes and Intermediates – The Shed, October 9, 2019 – March 22, 2020," *Arts Summary – A Visual Journal*, 13 October 2019, n. p.

6 Hans Ulbrich Obrist with Agnes Denes, "Holding the Universe in the Palm of Your Hand," in *Absolutes and Intermediates*, ed. Emma Enderby (New York: The Shed, 2019), 12.

7 Cf. Serge Guilbaut, *How New York Stole the Idea of Modern Art*. University of Chicago Press, Chicago, 1985.

8 Quoted in Peter Selz, "The Artist as Universalist," in *Agnes Denes*, ed. Jill Hartz (Ithaca, NY: Herbert F. Johnson Museum of Art, Cornell University, 1992), 147.

9 Agnes Denes, *The Art of the Third Millennium – Creating a New World View* (1996). See pp. 10–13 in the present catalogue.

10 Agnes Denes, *Strength Analysis – A Dictionary of Strength* (1971). See pp. 40–41 in the present catalogue.

11 Ibid.

12 Denes 2008.

13 Agnes Denes, *Dialectic Triangulation – A Visual Philosophy* (1968). See pp. 38–39 in the present catalogue.

14 Ibid.

15 Agnes Denes, "The Human Argument (1969–1970)," in *Absolutes* 2019, 58.

16 Agnes Denes, *Isometric Systems in Isotropic Space – Map Projections* (1973–1979). See pp. 66–75 in the present catalogue.

17 Cf. *Absolutes* 2019, 107.

18 Denes 2008, 21–65.

19 Ibid., 21.

20 Ibid.

21 Cf. Hartz ed. 1992, 74.

22 Agnes Denes, *Kingdom Series* (1972). See pp. 122–23 in the present catalogue.

23 Cf. *Absolutes* 2019, 236–37.

24 Cf. ibid.

25 Agnes Denes, "On Spirituality," in Denes 2008, 205.

26 On this topic, see Oliver Botar, *Prolegomena to the Study of Biomorphic Modernism, Biocentrism, Laszlo Moholy-Nagy's New vision and Erno Kallai's Bioromantik.* PhD Diss., University of Toronto, 1998, and Sándor Hornyik, A világ művészi képletei. Az elvont művészet és a világ új képe az Európai Iskola idején," [Artistic formulae of the world. Abstract art and the new world image at the time of the European School], in *Európai Iskola. Veszélyes csillagzat alatt (1945–1948)* [The European School. Under a dangerous constellation (1945–1948)], ed. Gábor Pataki (Szentendre: Ferenczy Múzeumi Centrum, 2024), 171–80.

27 Ernő Kállai, "Tárgymutató [Index]," in *Új Világkép* [New world image], with a foreword by Kázmér Fejér and picture explanations by Ernő Kállai, Galéria a 4 Világtájhoz, Budapest, 2–23 February 1947, 11.

28 *Structure in Art and Science*, ed. György Kepes (New York: George Braziller, 1965), vii.

29 Agnes Denes, *The Art of the Third Millennium – Creating a New World View* (1996). See pp. 10–13 in the present catalogue.

30 *Absolutes* 2019, 74.

31 Agnes Denes, *Pyramids* (1984, 2015) See pp. 48–63 in the present catalogue.

32 Ibid.

33 Ibid.

34 Ibid.

35 *Absolutes* 2019, 21–22.

36 Model for *Probability Pyramid – Study for Crystal Pyramid* (2019). Ibid., appendix.

37 Agnes Denes, *Isometric Systems in Isotropic Space – Map Projections* (1973–1979). See pp. 66–75 in the present catalogue.

38 Agnes Denes, *Manifesto* (1969). See pp. 8–9 in the present catalogue.

39 Agnes Denes, *Matrix of Knowledge* (1969–1970). See pp. 42–43 in the present catalogue.

40 Quoted in, Kathleen McGuigan, *Nothing Like a Dame*, 1 November 2019, n. p.

41 Cf. Heather Davis and Etienne Turpin, "Art and Death. Lives Between the Fifth Assessment & the Sixth Extinction," in *Art in the Anthropocene. Encounters among Aesthetics, Politics, Environment and Epistemologies*, eds. Heather Davis and Etienne Turpin (London: Open Humanities Press, 2015), 14; Lippard's most recent work on the art of Agnes Denes, "Pomethea of Paradox," in *Absolutes* 2019, 209–12.

42 Lucy R. Lippard, *Six Years: The Dematerialization of the Art Object from 1966 to 1972* (Berkeley, Los Angeles – London: University of California Press, 1996) (first ed. 1973).

43 On this, see Lucy R. Lippard, *Overlay. Contemporary Art and the Prehistory* (New York: Pantheon Books, 1983).

44 Agnes Denes, "The Paradox of Eco-Logic. Individual Creation vs. Social Consciousness.," in Denes 2008, 218.

45 Agnes Denes, *Rice/Tree/Burial* (1977–1979). See pp. 80–99 in the present catalogue.

46 Agnes Denes, *Ecological Practices* (1969). See pp. 78–79 in the present catalogue.

47 Cf. Ben Tufnell, *Land Art* (London: Tate Publishing, 2006); Thomas McEvilley, "Philosophy in the Land: Agnes Denes," *Art in America 92*, no. 10 (2004): 160; and *Art in the Land. A Critical Anthology of Environmental Art*, ed. Alan Sonfist (New York: E. P. Dutton, 1983).

48 Agnes Denes, *Wheatfield – Confrontation* (1982). See pp. 100–13 in the present catalogue.

49 Caroline A. Jonas, "Wheatfield and the Anthropogenic Image Bind," in *Absolutes* 2019, 221–28.

50 Ibid., 224.

51 Agnes Denes, *Tree Mountain – Time Capsule* (1992). See pp. 114–17 in the present catalogue.

52 Ibid.

53 See Tufnell 2006 and McEvilley 2005.

54 Cf. *Art in the Land. A Critical Anthology of Environmental Art* (New York: Dutton, 1983).

55 Agnes Denes, *The Art of the Third Millennium – Creating a New World View* (1996). See pp. 10–13 in the present catalogue.

56 Agnes Denes, *Stelae. Messages from Another Time*. See pp. 142–43 in the present catalogue.

57 Agnes Denes, *Noah's Ark – A Spaceship* (1982). See pp. 144–45 in the present catalogue.

58 *Budapest* 2008, 130–31.

59 On the ecological interpretation of the theme of Noah's Ark, see Jeffrey Jerome Cohen and Julian Yates: "Ark Thinking," in *Ecologies, Agents, Terrains*, eds. Christopher P. Heuer and Rebecca Zorach (New Haven – London: Yale University Press, 2018), 243–65.

60 The installation was realised in the framework of the Healing Arts project in 2021: https://www.youtube.com/watch?v=HJHgbjwgKFk.

Digging Deep is What Art is All About[1] On Agnes Denes's Environmental Thinking and Practice

When, in 1968, Agnes Denes authored and performed *Rice/Tree/Burial* (fig. 18, cat. no. 26), the first action considered to have expressed environmental concerns, the level of public awareness of ecological processes and of man's responsibility in harming nature was generally very low. Although a few years earlier, the publication of Rachel Carson's environmental science book *Silent Spring*[2] marked a turning point as it documented the massive impact of chemical pesticides – especially DDT – on insects, which subsequently resulted in the disappearance of birds, the attention paid to environmental questions only started to gain international publicity a decade later, with initiatives such as Earth Day created in 1970, or the Greenpeace organisation founded in 1971. To say that Agnes Denes is a visionary artist would therefore be a weak figure of speech.

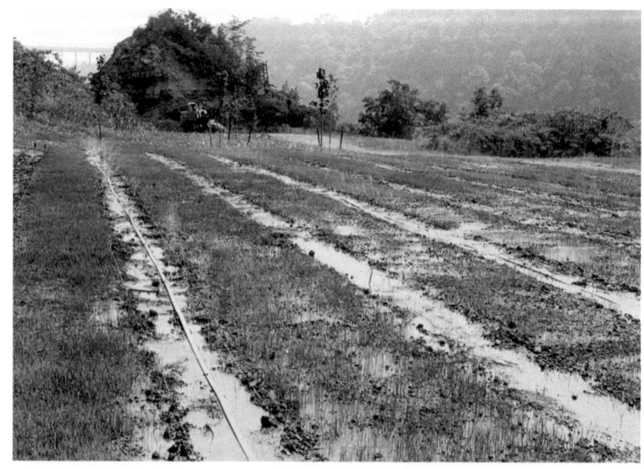

(fig. 18) Rice/Tree/Burial Project (Rice Planting), 1977–1979/2012 [cat. no. 26]

Róna Kopeczky

Probably one of the less obvious and rarely thematised aspects of Agnes Denes's conceptual environmental practice is the way she changes a centuries-long paradigm deeply rooted in – Western, European – collective memory and culture. Before the 16th century, – Western, European – daily interaction with nature was integrative and harmonious, the constellation that the individual, society and cosmos formed was seen as one organism in which each of them had its place and evolved symbiotically with the others. In this constellation, nature was considered as a nurturing, generous motherly entity on one hand, but also a wild, uncontrollable atmospheric force that could possibly provoke harsh weather and catastrophes, on the other. These two complementary – both feminine – images were "the projections of human perception onto the external world".[3] In the course of the 17th century, with the massive and accelerating process of mechanisation in agriculture and then in mining, the idea of culture developed as a mechanised, rationalised masculine metaphor in opposition to the nurturing, motherly imagery that was associated to earth and soil. In regard to the unpredictable – feminine as well – character of nature, culture generated another determining idea, a pattern of behaviour for the modern world: domination and control.

The image and belief system prevalent since antiquity in which nature was considered as a sacred, life-giving, and nurturing female living organism, respected and cared for, began to expire, and gradually faded away. The new images of control, domination, and exploitation that replaced this archetypal image of nature and the ethical constraints it brought with itself, became cultural[4] justifications for the violent intrusion of machines into nature and of metallic tools into the ground. In the 18th and 19th centuries, the Industrial Revolution needed, therefore produced these contradictory images and their normative associations as it developed its technological, commercial, and industrial apparatus that directly altered the soil[5]. Between the 16th and the 21st centuries, these cultural justifications have therefore strengthened, solidified, and shaped the nature (feminine) versus culture (masculine) division that prevails until our present days.

In the light of our civilisation's system of thought legitimating that culture (man) necessarily and unavoidably aggresses and modifies nature for his own survival, and automatically functions according to this dichotomy,

Agnes Denes's practice subverts, questions, supplants and invalidates in many ways. First of all, by directing, as a woman, her artistic interest and action towards the outside, a territory and concept that across centuries, became the privileged realm of men; by doing so, she overthrows the social determinism that assigned women indoors, in the safety of closed, small spaces, not only in everyday life, but also in art. As a logical prolongation of the paradigm, it is worth highlighting that the land art or earth art movement also counted a vast majority of male artists, such as Robert Smithson, Richard Long, Walter de Maria, Dennis Oppenheim, Jan Dibbets, Hans Haacke, James Turrell, Andy Goldsworthy or Giuseppe Penone, just to name a few. These artists worked in natural open space to leave their mark, reproducing the romantic gesture of man dominating nature, with a desire, a fixation for permanence; among their conceptual reasons to do so, sensitivity towards the environment was not a priority. As Megan O'Grady articulates it: "Compared to the grandiose, earth-gouging works made with bulldozers in inaccessible locales, like Smithson's *Spiral Jetty* or Michael Heizer's *City*, a more than 2 kilometre-long minimalist sculpture in the Nevada desert that has been under construction and closed to the public since its inception in 1972, Denes's work is both approachable and ecologically minded. *Wheatfield*, along with her later work – *The Living Pyramid* (2015), a grassy construction in a park in Queens, or *A Forest for Australia* (1998), the reforestation of an Australian water treatment site – are not solitary confrontations between artist and environment but rather a kind of public offering. Today, land art appears as an almost perfect distillation of the art world's history of male privilege, with its conviction that man is entitled to space to roam, to make his mark; women, however never enjoyed that privilege. Denes's work is about how we look at the earth itself, rather than an attempt to make her mark upon it".[6]

Visualising the invisible[7]

It is also essential to highlight the fact that Agnes Denes's environmental practice is not anthropofuge; the artist's intention is neither to direct the gaze away, nor to expel humanity from her universe, quite the contrary. To include local communities is central to her practice, insofar people involved can have more than just a scopic involvement in being actors, contributors, and spectators of her pieces. Probably her best-known work,

Wheatfield – A Confrontation (1982) (fig. 19, cat. nos. 27–41), stands as a visionary and transgressive act, a monument to identify misplaced priorities questioning controversial global issues and endless contradictions, in which she planted, grew, and harvested a two-acre area of wheat on a landfill facing Wall Street and the World Trade Center.[8] Making a simple, trivial wheat field visible in such an exceptional way certainly was a spectacle. From their office windows, hundreds of executives and employees could witness and enjoy the processes of cleaning the land from debris, planting, harvesting and the growth of the wheat. *The Living Pyramid* (2015) (fig. 20) composed of terraces filled with soil and a large variety of grasses and flowers, was completed not only as a site-specific installation but also as a participatory piece, with people being responsible for its planting and caring, therefore morally engaging and being committed to the piece, and by extension, to local and global environment. The same sense of awareness and custodianship is being cultivated by the *Sunflower Fields*[9] (2021 – ongoing) Agnes Denes gifted to the Autostrada Biennale in Kosovo, and which were planted and taken care of by local communities and inhabitants of two different cities in 2021 and 2023.

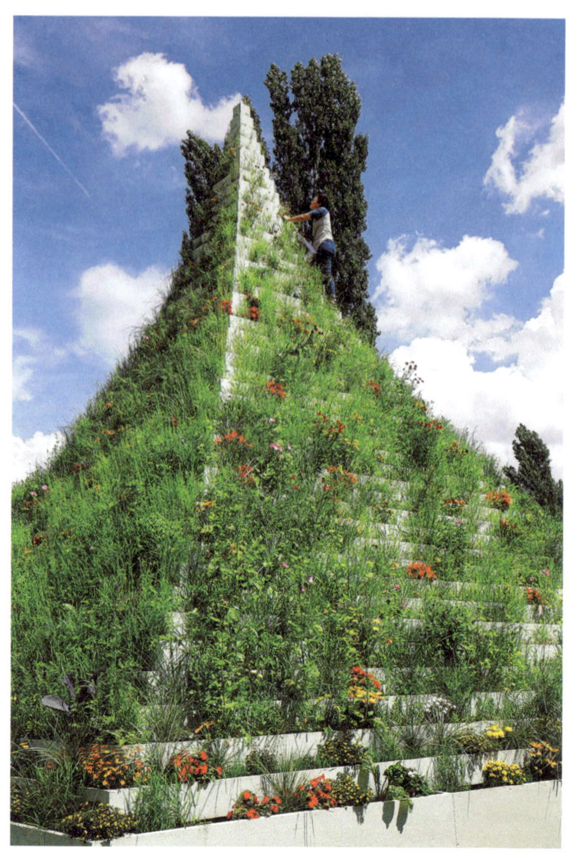

(fig. 20) <u>The Living Pyramid</u>, 2015/2017
documenta 14, Kassel, Germany

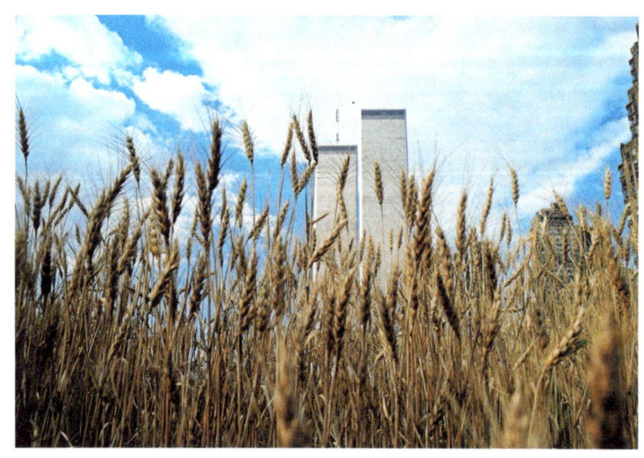

(fig. 19) <u>Wheatfield -
A Confrontation: Battery Park Landfill, Downtown
Manhattan - Cloudy Sky,</u> 1982/2024 [cat. no. 36]

Seeing reality and still being able to dream[10]

Secondly, the artist introduced the notion of concern and care, recognising and voicing the fragility of our world. From her first private action in the land entitled *Rice/Tree/Burial* (1968; 1977) to her flag piece *The Future is Fragile, Handle with Care* (2021) (fig. 17, cat. no. 44), Agnes Denes's environmental practice therefore roots in her understanding and her acceptance of the ephemerality and finitude of life. Her environmental concern appeared in the acts of reparation, reclamation or cleaning that composed her actions – working with landfills, cleaning contaminated soil with rice in *Rice/Tree/Burial* (fig. 21),[11] cleaning a land plot filled with construction debris for weeks before planting her *Wheatfield*, or allowing the bioremediation and rehabilitation of exhausted land by planting a forest on top of a gravel pit with her *Tree Mountain* (figs. 22–23, cat. nos. 42–43), project, not to speak about other lesser known or unrealised pieces that sought solutions to environmental issues such as general ecological stress, rising sea level, erosion, desertification or even global warming: *Antarctic Time Capsule* (1980–1986) (fig. 25), *A Forest for Australia* (1998), *Nieuwe Hollandse Waterlinie-25 Year Masterplan, The Netherlands* (2000); or *Mega-Dunes and Barrier Islands* (2013), among others.

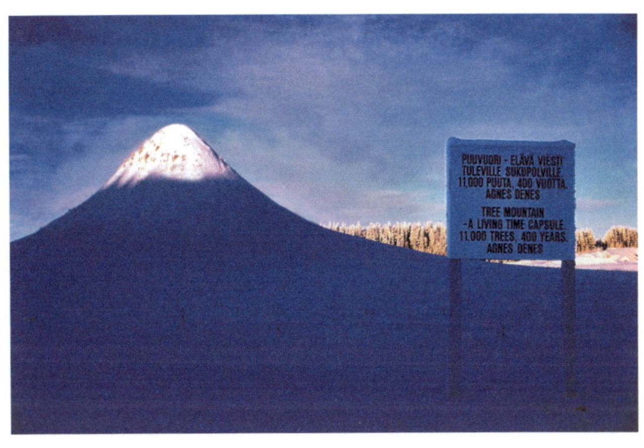

(fig. 22) <u>Tree Mountain - A Living Time Capsule - 11,000 Trees, 11,000 People, 400 Years - Winter View</u>, 1992-1996

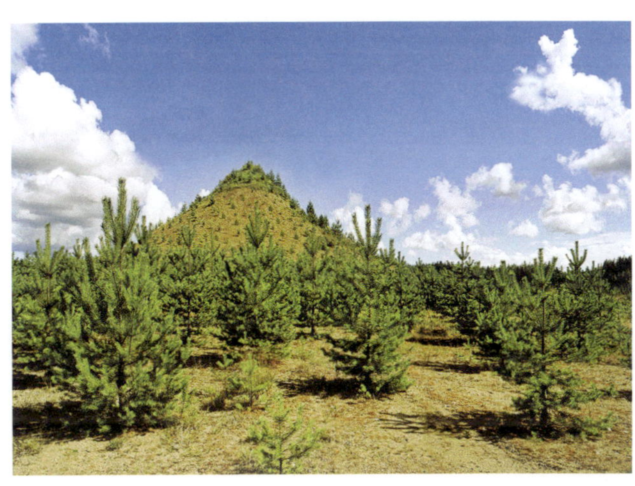

(fig. 23) <u>Tree Mountain - A Living Time Capsule - 11,000 Trees, 11,000 People, 400 Years - Summer view</u>, 1992-1996

Beyond these diverse acts of reparation lay the humility and duration of physical labour. Planting rice for *Rice/Tree/Burial* then watering it by hand; cleaning a construction site, evening eighty truckloads of topsoil, then digging 285 furrows by hand for a field of wheat to be planted;[12] or forming the mountain according to her calculations and instructions, then planting, together with locals and volunteers, eleven thousand pine trees that would draw the mathematical pattern of *Tree Mountain – A Living Time Capsule* (1992–1996). All these preparation works highlight that beyond imagining and conceiving, the efforts and physical challenges are an essential part of the creative process; "... the risks we took and the hardships we endured were all part of the basic concept", the artist states in her writings about the *Wheatfield* project.[13]

(fig. 21) <u>Rice/Tree/Burial Project (Burial of the Time Capsule) [cat. no. 26]</u>

Understanding the finitude of human existence and still striving to create beauty and provocative reasoning[14]

Thirdly, Denes has elaborated and conceived projects that are meant to outlive her and develop independently from her, reversing the hierarchic system in which the work of art is subordinated to and closely tied to the ego and life of the artist. This expresses fully in the project *Tree Mountain* (figs. 22–23), in which the planted Finnish pine trees, with an average life expectancy of 300 to 400 years, are meant to gradually restore a whole ecosystem and grow into the first man-made virgin forest. Planted by the artist with the help of eleven thousand volunteering helpers, *Tree Mountain* was at its inception a piece made for people to possess, to feel theirs. As Denes states it in the concept of this piece: "People who planted the trees received certificates acknowledging them as custodians of the trees. The certificate is an inheritable document valid for twenty or more generations in the future, the first such document involving the future in human history."[15] Not only are the planted trees meant to live throughout centuries after Denes has conceived and implemented this large earth work, they have also been gifted to the persons participating in the planting, dissipating the habitual artist's ownership status in relation to the work created. In this respect, the certificate each planter received directly connect with the notion developed by French philosopher Michel Serres in *The Natural Contract* (1990), according to which the Rousseauian social contract that binds and engages man to man is to be augmented with a contract between man and nature, as nature is a full-pledged protagonist in its own right.[16]

Although smaller in scale than *Tree Mountain*, *The Living Pyramid* and its multiple re-staged versions[17] do reach a similar effect in the way they are being cared for by locals, while reconnecting them to the natural circle of life that the structure of the pyramid itself follows by being itself dismantled when plants die in autumn. As discussed by Jonathan Goodman: "In summary, the changes occurring to The Living Pyramid after its exhibition is over parallel the changes that take place in nature itself – we move from construction to dissolution to construction again. ... [The] dismantling [of the Living Pyramid] recognizes that most culture today is impermanent. This does not mean it is of small value – quite the contrary,

the piece gains in worth for its momentary resistance to forces, mostly human and economic in nature, that would deny its worth."[18]

In the *Wheatfield* project (fig. 24), the crop was harvested, then sent all over the world to deprived areas to be replanted, in order to multiply and alleviate world hunger: "The harvested grain travelled to twenty-eight cities around the world in an exhibition called *The International Art Show for the End of World Hunger*, organized by the Minnesota Museum of Art (1987–1990). The seeds were carried away by people who planted them in many parts of the globe."[19] As an undeniable proof of Agnes Denes' long-lasting impact, of the actuality of her practice, and of growing awareness and sensitivity towards environmental issues that she certainly contributed to, *Wheatfield* was replanted in London in 2009, Milan[20] in 2015, as well as in Basel[21] and Bozeman, Montana in 2024.

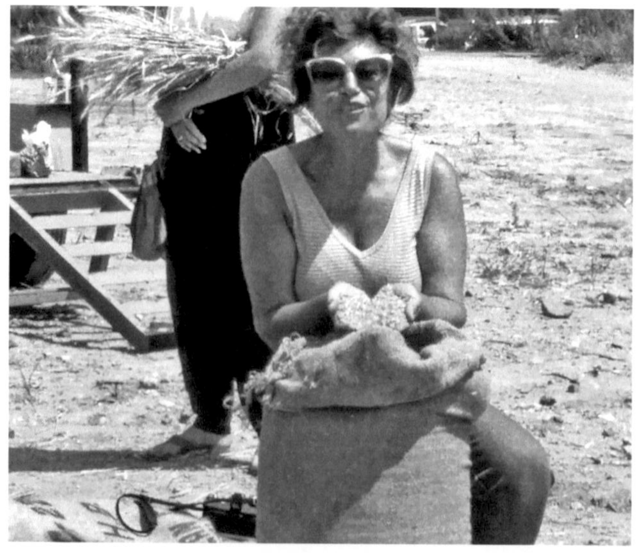

(fig. 24) <u>Wheatfield - A Confrontation</u>, 1982/2023 (still from the video) [cat. no. 62]

Another example of her artistic intention is the motif of time capsule that she started to integrate into her project with the reiteration of *Rice/Tree/Burial* in 1977. On this occasion, she buried the haiku she wrote, keeping no copy of it (fig. 18): "I buried my haiku poetry, giving up everything that I'd written up to that point ... I divested myself of the whole thing. I meant to give up something precious to the ground."[22] A trace, a message, or sometimes even a dictionary of our times preserved for the *Homo Futurus*,[23] time capsules are a recurring element in Denes's projects. In light of global warming and our dramatically rising temperatures, the project entitled *Antarctic Time Capsules* (fig. 25) conceived as early as 1980–1986 is probably the most relevant for the present. Predicting the accelerating melting of ice caps, Denes planned to bury several time capsules with different planned release time, containing different information regarding our civilisation deep into different glaciers, but above ice shelves so that "if glaciers continue to advance at their present rate, the first three capsules would be released, five, then, and fifty thousand years from now, and they would carry information ... aimed at a surviving population in need of such information ... Global warming may accelerate the melting and another ice age might slow it down for tens of thousands of years, but the capsules would be released in the correct sequence. Until then, they will remain safe unless the glaciers themselves are suddenly destroyed, which would require a truly major change in the global climate."[24]

(fig. 25) <u>Antarctic Time Capsules</u>, 1980-1986

As a fourth point, *Wheatfield* illustrates how Denes's approach stands in contrast with land artists who take artistic practice into the natural environment; by taking back nature in the city, she does the opposite and again, bridges the centuries-old nature-culture divide. It would be a simplified description of the project to summarise it by saying that wheat grew at the foot of skyscrapers. The crop did much more than just growing, it attracted insects and spiders, which themselves attracted rodents and birds. A whole ecosystem started to rebuild itself in just four months, and spring was not silent anymore.

From a philosophical point of view, Denes's conceptual approach would stand close to the notion of ecosophy elaborated in 1989 by French political philosopher and psychoanalyst Félix Guattari and Norwegian philosopher Arne Næss, the father of deep ecology. This notion, described as a philosophy of ecological harmony or equilibrium states that traditional environmentalist perspectives maintain the dualistic separation of human (cultural) and nonhuman (natural) systems, and therefore obscure the complexity of the relationship between humans and their natural environment. Therefore, the need for an ecological framework which understands the interconnections of social and environmental spheres. As a pioneer of conceptual environmental art, Agnes Denes did not refer to this theory explicitly but coined in 1971 the notion of Eco-Logic, which, similarly to the abovementioned, emphasised the importance of ecological thinking and action.

Eco-Logic and dialectical triangulation

As the last point of this essay, it is essential to underline Agnes Denes's expressed intention to "unite the human intellect with the majesty of nature"[25] which also advocated for a dialectic and non-hierarchic way to achieve harmony between man and environment. Her first exercise in Eco-Logic, *Rice/Tree/Burial*, originally performed in 1968 as a private ritual, then reiterated one decade later in 1977, comprised three, interconnected, dialectical phases. The first component was planting rice to represent life and growth, the seed itself denoting the nucleus, first principle or cause, and the beginning. The second element was the chaining of trees, an action that indicated interference with life and natural processes, but also linkage, connective units and associations, flexibility and restraint. As the artist herself described it: "The texture of the forest, having been interrupted by the reordering of its elements, yielded unique structures of isolated or combined sculptural forms. The chains became additional limbs and blended into their surroundings to become visible only in certain lights, angles, and perspectives, conveying the conflicting and interdependent aspects of art and existence, illusion and reality, imagination and fact. The chained trees stood as monuments to human thought versus nature."[26] The third phase was marked by the burying of the artist's haiku poetry to symbolise not only our intimate relationship with the Earth, passing, and returning to the soil, but also generation, as well as life-giving and through it, the birth of an idea or concept, the essence of thinking processes (consciousness, deductive reasoning, and the logic of emotions) and invention, i.e., creation itself.

The three interconnected and interdependent acts of this eco-philosophical piece constituted the first expression of triangulation (thesis, antithesis, synthesis) in Agnes Denes's practice. This concept would also unfold in her early programmatic philosophical drawings, including *Dialectic Triangulation: A Visual Philosophy* (1968–1983) [cat. no. 1] *The Human Argument* (1969), *Matrix of Knowledge* (1970) [cat. no. 3] *Isometric Systems in Isotropic Space – Map Projections: Pyramidal Projection* (1973) (fig. 26) and in later large-scale land art works such as *Wheatfield* or *Tree Mountain*.

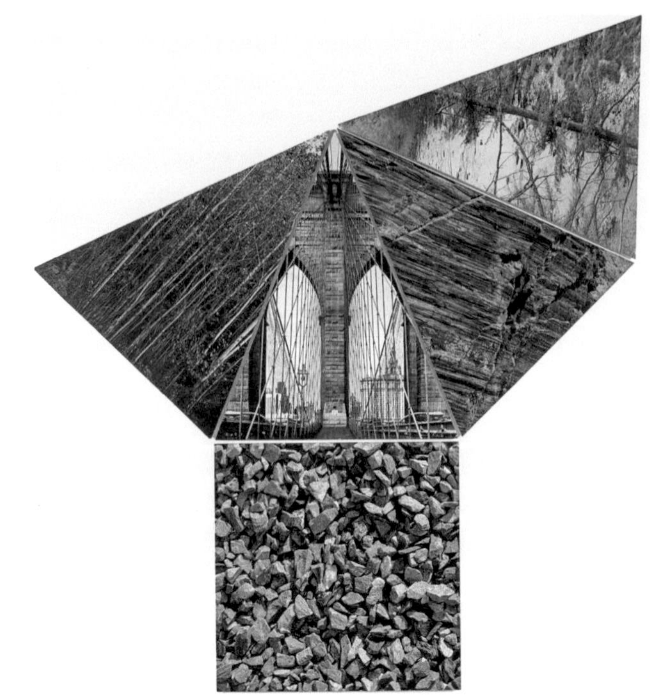

(fig. 26) Isometric Systems in Isotropic Space - Map Projections: Pyramidal Projection, 1973/2018

Working with paradox[27]

These are the opening words of Agnes Denes's *Manifesto* (1969) and one of the strongest pivotal forces of her creative approach. For the artist, this paradox refers to what she often calls the human predicament, i.e., the tension that lies between achievable conditions of global survival – the power of imagination and human intellect being one of those conditions – and logic that demonstrates how, despite being in its centre, we stay prisoners of our own system. In regard to her environmental practice, this might be framed more precisely as an eco-paradox, a tension arising between ecology and economics, and therefore between the culturally justified need of production, consumption, and the instinctive desire for the long-lost harmony and balance in the earth's ecological systems. The paradoxical situation in which a wheat field was planted by hand under Wall Street, the citadel of immaterial labour occurring in a sterile, artificial office environment, and in which abstract economic, capitalistic, and commercial were confronted by the very much concrete life cycle of a crop framed by seasons, as well as by the most basic human need that food represents, was already thoroughly discussed. Another perspective emerges, as articulated by Caroline A. Jones: "Confronting agrilogistics, the artist insisted on 'withholding' any processing or use value of the harvested wheat: 'The material is planted and cultivated for the sole purpose of withholding it from a product-oriented system. Isolating this grain from further processing (production of food stuffs) becomes like stopping raw pigment from becoming an illusionistic force on canvas.'[28] By contrast, Denes resisted the postures of male polemics against 'illusionistic force[s]' to weave her cherished grains or wheat into a project seeding future crops in impoverished communities around the world. … She explicitly refused to put the wheat into a commodity exchange market, instead giving it freely to those in need."[29]

Using intellect and instinct to achieve intuition[30]

In her protean artistic practice and deeply humanistic, classical modernist manner unfolding since the 1960s, Agnes Denes has been embracing philosophy, mathematics, linguistics, psychology, history, sociology, poetry, and music, closely intertwining science and art in a subtle mystery of knowledge. Her visual investigations and formulations, writings and environmental actions unfold as sensitive, long-life projects that are planned as a benign solution and as a gift for future generations to enjoy, but also to care for. As French philosopher Baptiste Morizot argues, the ecological crisis is first and foremost a "crisis of sensitivity"[31] (fig. 27). Denes's environmental practice is a remedy to that; not only do her artworks respect and stand as monuments to the natural cycles of life, they also unfold as social pieces, offer people a sense of agency, and encourage them to reconnect and reengage with a world – they know – they lost long ago.

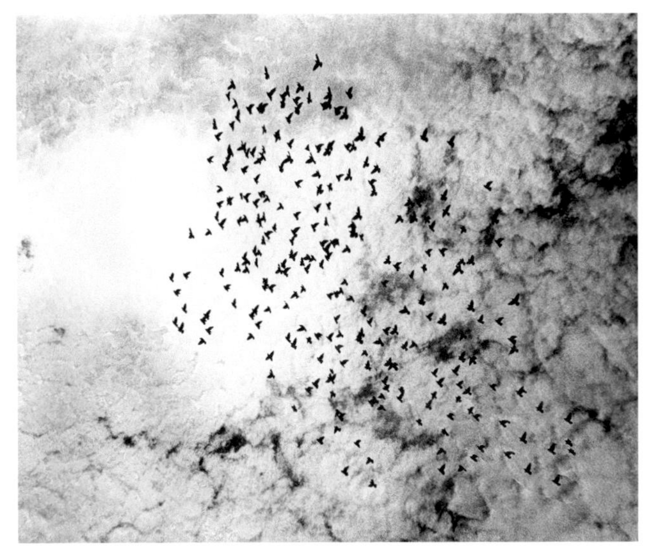

(fig. 27) <u>Bird Project –
A Visual Investigation
of Systems in Motion</u>, 1948/1979

1   Agnes Denes, *The Human Argument, The Writings of Agnes Denes*, ed. Klaus Ottmann (Putnam, Conn.: Spring Publications, 2008), 164.

2   Rachel Carson, *Silent Spring* (Boston: Houghton Mifflin), 1962.

3   "Ces deux imaginaires étaient associés au sexe féminin et constituaient des projections de la perception humaine sur le monde externe." Carolyn Merchant, *La nature comme femme et sa destruction par la science moderne* (Marseille: Éditions Wildproject, 2021), 18.

4   "Cultural" here is used with the meaning attitudes, behaviour, opinions, etc. of society.

5   Such as mining, deforestation, drainage of the soils, diversion of water, etc. For a broader context on this topic, see the determining text for eco-feminist thinking authored by Carolyn Merchant, *The Death of Nature* (San Francisco: Harper&Row, 1980).

6   Megan O'Grady, "Women Land Artists Get Their Day in the Museum," *New York Times Magazine*, 21 November 2018. With Agnes Denes's words: "Land Art was done by artists who needed more space than their studios. They had nothing to do with environmental concerns about which they couldn't care less." "Holding the Universe in the Palm of Your Hand – Hans Ulrich Obrist with Agnes Denes," in *Absolutes* 2019) 21.

7   Agnes Denes, *Manifesto*. See pp. 8–9 in the present catalogue.

8   In a meaningful synchronicity, Joseph Beuys' controversial piece entitled *7000 Oaks – City Forestation Instead of City Administration* was first realised in this same year,

in the frame of documenta 7, with similar motivations and equally, with the help of volunteers.

9 https://autostradabiennale.org/exhibitions/sunflower-fields-2021-ongoing-prishtina/ (last accessed: 29 June 2024).

10 Agnes Denes, *Manifesto.* See pp. 8–9 in the present catalogue.

11 Rice grew red as a sign of polluted soil: "Only Two Months Later Will I Learn / That My Field was Contaminated / That in Spite of / One Foot of Fresh Soil / I Grew Radioactive Rice". Agnes Denes, "Planting the Rice Field (haiku)," in Budapest 2008, 83.

12 Denes 2008, 164.

13 Ibid., 162.

14 Agnes Denes, *Manifesto.* See pp. 8–9 in the present catalogue.

15 Agnes Denes, *Tree Mountain – A Living Time Capsule-11,000 Trees, 11,000 People, 400 Years*, 1992–1996, (420 × 270 × 28 metres), Ylöjärvi, Finland. http://www.agnesdenesstudio.com/works4.html (last accessed: 10 July 2024).

16 Michel Serres, *Le contrat naturel* (Paris: François Bourin, 1990).

17 The piece was and will be reiterated at documenta 14 in Kassel (2017), Sakıp Sabancı Museum Istanbul (2022), or MUDAM Luxembourg (2025) among other venues.

18 Jonathan Goodman, "Agnes Denes at Socrates Sculpture Park," in *Sculpture Nature* (blog), https://sculpturenature.com/en/agnes-denes-au-socrates-sculpture-park/ (last accessed: 9 July 2024).

19 Agnes Denes, Wheatfield – A Confrontation, Battery Park Landfill, Downtown Manhattan, New York. http://www.agnesdenesstudio.com/works7.html (last accessed: 15 June 2024).

20 Agnes Denes's *Wheatfield* was re-enacted in Milan as part of the city's regeneration project and Expo, on the invitation of Fondazione Riccardo Catella and Fondazione Nicola Trussardi: https://www.fondazionenicolatrussardi.com/en/mostre/wheatfield_/ (last accessed: 18 July 2024).

21 *Honouring Wheatfield* was realised in the frame of the Art Basel Art Fair, 2024. This version is meant to be harvested, turned into flour, baked into bread and distributed to people in need in the frame of a communal event and experience: https://www.artbasel.com/stories/ecology-pioneer-american-artist-agnes-denes-basel-messeplatz-wheat-field-climate-change-awareness (last accessed: 18 July 2024).

22 "Holding the Universe in the Palm of Your Hand – Hans Ulrich Obrist with Agnes Denes," in *Absolutes* 2019, 21.

23 In 1977, along with a letter addressed "Dear Homo Futurus", the artist buried a time capsule containing microfilmed responses to a questionnaire that had travelled around the world. It listed existential questions concerning human values, the quality of life, and the future of humanity such as: "Do you believe humanity will become extinct one day?", "Which do you think will prove ultimately more important to humanity – science or love?", "What would you say the human purpose is?" or "What is ultimate reality?" Agnes Denes, "Questionnaire," See p. 83 in the present catalogue.

24 Agnes Denes, *Antarctic Time Capsules* 1980–1986. In: *Budapest* 2008, 100.

25 Agnes Denes, *Tree Mountain – A Living Time Capsule–11,000 People, 11,000 Trees, 400 Years*, See pp. 114–17 in the present catalogue.

26 Agnes Denes, *Rice/Tree/Burial with Time Capsule*, http://www.agnesdenesstudio.com/works2.html (last accessed: 15 July 2024).

27 Agnes Denes, *Manifesto.* See pp. 8–9 in the present catalogue.

28 Elizabeth Manchester, "Dennis Oppenheim: Directed Seeding – Cacelled Crop, 1969," online catalogue entry, March 2007, Tate Museum, London, accessed December 14, 2018, https://www.tate.org.uk/art/artworks/oppenheim-directed-seeding-cancelled-crop-t12402.

29 Caroline A. Jones, "Wheatfield and the Anthropogenic Image Bind," in *Absolutes* 2019, 226.

30 Agnes Denes, *Manifesto.* See pp. 8–9 in the present catalogue.

31 "… the ecological crisis is also a crisis of sensitivity – a crisis of our sensitivity to living things. By crisis of sensitivity, we mean an impoverishment of what we can feel, perceive, and understand, and the relationships we can develop with living things." Estelle Zhong Mengual and Baptiste Morizot, "The Illegibility of the Landscape. The Ecological Crisis as a Crisis of Sensibility," *Nouvelle revue d'esthétique* 22, no. 2 (2018): 87–96.

Catalogue
    Works in the
    Exhibition
    with Texts
    by Agnes Denes

Philosophical Drawings

Philosophical Drawings

Dialectic Triangulation:
A Visual Philosophy

Dialectic Triangulation is an art definition. It refers to
a process leading to the visualization of mechanisms and
hypotheses. It is the applicatin of inquiries to aspects of
human existance and knowledge.

Functionally, *Dialectic Triangulation* is a simplification
and systematic rebuilding of complexes on any subject
or matter by application of various methods (listed
below). One builds progressive trichotomies failing and
succeeding in a dialectic method, each time arriving
at a better thesis on a higher level. Dialectic means
a forever rising knowledge, a deepening awareness or
consciousness through wich the trinities are argued and
re-grouped. Triangulation is the activating force which
institutes the interaction of static states. It is also the
combination of intellect, instinct, and intuition.

Dialectic Triangulation is a clarification of ideas and the
revaluation of accepted knowledge. It raises a concern
by exposing the workings of hypotheses instead of
hiding them behind symbols - that of art as illusion.
It probes to locate and expose the center of things,
the true inner core of inherent but not yet understood or
disclosed meaning. This type of art is analytical; it goes
beyond illusionism and deals with realities.

TYPES OF TRIANGULATIONS:

a　　inanimate tri-groups representing all of genus,
　　　class, or category
b　　re-grouping or classification
c　　accepted facts examined, their validity and
　　　importance reestablished or denied
d　　mapping perceptual and ideatinal errors
e　　analyzing and diagramming various distortions
　　　and losses in communication
f　　arriving at a conclusion derived frm two
　　　propositions
g　　arriving at a mean between two extremes
h　　building propositions for dimensional expansion
i　　building propositions through deductive trisection
j　　constructing a proposition from "pure ideas"
k　　pure idea groups activated through controversy
l　　interdependent or progressive ideas becoming
　　　effective through succesive stages of
　　　advancement
m　　threefold theories interchangeable, and those
　　　forming argumentative conclusions
n　　seeking arguments with universal validity
o　　seeking reality and truth

Dialectic Triangulation: A Visual Philosophy
(including The Human Argument), 1968-1983 [cat. no. 1]

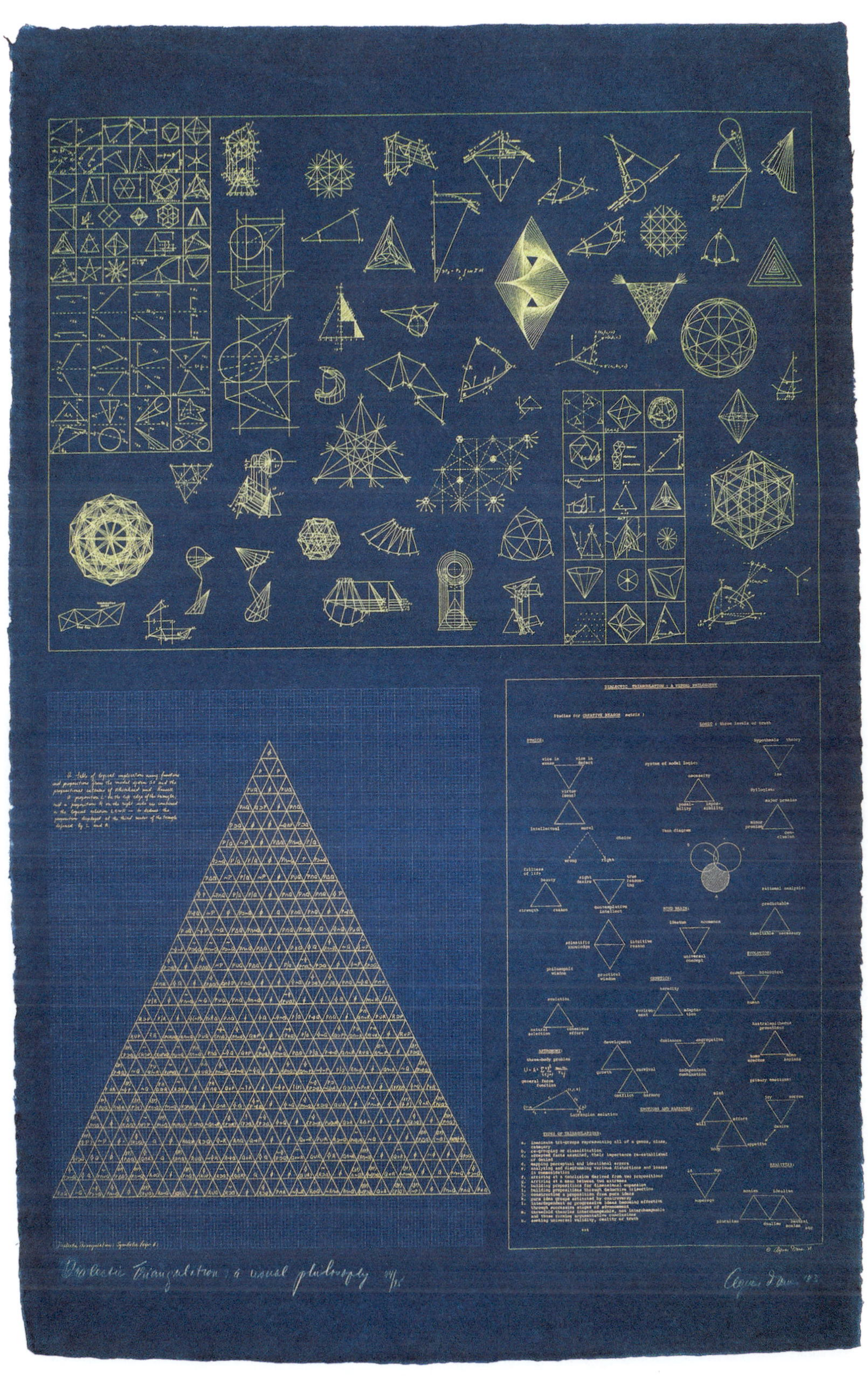

Strength Analysis –
a Dictionary of Strength, 1967–1971

Strength Analysis – A Dictionary of Strength is an anthology as well as a dictionary, an inquiry into linguistics and the structure and nature of language as it affects human understanding. It is an experiment in semiotics and semantics, in the creation of intangible, incorporeal kinetic sculpture and in the formalization of the meaning and essence of "strength".

I began working on *Strength Analysis* in 1965 while studying at Columbia and concluded the project in 1971, seven years later. During this interval I read the entire *Webster's Unabridged International Dictionary* and removed or, rather, extracted every word signifying "strength" in one form or another.

The words that had lain in the dictionary, alphabetized into a purely lexical capacity, freed from their inertia, were now emerging as new entities, forming a strange new "body of strength". They were being awakened while the idea of strength was being reevaluated, gaining new significance. They were coming to life to form a structure made of words, translucent and buzzing like a beehive. Held together by their own strength, the words created an undulating form like a swarm of bees moving about. Alive and constantly changing, nevertheless it was a sculptural, three-dimensional form, a semantic substance possessing object boundaries.

As the number of words grew so did their intensity. They seemed to aid each other in strength and grew stronger.

As I moved through the dictionary, the strange, amazing characteristics of language and the nature of words were unfolding. Their meaning fluctuated, changed constantly, when compared to each other. Even though with certain words an image would instantly jump to mind, often, when compared with others, the initial image blurred, and multiple, overlapping or sub-meanings broke forth. The words would not only modify, overlap, substitute, or dominate, but stretch until they finally moved out of each other's realm and began to take on entirely different meanings, often dependent on the circumstances in which they were used.

In addition to their connotations and ambiguities, their usage was also intriguing: how they get worn out through time and misuse – manipulated, exploited, twisted, and abused by one generation and resurrected by another; how they are reduced to cliches and slogans rarely to regain their dignity; how they often become dull and meaningless from latent connotations having attached themselves like barnacles; how they develop official multimeanings, especially in an age of specialization, and walk around like split personalities; and most important, how they get rediscovered from time to time and manage to bounce right back as new life is pumped into them through fresh applications. Words can be harnessed but seldom tamed.

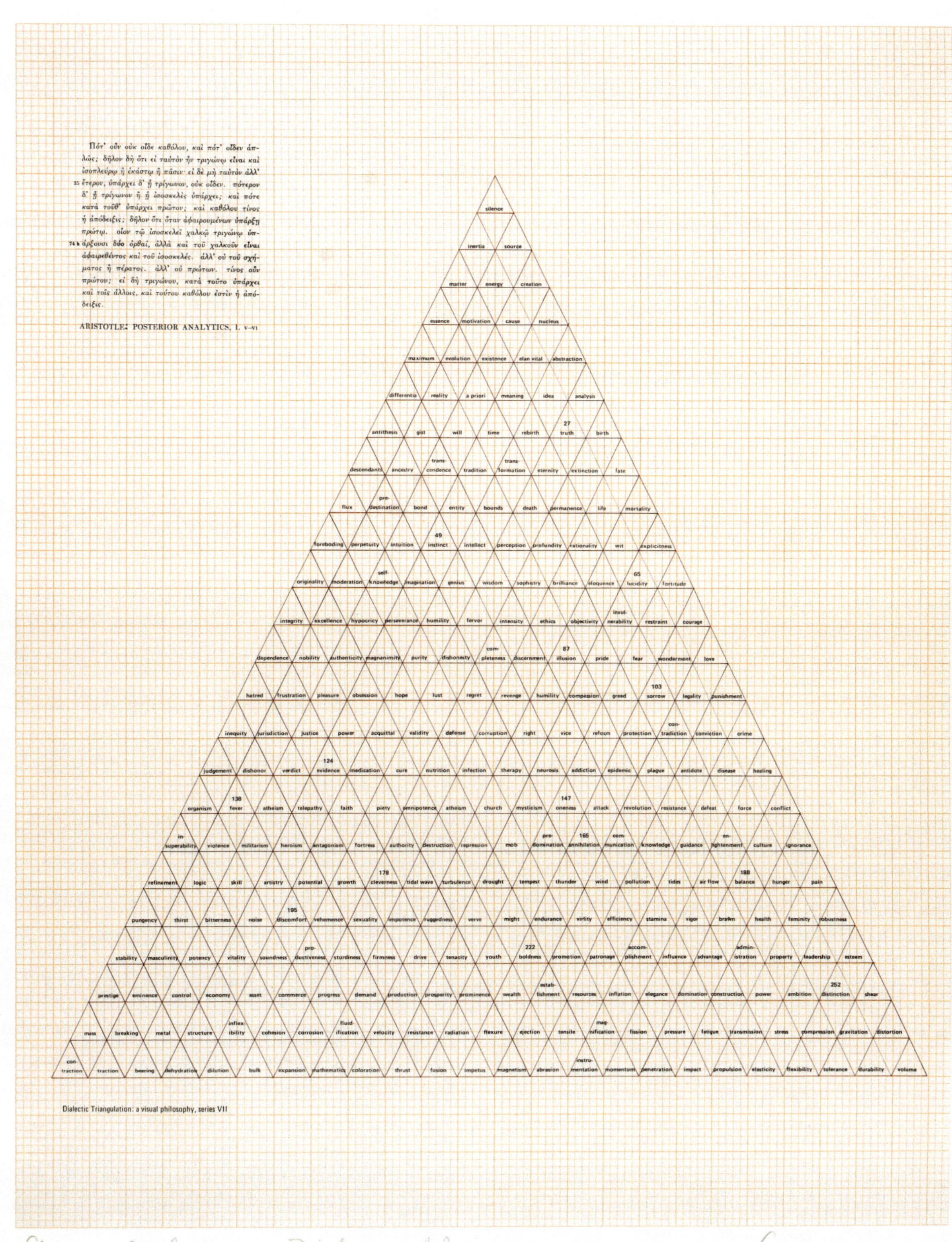

Dialectic Triangulation: a visual philosophy, series VII

Matrix Of Knowledge, 1969-1970

Matrix of Knowledge is a comment on future computerized, "censored" knowledge, a predictable result of increasing specialization and information overload leading to undue condensations, generalizations, or elimination of important information. The work anticipates a future in which evolution will be speeded up or slowed down at will and information will be dehydrated and coded for storage to be hydrated for consumption at chosen intervals.

Matrix of Knowledge presents an entire field, branch of science, or a human life at a glance the way a youth of the future might receive abridged and pre-selected educational material.

The sum of accumulated information doubles every seven to ten years. In the future this overload will increase until abridgments and reductions will appear at the pressing of a button on a systems analyzer, decoder, or computer. *War and Peace* may be reduced to a succinct paragraph if not eliminated altogether to appear only as a title under the heading "Russian Writers and their Work". No one will have the time or the inclination to read an entire book, or so many books, and individual thinking will diminish.

A youth today may read less than 500 books or their equivalent to be well educated. This number could easily jump to 10,000 or 20,000 in the near future. When having to read and learn that much becomes more than the mind can handle, reduction, pre-selection, and elimination will be the answer.

But who shall make these decisions – by what method and criteria? The individuals will certainly not be able to do it. A system will have to be set up to reduce incoming data at the risk of losing free choice. Mass media is already making choices for us, and specialization is also leading in that direction by trapping valuable data within each specialty where it remains undigested, hindering accurate deductions and combinations as the flow of communicationis blocked (Octopus Theory*).

Matrix of Knowledge was originally designed for the "Software" exhibition dealing with "Information, Technology and Its New Meaning in Art". The work uses data structure scheduling events in 3-D space. A crystallographic connective system confronts the viewer with the challenge of comparing ideas using pre-selected, condensed information making the selection process just as complicated even though the ideas are "packaged".

In one program visitors could create their own lives, where only Birth and Death were unchangeable – prefixed givens.

Matrices were built in *Creative Reason, Evolution, Politics and Systems or Ism-Isms, Emotions and Passions, Tree of Porphyry,* and *A Man's Life.*

Trigonal Ballet, also created for the "Software" show, was a very early form of computer animation using mathematics and sound. It gave the matrices layered dimensionality and an infinity effect achieved through tunnels of vanishing triangles. One was able to travel into the deep past and distant future while noting evolutionary changes.

* This concept is further developed in the *Book of Dust* as the "Octopus Model".

© Agnes Denes 1969–1970

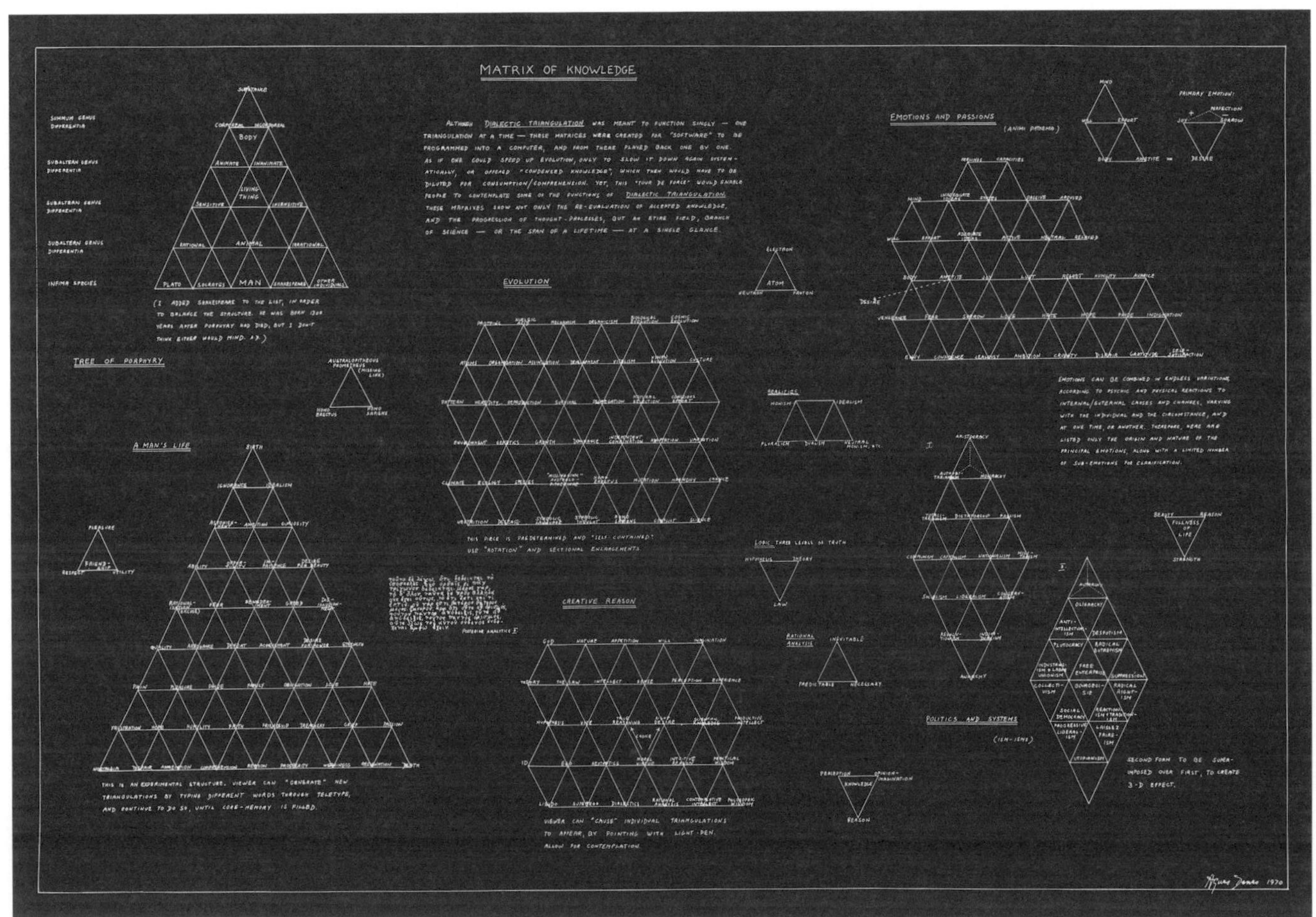
MATRIX OF KNOWLEDGE
TREE OF PORPHYRY
A MAN'S LIFE
EVOLUTION
CREATIVE REASON
EMOTIONS AND PASSIONS
POLITICS AND SYSTEMS

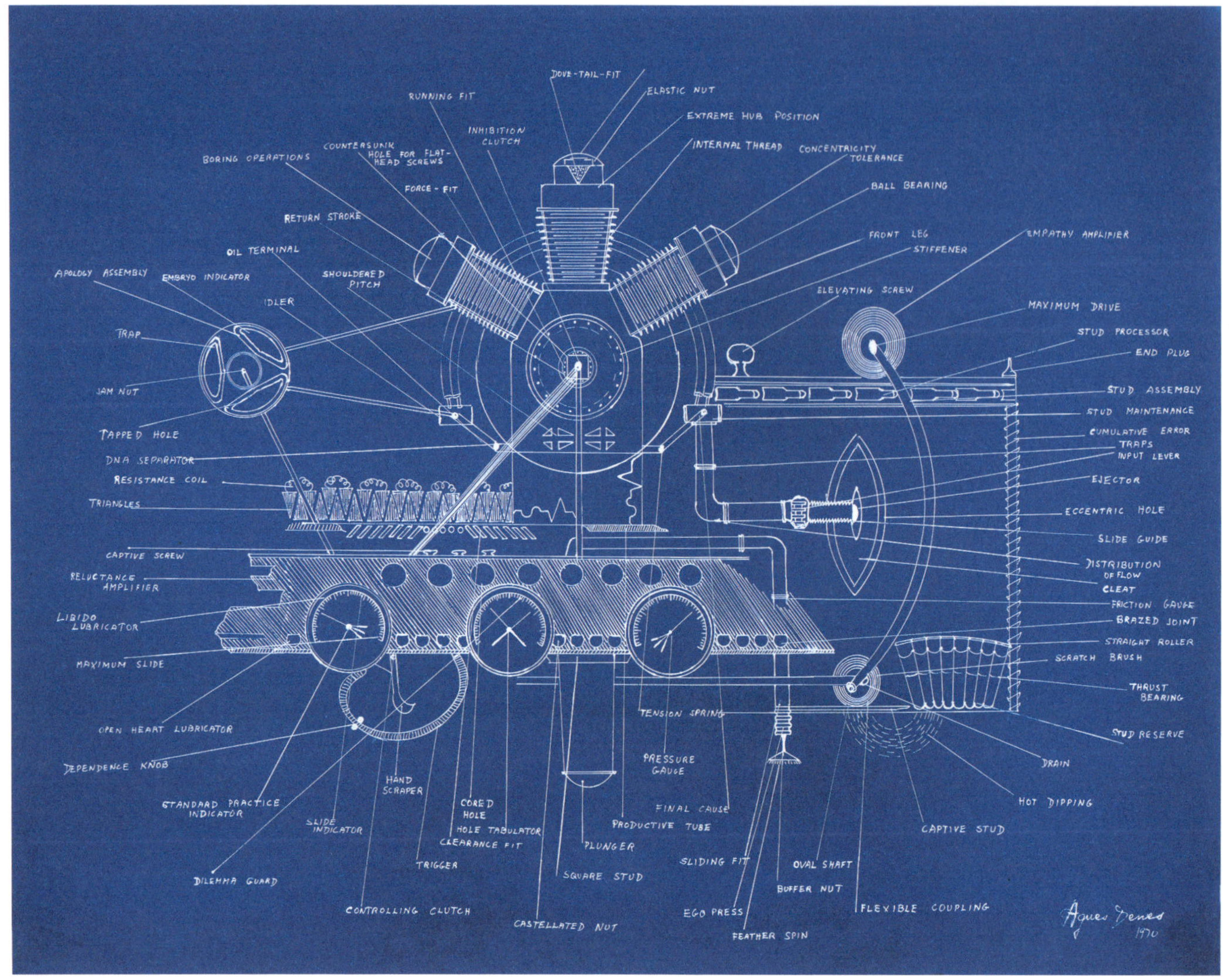
DOVE-TAIL-FIT
RUNNING FIT
ELASTIC NUT
EXTREME HUB POSITION
INHIBITION CLUTCH
INTERNAL THREAD
CONCENTRICITY TOLERANCE
BORING OPERATIONS
COUNTERSUNK HOLE FOR FLAT-HEAD SCREWS
FORCE - FIT
BALL BEARING
RETURN STROKE
FRONT LEG STIFFENER
EMPATHY AMPLIFIER
OIL TERMINAL
APOLOGY ASSEMBLY
EMBRYO INDICATOR
SHOULDERED PITCH
ELEVATING SCREW
MAXIMUM DRIVE
IDLER
TRAP
STUD PROCESSOR
END PLUG
JAM NUT
STUD ASSEMBLY
STUD MAINTENANCE
TAPPED HOLE
CUMULATIVE ERROR TRAPS
DNA SEPARATOR
INPUT LEVER
RESISTANCE COIL
EJECTOR
TRIANGLES
ECCENTRIC HOLE
SLIDE GUIDE
CAPTIVE SCREW
DISTRIBUTION OF FLOW
RELUCTANCE AMPLIFIER
CLEAT
FRICTION GAUGE
BRAZED JOINT
LIBIDO LUBRICATOR
STRAIGHT ROLLER
SCRATCH BRUSH
MAXIMUM SLIDE
THRUST BEARING
OPEN HEART LUBRICATOR
STUD RESERVE
DEPENDENCE KNOB
TENSION SPRING
DRAIN
PRESSURE GAUGE
HAND SCRAPER
STANDARD PRACTICE INDICATOR
CORED HOLE
FINAL CAUSE
HOT DIPPING
SLIDE INDICATOR
HOLE TABULATOR
PRODUCTIVE TUBE
CAPTIVE STUD
CLEARANCE FIT
PLUNGER
SLIDING FIT
DILEMMA GUARD
TRIGGER
SQUARE STUD
OVAL SHAFT
CONTROLLING CLUTCH
CASTELLATED NUT
EGO PRESS
BUFFER NUT
FLEXIBLE COUPLING
FEATHER SPIN
Agnes Denes
1970

<u>Liberated Sex Machine</u>, 1969–1970/2013 [cat. no. 4]
<u>Liberated Sex Machine</u>, 1969–1970/2013 [cat. no. 5]

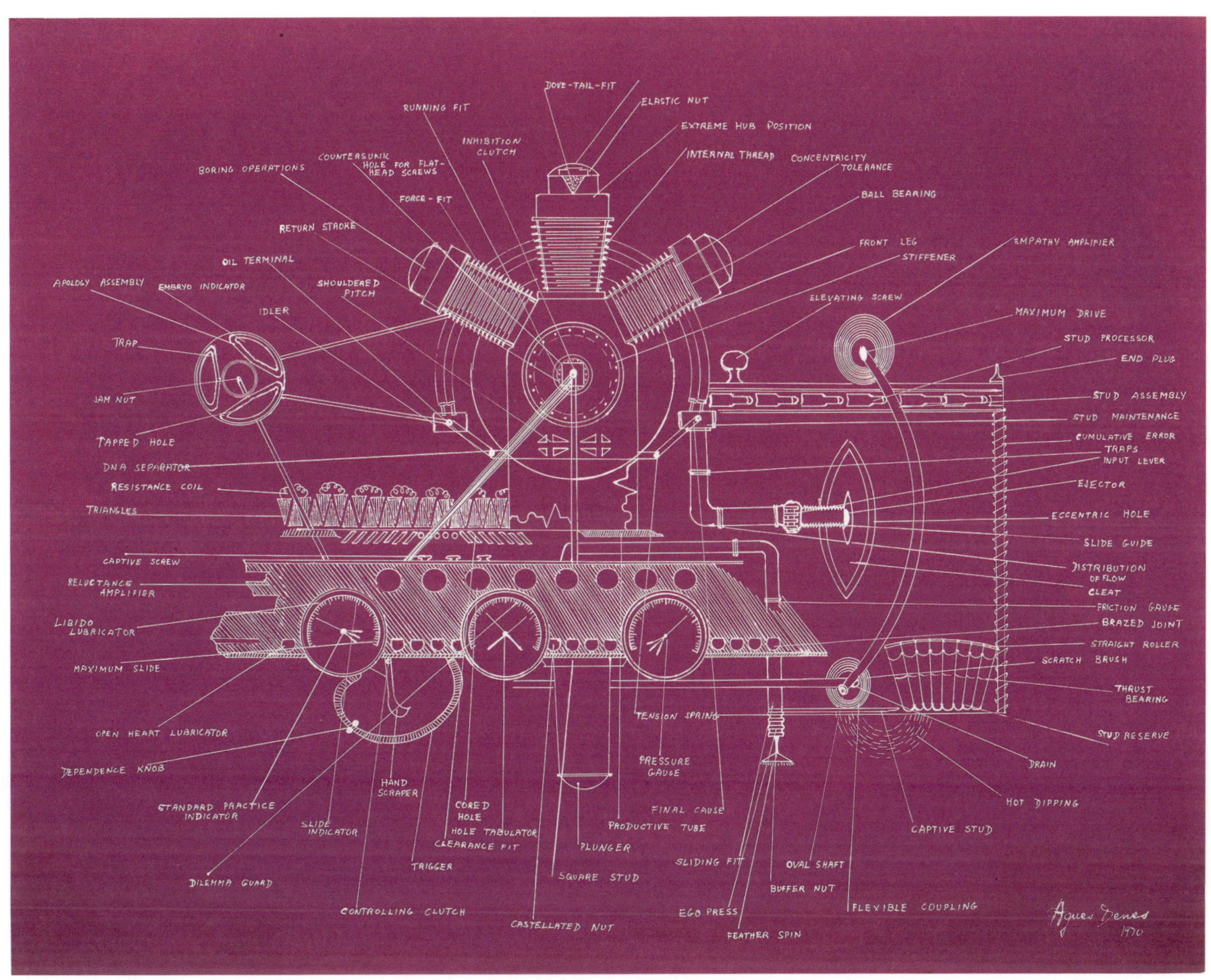

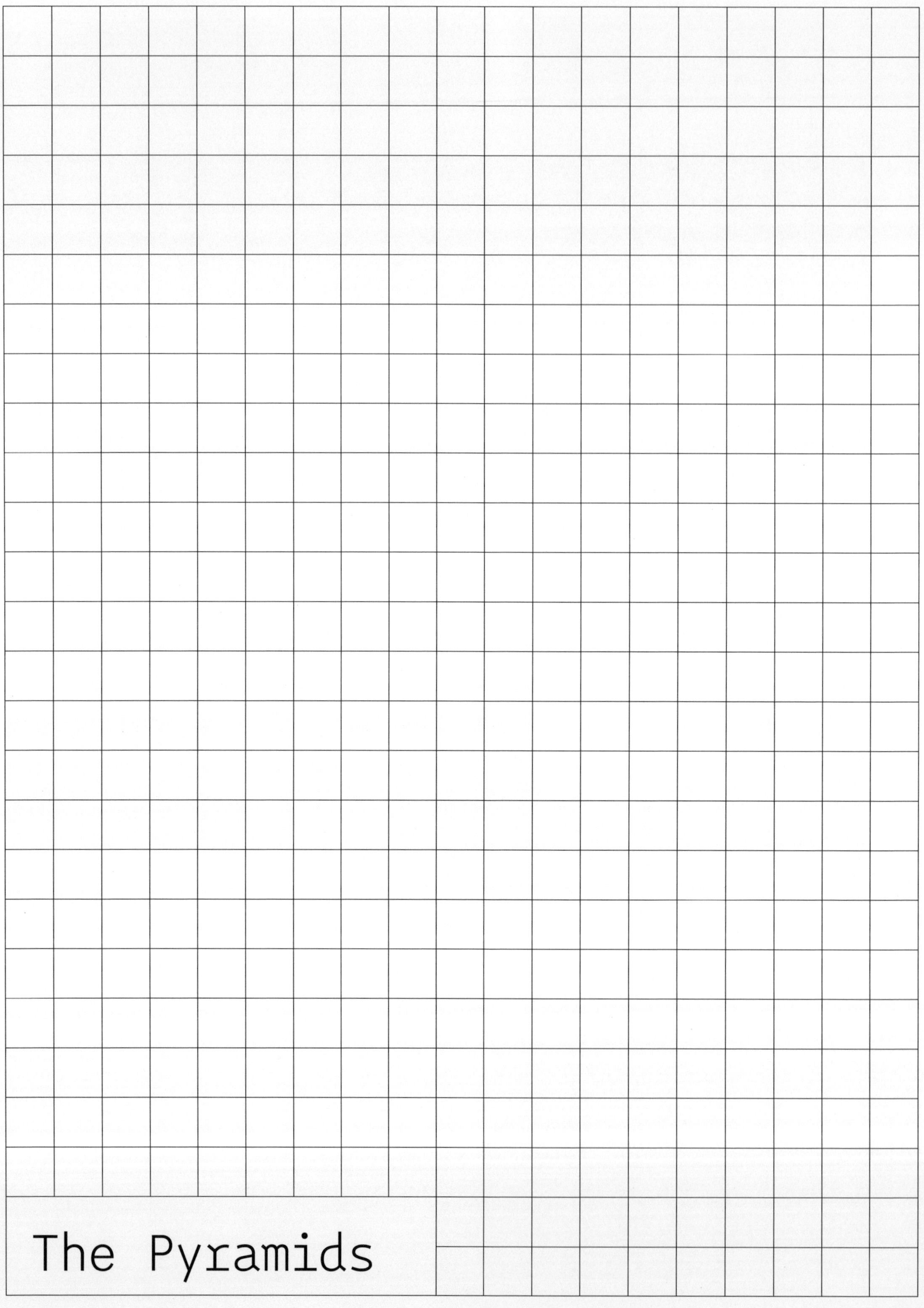

The Pyramids

The Pyramids

The Pyramids

The pyramids appear in my work in a variety of forms from the Snail Pyramid, Egg and Fish Pyramid to pyramids of thought processes, mathematics, forests humanity, survival. These pyramids have little to do with their ancestor pyramids of Egypt, rather they represent social structures, in the form of visual philosophy conveying ecological, social and cultural issues with a purpose to answer humanity's problems, issues of concern and seek benign solutions.

There are real pyramids and exotic ones, imaginary and philosophical, they represent logical structures, architectural innovations and some build societies. They represent the past and the possible future we will invent. Some pyramids are not exactly pyramid shaped and their meaning spans all of human existence.

They may depict a society in the process of tampering with its destiny, with comparisons made to the rise and fall of previous advanced societies that have interfered with their evolution.

Some pyramids form matrices that embrace logical symbols, permutations working out human theoretical concepts, and there are those that represent irony or beauty like the *Crystal Pyramid,* a massive edifice with its millions of reflections.

The materials of the pyramids are diverse as well, they can be stone, etched glass, plantings and even silk. They can be invisible as thought processes, logic and mathematics; or trees when they form a forest; conceptual, shaped like a nautilus when a future city; motion when they seem to awaken; birds when they fly; history when they probe the ancients.

Some pyramids contrast civilizations, others tackle linguistics, some seek origins, the power of nature's innocence and of true beginnings. Some depict the human predicament, and the glory of accomplishments, traditions and overcoming them. Some are made of tiny individuals who perform brilliant tasks, contrasting the magnificence of their collective accomplishments with the insignificance of the individual components. These are the *Masterbilders* who build the *City of Fools.* They map human parameters within the changing aspects of reality and their mathematics represent our striving for perfection, and what's most endearingly human, our weaknesses and flaws.

Some pyramids float in apparent weightlessness, while others are made of the weight of conscience. But what they all convey is the human drama, our hopes and dreams against great odds. They represent the paradoxes of existence and like grand mandalas, define our destiny.

This new work of the *Living Pyramid* is planted material, yet a new meaning. Transformed into blossoms, the Pyramid renews itself as evolution does to our species. The rigid angle becomes an arc to reach above, to reach what it wishes to reach.

It is not just planting, but planting the paradox, a structured edifice of soil and grain, not on a farm or field but in the heart of a busy mega-city. It is planting the seed into soil and human minds.

© Agnes Denes 2015

The Pyramids, 1969–

The Pyramid Series begins with an abstract mathematical theory of probability from which a number system is derived and rendered into visual form for the purpose of exploring its underlying structure, the inner workings of its otherwise invisible transformations. The number system represents a universal concept and *The Pyramids Series* becomes the vehicle through which analytical propositions can be visualized.

As the anatomy of form changes, layers of appearances and assumptions are peeled away to allow elusive processes to emerge. The structure is dissected, reshaped, and fragmented to reveal the most intimate logical patterns. Thus a process develops that probes the essential nature of systems, penetrating down to the core even more basic than skeletal structure or anatomy to seek the formation of form itself.

On this edge new patterns are found and isolated. A reality of changing illusions emerges in flawless, pure forms that remain "perfect" (their own essence) for a moment, instantly metamorphosing into new systems and processes whose origin and destiny are predetermined.

Stations of the Pyramids

In *Pascal's Triangle* (1973–1974) a mathematical solution for the relative probability of accidental repetition of chance occurrences results in a dynamic, spiraling number system. Each line of this pyramid of binomial coefficients is constructed by writing the sum of each pair of adjacent numbers of the line above and putting "1" at each end. The relative probability is given by one particular term divided by the sum of all terms in that line.

Starting with the equilateral triangle, the expansion accelerates so rapidly that if the structure were continued to a height of 22.9 feet, the base would be one mile long. If the base were extended from here to the sun (93 million miles), the tip of the structure would still be only 133 miles high.

Although Pascal's triangle is known and discussed by mathematicians, it has never before been realized in visual form, exposing previously unknown properties that can lead to new discoveries. For example, the drawing reveals that the theory is a three-dimensional, spiraling number system that fits around a shell (shell mathematics), pointing to basic patterns unifying rational thought and nature.

Fragmentations (1973–1974). The network of numbers is removed to show the elusive underlying structure and elegant patterns of its logic (See *Logic of Systems/ Systems of Logic, Patterns of Motion, Pascal's Triangle*).

Probability Pyramid – The Perfect Pyramids (1974–1980). In these new three-dimensional forms and structures, the numbers are transformed into pyramidal stone blocks retaining the curvature and logic-design of the original mathematics. Their "perfection" is the language of mathematics and logic, simple and unadorned, pure as nature's striving toward a kind of perfection by weeding out what is superfluous and making do with only the essentials. Built from the core, the nucleus, they have a natural strength, the power of innocence, that of true beginnings. They communicate their reason for being in the world with complex simplicity. Their "perfection" is also the ideal measure of principles and values within a universal concept. Therefore, the pyramids can now convey these concepts and form monumental structures such as Crystal Pyramid, which reflects its own infinity.

4,000 B.C. (1973) confronts two civilizations, contrasting and drawing analogies between us and the ancient Egyptians whose structures were heavy and everlasting, their thinking "dichotomous". They tended to think in two absolutes, choices limited to two, and a static world view. They believed in day and night (light and dark), life and death, aridity and fertility, and had two gods, the sun Ra and the river Osiris. In contrast, with more advances in science and technology, we seem to have tendencies toward a more "trichotomous" approach to life, culminating in an evolutionary world view and complex theories. Trichotomy, the division into threes, here refers to the building of more complex systems or the breaking down into more intricate divisions, which does not necessarily mean that we are smarter, only more complex. We believe in change and evolution and have tampered with our destiny. Did they as well? Do civilizations that transcend themselves die out? The Egyptians did.

4,000 Years – "If the Mind . . ." (1975). In this work I transliterated one of my statements regarding the nature of art into Middle Egyptian hieroglyphic writing, thus spanning four thousand years of change in communication, language, and concepts. Middle Egyptian – chosen for its purity and richness, and as the best representative of this civilization – made literal translation impossible. Consequently, the limitations of a vocabulary that had served another time and place transformed this philosophical statement born in the twentieth century into sheer poetry.

Probability Pyramid – The Crystal Pyramid (1976) is a one-of-a-kind superstructure that represents our era, as the pyramids of Egypt defined, for all time to come, the Egyptians. It is to be constructed from over 100,000 glass blocks for total light transmission and refraction, with inverted half-vaults shaping the crystal walls adapted to relativity theory and the probability curve. *Crystal Pyramid* appears suspended over a mirror of water, which reflects its oblique form. Access to the pyramid is from the ground below through an underwater tunnel (visible from above through a glass ceiling), which opens into the large interior where myriads of crystal-like reflections create the effect of infinity.

Crystal Pyramid is the opposite of the Egyptian pyramids and their opaque, rigid, heavy mass. Its rhythmic form, iridescence, and apparent weightlessness sets it apart to represent our era and symbolize our civilization in the centuries to come. It is a paradox in concept and design, an elusive temple dedicated to the human spirit and skill. It is at this point that *Crystal Pyramid* joins its Egyptian counterparts in

combining logic, science, and poetry with engineering skill and architectural know-how to address itself to issues that are timeless.

Compared with the usual density and opacity of buildings, this structure is transparent and elusive in its forever-changing effects – a comment on our ideas, on our destiny, and on a universal scheme we can never totally comprehend.

Citadel for the Inner City – The Glass Wall (1975–1976). A long narrow pyramid-shaped wall is constructed from solid glass blocks whose intrinsic design is the binomial expansion system. It is slightly curved, transparent, and elusive to behold, a total contradiction to what is expected of a wall or fortress. It distorts and fragments reality, offering constantly changing illusions instead.

In *The Master Builders* (1979). an army of tiny people enters a world of constant flux. Born of a mathematical concept, they assume various states of being and activity, leaving perfection behind but retaining the system and structure.

The probability curve of Pascal's triangle is reintroduced as the *Master Builders* form new patterns of evolutionary ambiguity. This is the moment when pattern turns into form and begins to spin the logic that shapes the web to become both skeletal structure and its covered flesh.

Pascal's Perfect Probability Pyramid & The People Paradox – The Predicament (1980) depicts a society composed of individuals who stand in protected isolation, alone but without privacy. They cannot escape the structure yet seem to be fooled by illusions of freedom. Representing alienation in togetherness and uniqueness in uniformity, they assume the journey of living paradox. Although each figure is different, carefully drawn to represent distinct individuals acting out countless lives (there are over sixteen thousand people in the drawing), ultimately they all seem identical and indistinguishable. The dissimilarities are almost imperceptible yet become quite noticeable at close scrutiny. The pyramid they form is a society of visual mathematics in which they are but patterns and processes, number components of a mathematical system who believe they are unique entities.

The endless contradictions they seem to accept into their lives, their ability to know so much and understand so little, makes them very endearing. They are emotionally unstable yet manage complicated technological miracles and do not seem to realize that their great advances have interfered with their own evolution.

The magnificence of their collective accomplishments and the insignificance of the individual component are unmistakable. Not a single tiny figure can walk away from the structure – they ARE the structure. They are the anatomy and the form and it is their illusions of freedom and the inescapability of the system that forms the ultimate paradox. They span a delicate balance between universals and the self, between the moment and eternity, and with great courage proceed to build the Perfect Pyramids.

Theories Tampered With – The Second Predicament (1982) depicts a society in the process of tampering with its destiny. We become witnesses to the gradual but drastic changes in the patterns and functions of a design forced to form a bottleneck. One wonders what effect this drastic change will have on the inhabitants, how the tiny figures will react to being forced through the bottleneck, and how it will affect their personalities and duties. When the system quietly explodes, setting off ripples of inevitable consequences, the inhabitants do not seem to notice or mind. They seem more at ease now, as if having gone through the bottleneck and survived was all that mattered.

In *The Magic Mountain I* (1982) the populace seems quite content as they stream and traverse down the slopes forming the landscape. But in *Magic Mountain II* (1985) a quiet unrest can be detected. One must look very closely to notice that some of the solitary figures have broken formation, have detached themselves from the paths of precision. Almost imperceptibly, a small crowd is beginning to gather at the bottom of the slopes. They seem unaware that by breaking away the landscape will disintegrate. Later drawings reveal the consequences that follow.

Snail People – The Vortex (1989). The third predicament concentrates on the plight of very sophisticated individuals who form a complicated structure. As they reach the center they seem to be caught in a vortex, pulled by eddies in opposite directions. There are two whirlpools spinning toward each other, but since one group is on the inside, the other on the outside of its universe, they are separated by dimensions the inhabitants can never traverse.

Tower of Babel (1983). The biblical tower of confusion is redesigned with state-of-the-art technology, eventually to become its own Shadow, the poetry of its architecture.

The City (1985). The individual's dilemma is superseded by the predicament of the species. The ruins of super-sophisticated pyramids represent technological miracles produced by restless, noble but unstable creatures and tell of ideas that flourished or else were destroyed by a race that was capable of greatness yet somehow remained no different from others before it. They toy with their destiny and leave great ruins. But each civilization has its own method and reason for becoming extinct or surviving and as such, this one is unique.

The City is an important place. This is where things get sorted out, where innocence and decadence walk hand in hand. It is the belly as well as the brain of the animal. *The City* is not unhappy though it may be unaware. There is a lot of excitement going on here as they are busy creating the best ruins yet for future generations to ponder and be filled with awe.

The Perfect Pyramids and the City of Fools (Model for a Flawless Ruin), 1986. The City is filled with pyramids built by the *Master Builders* according to the map of *The First Predicament*. Now we are beginning to understand why the pyramids are called perfect and why they must leave perfect ruins, and soon we shall also know about the City of Fools.

A symbiotic relationship exists between *The City* and the *Master Builders*, who support the *City* while it supports them. Meanwhile, a much more complicated hierarchical situation runs concurrently on many levels. Just as cells in a body come together to form organs which in turn form complete organisms, the inhabitants form neighborhoods, then cities and societies. Great interdependence is essential to both: cells working together can accomplish what an individual cell cannot, and the inhabitants together can do what alone they cannot. It gets complicated when the organism becomes too complex and thus susceptible to changes in its equilibrium. The more complex the system, the easier it is for the balance to be disrupted. Whether the breakdown occurs internally or externally, the interdependence is such that the organism breaks down on all levels of its hierarchy. Cells as individuals may live on, often to form new organisms. The species goes on and new art is made.

The Map of the City (1987).
Layout: four-point perspective.

The Inner City contains the *Neighborhood of Consistency* and the *Square of New Roots*. The square is filled with statues representing individuals sitting on various animals such as tigers, dinosaurs, fishes, and pigs.

The Citadel of Pride is deep in the mountains surrounded by fabricated ruins interspersed with those created by natural causes. *The Archives of Human Values,* which is deteriorating, faces the *Pillars of Assumptions*, inscribed by the elders, and the *Temple of Narcissism*, a cave of reflecting crystals. *The Boulevard of Skills* crosses *Terror Park*, and just below it lies the *Avenue of Intentions* leading to *Power Drive* and *Error Lane.*

The major square in the center of town is called *Common Ground,* which is used for interrogations, punishments, dedications, and celebrations – often simultaneously.

The Perfect Pyramids are found throughout the *City.* Their interiors are somewhat different but the exteriors are all identical – only the sizes vary.

Plaques are everywhere, honoring physical excellence and training, accuracy and speed. *The Master Builders* are everywhere, swarming over the *City*, ceaselessly on the run. They all go to sleep every night to rejuvenate themselves and awake more or less at the same time. They feed themselves by eating other animals, fruits, and plants of the land. Each is bound by a skin container separating it from the others and from the rest of the world, creating a subjective self-state with a trapped consciousness and a fixed perspective from within. They take great pride in their organization and accomplishments and in the *Perfect Pyramids.*

The inhabitants tend to their young with great affection but cannot help contaminating them, so that each new generation grows up with more or less the same propensities and parameters. Thus misconceptions are nurtured and propagated until these are totally ingrained in their culture. Everything repeats itself endlessly. They are trying to find some use for the elderly because they are embarrassed by them, reminded of their own frailty.

The City is divided by a river called *You Can't Step Into Me Twice.* The two banks thus created are *the Left* and *the Right Hemispheres*. One is considered to be evil and the other good. Everything inside the bodies of the inhabitants also comes in pairs. They have two eyes, nostrils, lungs, brains, hands, feet, and so on.

There are guards everywhere who watch that the river flows, egos are replenished, and promises are kept. The guards are not supposed to wash in the river but they do. The outskirts of the *City* are terribly neglected. Nothing lives there but the stones, waiting to become blocks for the *Perfect Pyramids.* Occasionally, an elderly or a defective is found and, once, someone claimed to have seen a mystic.

All the *Restless Pyramids* (1983–) are related and they are born *When the Pyramids Awaken.* Realizing they are organic forms, the pyramids lose their rigidity and stillness. They begin to stretch and sway, as they break loose from the tyranny of being built, knitted into form. They proceed to unglue their units, the program and method that bind their cell structure. Once their elements are free, the *Restless Pyramids* become flexible to take on dynamic forms of their own choosing.

At this point they decide to fend for themselves and create their own destiny. They also begin to look out for the inhabitants, for whom they create environments.

This is the birth of giant *Fish Pyramids*, *Flying Bird Pyramids*, and pyramids in the shape of an *Egg* or a *Teardrop*. They are created for a different world in which the inhabitants will live in space, hovering above Earth, or else live on Earth in self-contained environments. These structures have little of "science fiction" about them; rather, they are pure technology with yet another kind of "perfection", that of the flexibility of natural systems. They have a look of freshness and vulnerability. They are the future and the future is always vulnerable and unused.

The Egg Pyramid – Self-Contained, Self-Supporting City Dwelling (1984) is a structure designed to house and completely sustain its inhabitants, providing food, education, health care, entertainment, and other needs.

Flying Bird Pyramid for the Twenty-Second Century (1984) and *Flying Half Bird* (1984) are the first space environments/stations with flexible, self-regenerating, and easy-to-repair units or modules resembling natural systems.

Fish Pyramid – A Floating Water Habitat (1984) is a resilient and versatile water habitat, a floating city that supports life on or under water as either becomes necessary.

Teardrop in Space (1984) is a floating monument.

These benevolent forms direct their own destiny depending on neither the *City of Fools* nor *The Paradox* for their principles of "perfection". Like grand mandalas, they define our destinies.

The copyright dates of these works correspond to the dates given above. This is an ongoing project.

© Agnes Denes 1984

The Pyramids as They Were, 1994 [cat. no. 6]
When the Pyramid Awakens, 1994 [cat. no. 7]

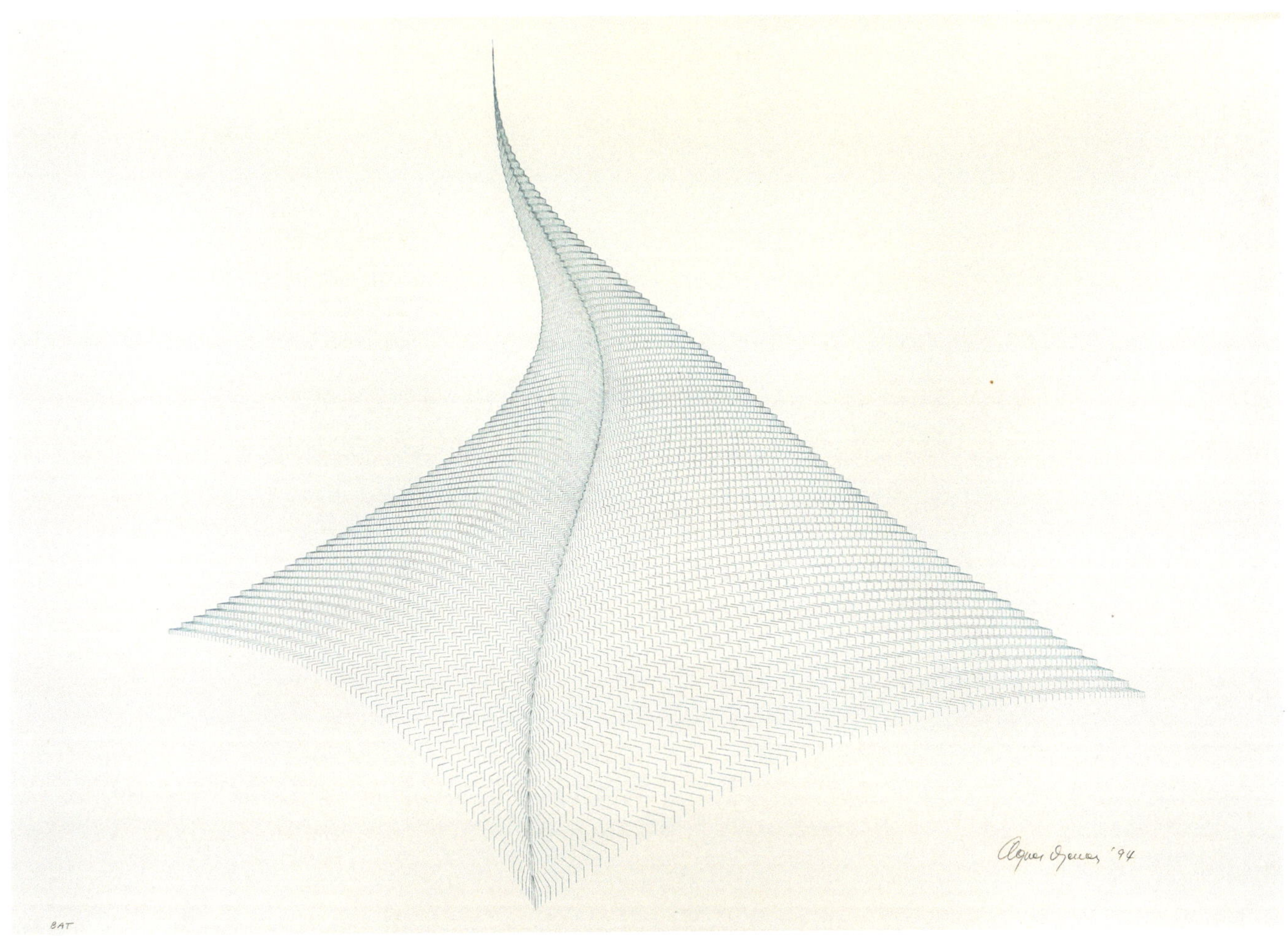

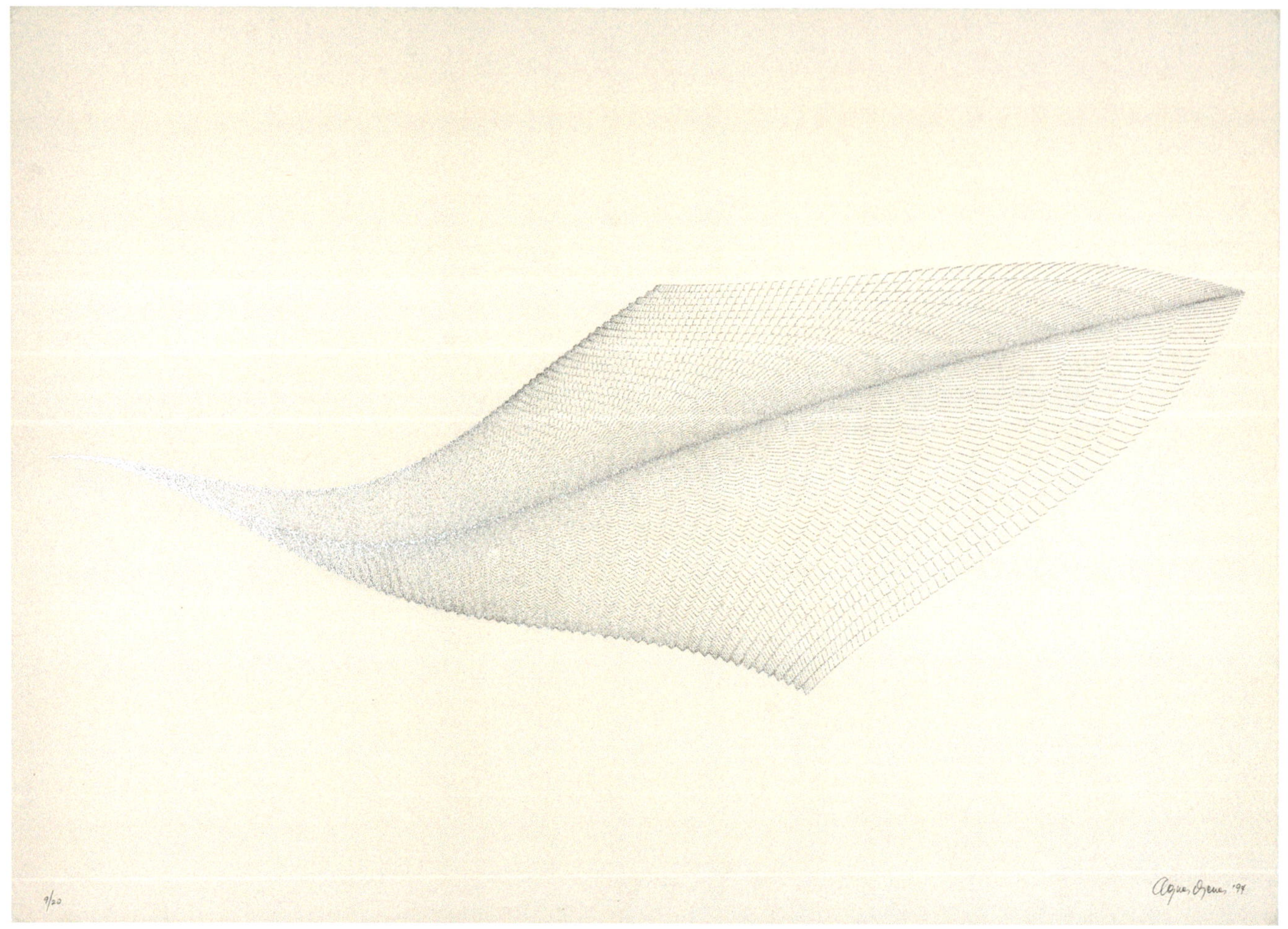

Fish Pyramid - Noah's Ark for the New City, 1994 [cat. no. 8]
Flying Bird Pyramid, 1994 [cat. no. 9]

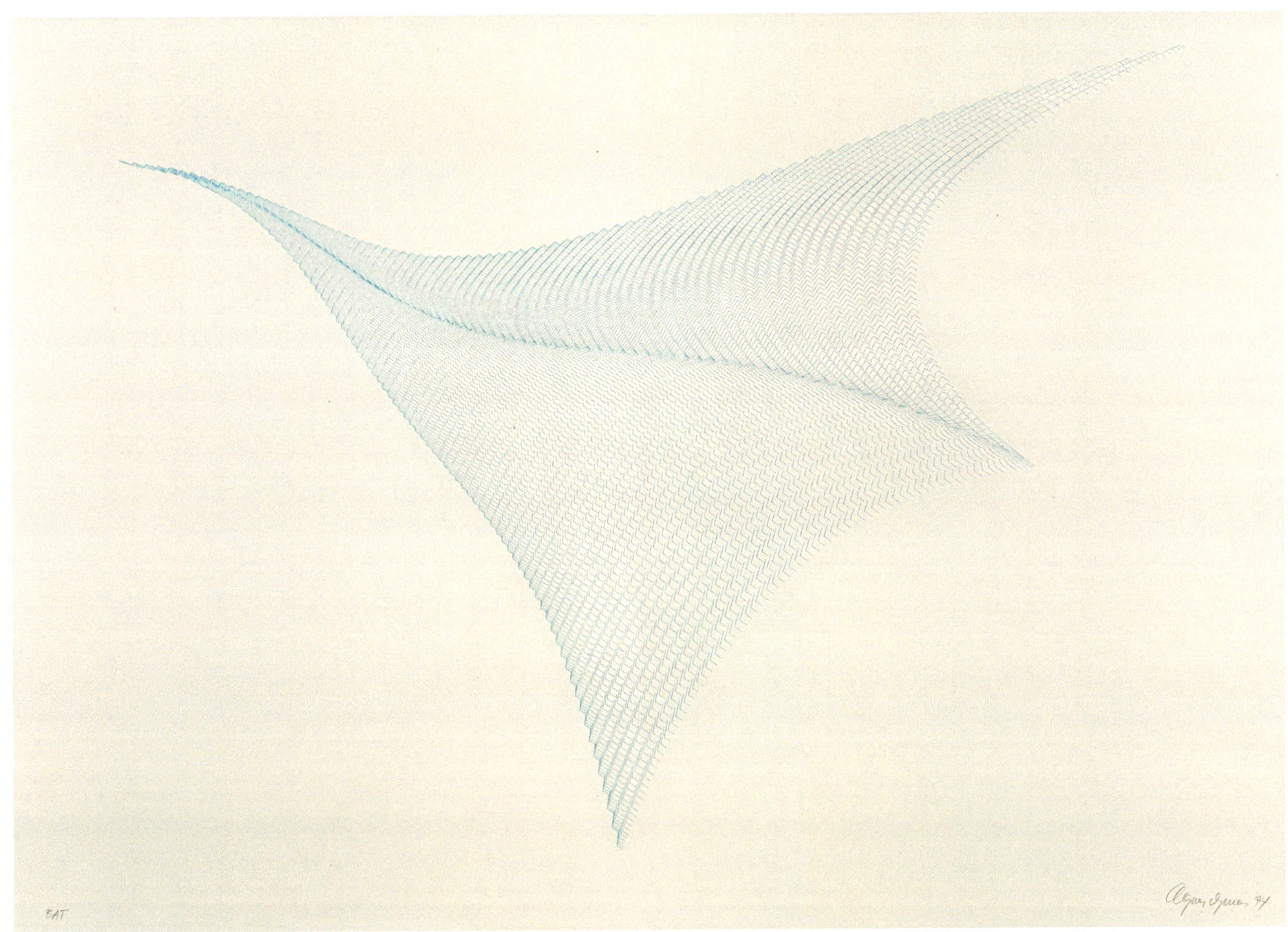

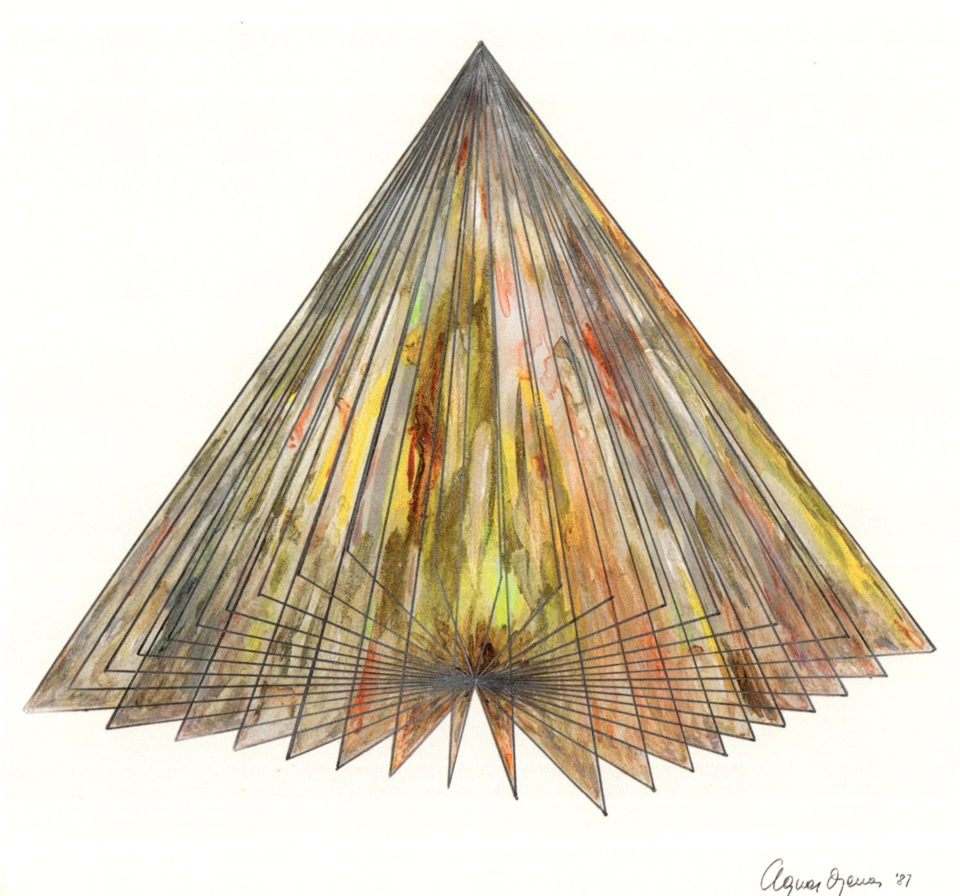

Pyramid, 1987 [cat. no. 10]
The Reflection, 1981 [cat. no. 11]

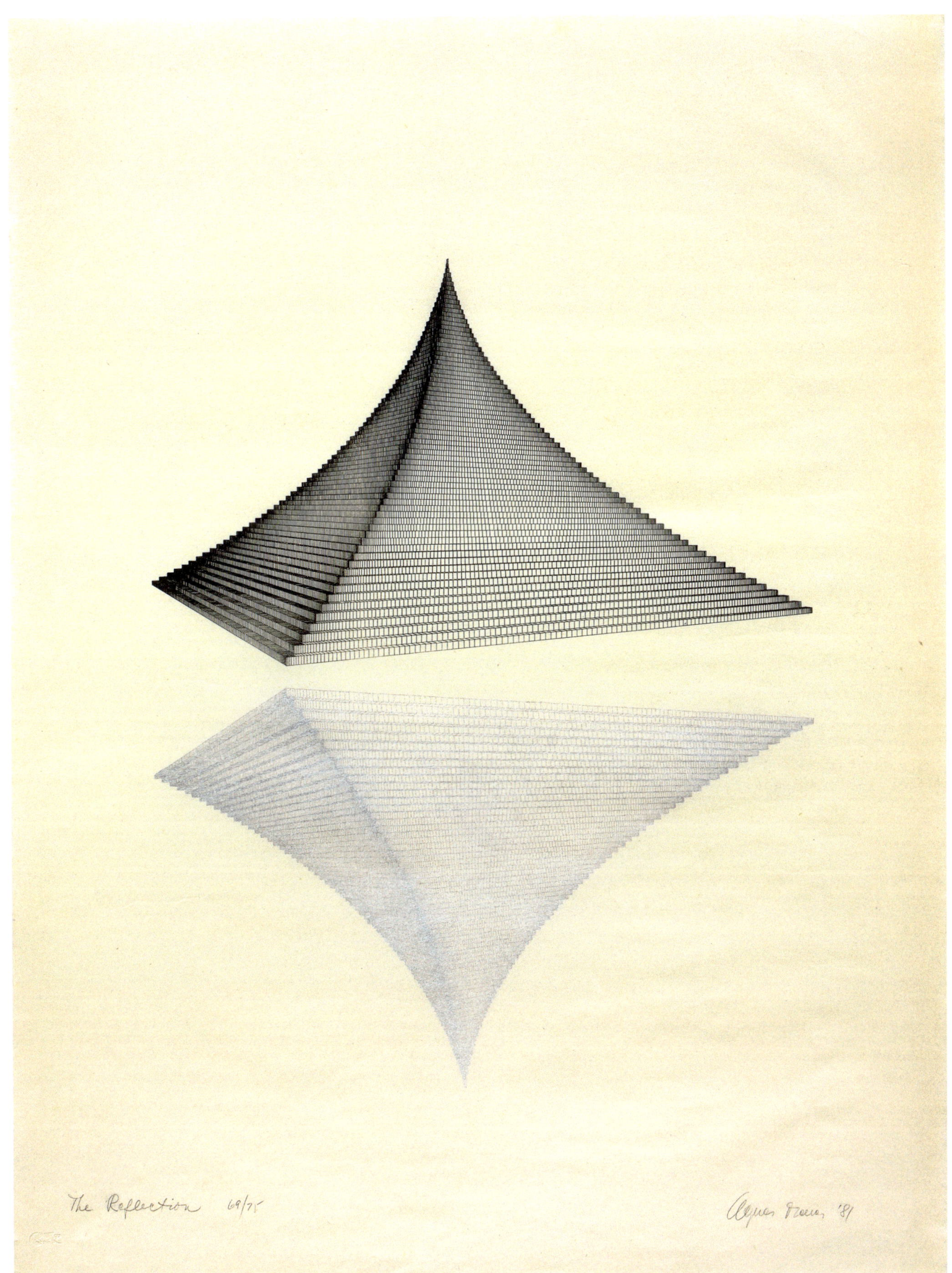

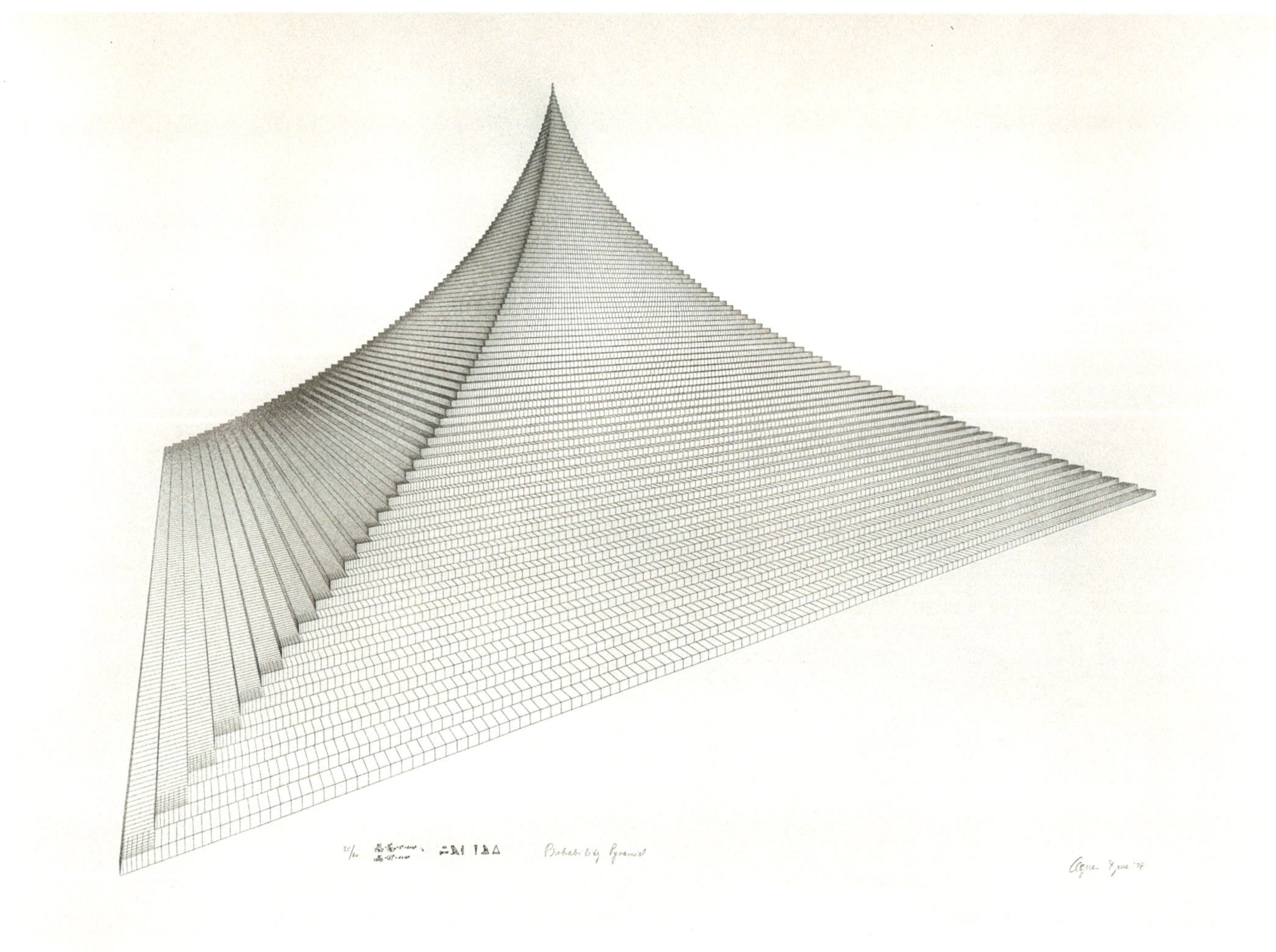

Probability Pyramid, 1978 [cat. no. 12]
Probability Pyramid II, 1981 [cat. no. 13]

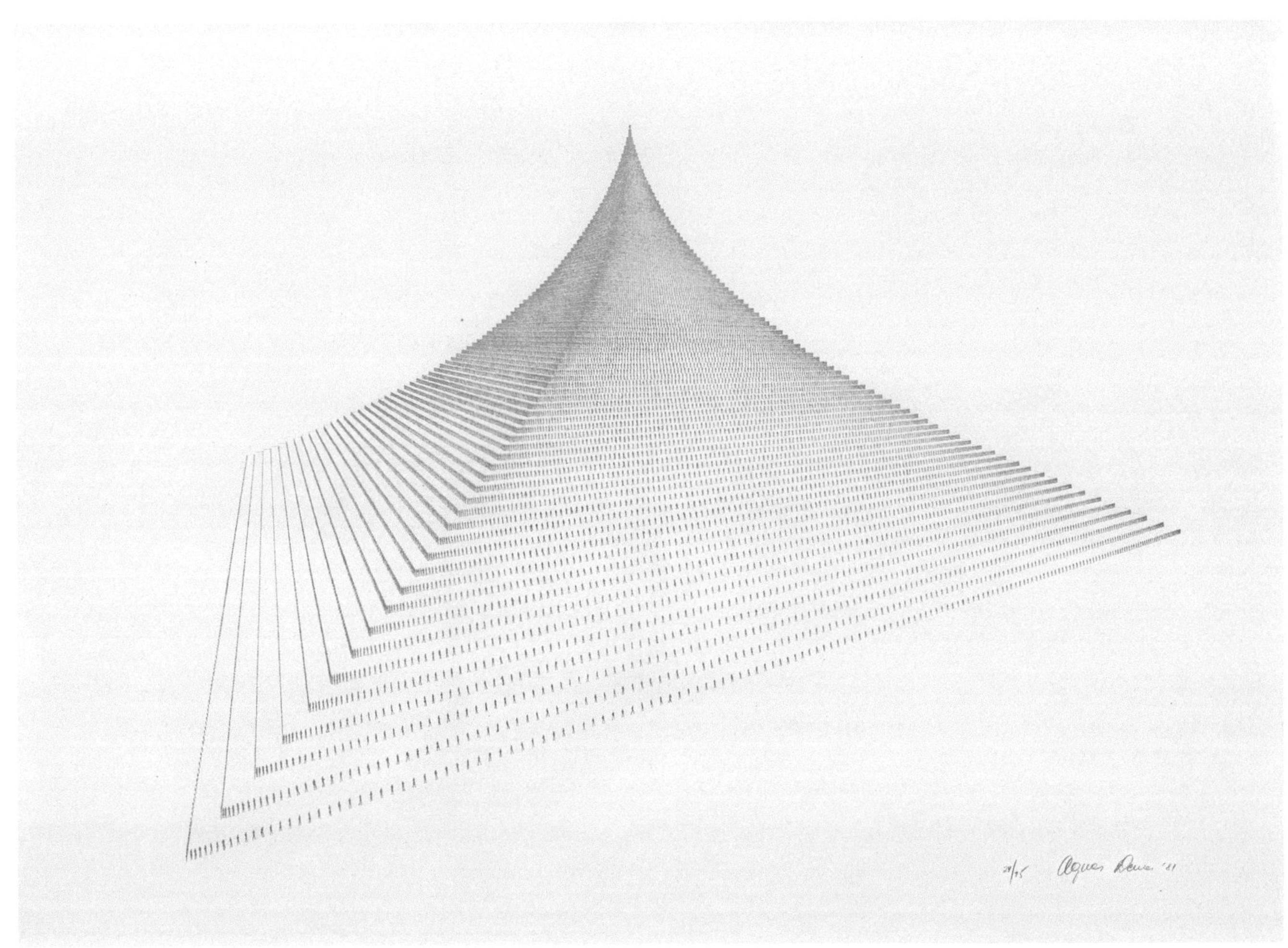

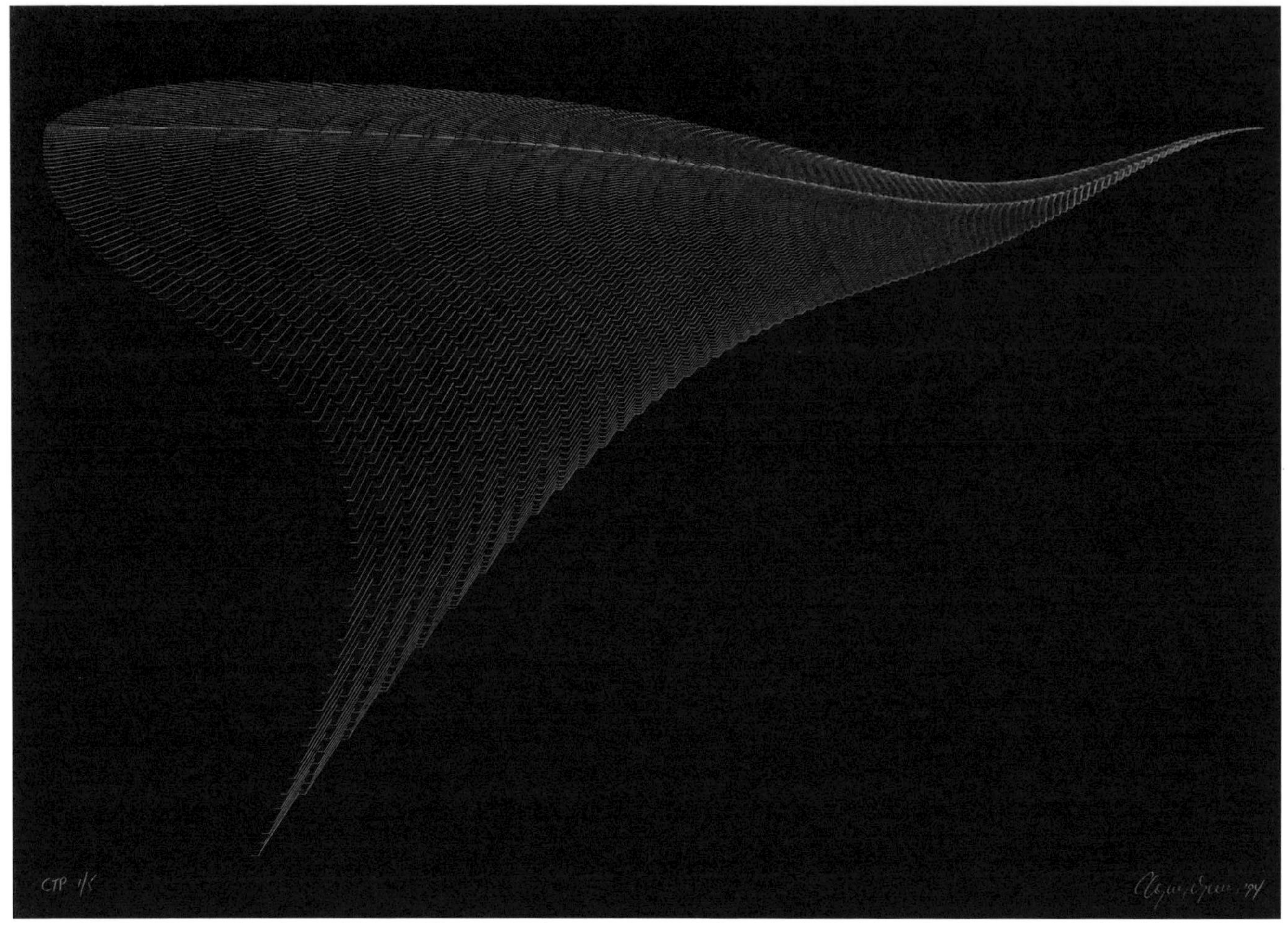

<u>Half Bird - A Flexible Space Station</u>, 1994 [cat. no. 14]
<u>Flying Fish Pyramid - A Floating Water Habitat</u>, 1984 [cat. no. 15]

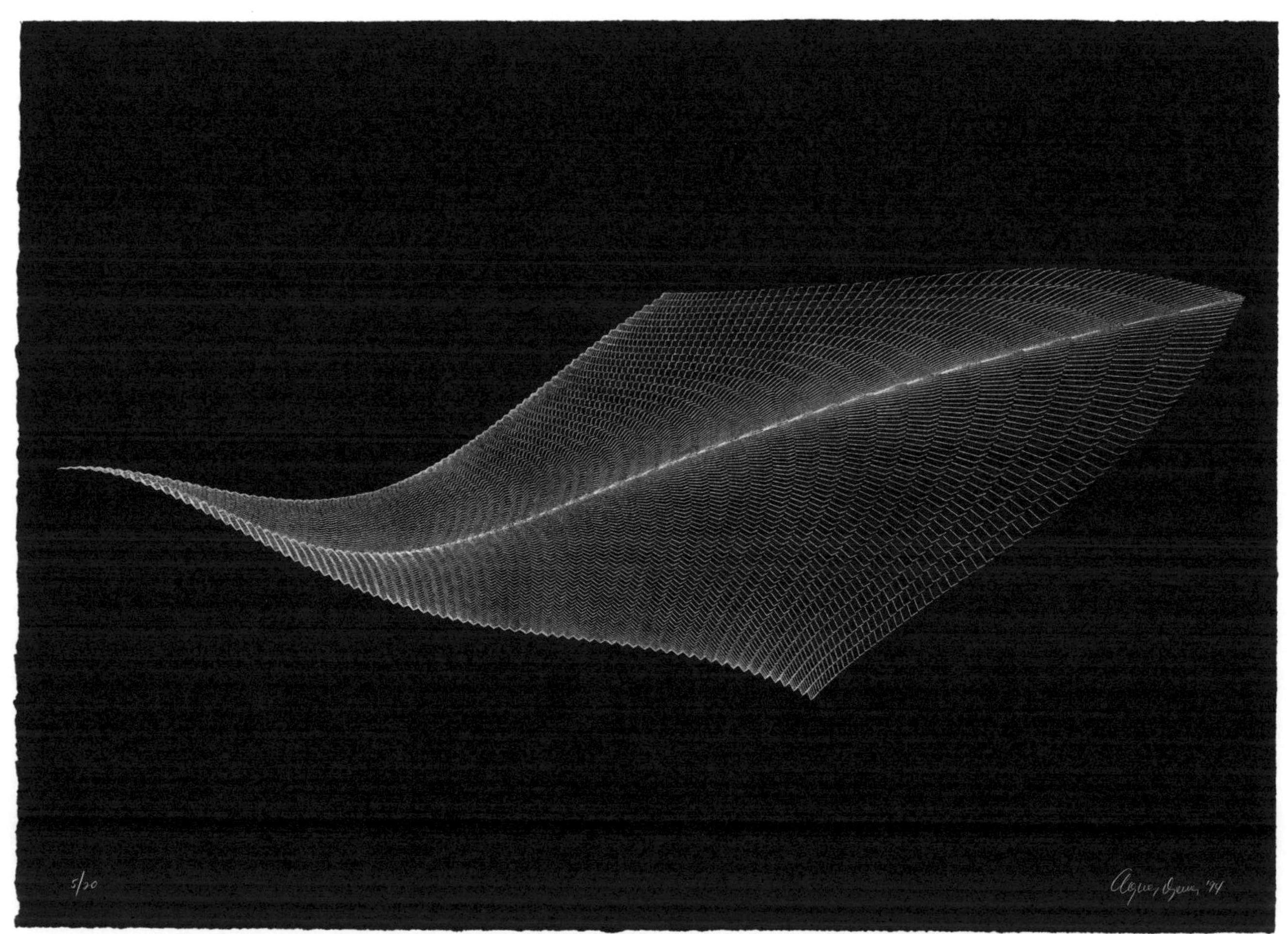

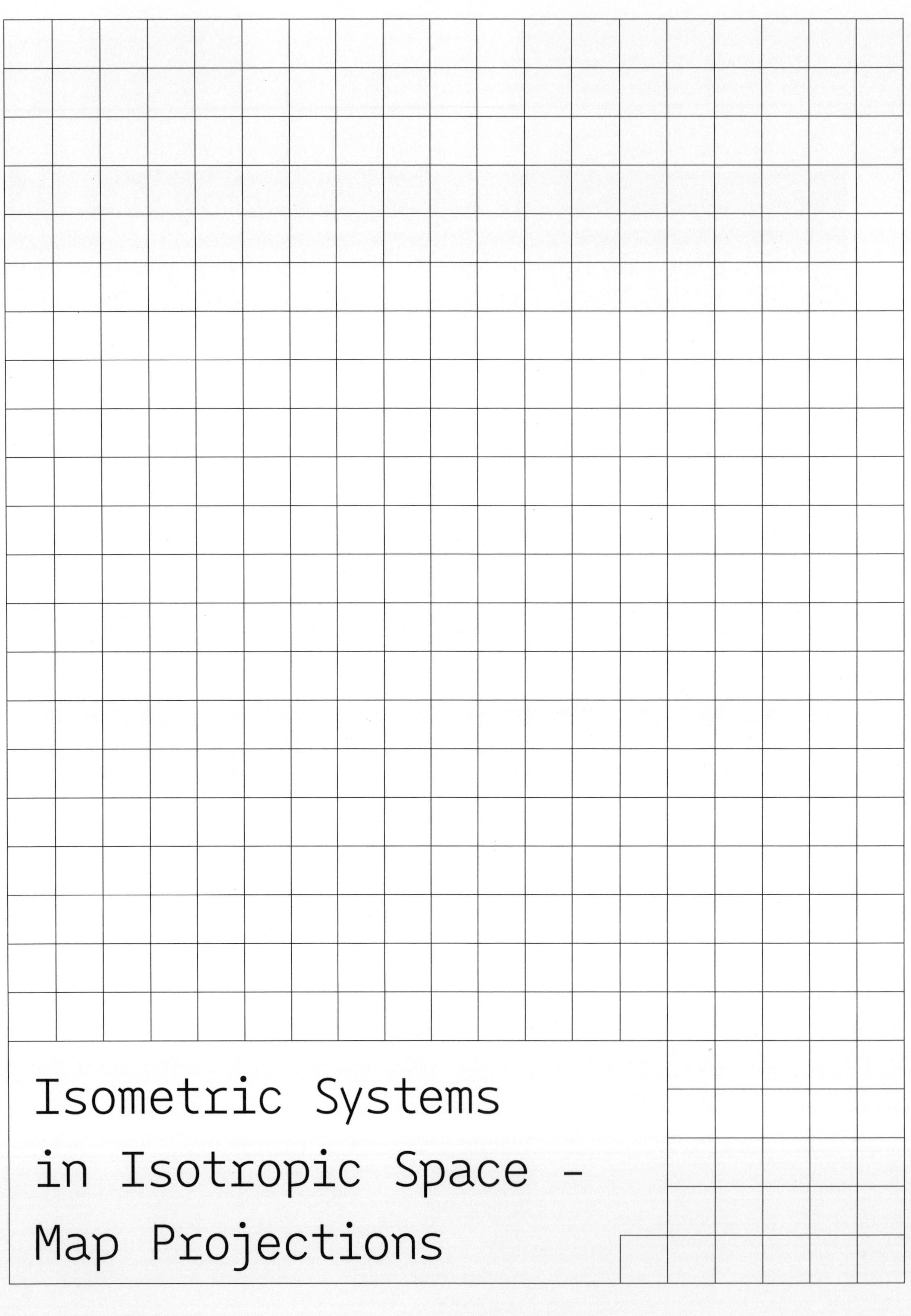

Isometric Systems in Isotropic Space – Map Projections

Isometric Systems in Isotropic Space - Map Projections

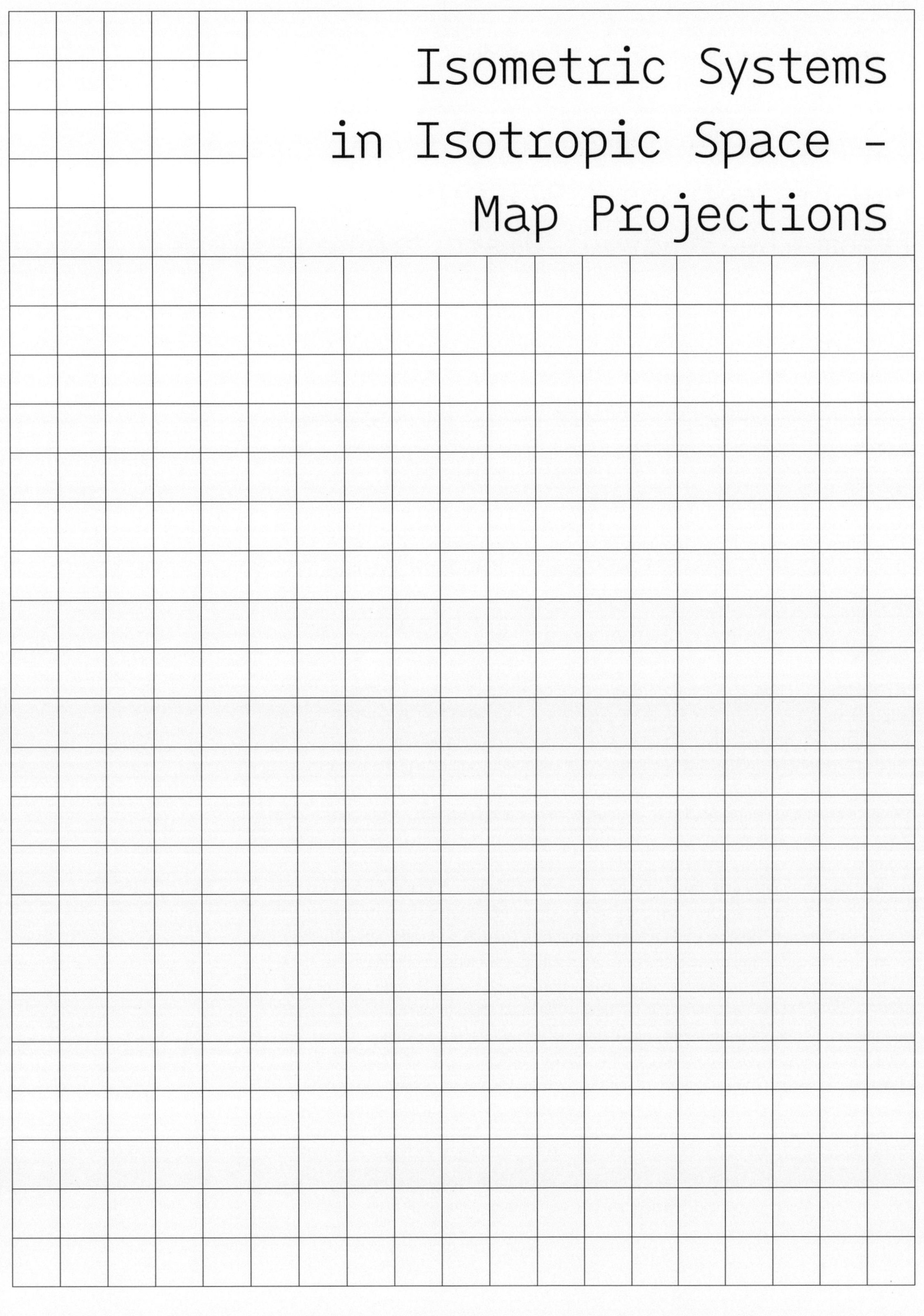

Isometric Systems in Isotropic Space - Map Projections, 1973-1979 (from the Study of Distortions series)

Map Projections, like most of my work, maps human perimeters within the changing aspects of reality and involves distortions and perspective, probability and space relations, transformations and interactions of phenomena. In essence, mathematical forms are projected over fluid space to create distortions of our globe into the pyramid, the cube, and the dodecahedron (three polyhedra); the doughnut (tangent torus); the egg (sinusoidal ovoid); the snail (helical toroid); and the lemon (prolate ovoid). Additional forms are the hot dog and the geoid.

Entropy (amorphous continents) envisions and maps unique phenomena in the creation or final entropy of global systems and universal coordinates in space/time.

Fragmentation (an integral part of my work for the past ten years, closely aligned with *Study of Distortions*) is here applied to the floating continents.

Map Projections creates sculptural form in celestial space and presents analytical propositions in visual form. It is a tantalizing game if one learns to read between coordinates and doesn't mind making sport of the human predicament. It takes place in hypersphere using all of our space – our entire orbiting home in the universe. *Map Projections* is sculptured reality, based on the conflicting and interdependent elements of art and existence, illusion and reality, imagination and fact, chaos and order, irrationality and reason. It projects a dynamic world of rapidly changing concepts and measures, where the appearances of things, facts, and events are assumed manifestations of reality and distortions are the norm. In this new relativistic existence, objects become processes and forms are patterns in motion. Matter is a form of energy and our own human substance is but spinning velocity. There is no solid matter and no empty space; time becomes an earthbound reality but remains an enigma in the fourth dimension. Even the laws of nature may undergo evolutionary changes and one becomes aware of the relativity of reality. Knowledge must be reassessed to cope with the new concepts of probability and catastrophe theories, curved space, black holes, the uncertainty principle, and possible other universes. We must create a new language, consider a transitory state of new illusions and layers of validity, and accept the possibility that there may be no language to describe ultimate reality, beyond the language of visions.

Map Projections enters art in the form of process, involving the pleasures of doing – shaping, transforming, splitting, erasing, and the excitement of the search, the hunt, the analysis, the discovery.

Isometric Systems in Isotropic Space - Map Projections:
Pyramidal Projection (Budapest version), 1973/2018 [cat. no. 16]

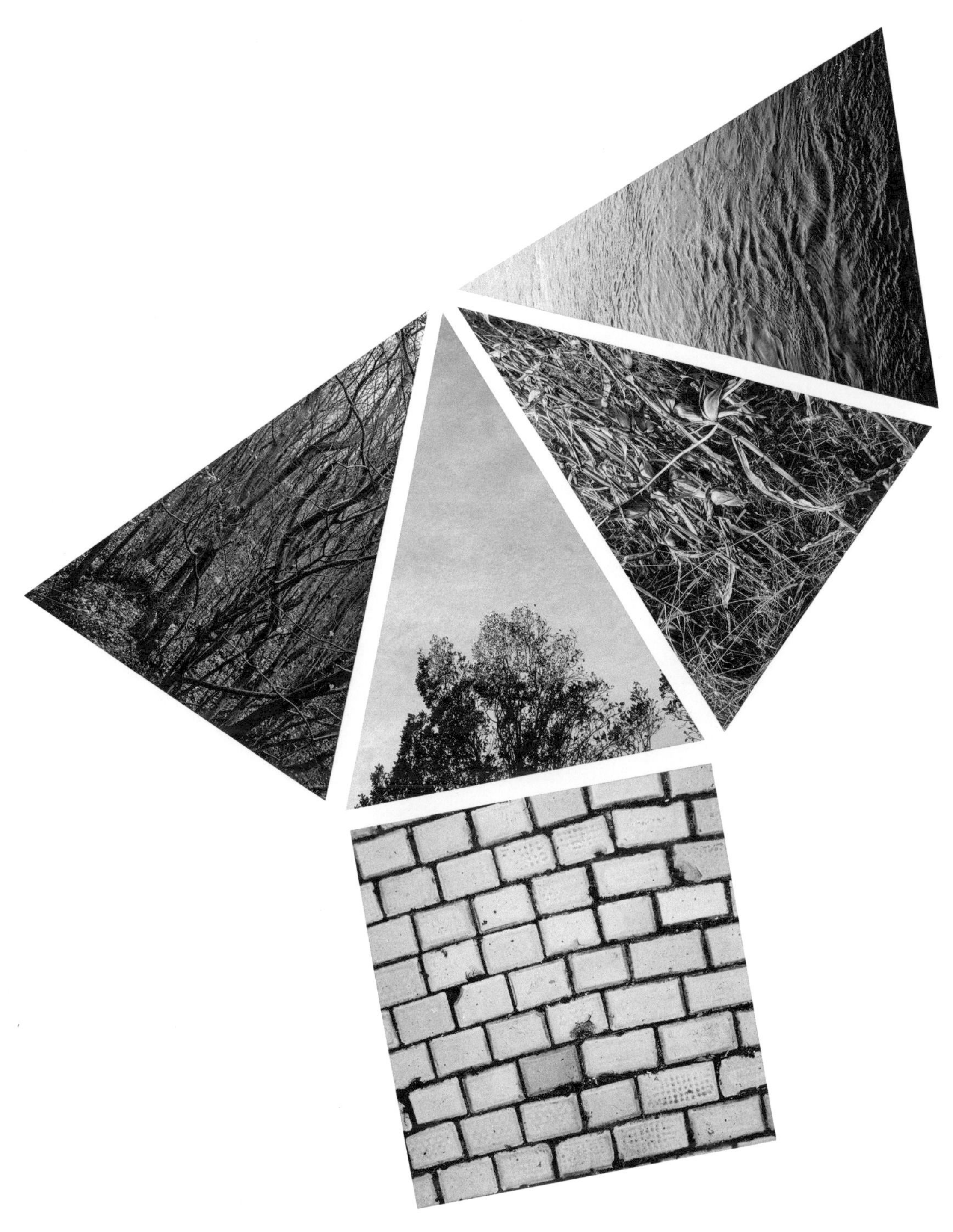

Point of departure: rejection of existing information, zero dimension. Followed by the amassing of new data, assessment and choice. The anatomy of form is studied, vectors are built, earth measurements and scale factors rearranged, grid systems created and dimensions added. And when the perfect form slowly emerges, it is carefully obliterated, dissected and pulled apart, not only to find further beauty but to gain other perspectives. The live skin of the globe is peeled, the dynamic mantle stripped bare to expose the membrane of grids and coordinates down to the core of gravitational mass, the nucleus. At this point elusive processes and invisible structures begin to emerge. Longitude and latitude lines are unraveled to form networks of consciousness on new levels of awareness. The remaining points of intersections are cut, and the continents allowed to drift. Gravity has been tampered with, earth mass altered, polar tension released. The north pole is forced to meet the south or they are pulled apart.

The consequences are then observed, weighed, and reassessed. There is change in orbital rotation, chemical structure, physical operations, gravitational pull, time dilatations, tidal waves, compression and expansion of matter, and of course, whatever the necessary effects are on us, inhabitants. The remaining degrees float in space to map the moment, eventually to realign themselves around new forces and form new loyalties. The boundaries have been transgressed, the orbital spin arrested, and momentum held still in conceptual form.

But the hard-won knowledge is once again relinquished, and new forms and possibilities are sought. And there you have it. Substance and matter, structure and system blend with first causes, final causes, and the ex nihilo. Polar implosion, velocity, momentum, inertia, the quest, the hunt. Searching for the logic of matter, a glimpse at the formation of form, knowledge gained and abandoned, the game won or lost. And the game is all there is.

© Agnes Denes 1976

Isometric Systems in Isotropic Space - Map Projections:
The Hot Dog, 1976 [cat. no. 17]

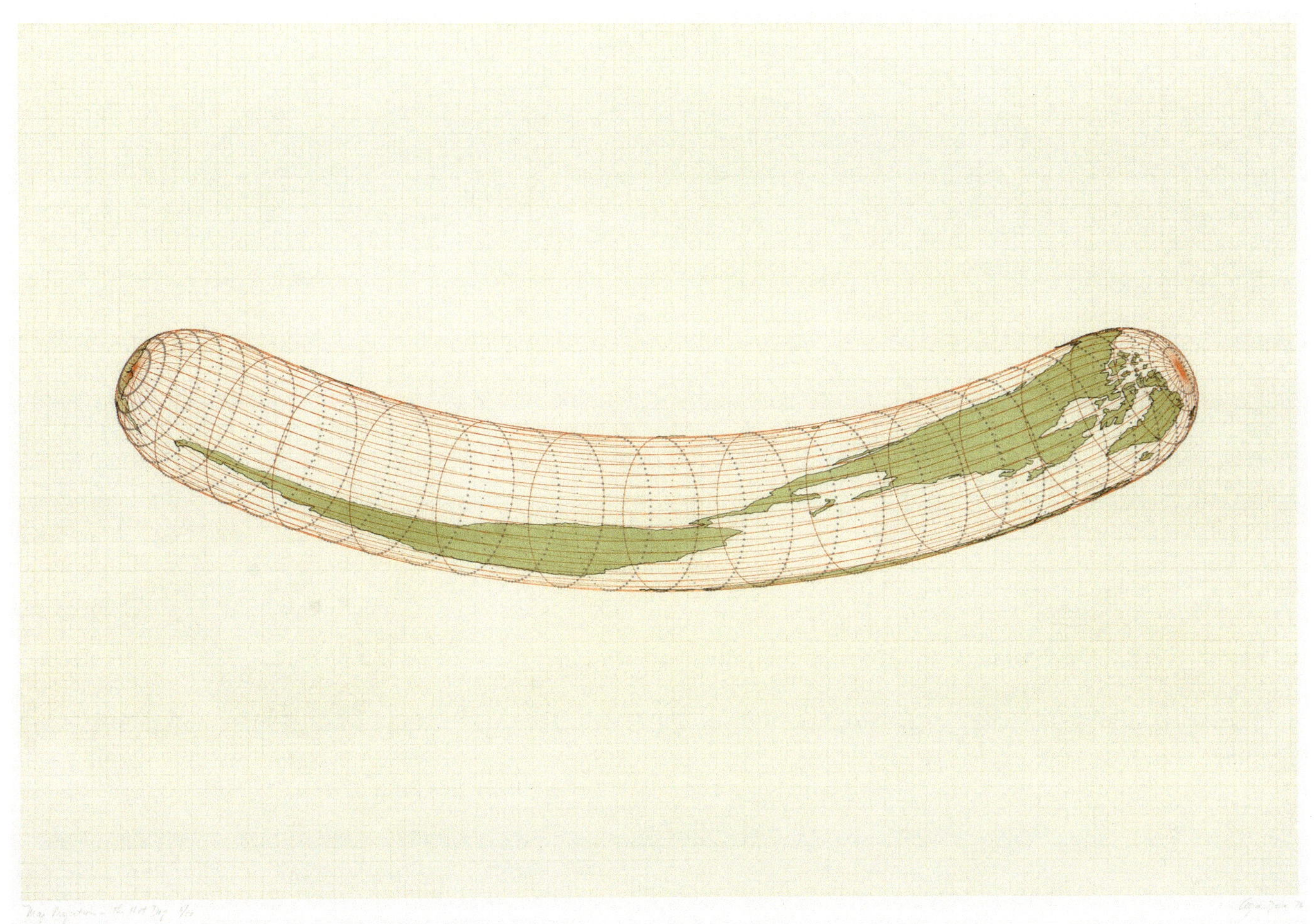

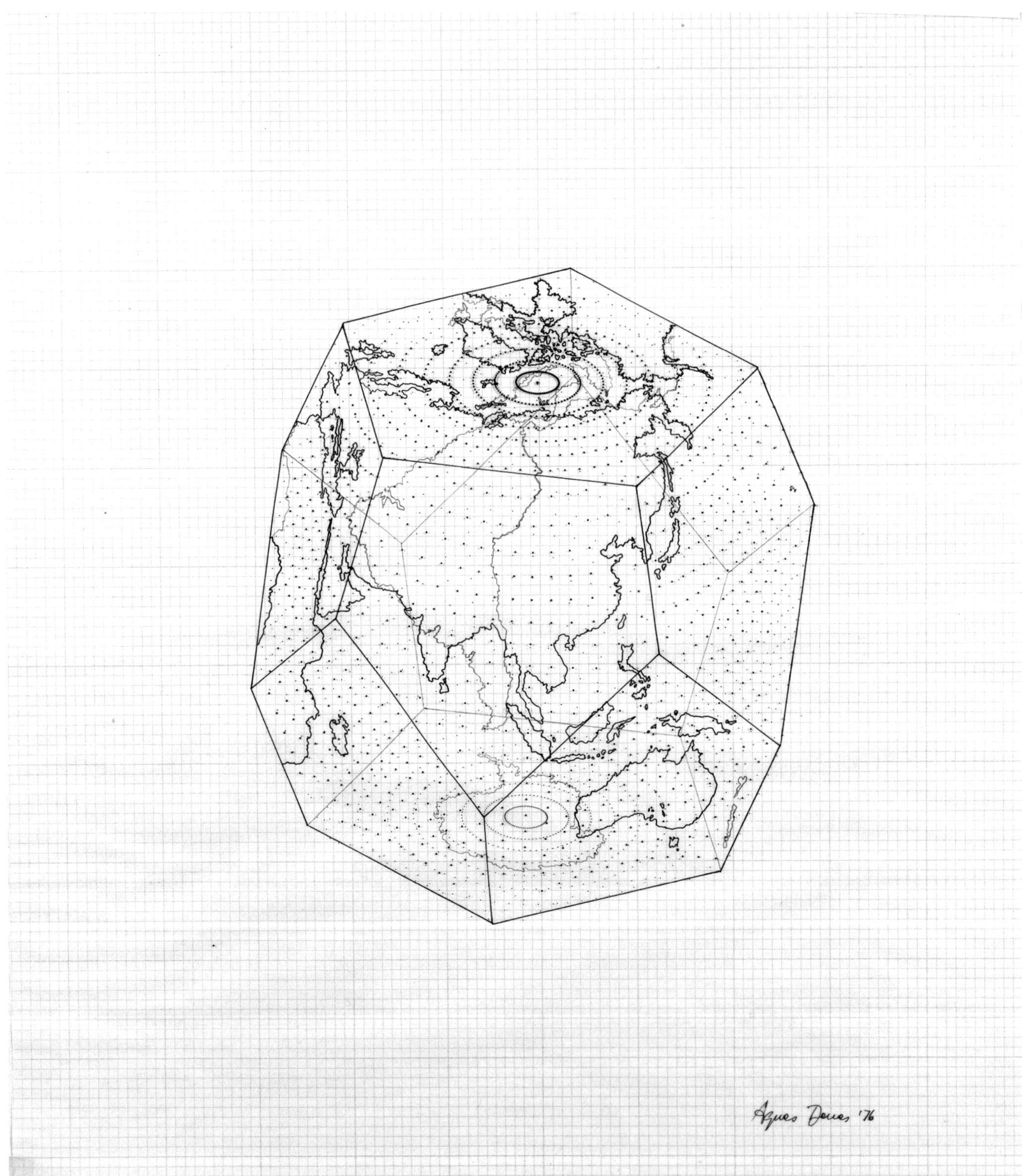
Agnes Denes '76

Isometric Systems in Isotropic Space - Map Projections:
The Dodecahedron, 1976 [cat. no. 18]
Isometric Systems in Isotropic Space - Map Projections:
The Snail, 1978 [cat. no. 19]

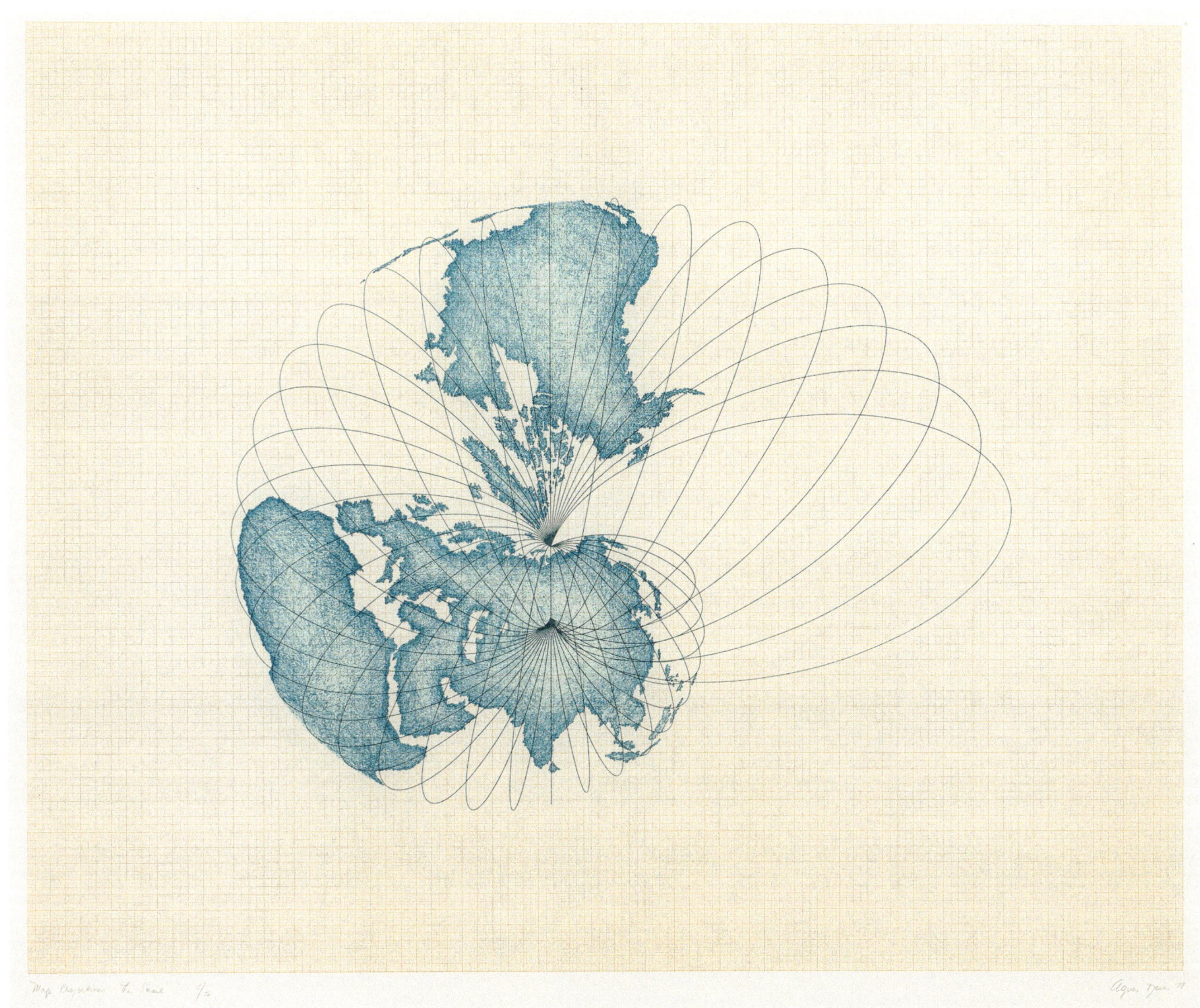

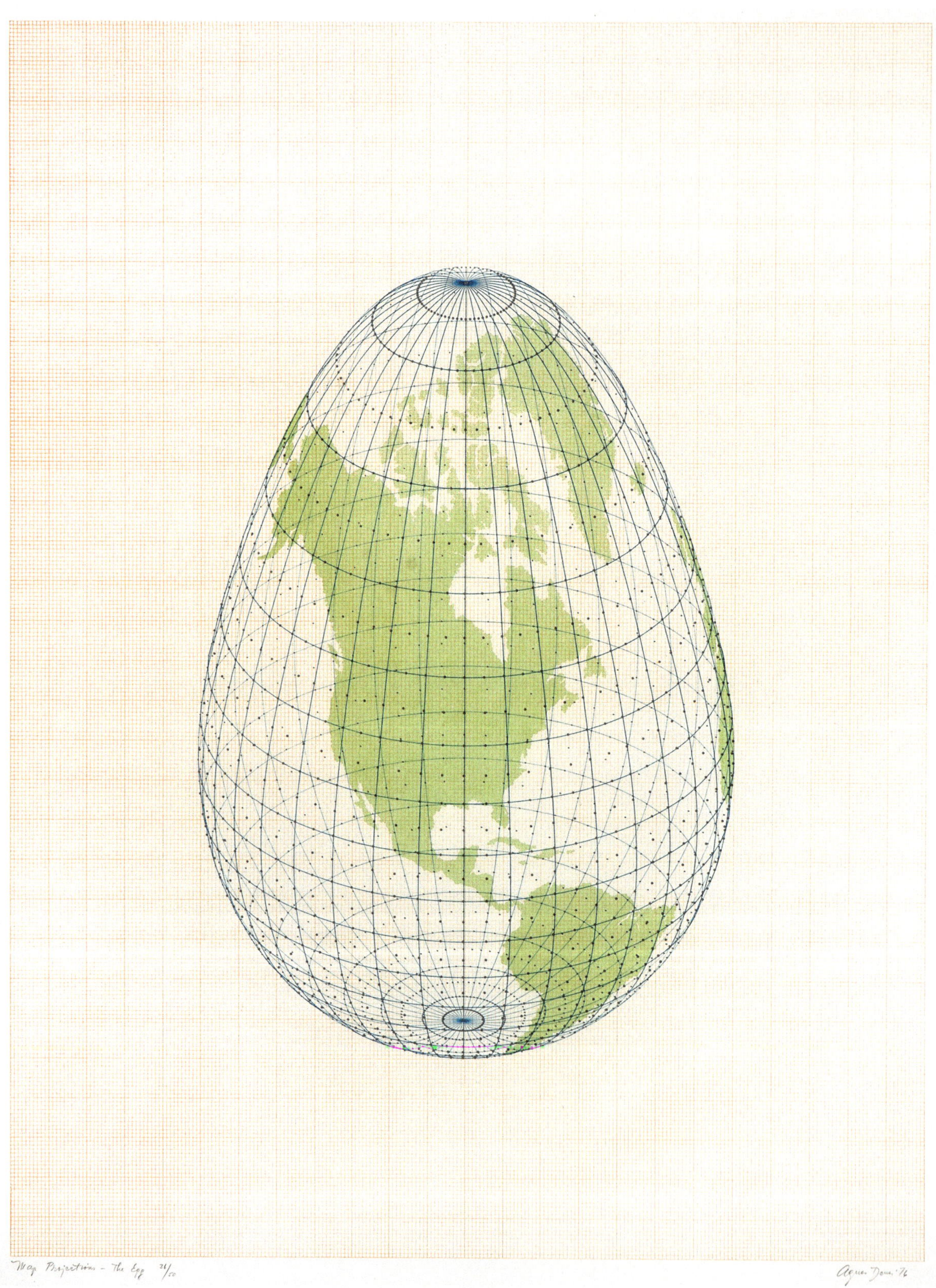
"Map Projections - The Egg" 24/50
Agnes Denes '76

Isometric Systems in Isotropic Space - Map Projections:
The Egg, 1976 [cat. no. 20]
Map Projections: The Snail, 1974 [cat. no. 21]

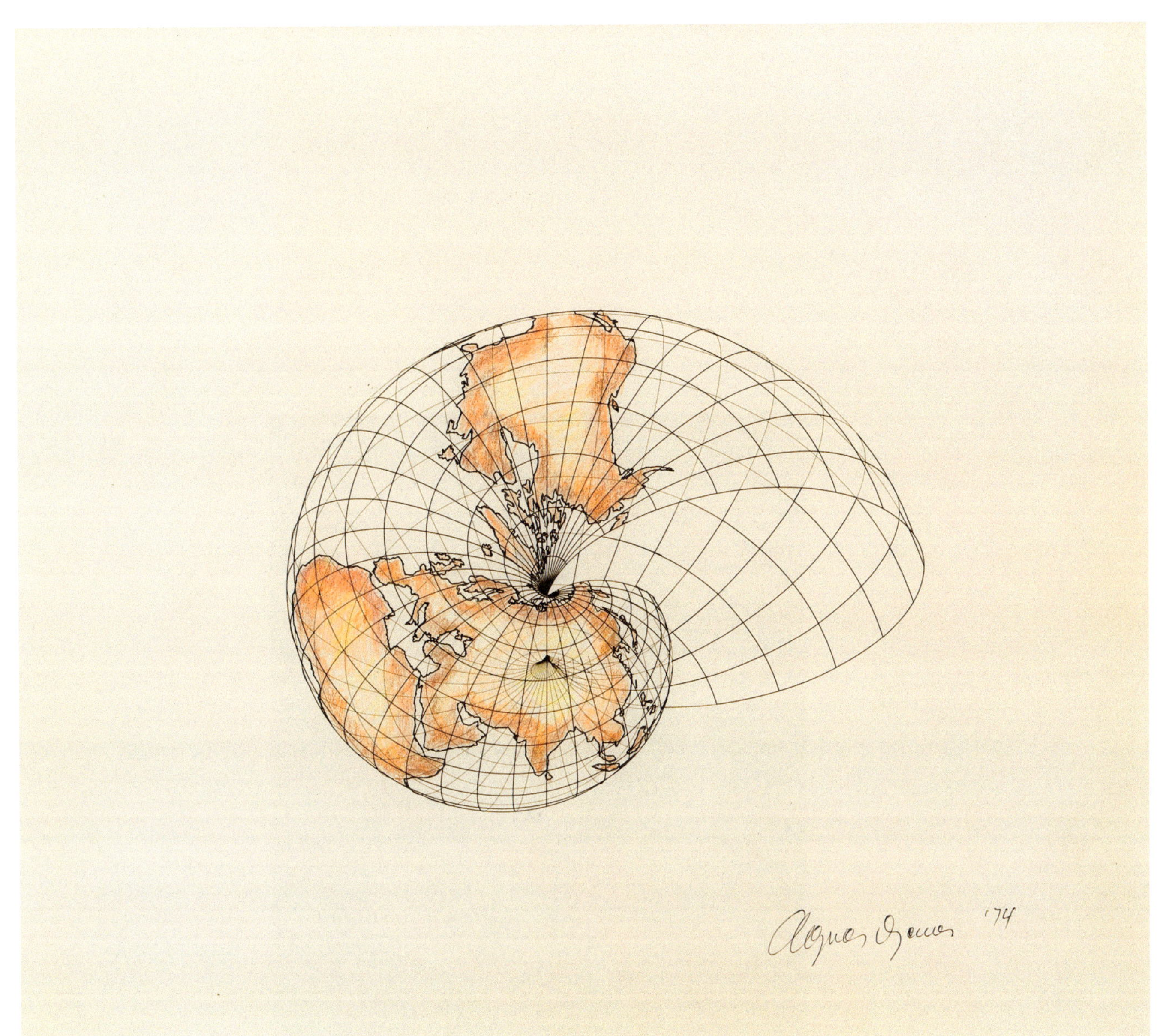

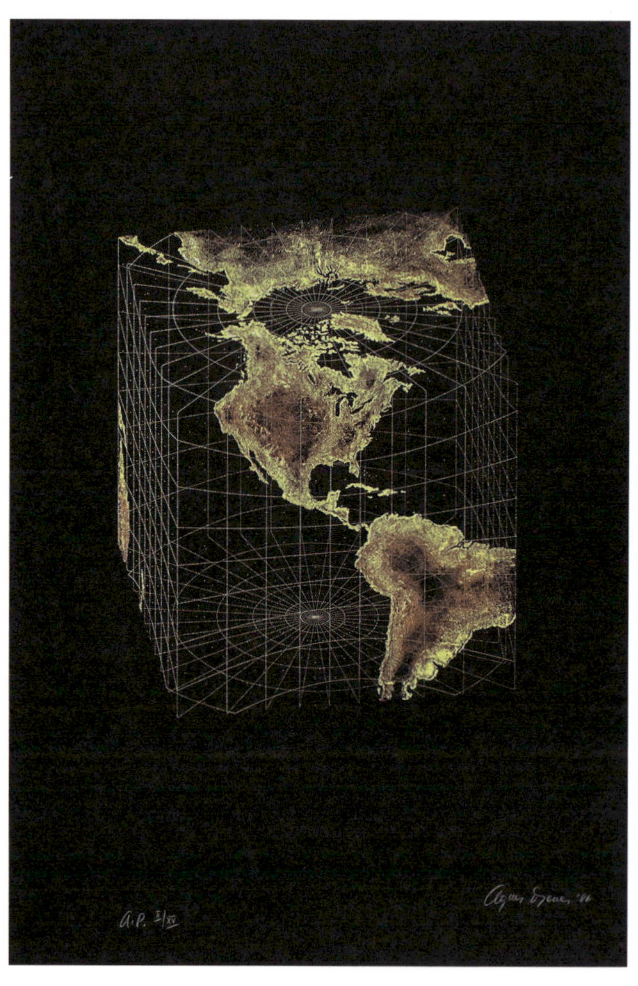

<u>Isometric Systems in Isotropic Space - Map Projections: The Cube</u>, 1986 [cat. no. 22]
<u>Study of Distortions; Isometric Systems in Isotropic Space -</u>
<u>Map Projections: The Cube</u>, 1975 [cat. no. 23]
<u>Isometric Systems in Isotropic Space - Map Projections: The Doughnut</u>, 1980 [cat. no. 24]

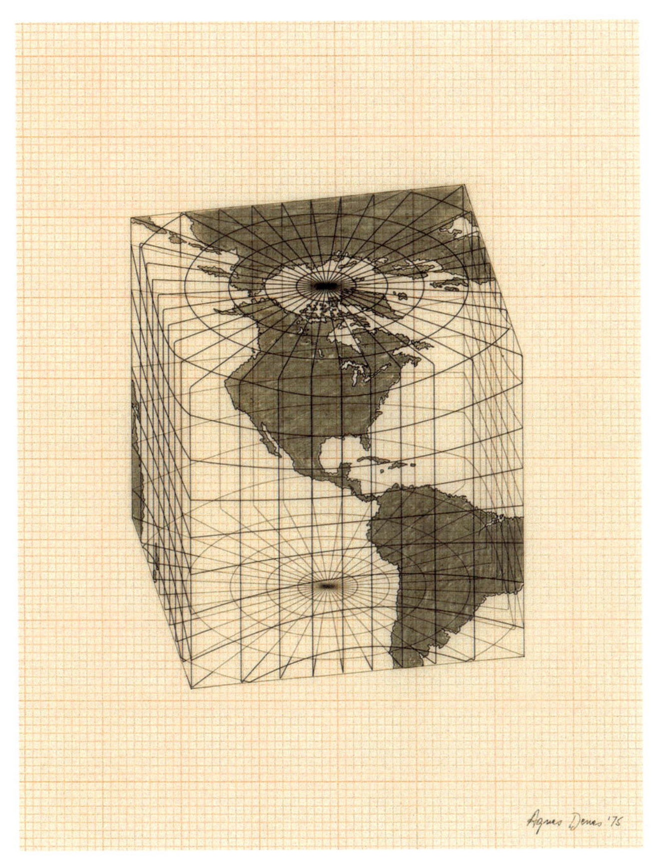

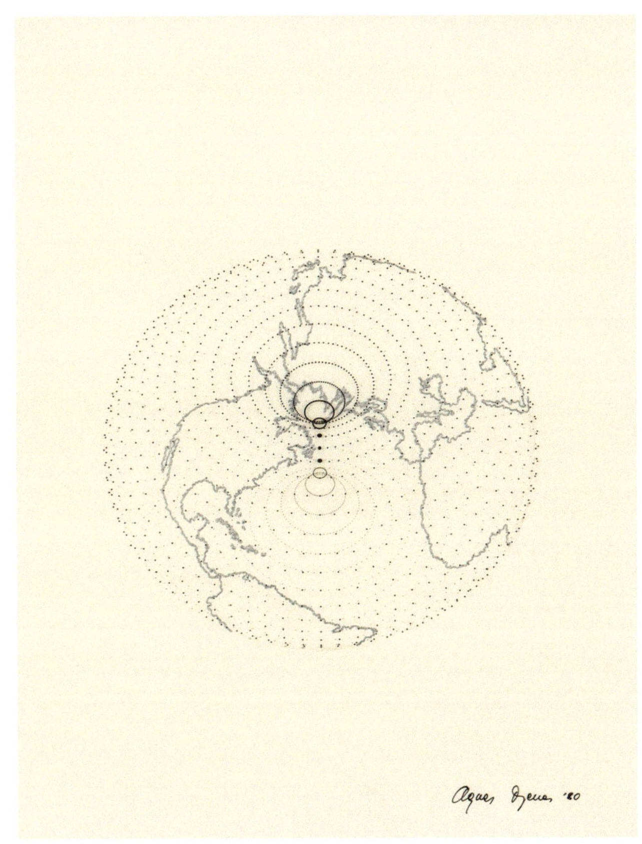

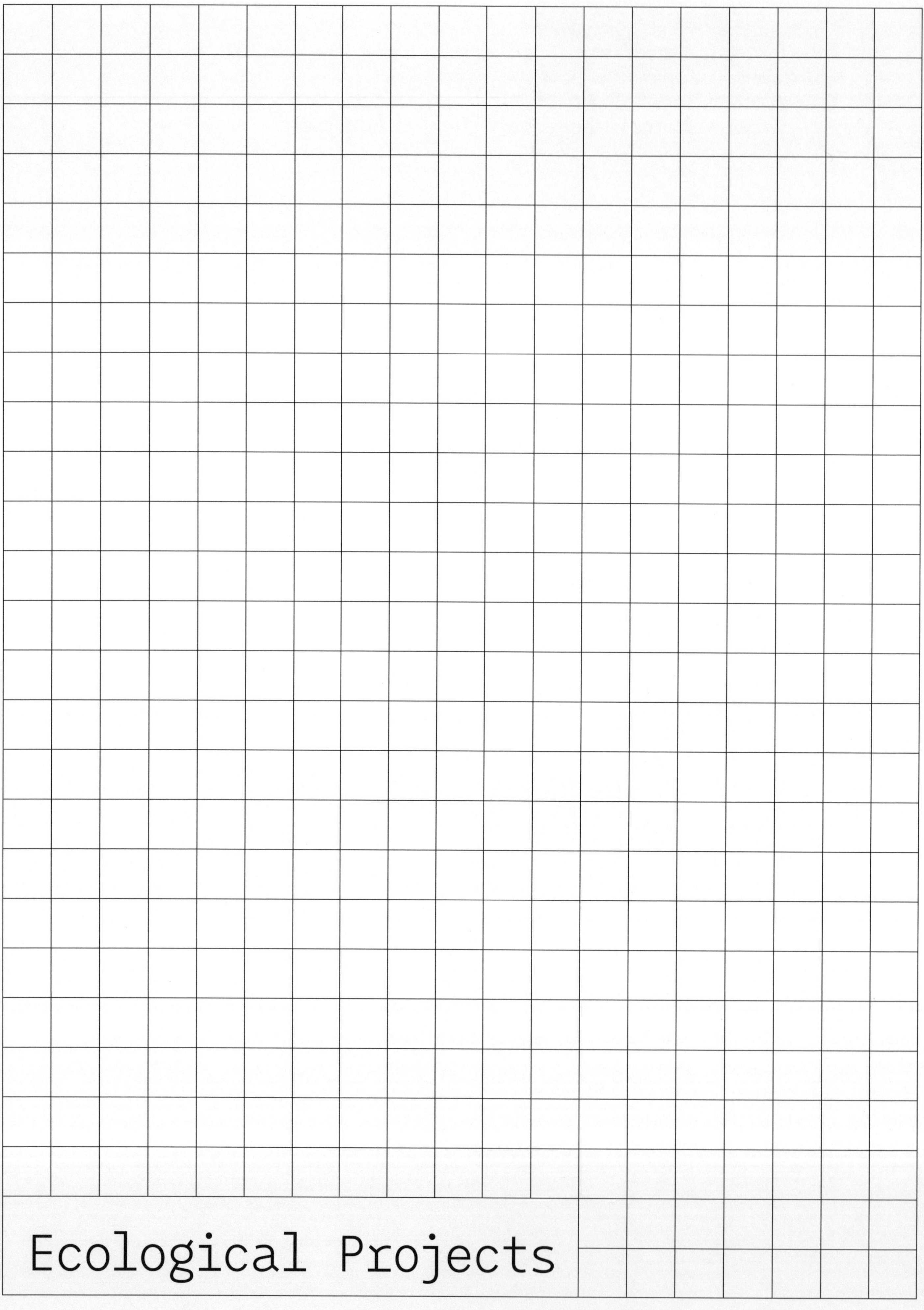

Ecological Projects

Ecological Projects

Exercises in Eco-Logic, 1969

The first visual transitional triangulation was realized in the summer of 1968, in Sullivan County, New York.

RICE was planted to represent interference with life/growth; TREES were chained* to represent interference with life/growth; and HAIKU was buried** to represent the idea, the abstract, the absolute.

We begin with something vital or controversial – LIFE; find its opposite – DEATH; then proceed to establish a connective link, intermediate rationale, which modifies the first two (deductive, assertive, or expository) and transitions them to a higher trichotomy – IDEA.

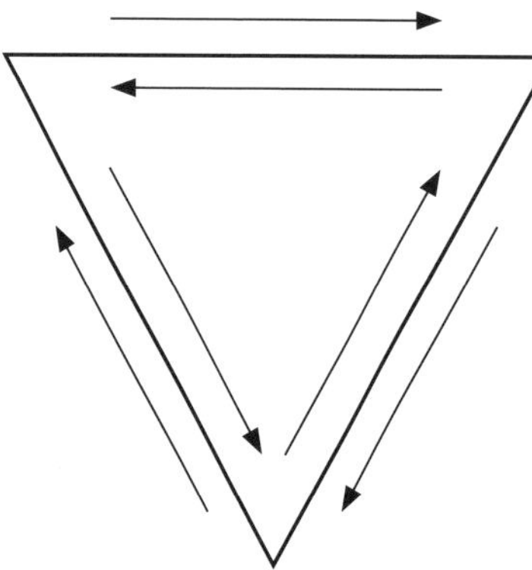

RICE PLANTING
(thesis)

life
causation
semination
creation
cultivation
growth
development
transition
impermenance
mortality

TREE CHAINING
(antithesis)

death-interference
with life & development
inhibition
restraint
modification
variation
mutation
transition
endurance
adaptation
change
survival
life

HAIKU BURIED
(synthesis)

induction
semination
idea/reason
succession
development
preservation of concepts
survival
growth/evolution
continuum
transcendence

*   TREE CHAINING: testing the strength of an idea to determine which is stronger: thought or nature.

** HAIKU BURIAL: Haiku poetry written before 1968 buried in an airtight container, twelve feet deep.

© Agnes Denes 1969

<u>Rice/Tree/Burial Project (Original Creation in Sullivan County, New York),</u>
1968/2009 [cat. no. 25]

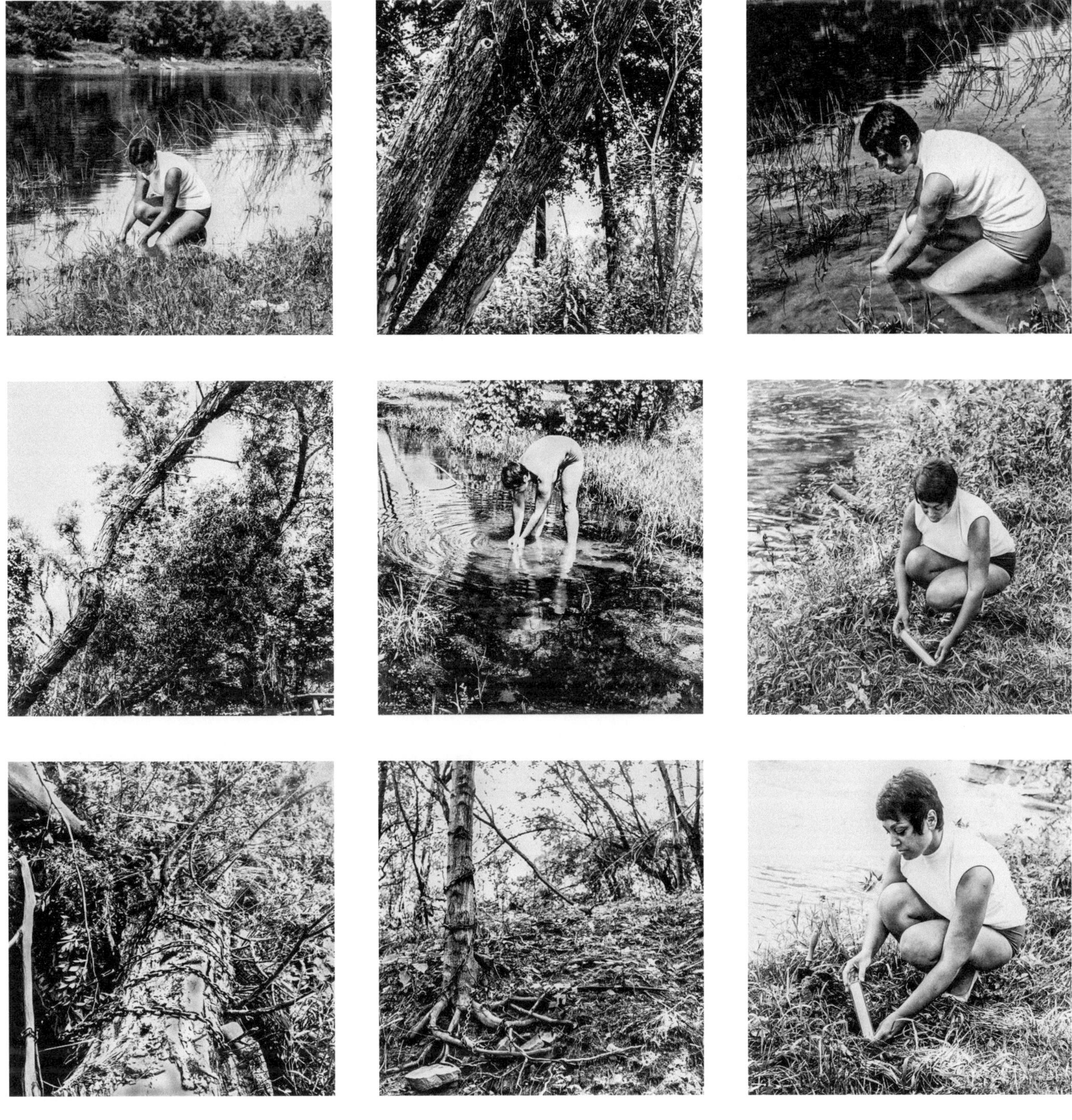

Rice/Tree/Burial, 1977–1979

Artpark, Lewiston, New York
(Cibachrome and black-and-white photographs)

Rice/Tree/Burial was first realized in 1968 in Sullivan County, New York, in a private ritual. It was a symbolic "event" and announced my commitment to environmental issues and human concerns. It was also the first exercise in Eco-Logic.

I planted rice to represent life (initiation and growth), chained trees to indicate interference with life and natural processes (evolutionary mutation, variation, decay, death), and buried my Haiku poetry to symbolize the idea or concept (the abstract, the absolute, human intellectual powers, and creation itself). These three acts constituted the first transitional triangulation* (thesis, antithesis, synthesis) and formed the Event. According to evolutionary theories, Event is the only reality, while the reality we perceive is forever changing and transforming in an expanding evolutionary universe in which time, space, mass, and energy are all interconnected and interdependent.

Rice represented a universal substance referring to sustenance and the life-giving element, while the seed itself denoted the nucleus, first principle or cause – the beginning. The act of sowing implied the source of growth, the introduction of a thing into another environment in order to initiate a process, the setting of something into motion (fertilization, conceiving, induction).

The chaining of trees signified linkage, connective units and associations, flexibility and restraint. It implied bondage, defeat, interference with growth – decay. The act of chaining brought attention to the mysterious life-force of an organism and its partial triumph over boundaries and restraints – its uneven, limited transcendence. Chaining trees also expressed choice, the selection and defining necessary in the creative process.

The texture of the forest, having been interrupted by the reordering of its elements, yielded unique structures of isolated or combined sculptural forms. The chains became additional limbs and blended into their surroundings to become visible only in certain lights, angles, and perspectives, conveying the conflicting and interdependent aspects of art and existence, illusion and reality, imagination and fact. The chained trees stood as monuments to human thought versus nature.

The burial of my haiku formed the essence of thinking processes (consciousness, deductive reasoning, and the logic of emotions). It represented the concept as essence of invention, which connects and defines life and death and acts as modifier and rationale for both.

I kept no copies of my poetry, thereby relinquishing, "giving up to the soil", something personal and precious – an act that also symbolized the self-denial and discipline required by this new analytical art form.

The act of burial, or placing into the ground and receiving from it, a cause-and-effect process, marks our intimate relationship with the earth. On the one hand, it indicates passing, returning to the soil, disintegration, and transformation; on the other, generation and life-giving, placing in the ground for the purpose of planting. It is also as a metaphor for human intelligence and transcendence through the communication of ideas – in this case, to future descendants.

All three imply change from one form to another, cyclic phenomena, transformation – as from chaos to order and back. Consequently, all three idea representatives or metaphors – the rice, the tree, the burial – become analogous, interactive and interdependent, creating the tension of opposing forces acting on each other and the momentum necessary to pass from one state to another and into further propositions. Their interaction creates a counterbalance as they pass into each other's realm or meaning to become successively interchangeable through their inherent polarity.

The ritual marked the beginning of my involvement with the creation of a "visual philosophy", a complex process which explores essences as forms of communication. It finds methods to put analytical propositions into visual form, defines elusive processes and creates analogies among divergent fields and thought processes. It challenges the status quo and tests its own validity.

In the summer of 1977, the ritual was re-enacted and realized on a full scale at Artpark (Lewiston, New York), completing the first cycle in the evolutionary process of my work and marking an important phase in its development. This periodical summation is a natural evolutionary phenomenon. Organisms probe their environment to find best possible ways to survive by developing memory and the ability to compare. In our limited existence this long view of reaching back and re-examining provides answers as to where we have been and where we are going.

I planted a half-acre rice field 150 feet above the Niagara gorge. The site marked the birthplace of Niagara Falls between Canada and the U.S., twelve thousand years ago. The rice grew up mutant, an unforeseen consequence of Artpark having been a dump-site near Love Canal.

I chained the trees in a sacred forest that was once an Indian burial ground, long since looted and desecrated, working under the watchful eyes of the Indians who seemed to hover over us in the trees and cover our bodies in the form of eerie spiders.

I then climbed out to the edge of Niagara Falls and filmed it for seven days, adding the forces of nature, as a fourth element, to this cycle of dialectics. With this act I also affirmed that my art functioned on the edge of the unknown in a delicate balance of the universals and the self, of the moment and of eternity – and was not afraid to assume the risks such art must take.

The shaky ledge from which I filmed had been dynamited to control the retreat
of the falls. Soon after my filming, it fell into the white foam below.

The time capsule was buried at Artpark at 47°10' longitude and 79° 2' 32" latitude.
It contained no objects other than the microfilmed responses to a questionnaire that had
traveled around the world, and a long letter I wrote addressed "Dear Homo Futurus."

The questionnaire was composed of existential questions concerning human values, the
quality of life, and the future of humanity. The responses were primarily from university
students in various countries where I spoke or had exhibitions of my work. Within
the context of the time capsule the questionnaire functioned as an open system of
communication, allowing our future descendants to evaluate us not so much by the
objects we created – as is customary in time capsules – but by the questions we
asked and how we responded to them.

The microfilm was desiccated and placed in a steel capsule inside a heavy lead box
in nine feet of concrete. A plaque mar ks the spot: at the edge of the Indian forest,
surrounded by blackberry bushes. The time capsule is to be opened in 2979,
in the 30th century, a thousand years from the time of the burial.

There are, still within the framework of this project, several time capsules planned
on earth and in space, aimed at various time frames in the future.

   *   Dialectic Triangulation: A Visual Philosophy and Exercises in Logic* (1967–1969)

© Agnes Denes 1979

Questionnaire

Do you believe humanity will become extinct one day?

If so, should this influence our attitude or change our thinking and actions?

What governs your actions? Do you think there is a force influencing what happens?

What do you want out of life?

Why not more?

Are you religious? If so, do you think it could be habit or conditioning?

What do you care about most?

How do you feel about death?

What would mean the greatest happiness to you?

Do you hate anything?

What do you think hate is?

What is love?

Which do you think will prove ultimately more important to humanity--science or love?

If there are different kinds of love, what connects them?

What would you say the human purpose is?

What would you rather be, if you had a choice?

If we are results of a development, in what direction is that development moving?

What do you consider humanity's most important achievement?

If human curiosity is the result of a mind half used, do you think the mysteries
      will be solved when the mind is filled?

In what way do you feel that you are defeated?

In what way do you feel that you are triumphant?

What do you consider to be the major differences between humanity
      and „lesser" animals?

Do you think we are slaves to our customs?

How could we overcome this?

What would perfect existence consist of?

What is ultimate reality?

Do you think humanity should be more practical or more visionary
      (ethical, magnanimous, creative, humanistic, etc.)?

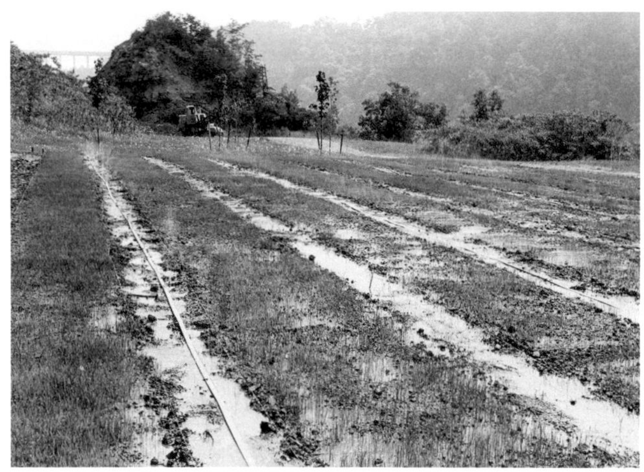

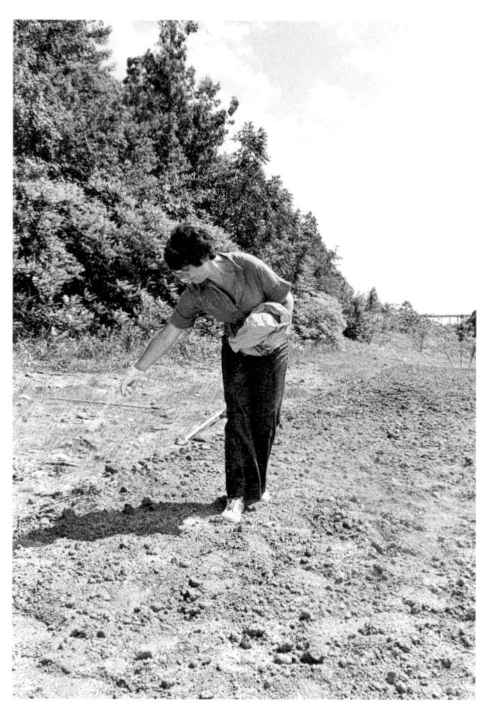

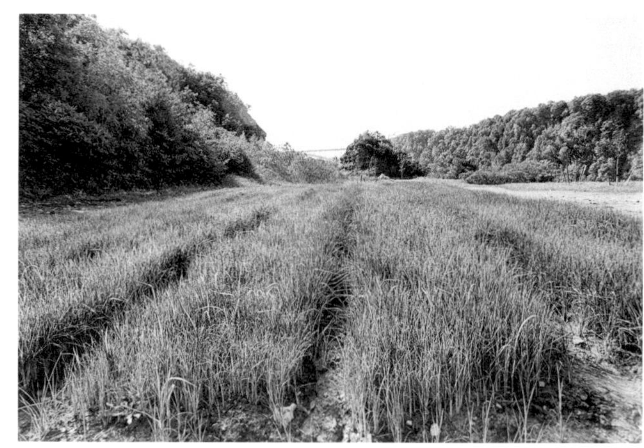

<u>Rice/Tree/Burial Project (Original Creation Artpark Lewiston, New York)</u>,
1977–1979/2012 [cat. no. 26]

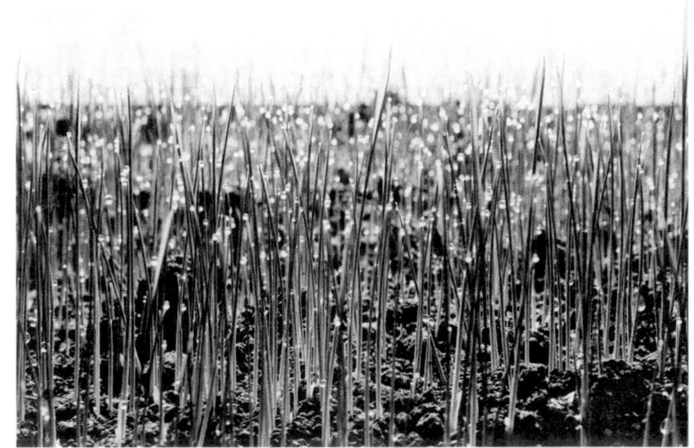

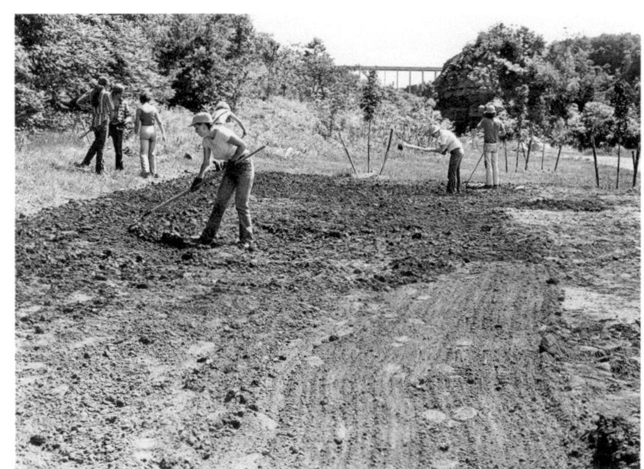

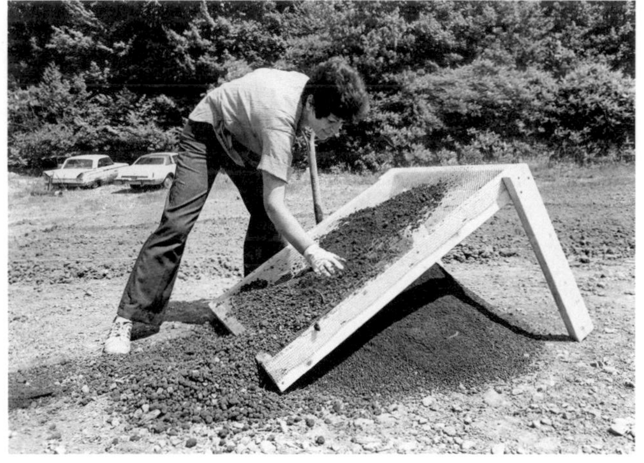

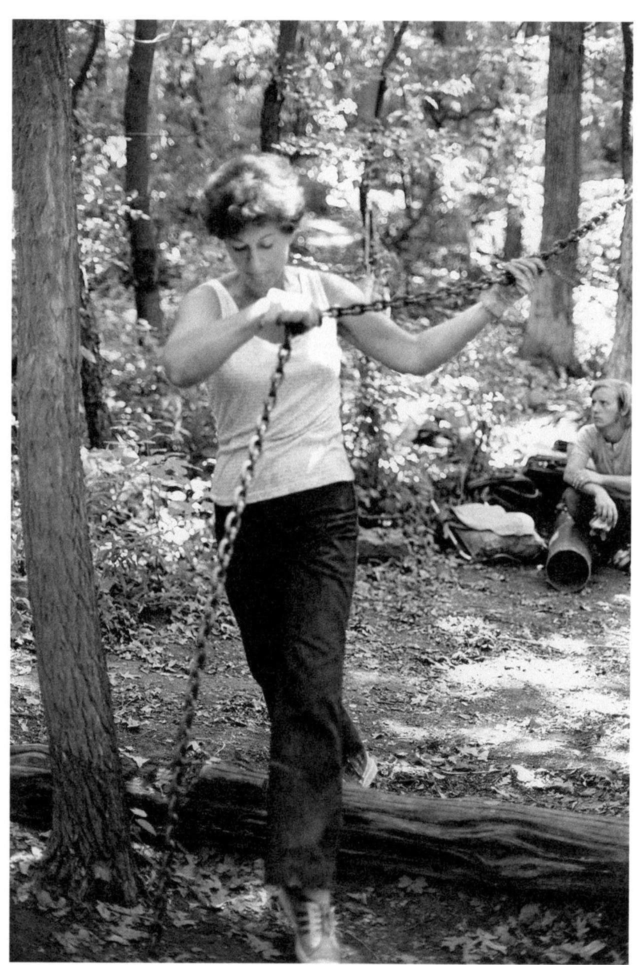

<u>Rice/Tree/Burial Project (Original Creation Artpark Lewiston, New York)</u>,
1977-1979/2012 [cat. no. 26]

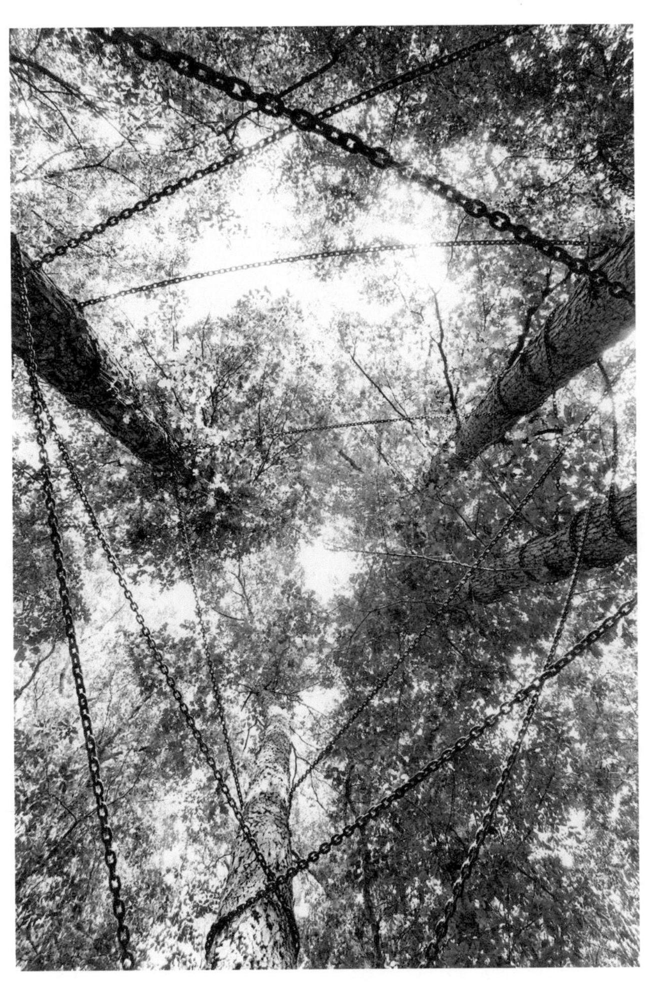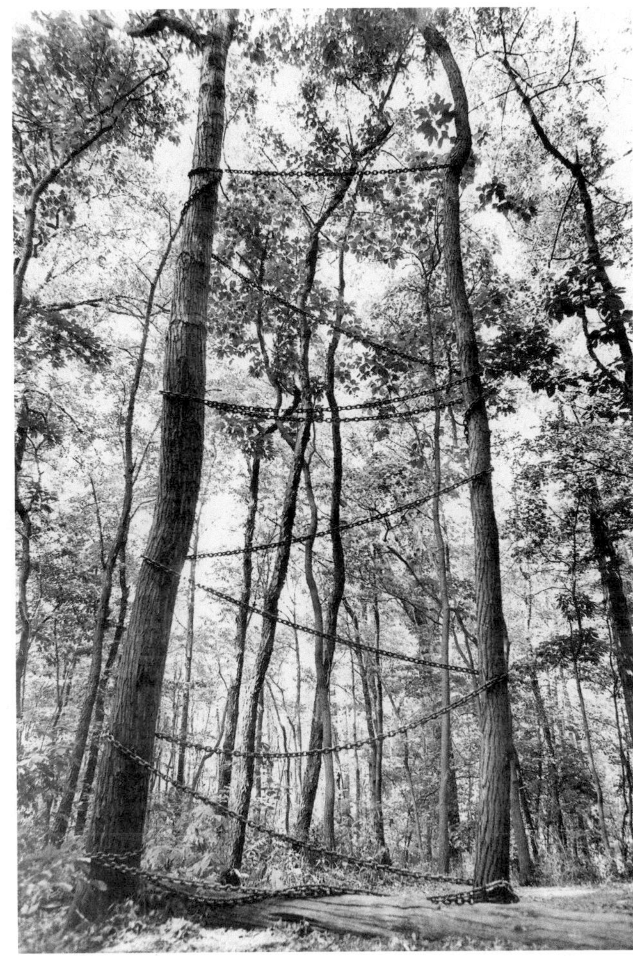

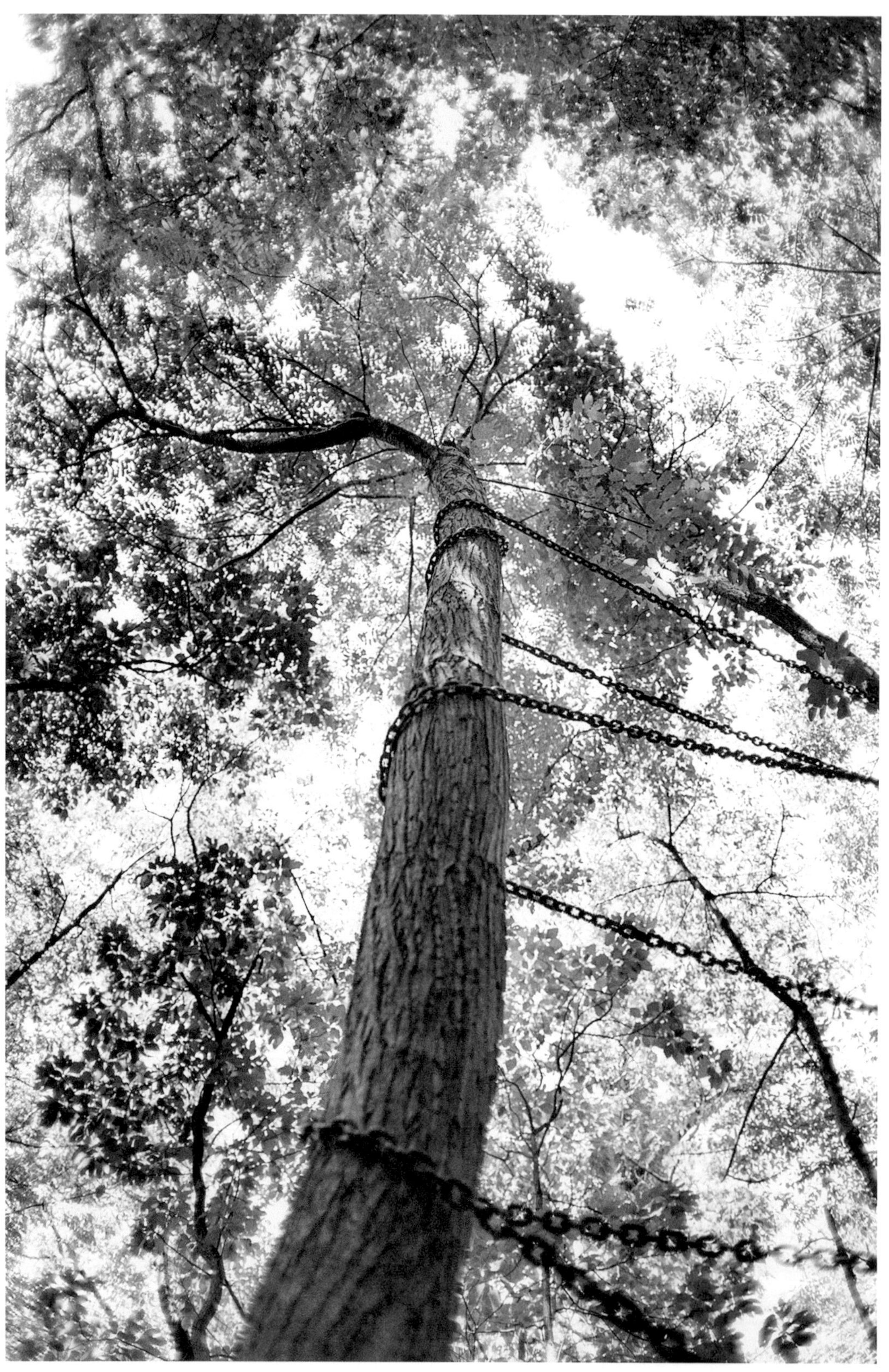

Rice/Tree/Burial Project (Original Creation Artpark Lewiston, New York), 1977-1979/2012 [cat. no. 26]

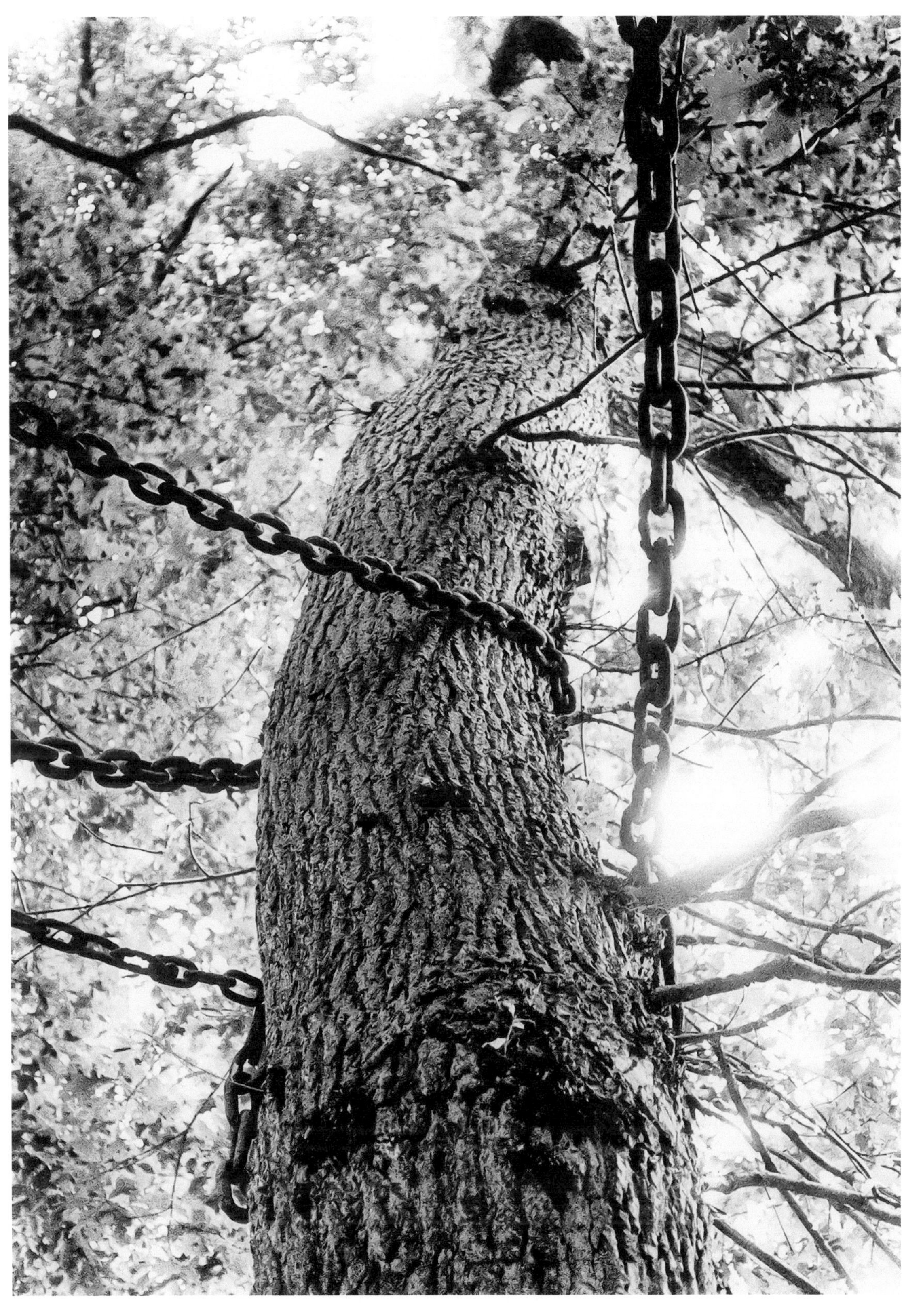

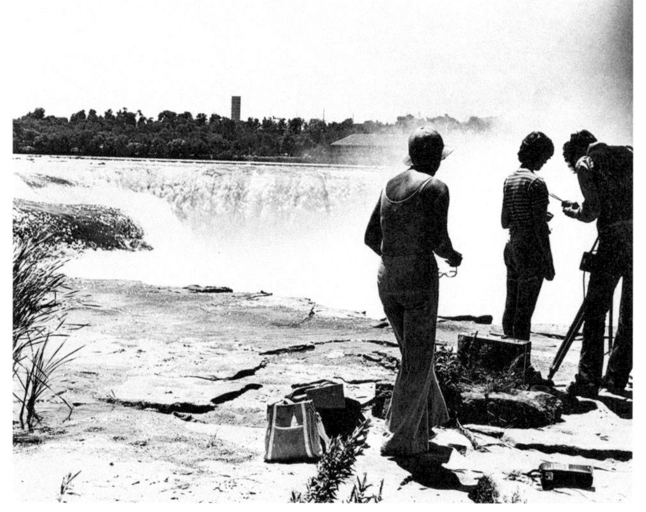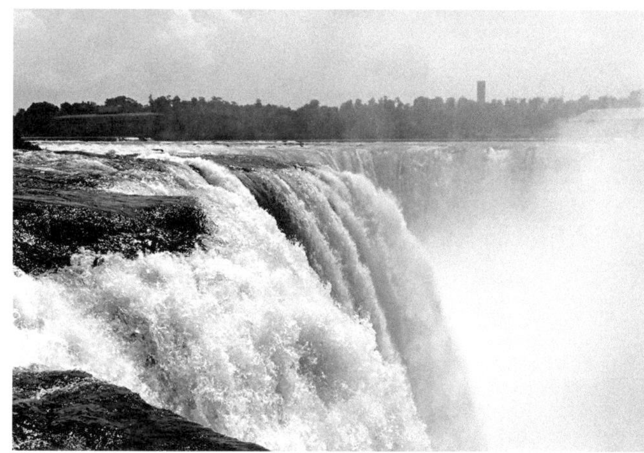

Rice/Tree/Burial Project (Original Creation Artpark Lewiston, New York), 1977–1979/2012 [cat. no. 26]

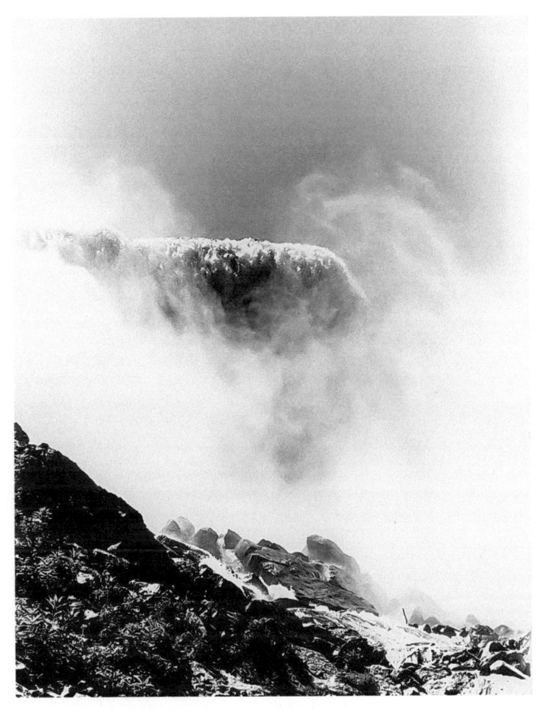

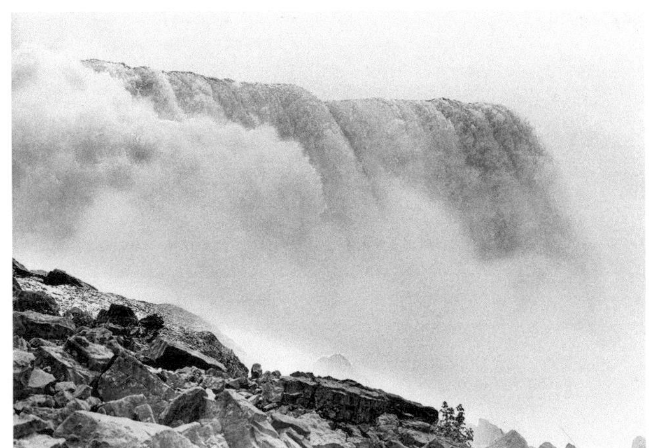

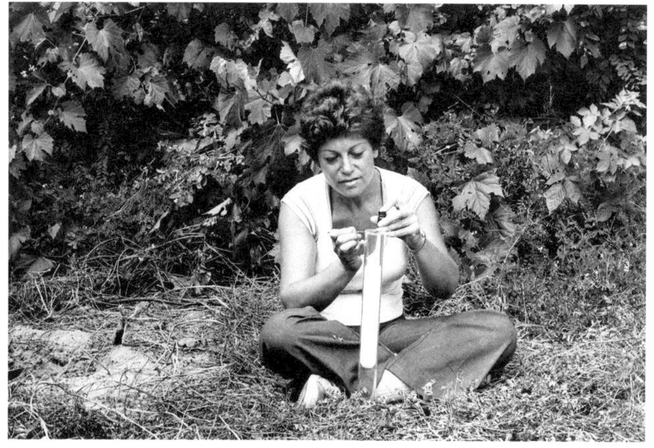 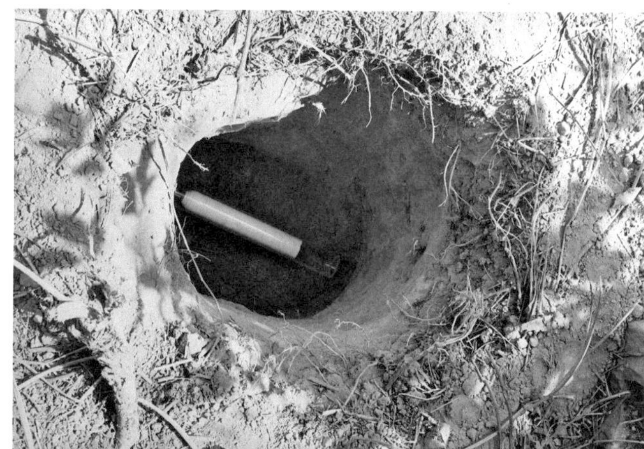

<u>Rice/Tree/Burial Project (Original Creation Artpark Lewiston, New York)</u>,
1977-1979/2012 [cat. no. 26]

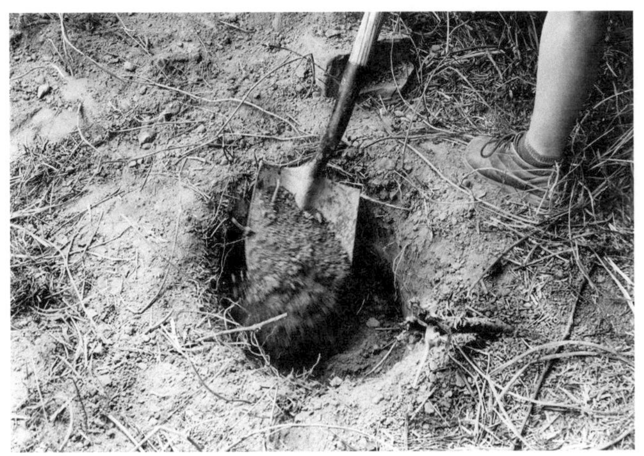

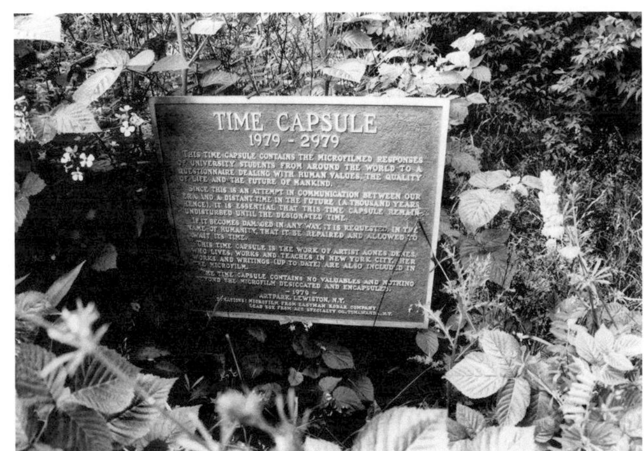

Planting the Rice Field

The Ritual of Preparing
                                        The Seedbed
Trucks Dumping Dirt
                    Roto Tiller Digs
                                    Bites into Rocky Clay Soil
                                                            Removing Rocks
Shoveling Raking Sifting Soil
                        Trying to Level the Ground with No Success
Without Levees Can't Flood the field
                                            Must Sprinkle-Irrigate
                                                There Isn't Enough Hose or Water
Volunteer Firemen Lend Us Quarter Mile Hose
                                        Frayed and Battered Full of Holes
But We Are Grateful!
                    Then Onto Designing Sophisticated Systems
                                                        To Even Water Pressure
Building Paddies
                    Mixing Nitrogen and Phosphate
                                                Then At Last   Semination!
The Seed Enters the Soil
                                            Sowing in Breathless Sunheat
Healthy Long Grain
                        Louisiana Bella Patna   Strain
                                                    Sweat Blurs Our Vision
A Storm Warning in the Drama of the Sky
                            Frantic Rush to Cover the Seeds with Sifted Topsoil
Then a Week's Wait for
                            Seed Birth
                                    Tender Yellow-Green Shoots Emerge
Pushing Through Rocks and Clods
                                    On Borrowed Soil   Life!
Niagara Falls was Born Here Twelve-Thousand Years Ago
                                                    Seedlings Fill the Field
An Inch of Growth a Day
                            Maturing Into
                                        The Most Brilliant Green Ever
People Come from Everywhere
                            The First Rice Field in the Northeast
And the Color of It!
                        Against the Humdrum Green Around
                                            One Develops Farmer's Mentality

Wishing for Gentle Rain and Good Yield
                                        Nurturing   Tending the Field
Spraying Propanil
                    Adding Fertilizer
                                                        Sinking Kneedeep into Soppy Irrigated Soil
                                                                    To Weed
               Then Covered with Mud and Sweat Collapsing
                                              Feet Dangling Over the Edge
Hundred and Fifty Feet Below Me the Fastmoving
                                          Swirling River Gorge
                      Where Niagara Passed 12,000 Years Ago
How was it then? Did the birds sing?
                        Who saw? Who Heard?
                                              I Keep Vigil
Behind Me the Full Grown Field
                        Rich and Lush I Listen to It
            Rustling in the Wind   Quivering in the Summer Rain

Only Two months Later Will I learn
                        That My Field was Contaminated
                                        That in Spite of
One Foot of Fresh Soil
                      I Grew Radioactive Rice.
                                                © Agnes Denes 1977

Chaining the Forest

Activity
                   Hauling Tons of Chains into the Forest
                                            Past Sacred Indian Burial Ground
Not Heeding The Warning
                               I Select the Trees to be Chained
Then Drag The Chains
                                                 Around the Trunks
         Pulling Lifting Circling Nailing Weaving
                                            In and Out of the Trees
Hoisting the Chains onto the Branches
                                      The Clank and Clatter of Steel Against Rock
Scraping Bark and Skin
                   Lifting and Hoisting
                                 Higher and Higher   Intruding
Straining an Stretching
                 While   Spiders Crawl and Dance   Over Us They
Seem to Have One Double-Jointed   Extra Leg   Used for Navigation
  Where Do They Come From?
                           Who and What Are They?
                                 No One Has Ever Seen Them Before
The Book We Find Does Not List Them   An Unknown Species
                               Spirit of Dead Indian We are Warned
The Trees Succumb
                   The Chains are Taut
                         The Portal is Done   Leading into the Chamber
And Deeper   In the Heart of the Forest
                   Higher Upon a Hill   Stands
One Magnificent Tree   Thick and Tall   More Than a Hundred Feet
                   To Be Chained   Into   A Sweeping Arc
                             The Church Steeple
And Around It   In Natural Formation Dozens of Trees Stand Vigil In a Crescent
Bending Over to Form
                   An Arched Roof
                               The Perfect Dome   For the
                                                   Cathedral !
Standing Inside its Stillness
                               I Am Inside the Only Cathedral
                   Really Made by God
Then suddenly
         The Foliage Forms a Running Figure   Seen Against the Sky
                                             Then Another

Sitting Cross-Legged with a Headdress

The Air is Stifling and Muggy

And We are Covered with Bites

I photographs The Indians in the Foliage

For My Doubt As Well As Others'

Toward Evening on the Third Day the Air Softens

And Cools

The Chains Become Limbs   The Trees Are Not Hurt

The P o r t a l The C h a m b e r and The C a t h e d r a l

Thought Versus Nature

The Chain Drawing is Complete   The Structure Lives

Antithesis Has Been Given Form

And It Isn't Death   Because Life is Only   H e r e n e s s

The Chains Now Look

Like Branches

And Dissolve Into Forest Texture

Mutation Is

Variation   The Forest is Different

But Change is Life   The Trees

Breathe With

The Chains   Silent Chains in the Night   In a Forest

Alive With

Fireflies and Night Sounds.

© Agnes Denes 1977

The Falls

Having Obtained Special Permit to Film the Falls from a Rock Jutting over the Edge
We Stand in the Midst of a Drama
Around Us the Rapids Broil
Frothing Foamy Watermass Swirls Fights Holds Back
Then Spills Violently Over the Edge
And Plunges into the Depth Below
Into a Pool of Foam Sliced by Rainbow
Rage Thunder Ceaseless Energy The Sun is White Heat
And the White of the Water Hurts the Eyes
At My Feet a Still Pool
Has Collected in the Hollow of a Rock
I Kneel to Drink and Cool My Hot Face
If I Lean Forward or Put my Arm Out
If I Reach Out I can Touch   Death
The Tumult and the Momentum is Too Frightening
Two Hundred Feet Below
Straight Down
Endless Deluge Sizzling Roaring Torrent   And Death
Just One Step
For an Interminable Timeless Moment I Feel a Silent Pressure from Within
A Frozen
Fearless Stillness Looking Out of Me at the Sun   Foam   Mist
Cascading Tons of White-Silver-Green Frost
This is the Whole World
The Mind Locks into its Profundity   And Knows
Understands   Everything
No Words are Adequate   This Chilling Peace
The Temptation to Let go and Cascade into Paradise
Without Fear
Just a Tremendous Impulse to Leap
And Standing There at the Summit Surrounded by this Magnificence   I Know
Majesty and Insignificance
And   All the Answers
Then Suddenly   The Thundering Resumes   Time Resumes
And I am Left   Limp
From the Intensity of the Moment
We Follow a Bird with the Camera
As It Flies Fearlessly Up Against the Flow of Water
The Stimulation Is Almost Unbearable
None of Us Speak   Silent Even Later
On the Way Back in the Car
Having Seen It   Felt It   Been to the Mountaintop
For Rice/Tree/Burial
The Fusion is Complete.

The Burial

The ritual is quite different here, searching for a spot untouched, private, between
rice field and forest, then finding it at the base of a lush hill at the edge of the forest
bordered by blackberry bushes, tall fern and shrubs. The preparation of the ground
consists of digging a deep hole for the time capsule. The soil is hard and the machine
makes an awful racket as it bites deeper into the bottom and hits something hard with
a sharp clank. Red-orange broken pieces surface from inside the earth – artifacts
of another time? Time capsule upon time capsule, why not? We dig some more,
shaping the cavity, it takes two days, while we prepare the time capsule, microfilmed,
desiccated safely tucked into a lead box to be opened in the thirtieth century. Not
much time but a lot if you are a human. No objects inside, only existentialist questions
and answers. The future will evaluate us by the questions we asked and the answers
we gave, not by the objects we made. We bury the capsule in nine feet of cement
replacing some of the earth. How will they ever get this out? I ask. If they can't figure
that out by 3000 A.D., says an intern, they don't deserve to find it. Great. Students are
smart. These are their responses in the capsule. From all over the world. The plaque
is placed marking the spot. The vegetation is knee-deep and the area looks almost
untouched. Communication has commenced spanning centuries. As the seed enters
the ground, as a person enters it for burial, so now human thought enters it seeking
to overcome human finitude and to find a foothold, some meaning through the cyclic
exchange between minds and epochs, whatever the outcome, the paradox has been
planted, the thought is in the ground.

© Agnes Denes 1979

Wheatfield - A Confrontation, 1982

Battery Park Landfill, downtown Manhattan, 2 acres of wheat planted
and harvested, Summer 1982

The Philosophy

My decision to plant a wheatfield in Manhattan instead of designing just another public
sculpture grew out of a long-standing concern and need to call attention
to our misplaced priorities and deteriorating human values.

Manhattan is the richest, most professional, most congested, and without a doubt,
most fascinating island in the world. To attempt to plant, sustain, and harvest two acres
of wheat here, wasting valuable real estate, obstructing the machinery by going against
the system, was an effrontery that made it the powerful paradox I had sought for the
calling to account.

It was insane. It was impossible. But it would call people's attention to having to rethink
their priorities and realize that unless human values were reassessed, the precious
quality of life, even life itself, was perhaps in danger. Placing it at the foot of the World
Trade Center, a block from Wall Street, facing the Statue of Liberty, was to be a careful
reminder of what this land had stood for and hopefully still does.

My work usually reaches beyond the boundaries of the art arena to deal with
controversial global issues, questioning the status quo and the endless contradictions
we seem to accept into our lives – namely, our ability to see so much and understand
so little, to have achieved technological miracles while remaining emotionally unstable;
our great advances, desirable, even necessary for survival, that have interfered with
evolution and the world's ecosystem; or for that matter the individual human dilemma,
struggle, and pride versus the whole human predicament.

Wheatfield was a symbol, a universal concept. It represented food, energy, commerce,
world trade, economics. It referred to mismanagement, waste, world hunger, and
ecological concerns. It was an intrusion into the Citadel, a confrontation of High
Civilization. Then again, it was also Shangri-la, a small paradise, one's childhood, a hot
summer afternoon in the country, peace, forgotten values, simple pleasures.

The idea of a wheat field is quite simple. One penetrates the soil, places one's seed of
concept, and allows it to grow, expand, and bear fruit. That is what creation and life is all
about. It's all so simple, yet we tend to forget basic processes. What was different about
this wheatfield was that the soil was not rich loam but dirty landfill filled with rusty metals,
boulders, old tires, and overcoats. It was not farmland but an extension of the congested
downtown of a metropolis where dangerous crosswinds blew, traffic snarled, and every
inch was precious realty. The absurdity of it all, the risks we took, and the hardships we
endured were all part of the basic concept. Digging deep is what art is all about.

Introduce a leisurely wheat field into an island of achievement-craze, culture, and decadence. Confront a highly efficient, rich complex where time is money and money rules. Pit the congestion of the city of competence, sophistication, and crime against open fields and unspoiled farmlands. The peaceful and content against the achiever. The everlasting against the forever changing. Culture versus grass roots.

Wheatfield affected many lives, and the ripples are extending. Some suggested that I put my wheat up on the wheat exchange and sell it to the highest bidder, others that I apply to the government for farmers' subsidy. Reactions ranged from disbelief to astonishment to being moved to tears. A lot of people wrote to thank me for creating Wheatfield and asked that I keep it going.

After my harvest, the four-acre area facing New York harbor was returned to construction to make room for a billion-dollar luxury complex. Manhattan closed itself once again to become a fortress, corrupt yet vulnerable. But I think this magnificent metropolis will remember a majestic, amber field. Vulnerability and staying power, the power of the paradox.

The Act

Early in the morning on the first of May 1982 we began to plant a two-acre wheatfield in lower Manhattan, two blocks from Wall Street and the World Trade Center, facing the Statue of Liberty.

The planting consisted of digging 285 furrows by hand, clearing off rocks and garbage, then placing the seed by hand and covering the furrows with soil. Each furrow took two to three hours.

Since March over two hundred truckloads of dirty landfill had been dumped on the site, consisting of rubble, dirt, rusty pipes, automobile tires, old clothing, and other garbage. Tractors flattened the area and eighty more truckloads of dirt were dumped and spread to constitute one inch of topsoil needed for planting.

We maintained the field for four months, set up an irrigation system, weeded, cleared out wheat smut (a disease that had affected the entire field and wheat everywhere in the country). We put down fertilizers, cleared off rocks, boulders, and wires by hand, and sprayed against mildew fungus.

"We" refers to my two faithful assistants and a varying number of volunteers, ranging from one or two to six or seven on a good day.

We harvested the crop on August 16 on a hot, muggy Sunday. The air was stifling and the city stood still. All those Manhattanites who had been watching the field grow from green to golden amber, and gotten attached to it, the stockbrokers and the economists, office workers, tourists, and others attracted by the media coverage stood around in sad silence. Some cried. TV crews were everywhere, but they too spoke little and then in a hushed voice.

We harvested almost 1,000 pounds of healthy, golden wheat.

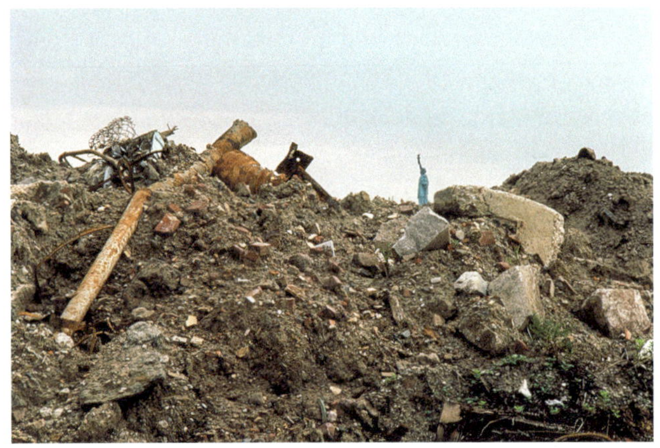

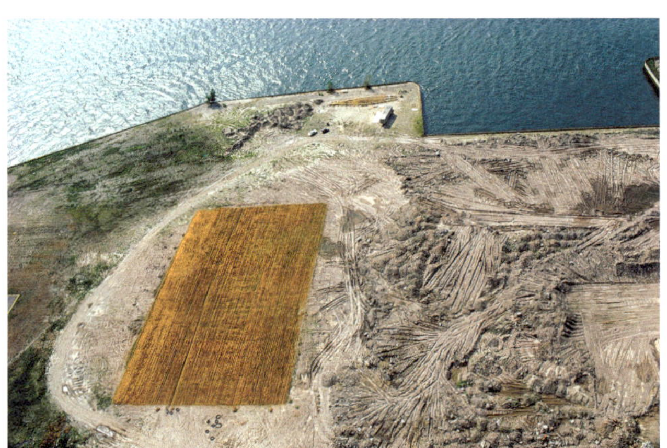

<u>Wheatfield - A Confrontation: Battery Park Landfill,</u>
<u>Downtown Manhattan - Before Planting</u>, 1982/2024 [cat. no. 27]
<u>Wheatfield - A Confrontation: Battery Park Landfill,</u>
<u>Downtown Manhattan - Aerial View</u>, 1982/2024 [cat. no. 28]
<u>Wheatfield - A Confrontation: Battery Park Landfill,</u>
<u>Downtown Manhattan - Green Wheat</u>, 1982/2024 [cat. no. 29]

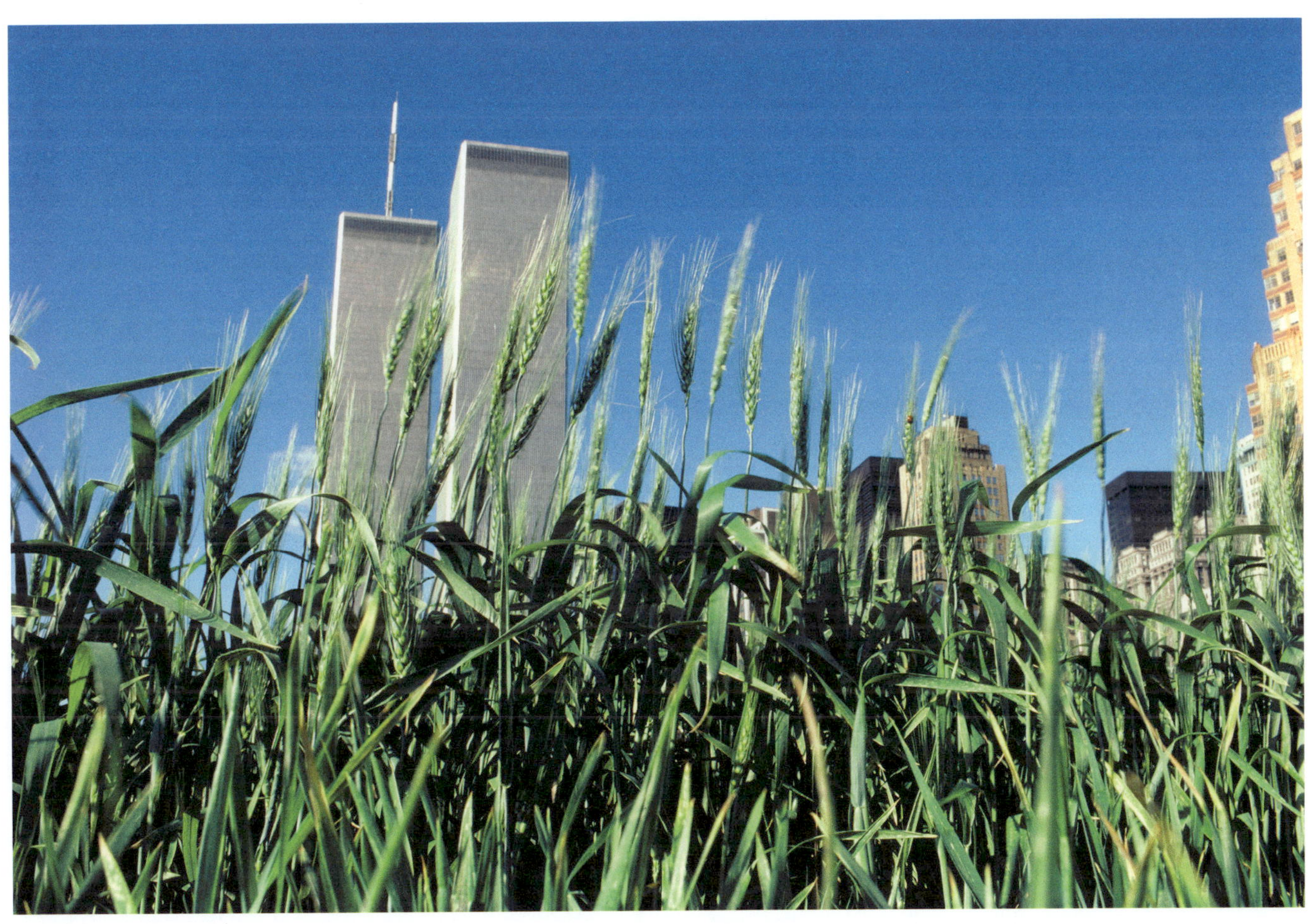

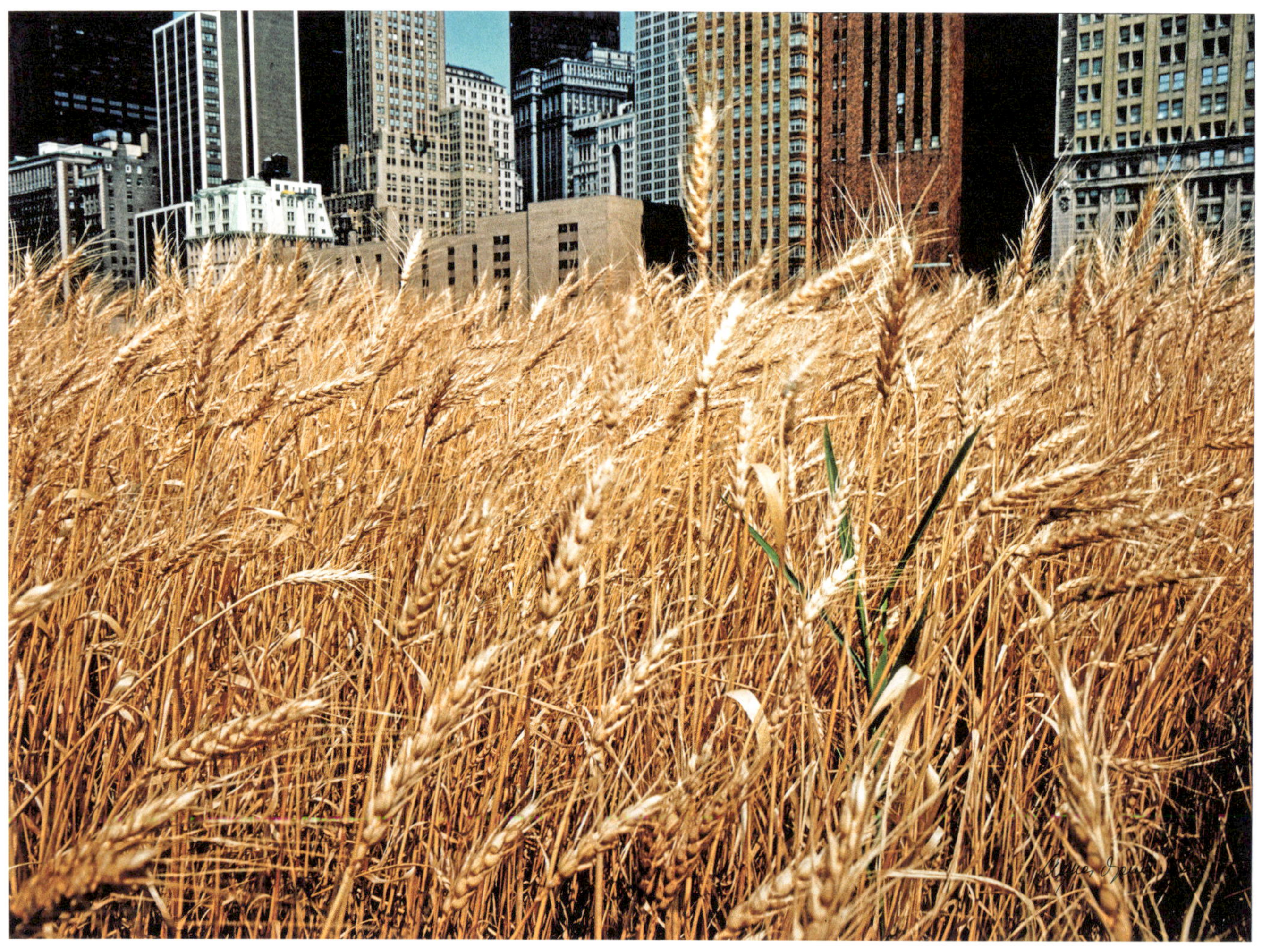

<u>Wheatfield - A Confrontation: Battery Park Landfill,</u>
<u>Downtown Manhattan - Golden Wheat 2</u>, 1982/2024 [cat. no. 30]
<u>Wheatfield - A Confrontation: Battery Park Landfill,</u>
<u>Downtown Manhattan - Blue Sky, World Trade Center</u>, 1982/2024 [cat. no. 31]
<u>Wheatfield - A Confrontation: Battery Park Landfill,</u>
<u>Downtown Manhattan - With Statue of Liberty Across the Hudson</u>, 1982/2024 [cat. no. 32]

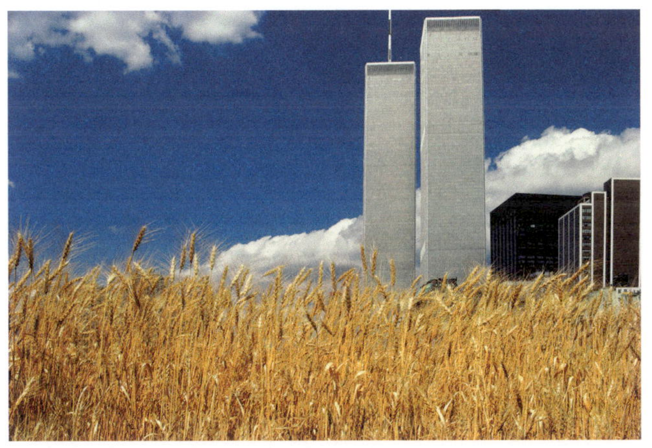
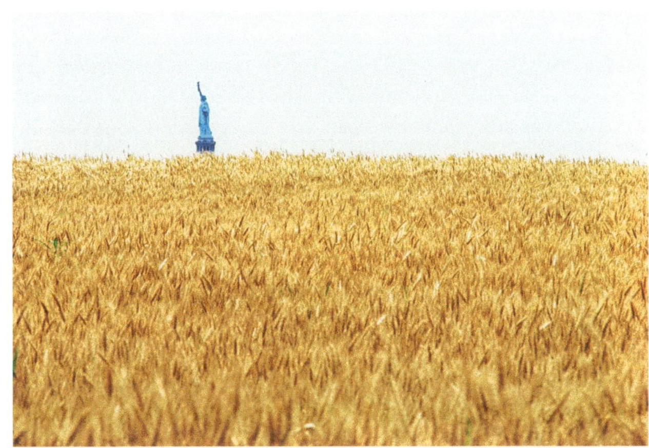

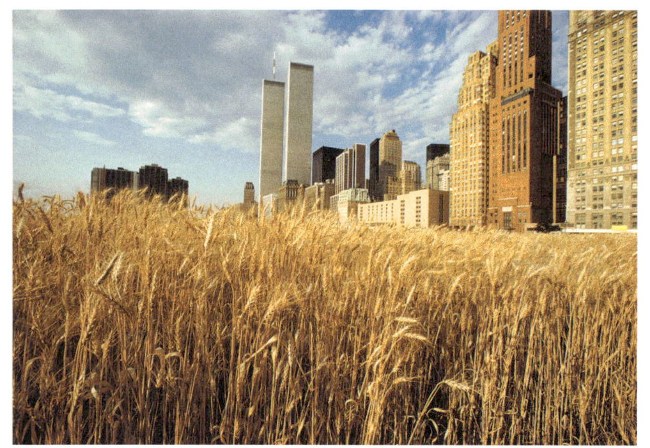

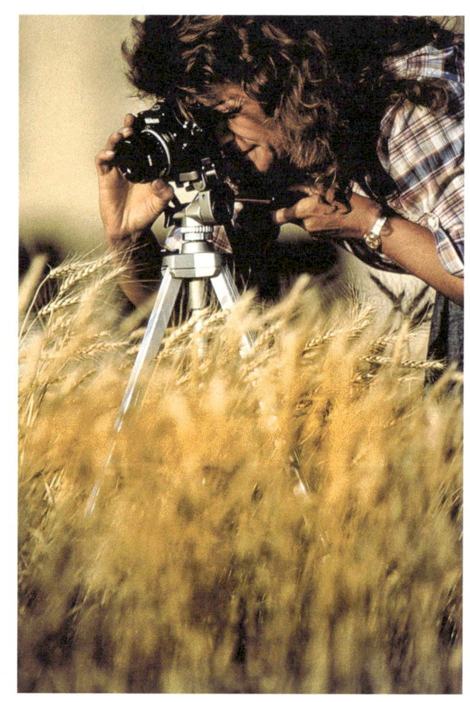

Wheatfield - A Confrontation: Battery Park Landfill,
Downtown Manhattan - With New York Financial Center, 1982/2024 [cat. no. 33]
Wheatfield - A Confrontation: Battery Park Landfill,
Downtown Manhattan - With Artist Photographing in the Field, 1982/2024 [cat. no. 34]
Wheatfield - A Confrontation: Battery Park Landfill, Downtown Manhattan -
Ocean Liner Passing Wheatfield on the Hudson, 1982/2024 [cat. no. 35]
Wheatfield - A Confrontation: Battery Park Landfill,
Downtown Manhattan - Cloudy Sky, 1982/2024 [cat. no. 36]

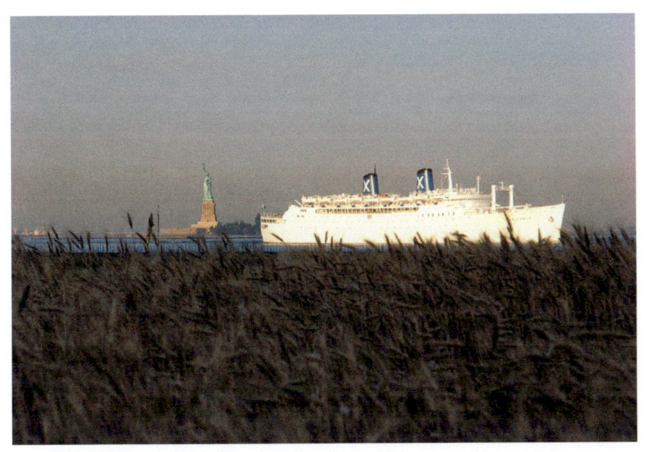
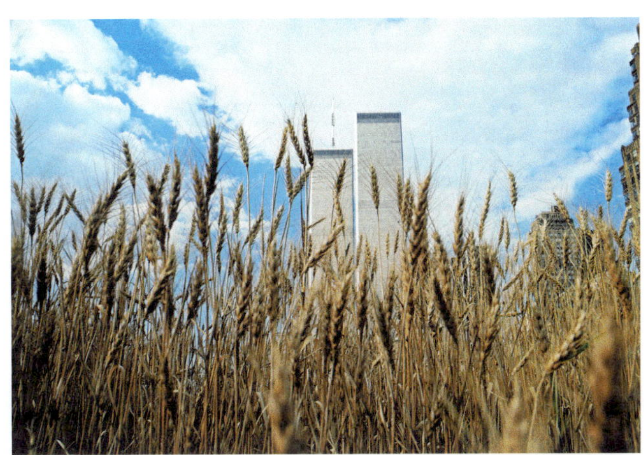

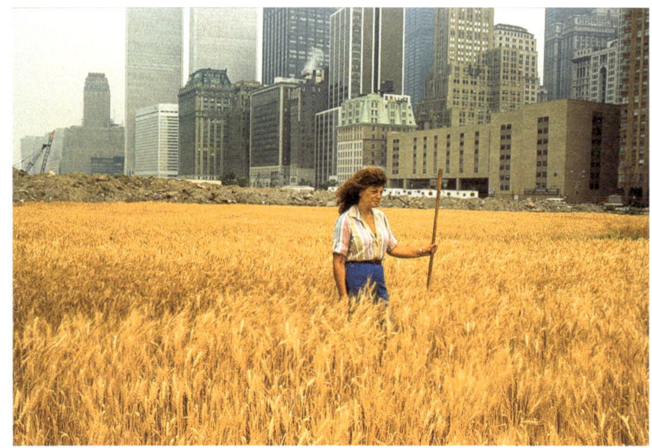 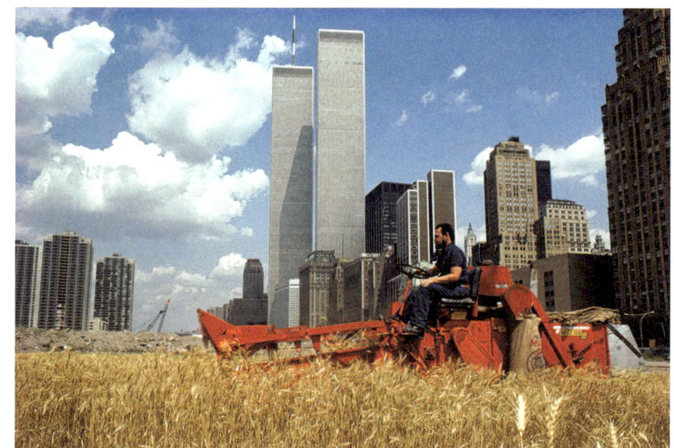

Wheatfield - A Confrontation: Battery Park Landfill,
Downtown Manhattan - With Agnes Denes Standing in the Field, 1982 [cat. no. 37]
Wheatfield - A Confrontation: Battery Park Landfill,
Downtown Manhattan - The Harvest, 1982/2024 [cat. no. 38]
Wheatfield - A Confrontation: Battery Park Landfill,
Downtown Manhattan - Harvest with Sailboat, 1982/2024 [cat. no. 39]
Wheatfield - A Confrontation: Battery Park Landfill,
Downtown Manhattan - Aerial View 2, 1982/2024 [cat. no. 40]

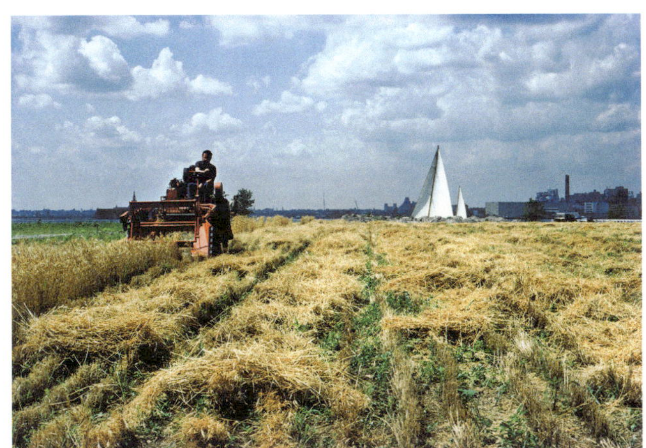
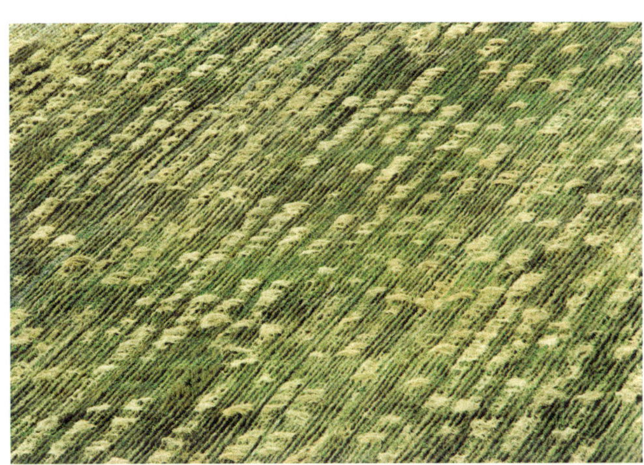

Wheatfield — A Confrontation

Preparing the planting of a field
in the middle of the city
Bringing in the soil
trucks unload the field
Laying down the rows
One block from Wall Street
Statue of Liberty across the Hudson
The sunset and 4 acres of Manhattan,
empty and all mine
50-page contract with the city
protects everyone but me
Three buildings in construction
four blocks away
Birth of a City of what will be condos,
office spaces – greed
My placing is important for the **Confrontation.**
Wall street to the right, the
Hudson to my left a foot away
And the Statue looking at me saying,
make me proud. I did. She did.
We look at each other every day.
Strong harbor winds,
cross winds of New York harbor
Afraid the seeds won't hold
get blown out of the soil
Digging deep furrows planting by hand
instead of broadcasting
So the seeds won't blow away,
Winds come but rains don't
Then it rains when you don't want it
Harsh harbor winds, cross winds,
Storms and dark angry skies
The arrival of living things
The famous performing spider,
yellow/black dance for the press
for TV crews and photographers
My assistant who nearly passes out
Had some mysterious illness
could not contain himself
People looking down from skyscrapers
talking about a slender woman working
in the field tending to everything,
a pinpoint in the distance, tireless

Managing things day in and day out
From early morning till late at night
Arrival of the bugs
Field mice, ladybugs, caterpillars,
field mice, dragonflies
Like a note from Wall Street
come praying mentis,
too tired to get the joke
New Jersey mollusks swim across
the surface tension of the Hudson
to great the field
slime-slid onto twigs and wheat stalks
Thousands of lady bugs
Oceanliners daily foghorn solute
Green wheat shoots pop up
Close ups shot from lying in the mud
I photograph every day
Wheat smut destroys wheat
everywhere in the country
TV crews ask why not us
We pick it by hand daily, we smile
the famous dancing spider,
TV crews delight
4th of July fear of field being trampled down
overrun by millions pushing to see the fireworks
Police barricades lent by police, helpful, kind,
People don't hurt what they love,
No vandalism, not a foot
Only a dog comes daily to pee on the field
every day, his expression of love
4th of July spray from tugboat
Red white and blue spray
Great honor honoring the field
Ocean liners come solute with their foghorn
All the while threat of the construction mafia
The Joe: attack of the hard hats—vandalism
Wall street brokers hang out,
watching the field grow
Working with insufficient funds,
assuming responsibility for a project
And doing it all while having no authority
just risk and responsibility
And a fifty page contract

that protects everyone but me
Running the whole production
without funds or experience
Nothing but bravado
to send an important message,
through a work of art
Eyes on the goal,
feeling no pain, discomfort,
mud, cold, heat, unbearable heat
Documenting the whole project, lying in mud,
Protecting only the camera and the shot
The weather helicopter takes me up for
aerial photos, getting seasick,
Then taking pictures from rooftop of 49th floor
Late at night exhausted
from having worked all day in the field
Making sandwiches daily for the volunteers,
Photographing everything, managing the project,
Paying bills, daily on the phone finding volunteers
While fighting the enemies around me
Then *The Joe,* head of the construction mafia,
Want me to go with him to Atlantic City,
When I don't, they steal my tools, lock the gates
So the volunteers couldn't come in or leave
Holding up the work with precious time table
Volunteers eventually roll under the gate to get in,
Where I've dug a space in the ground for them,
Finding a cross in the rubble,
told it was a good omen
Money returned by trucker
who admitted wanting to steal it
My precious few thousand dollars
Had no money for anything
Ten thousand to do the whole project
and put in twice that from my own,
still not enough, never any money
Jeering me, the stupid trusting woman
The key to the gate being denied
by mafia construction workers
*The Joe…*the leader, relentlessly want to bed me
Mafia attacks my equipment,
stealing or destroying them
Laughing behind my back
Good looking crazy broad
Try to get her into bed,
if not steel her tools

Volunteers throw stones off the field,
clearing the rubble
had only enough money for
one inch of top soil
The gratitude of volunteers:
 You saved me thousands in psychiatric fee;
Cured me of phobias; got the anger out of me,
she says while hurling the stones
throwing garbage off the field.
Filled with nothing but the strength
of naïve, creative enthusiasm
Looking only to the goal,
the commitment, the task ahead,
From moment to moment,
from catastrophe to solutions,
People stealing my little money, its miraculous return,
Small miracles all along, finding the cross in garbage,
Maria says could I keep it?
My money gets returned, disaster and accomplishment,
Reaction of volunteers: we'll never forget this
God Bless you
The locked gates open, then key to the gate finally won,
Brought over on a piece of cloth in a ceremony
Like the key to the city
Ending the struggle with the construction workers
The Joe, finally giving up to bed me
 hands me the key to the gates
Respect grows daily for the crazy broad
As the wheat grew they show off with it
Look at OUR WHEATFIELD they say
Want to see a wheat field in Manhattan?
The taxi driver says, I'll take you there
I've seen it I say.

Deciding not to harvest with scythes
not to cut off fingers or hands
Harvester chugs through the tunnel
to West Street in heavy traffic
Being against the company's politics
I'm forced to accept their help
The harvest,
people stand around and cry,
who died? The field? No it just gave birth
They just stand with eyes full of tears, silence
It was the only field in hundreds of years in Manhattan
I give the hay to the mounted police

of New York for the horses
Later the harvested seed is
put into huge canvas bags
Then for months having to save
it from rats and mice
You put anything into the world
and instantly become responsible for it
if a child or the seeds from
 a field of wheat
Museum travels the seed to 28 cities
around the world
Put into small bags
that people carry away
Plant in solidarity with my concept
around the world to become one with it
They beg me to keep the field going,
I can't. legal stuff,
Can the message survive?
don't destroy the earth, don't mismanage,
feed the hungry, wake up, be better.
Believe in your better self.

The last open space in Manhattan, gone
to become condos, offices, malls, hotels
But for one summer it was a field of golden wheat
survival blowing in the wind.

Lower Manhattan
New York City,
Summer 1982
© Agnes Denes

ADDENDUM

Another menace:
The woman assigned to oversee my project,
not up to it just there to make trouble
My assistant, the gardener from the city
says about her:
she is so uptight she'd break a rectal thermometer!
although he usually had no sense of humor
says even this with a straight face,
not in jest
he had to be restrained not to chase her
off the field a few times.
The guy had a tamper and at one time
I held him back from hitting her
she was a nervous person,
afraid of her own shadow,
but strong enough to bossing me around,
putting me in horrible situations
 withholding the press with stupid excuses,
She was put into charge without experience
and as coverup overdid her job
she withheld my spending money,
the little I needed for paying people,
enjoying my embarrassment,
interfered in everything none of her business,
made my life living hell which was
already overwhelmingly difficult.

Wheatfield - A Confrontation: Battery Park Landfill,
Downtown Manhattan - Green Wheat Turning Yellow, 1982 [cat. no. 41]

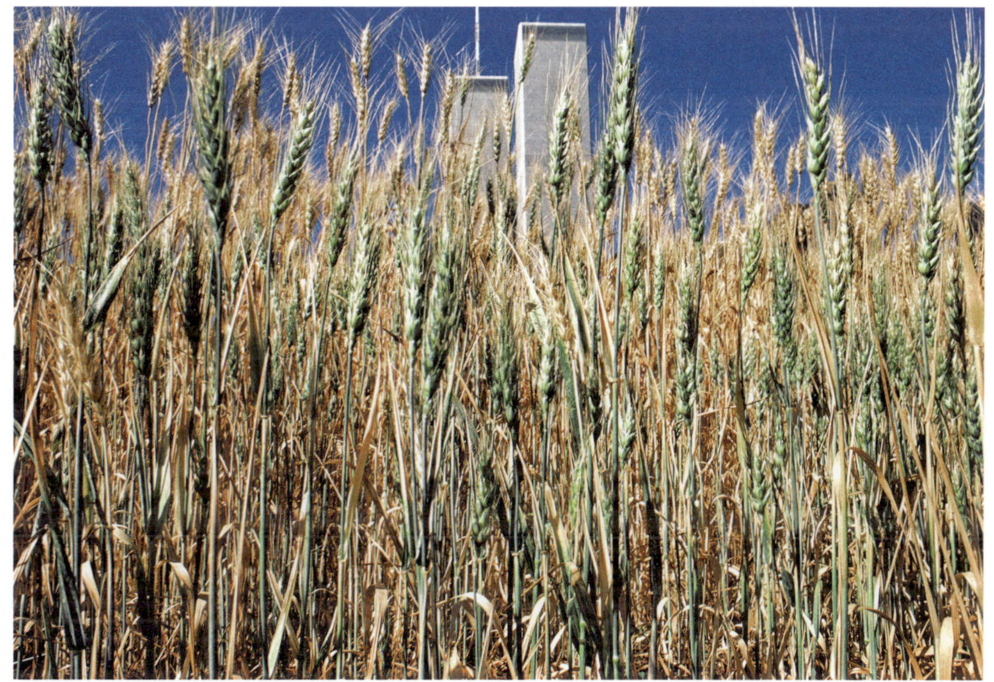

Tree Mountain — A Living Time Capsule

11,000 Trees, 11,00 People, 400 Years, 1982–1996
420 × 270 × 28 meters

Tree Mountain (1982–1996) is a collaborative, environmental project that touches on global, ecological, social, and cultural issues. It tests our finitude and transcendence, individuality versus teamwork, and measures the value and evolution of a work of art after it has entered the environment. *Tree Mountain* is designed to unite the human intellect with the majesty of nature.

Eleven thousand trees are planted by the same number of people according to an intricate pattern derived from a mathematical formula. The mathematical expansion changes with one's view and movement around and above the mountain, thus revealing hidden curves and spirals in the design. If seen from space, the human intellect at work over natural formation becomes evident, yet they blend harmoniously.

The projected size of *Tree Mountain* was 1.5 miles in length, .25 mile in width, and elliptical. Height was site-specific, depending on the incline, approximately 120 feet.

Originally I chose silver fir because these trees are dying out, and it is important that we preserve them. Otherwise, any tree could make up the forest as long as it can live three to four hundred years. The trees must outlive the present era and, by surviving, carry our concepts into an unknown time in the future. If our civilization as we know it ends, or as changes occur, there will be a reminder in the form of a strange mathematical forest for our descendants to ponder. In the end we settled on planting Finnish pine, as silver fir could not have survived the harsh Finnish winters.

Tree Mountain is a collaborative work, from its intricate landscaping and forestry to the funding and contractual agreements for its strange, unheard-of land-use of four centuries. The collaboration expands as eleven thousand people come together to plant the trees that will bear their name and remain their property through succeeding generations. All planters received an inheritable certificate valid for 400 years in the future. They can leave their tree to their heirs, be buried under it, and sell it at auction or by other means. The trees can change ownership, but *Tree Mountain* itself can never be owned or sold, nor can the trees be moved from the forest. Tree Mountain represents the concept, the soul of the art, while the trees are a manifestation of it. They are salable, collectible works of art, inheritable commodities, gaining stature, fame, and value as they grow and age as trees. But in the meanwhile they remain part of a larger whole, the forest. They are individual segments of a single, limited edition. The trees are unique patterns in the design of their universe. The certificate covering so many generations is first in human history.

And the trees live on through the centuries — stable and majestic, outliving their owners who created the patterns and the philosophy, but not the tree. There is a strange paradox in this.

Tree Mountain begins its existence when it is completed as a work of art. As the trees grow and wildlife takes over, as decades and centuries pass, *Tree Mountain* becomes a fascinating study of how the passing of time affects a work of art. It can become a thermometer of the evolution of art. Through changing fashions and beliefs, Tree Mountain can pass from being a curiosity to being a shrine, from being the possible remnants of a decadent era to being one of the monuments of a great civilization.

Tree Mountain is a living time capsule that benefits future generations with a meaningful legacy.

Note: Ten years after its creation, *Tree Mountain* was realized in full scale in the Pinziö gravel pits, Ylöjärvi, Finland, 1992–1996.

© Agnes Denes 1992

Tree Mountain - A Living Time Capsule - 11,000 Trees, 11,000 People,
400 Years (Triptych) 1992–1996/2013 [cat. no. 42]

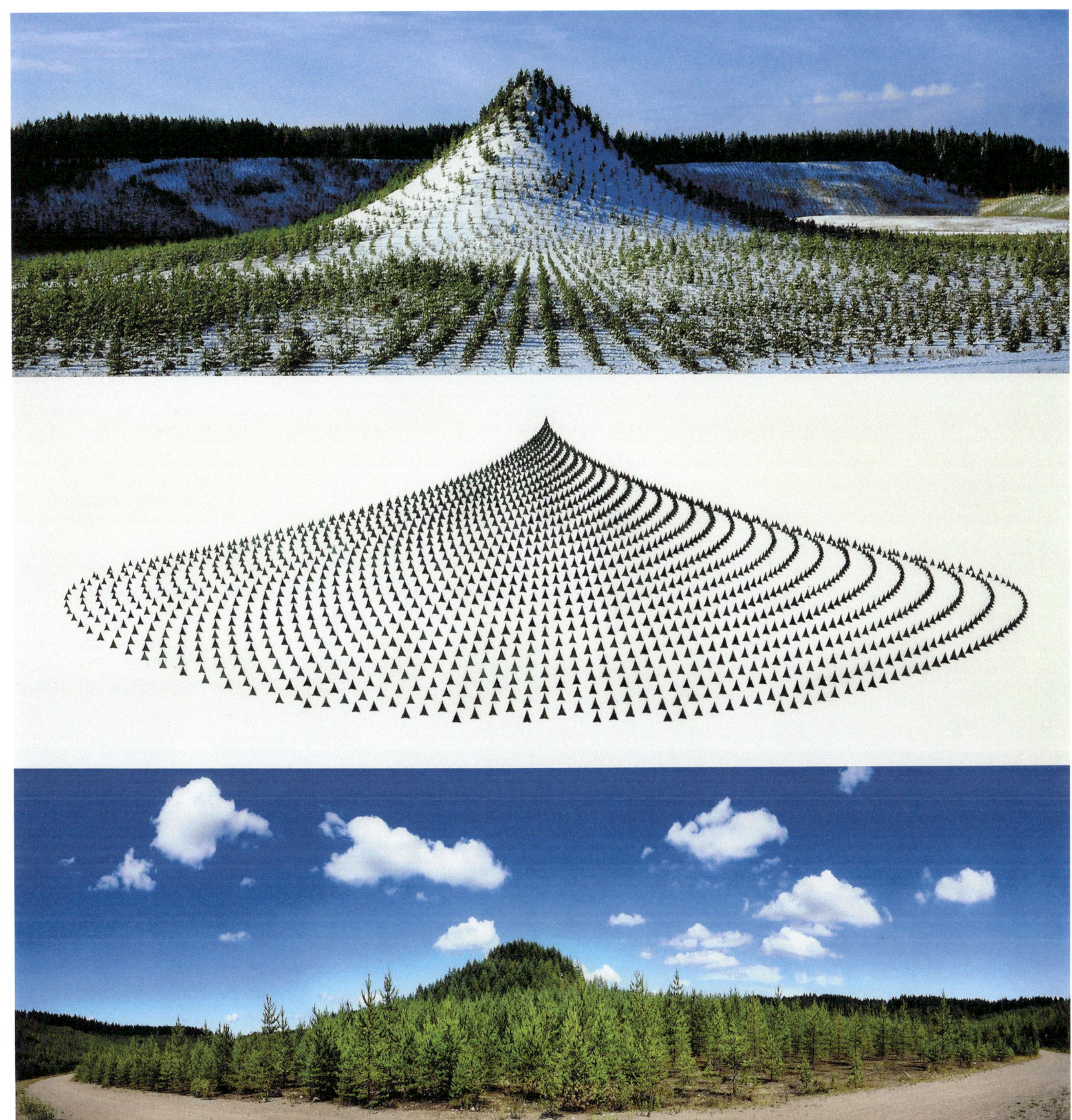

Tree Mountain – A Living Time Capsule
11,000 People, 11,000 Trees, 400 Years, 1992–1996
Ylöjärvi, Finland

Aira Kalela, Ministry of Environment, Finland

A huge manmade mountain measuring 420 meters long, 270 meters wide, 28 meters high and elliptical in shape was planted with eleven thousand trees by eleven thousand people from all over the world at the Pinziö gravel pits near Ylöjärvi, Finland, as part of a massive earthwork and land reclamation project by environmental artist Agnes Denes. The project was officially announced by the Finnish government at the Earth Summit in Rio de Janeiro on Earth Environment Day, June 5, I992, as Finland's contribution to help alleviate the world's ecological stress. Sponsored by the United Nations Environment Program and the Finnish Ministry of the Environment, *Tree Mountain* is protected land to be maintained for four centuries, eventually creating a *virgin* forest. The trees are planted in an intricate mathematical pattern derived from a combination of the golden section and the pineapple/sunflower pattern designed by the artist. Even though infinitely more complex, it is reminiscent of ancient earth patterns.

Tree Mountain is the largest monument on earth that is international in scope, unparalleled in duration, and not dedicated to the human ego, but to benefit future generations with a meaningful legacy. People who planted the trees received certificates acknowledging them as custodians of the trees. The certificate is an inheritable document valid for twenty or more generations in the future. The project is innovative nationally and worldwide – the first such undertaking in human history. This is the very first time in Finland and among the first ones in the world when an artist restores environmental damage with ecological art planned for this and future generations.

Tree Mountain, conceived in 1982, affirms humanity's commitment to the future well being of ecological, social and cultural life on the planet. It is designed to unite the human intellect with the majesty of nature. Tree Mountain was dedicated in June, 1996 by the President of Finland, other heads of state, and people from everywhere.

© Agnes Denes

Tree Mountain - A Living Time Capsule, Ylöjärvi Finland,
1992-1996/2013 [cat. no. 43]

The Future is Fragile

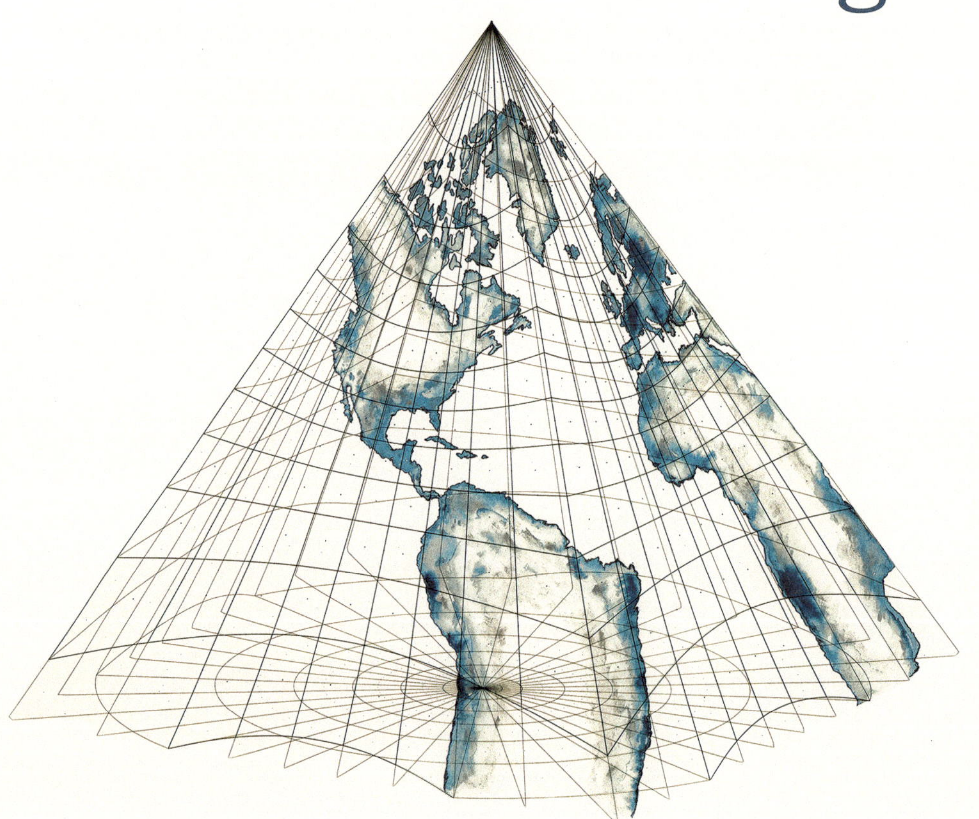

Handle With Care

The Future is Fragile, Handle With Care, 2021 [cat. no. 44]
The Future is Fragile, Handle with Care – Agnes Denes's flag
on the facade of the Museum of Fine Arts Budapest in October 2024

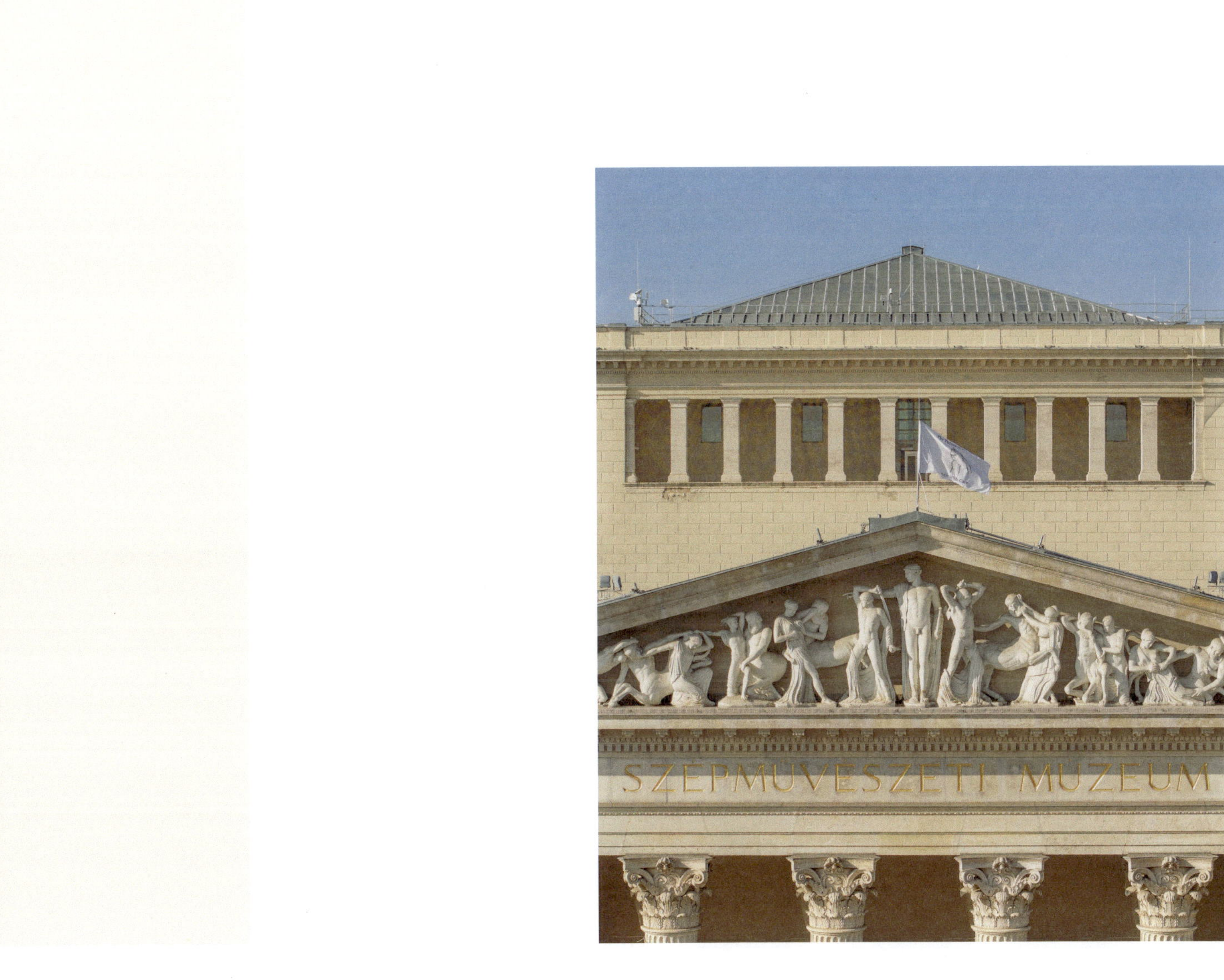

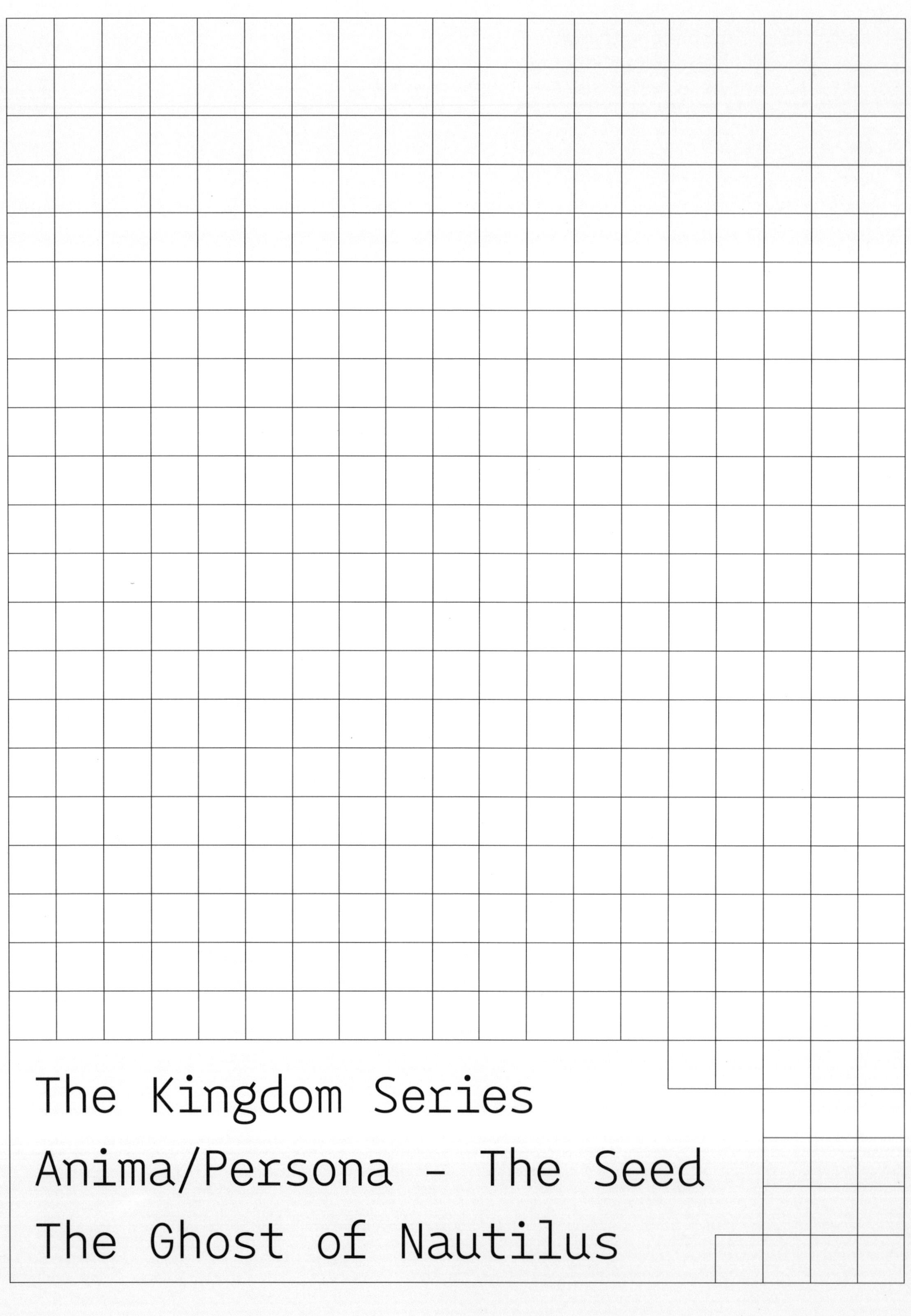

The Kingdom Series
Anima/Persona - The Seed
The Ghost of Nautilus

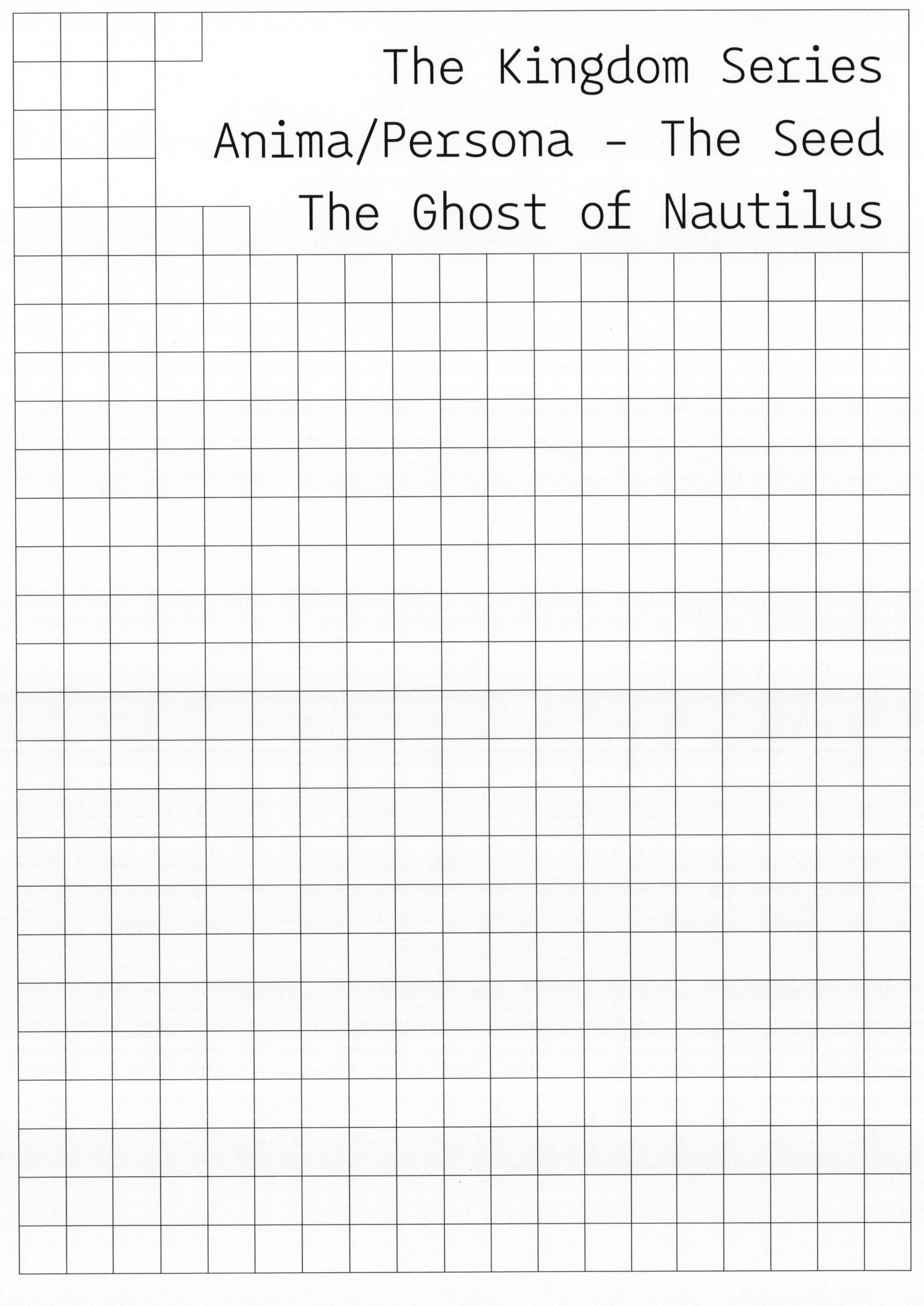

The Kingdom Series
Anima/Persona - The Seed
The Ghost of Nautilus

The Kingdom Series

The animal and plant kingdoms are explored through
X-rays, demonstrating the strange beauty and exquisite
anatomical structuring one may imagine but never
otherwise see in these forms.

© Agnes Denes 1972

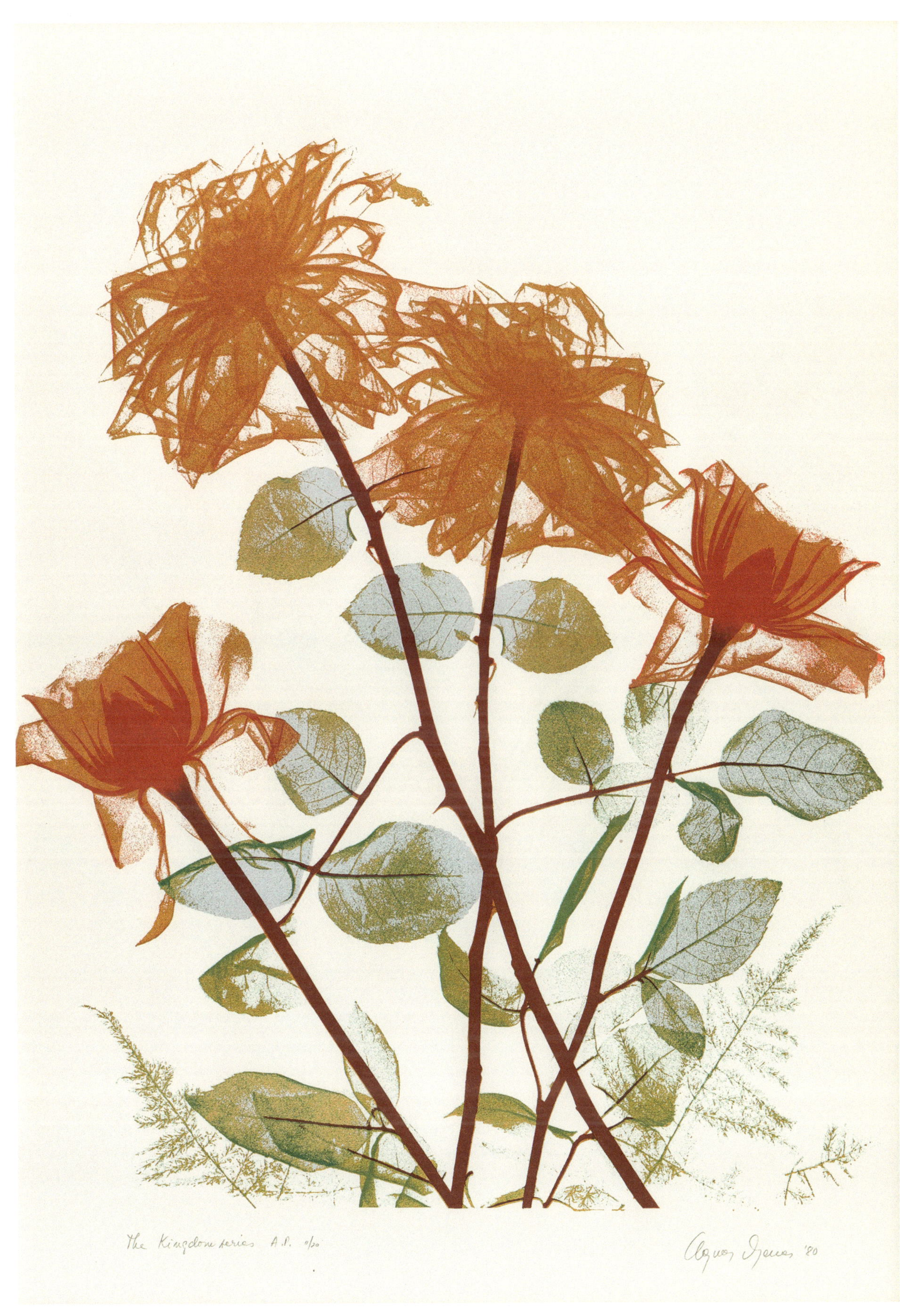
The Kingdom series A.P. */20
Agnes Denes '80

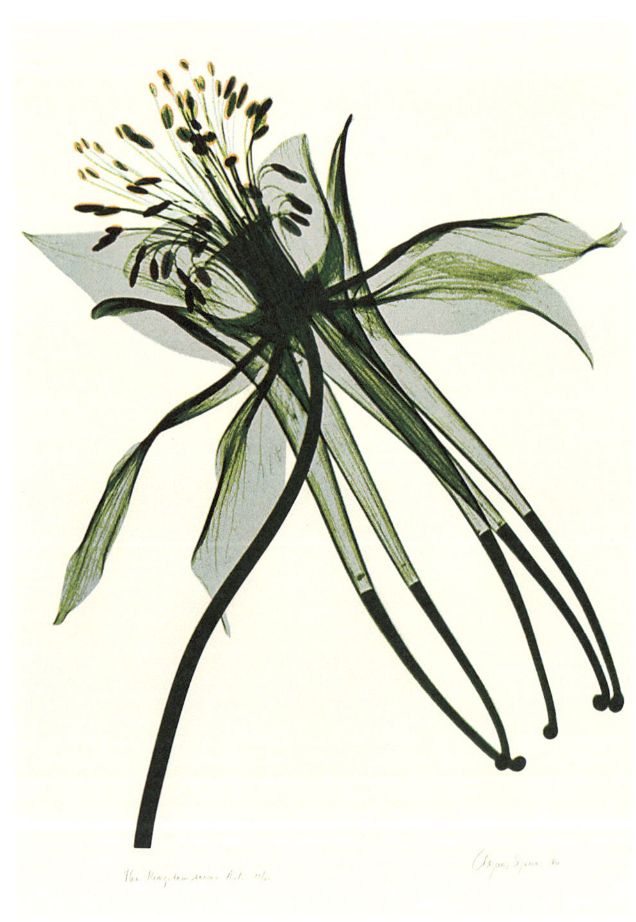

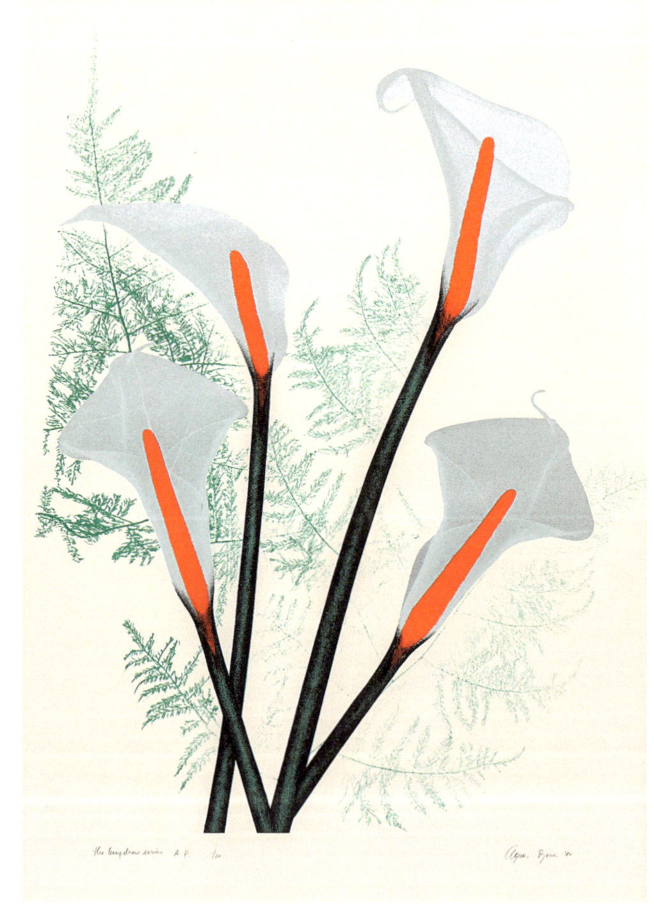

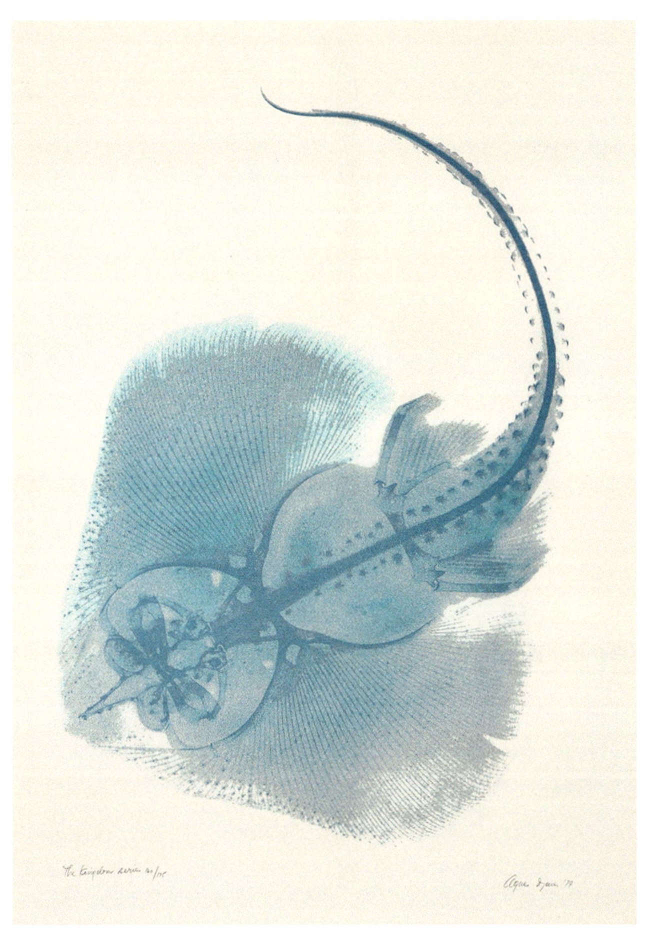

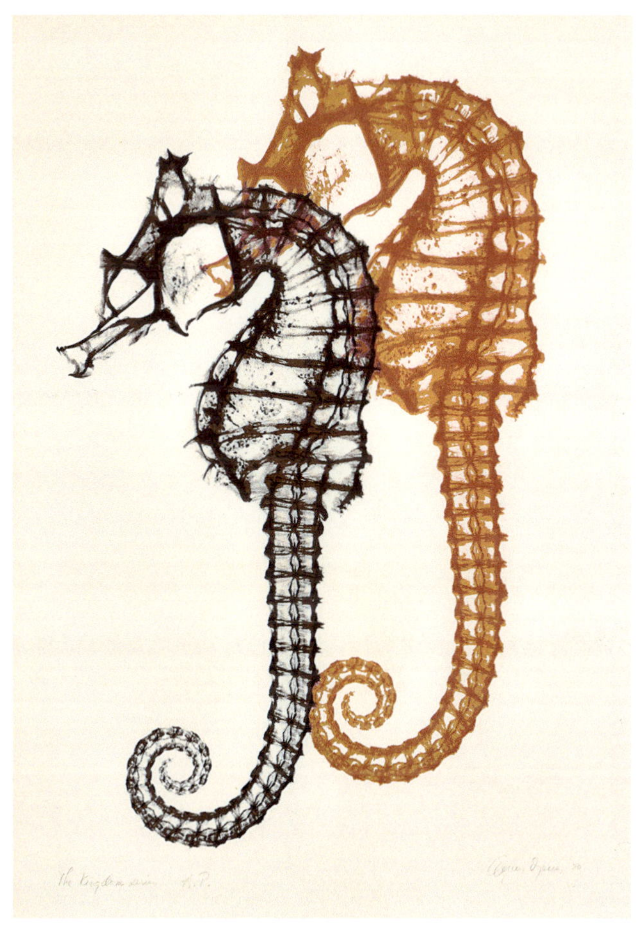

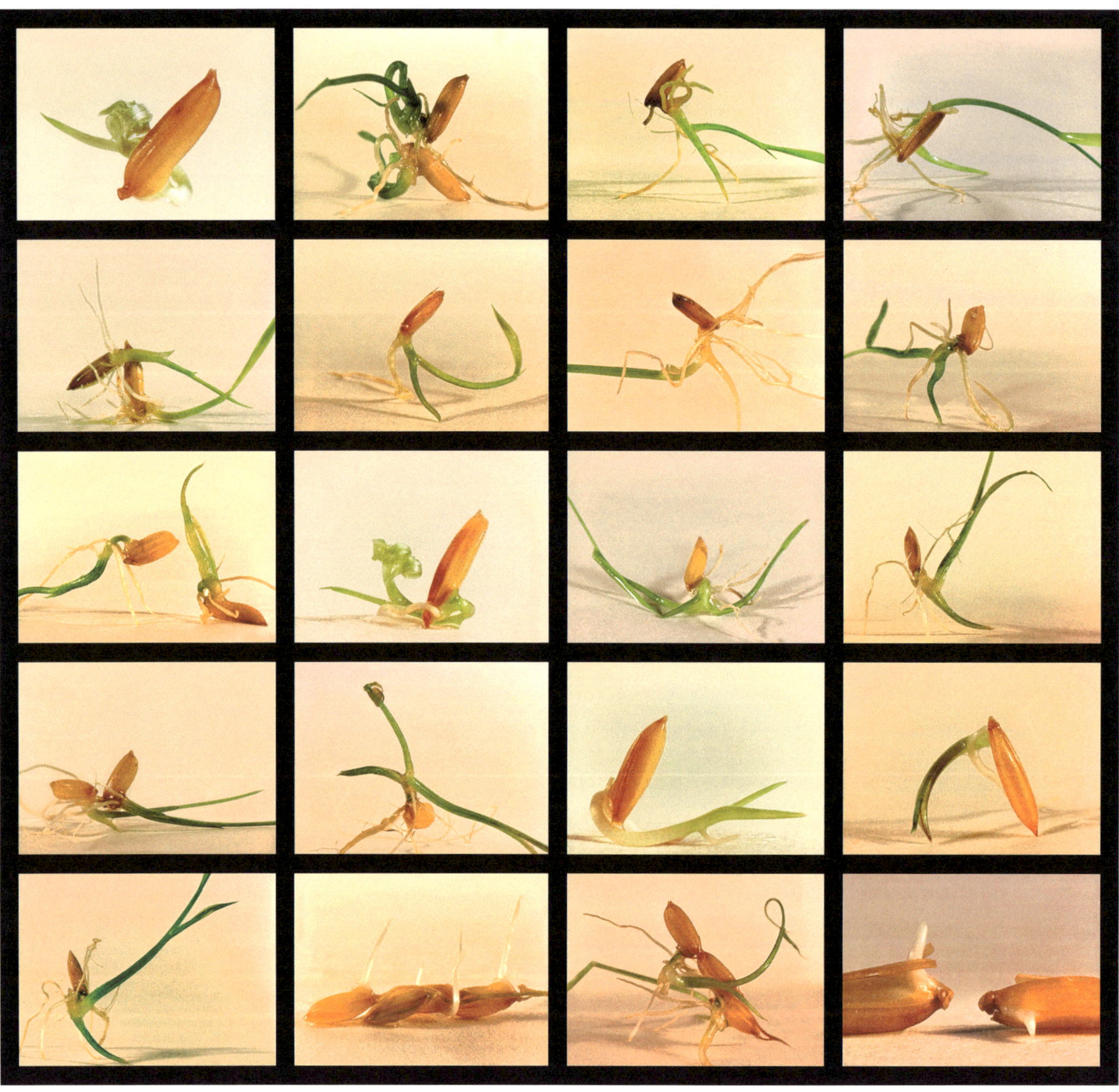

Anima/Persona - The Seed (white), 1978-1980/2019 [cat. no. 50]
Anima/Persona - The Seed (black), 1978-1980/2019 [cat. no. 51]

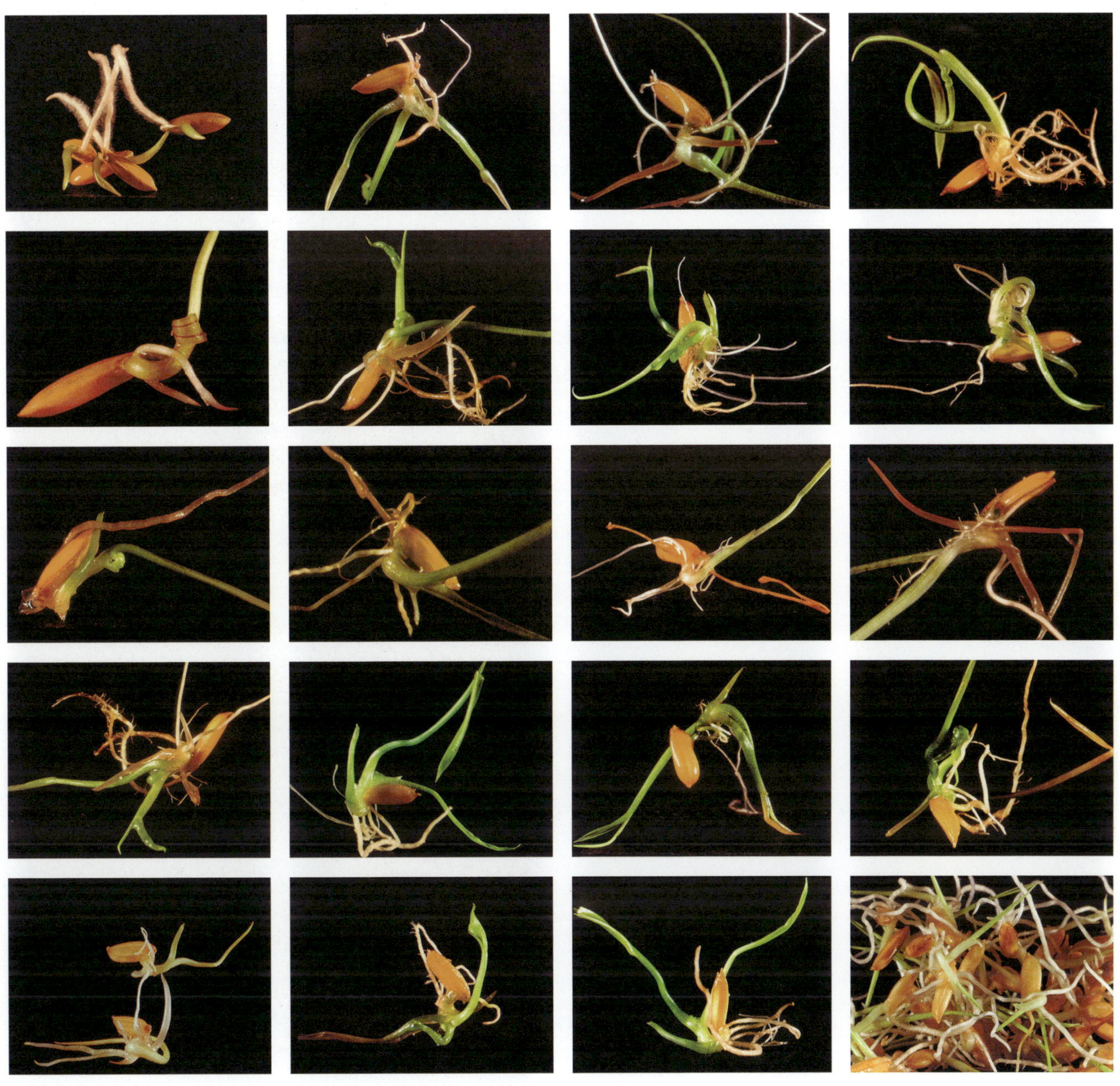

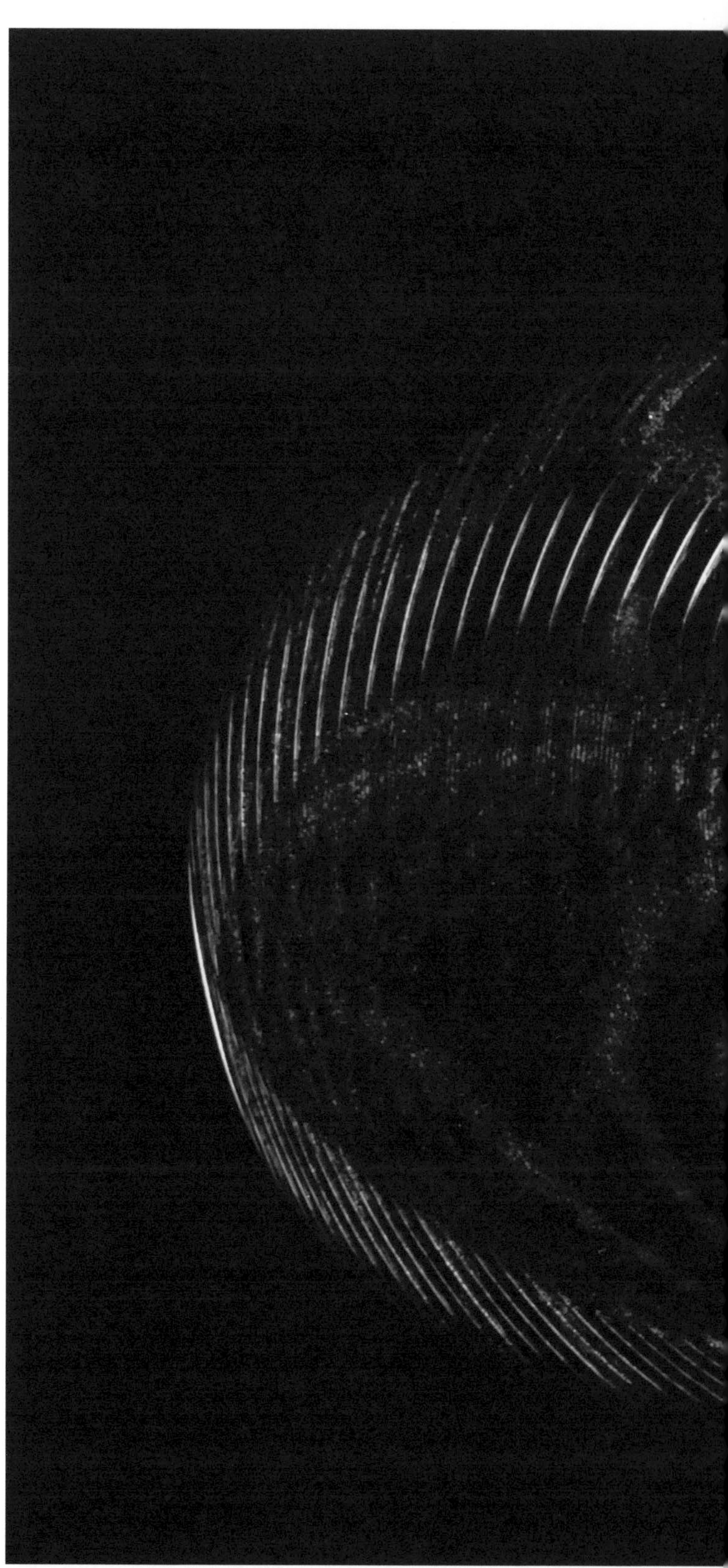

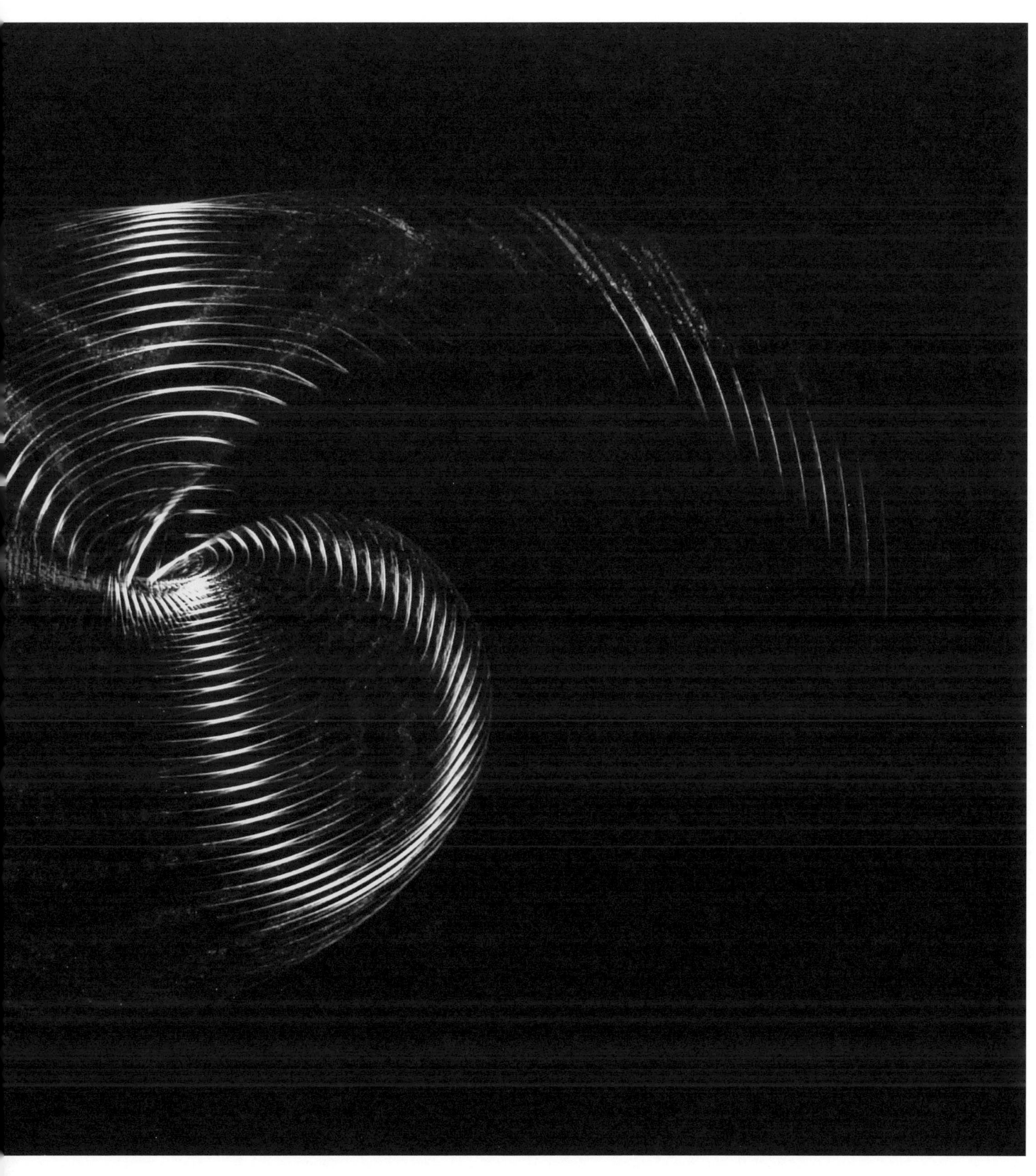

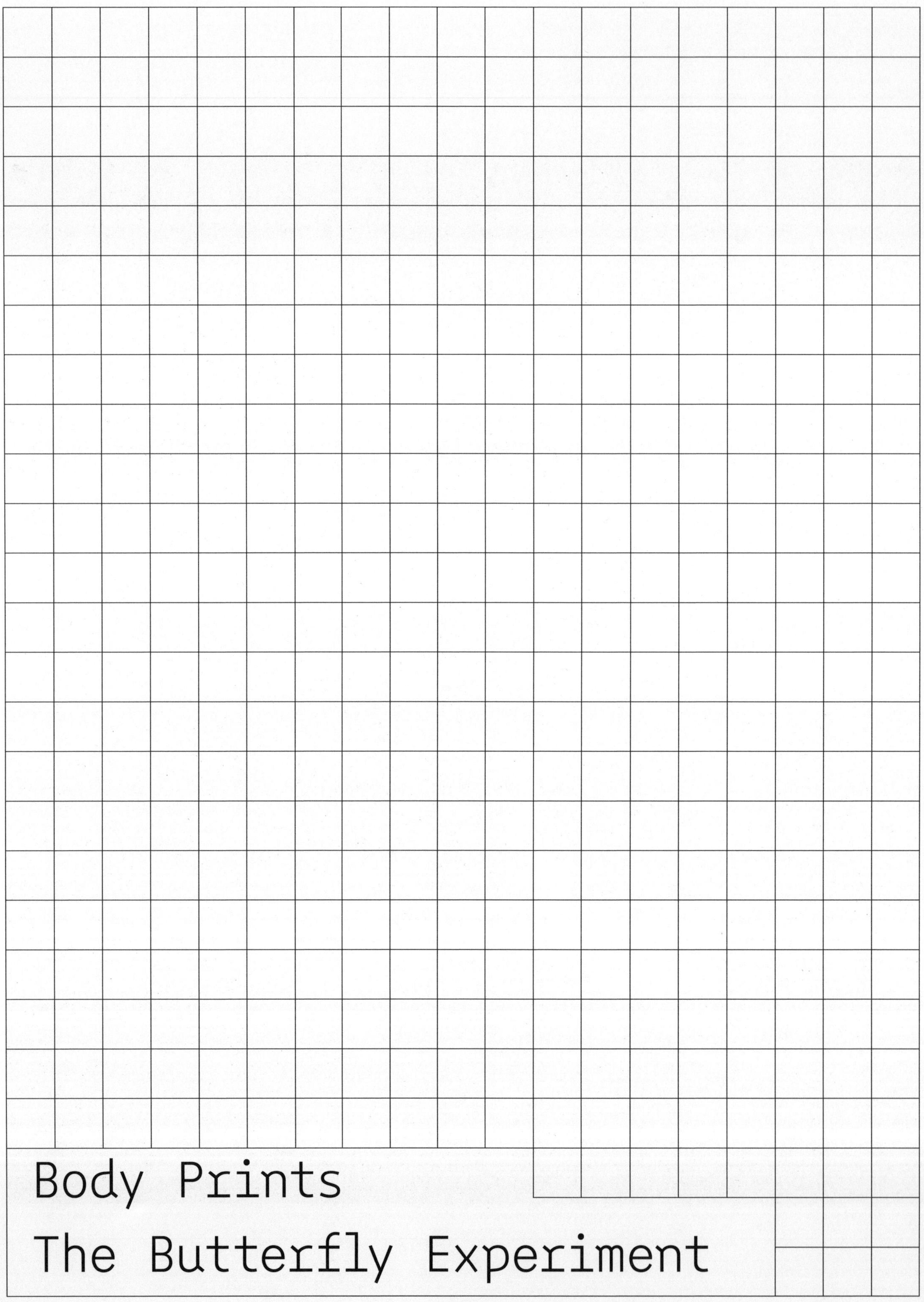

Body Prints

The Butterfly Experiment

Body Prints
The Butterfly Experiment

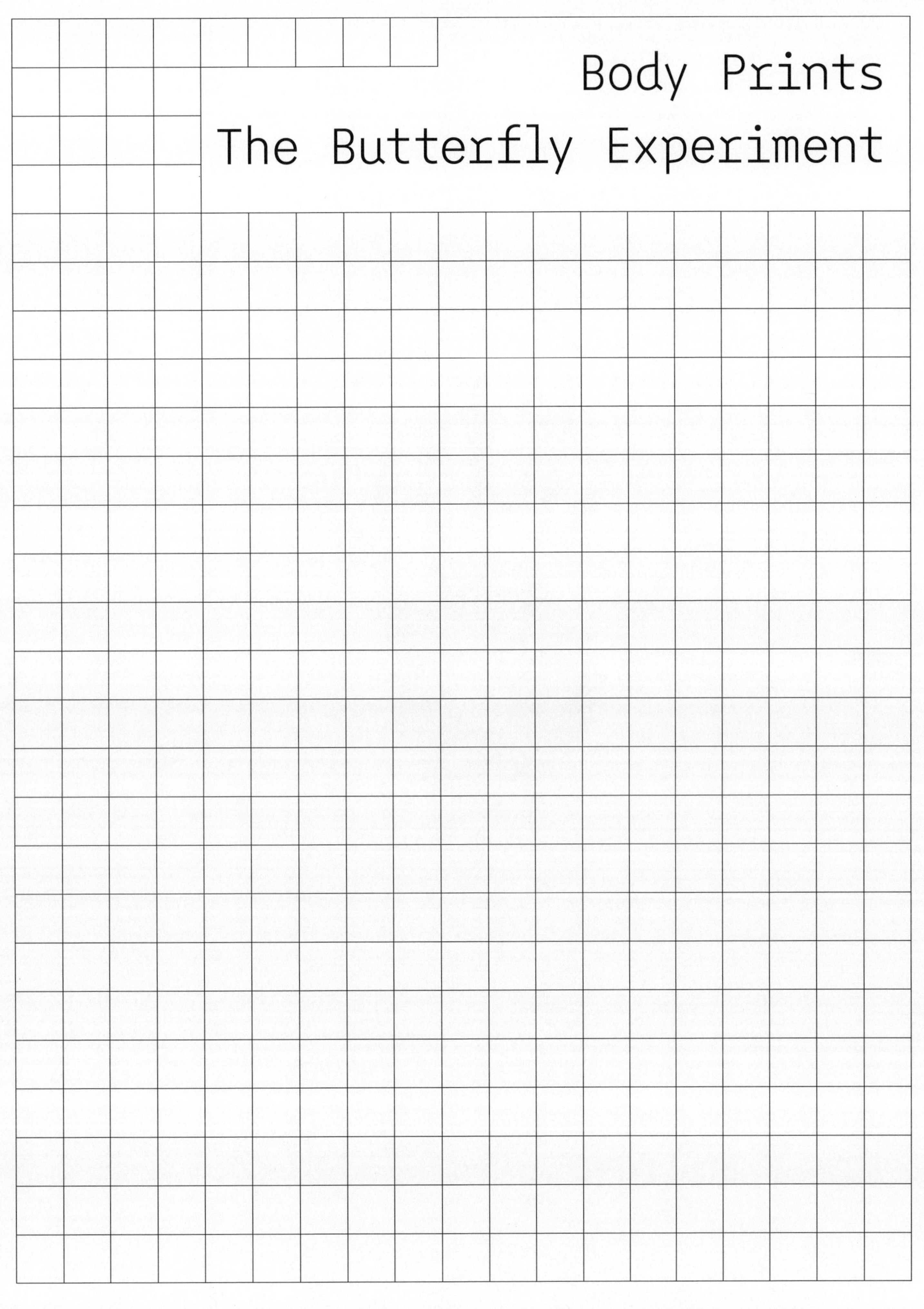

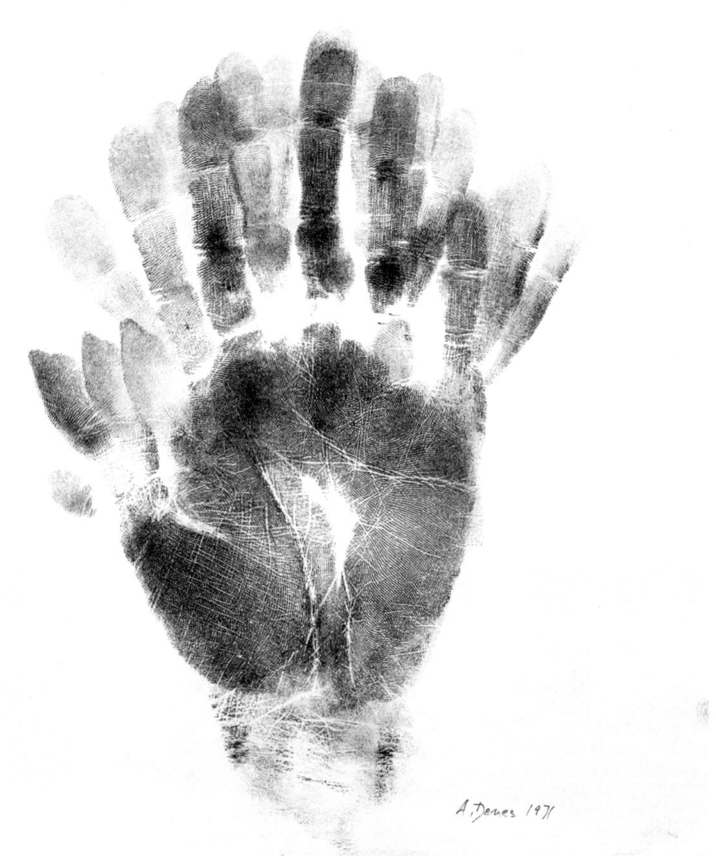

A. Denes 1971

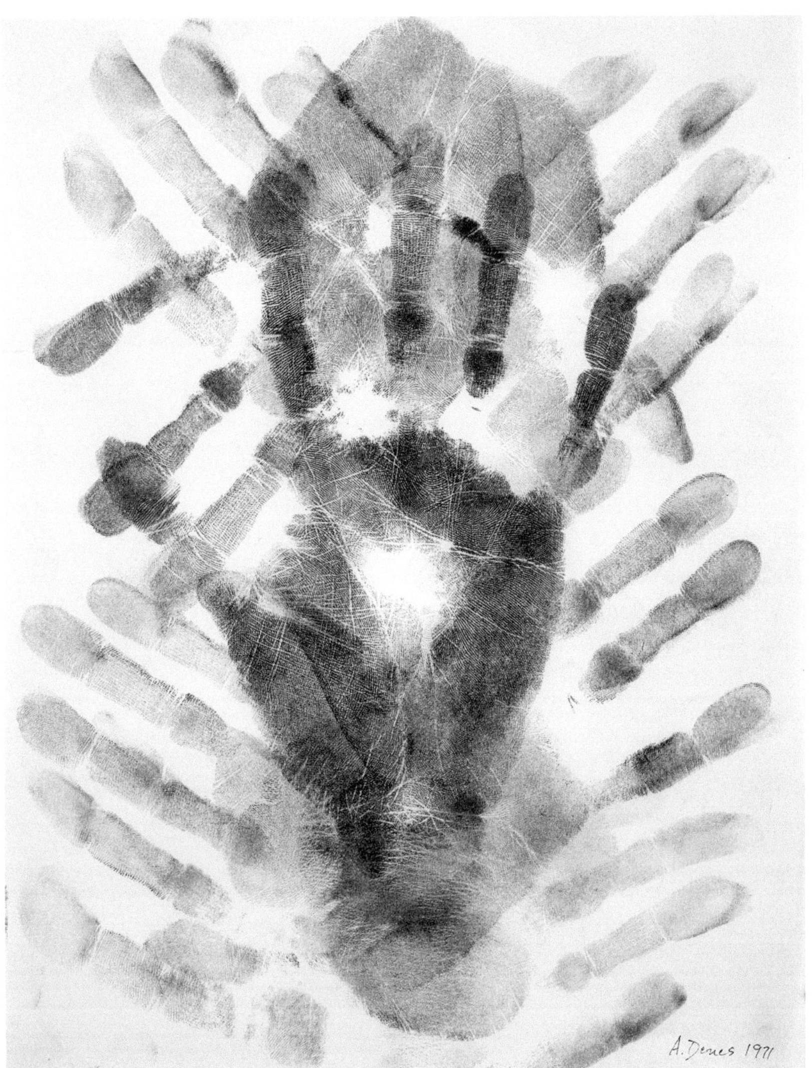

The Butterfly Experiment

"Since I have been losing movement in my fingers caused by a rare illness I can't
make art in the ordinary sense. The complicated fine line drawings and beautiful images
no longer in my control, I had to find ways of creating in other forms. You can't stop
creativity, it is like a torrent inside you, a volcano that keeps erupting. It took awhile to
teach myself to write on the computer keypad with unbending fingers. Now I am writing
two books. Then I began experimenting with creating images, and here are some
of the results.

The Butterfly Experiment is among these new works experimenting with how light
can transform works of art, play with the visual experience on an intellectual plane.
It vibrates, leaves you breathless. In a sense it is intelligent light. Letting the outer
layers light up the work I was able to create extraordinary visual experience. Showing
shadows and internal elements, the skeletal structure of form, as I did many years ago
in the *Philosophical Drawings*, or as with the *Flying Pyramids* when I experimented
with pure silver and gold powders to create art that not only lights up the work to glow
when light hits it, but that it can disappear from the paper in certain lighting, leaving
a shadow of itself.

But don't ask me how I did the *Butterfly Experiment*, or some of my later works,
because I don't know and can't repeat the process. Coming to the computer for the
first time to make art, I just kept creating, never thinking about documenting the process
in case I needed to repeat it. Today's students work with programs. I didn't. Just used
my computer and kept experimenting.

All my life when I lost one thing I loved, the force of creativity brought me another.
When I lost my language of poetry traveling to new countries, I made visual art and
wrote books. When this force and the world demanded more dimensions, I made
ecological art. When my body bent to illness; the creative force retaliated and
made art in the computer.

I still need more time, more forms of creativity; it's my oxygen, it's my sunlight."

© Agnes Denes 2017

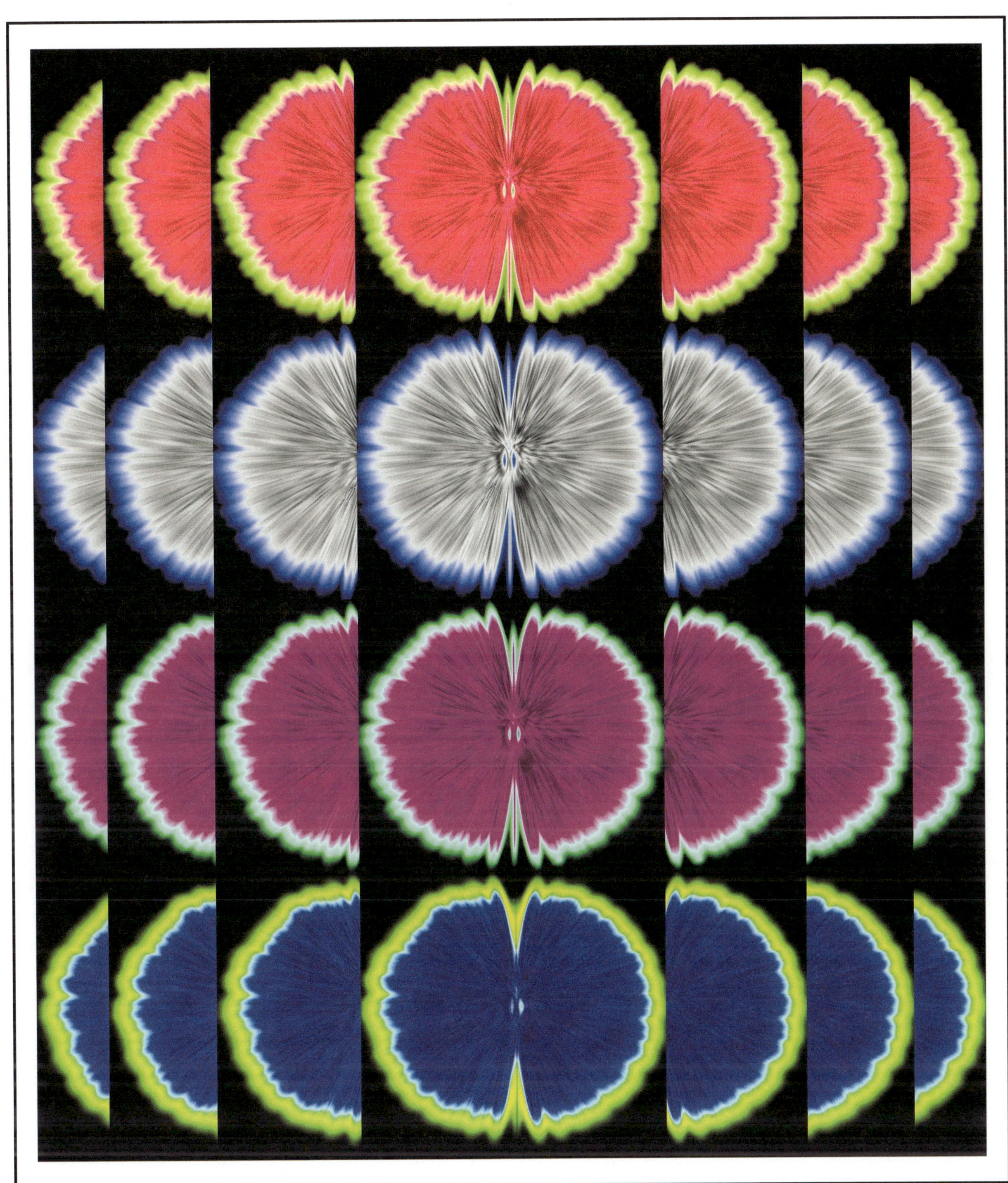

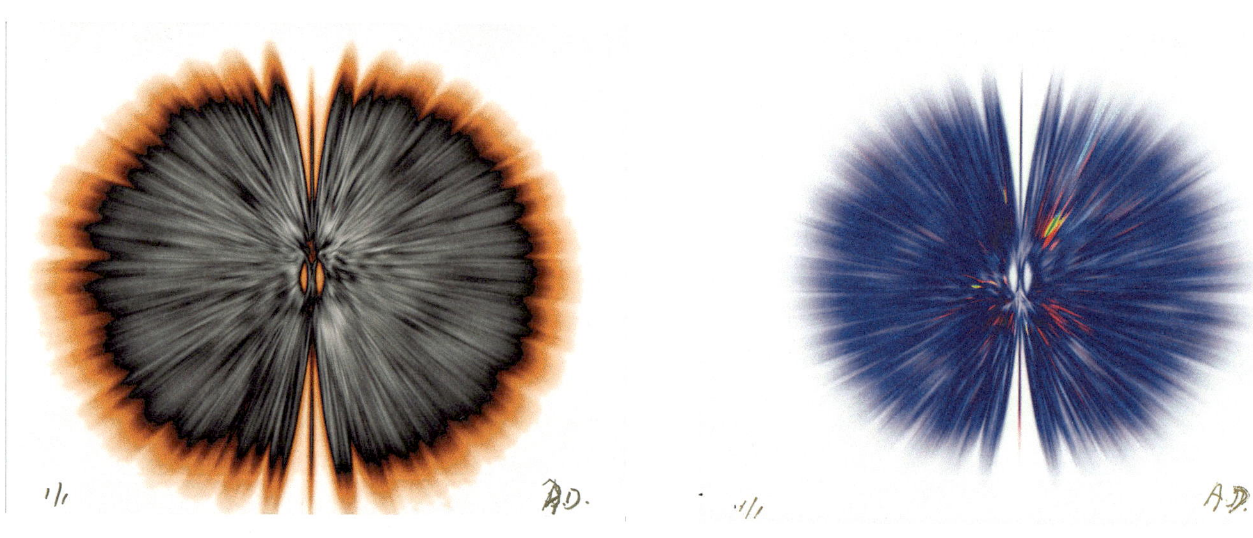

<u>Everything Realized</u>, 2020-2021 [cat. no. 56]
<u>Purple Rhapsody</u>, 2020-2021 [cat. no. 57]
<u>Butterfly Experiments in Grey</u>, 2015 [cat. no. 58]
<u>Butterfly Experiments in Blue</u>, 2015 [cat. no. 59]

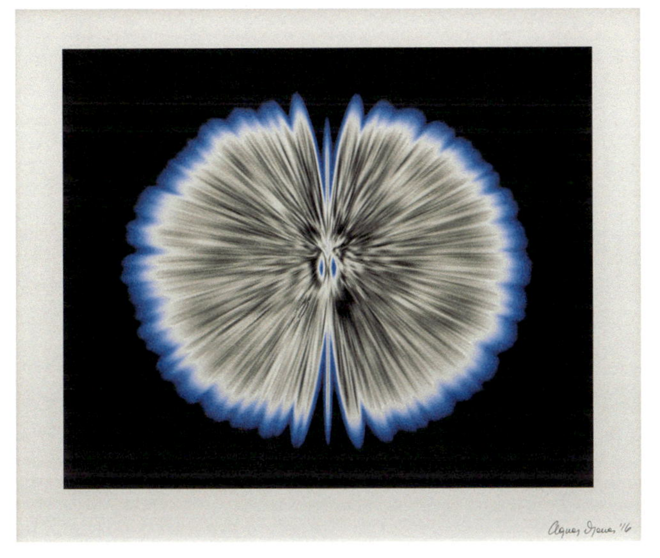

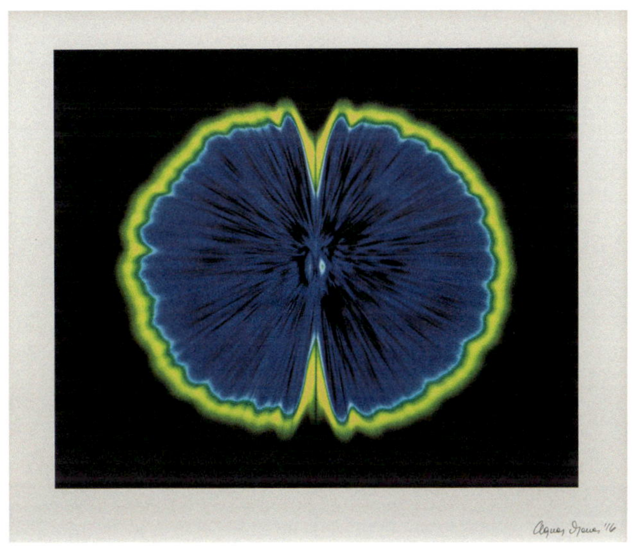

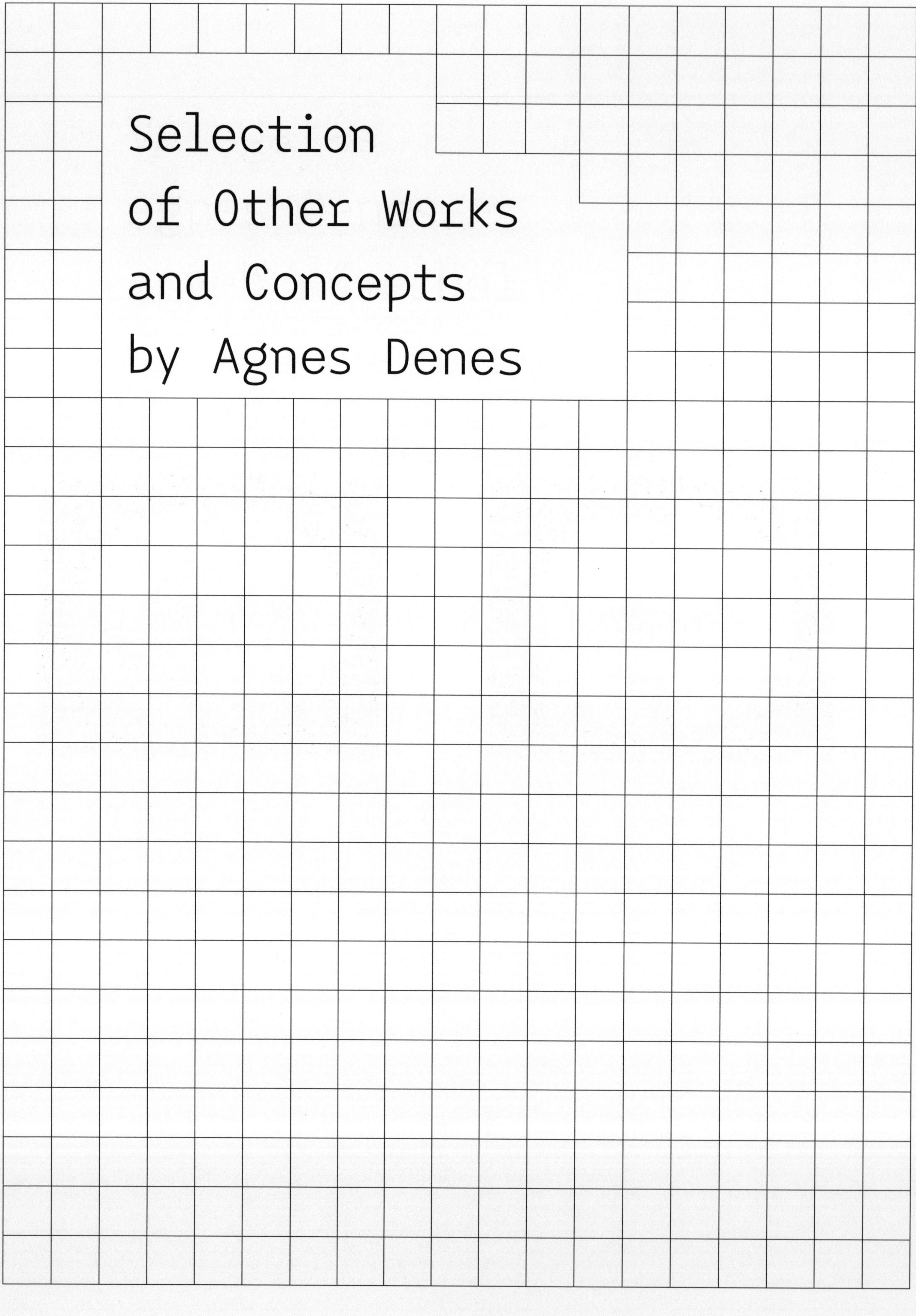
Selection
of Other Works
and Concepts
by Agnes Denes

Systems of Logic / Logic of Systems

Finalist Drawing for University City Science Center, Philadelphia
(steel cable and rods, 4 × 18 × 3 m, 1988)
Silver and India ink on mylar

*Systems of Logic/Logic of Systems** is a steel cable structure based on the mathematics of Pascal's triangle.

The number system represents a universal concept (the essence or nature of a thing) that becomes the vehicle through which analytical propositions are visualized (given form, created).

The network of numbers represents the "logic" that supports the structure, which itself represents the "system"; conversely, the system represents "structure". The number logic represents structural eloquence, as valid structuralization gives tribute to the basic beauty of logic. Underlying patterns and concepts determine the form, while the logic remains intact.

Pattern-finding is the purpose of the mind and the construct of the universe. There are an infinite number of patterns, some of which are known; those still unknown hold the key to unresolved enigmas and paradoxes. Thus formal and exclusively visual information can be refined to such an extent as to impart the most precise and significant information in addition to visual gratification.

This exercise in "visual mathematics" is a way of using universals and ultimates to arrive at true beginnings (formal cause - the cause of form).

As a three-dimensional form, *Systems of Logic* has an almost invisible substructure to which the steel cables are attached, then pulled taut, much like an inverted bridge with its supporting sides placed end to end, while the sloping centers are suspended in mid-air, pointing to the viewer at both ends. The steel cables allow the entire network to be seen, the order, repetition, and tension to be experienced.

On the horizontal plane, the effect is that of an engineering and architectural tour-de-force. Viewers may walk around the cable network and experience the pointed tips from a head-on perspective (6.5 ft. in height), while their own motion changes the designs created by the converging cables into moire patterns. The direct and pure translation of mathematics into form is obvious.

The visual mathematics is also evident in the vertical, but here the dominant effect is that of being surrounded by taut cables that seem to have minds of their own. One is inside mathematics, almost within its control.

In the vertical interpretation, the structure is seen from beneath, with the red, black, and silver cables converging at the top. As one looks upward to the apex, the cables appear to be suspended from the clouds, descending in a neat, tight formation around the viewer, like a tall, slim umbrella.

*This concept was developed into different forms from 1974 to 1988.

© Agnes Denes 1983

<u>Systems of Logic / Logic of Systems: The Human Argument in Steel & Crystal</u>
<u>With Sundial</u> — Finalist Drawing for University City Science Center Philadelphia,
1988 [fig. 28]
<u>Systems of Logic / Logic of Systems: Elliptical Superstructure</u>
— Finalist Drawing for University City Science Center Philadelphia, 1988 [fig. 29]

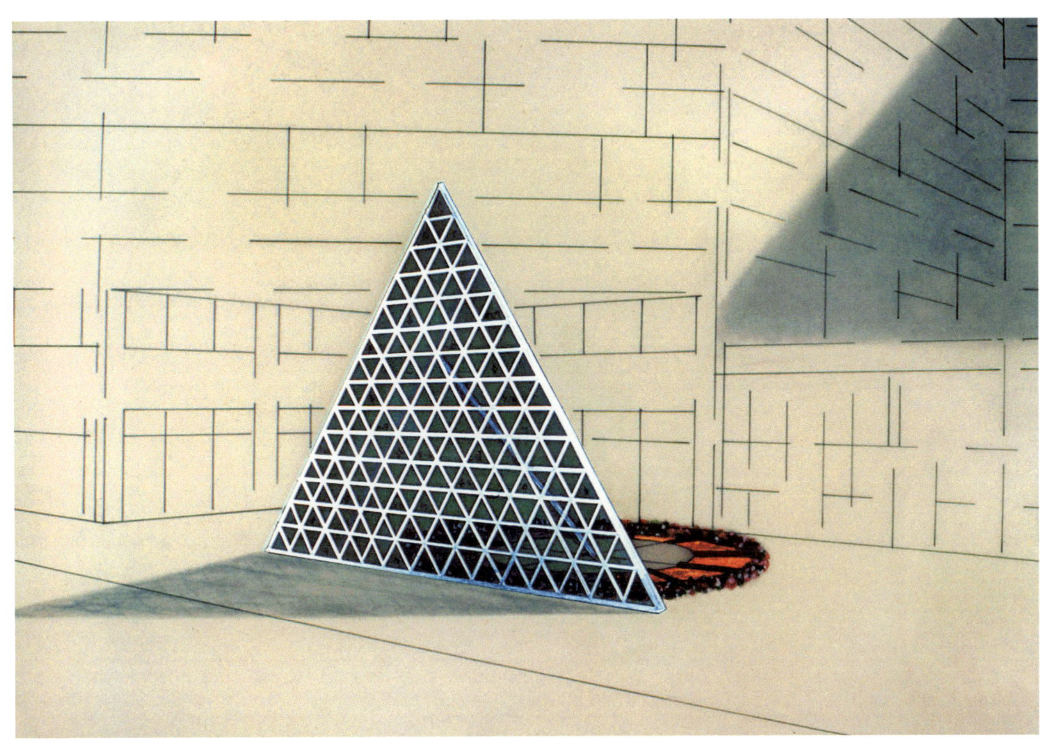

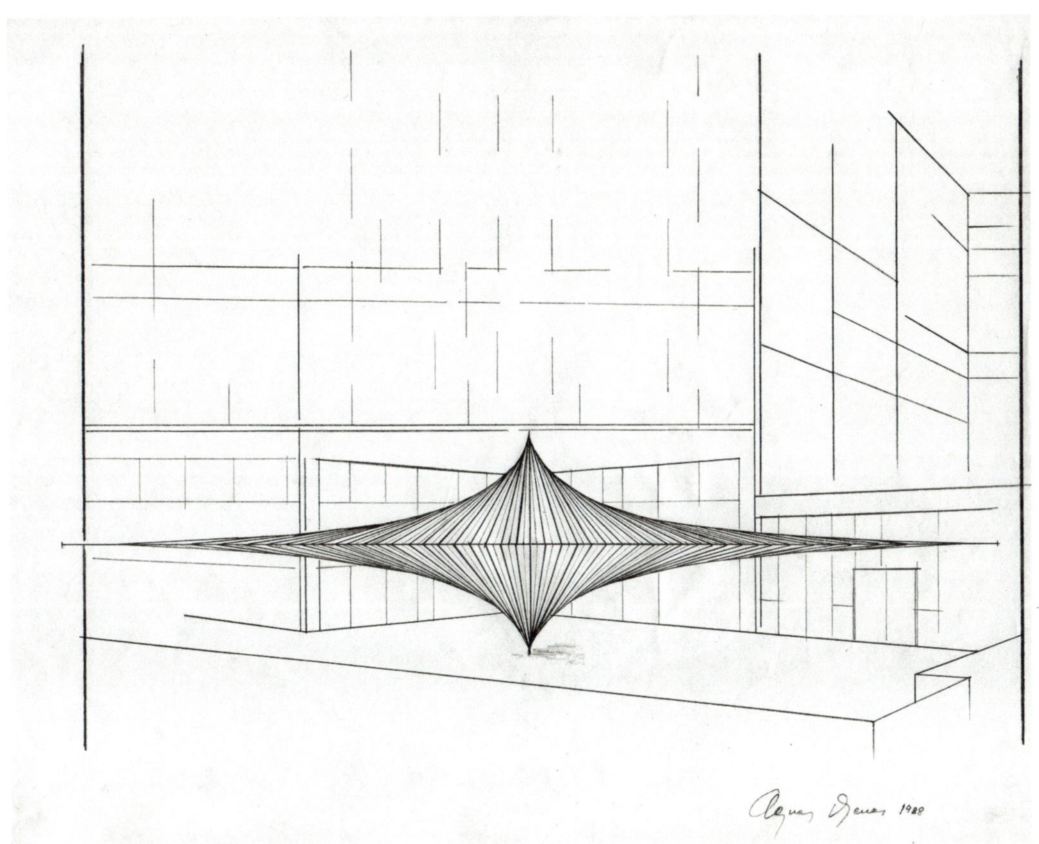

Stelae - Messages from Another Time - Discoveries of Minds and People, 1986

Hand-carved pink Portuguese marble
Hand-carved white Carrara marble
178 × 94 × 15 cm; each, and weigh 1.5 ton each stone

A well-known, important excavation from the ancient city known as Genoa of the Liguria Province, country Italy, European continent, late twentieth century. A major and unique find, extremely well preserved and restored to near original condition. The inscriptions have been deciphered and appear in translation below bearing the date 1986 A.D.

By studying the meaning of the symbols one arrives at a better understanding of the people who lived toward the end of the second millennium, a fairly advanced technological age in which major scientific discoveries were made that, as we know, had such an enormous effect on later centuries. A significant aspect of these tablets is that they include practically all major scientific breakthroughs for this period.

It is appropriate to note here that the very site of this exhibit was a church and monastery at the time, named Santa Maria di Castello, which had been built in an even earlier period, perhaps the thirteenth century.

Vandonia, 6000 A.D.

Transliteration:

1a–b Energy and mass in Special Relativity
2   Field equations in General Relativity
3   Principle of Least Action (basis of classical mechanics
4a   Expansion of the universe (the Hubble Law)
4b   The ultimate fate of the universe determined by Ω, the density parameter
5   Energy of photon - the particle-like behavior of waves
6   Fusion of hydrogen into helium (sun's source of energy -hydrogen burning into helium)
7   Photosynthesis - plants storing energy
8   The base of DNA and RNA as it encodes genetic information in chromosomes
9   Maxwell's equation for electromagnetism
10   Nuclear fission reaction in bombs and power plants
11   Thermonuclear fusion in an H-bomb
12a Schrödinger's wave equation, quantum mechanics - showing wave nature of matter
12b Uncertainty Principle (uncertainty built into quantum mechanics [Heisenberg])
13a–c–d Circuit diagram, symbol and truth table of NAND gate - basic building block of computers
13b Particle interactions in quantum field theory (Feynman diagram)
14   Wave function of the universe using relativity and quantum mechanics to describe the first moment of the universe.
1986 A.D.

Stelae — Messages From Another Time—Discoveries of Minds and People, 1986
Permanent Installation: Bucknell University, Lewiston, Pennsylvania, USA [fig. 30]

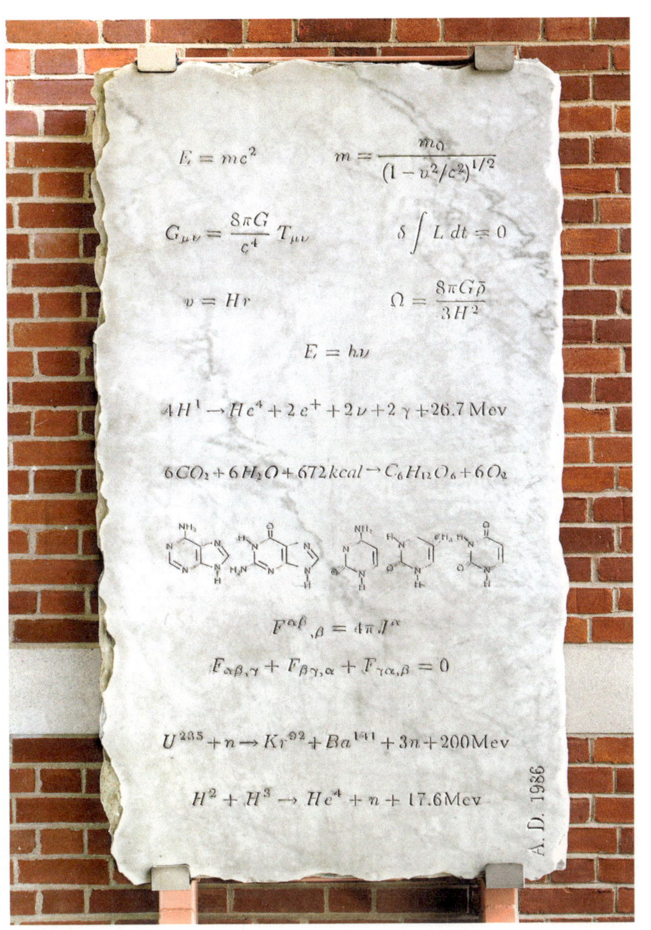

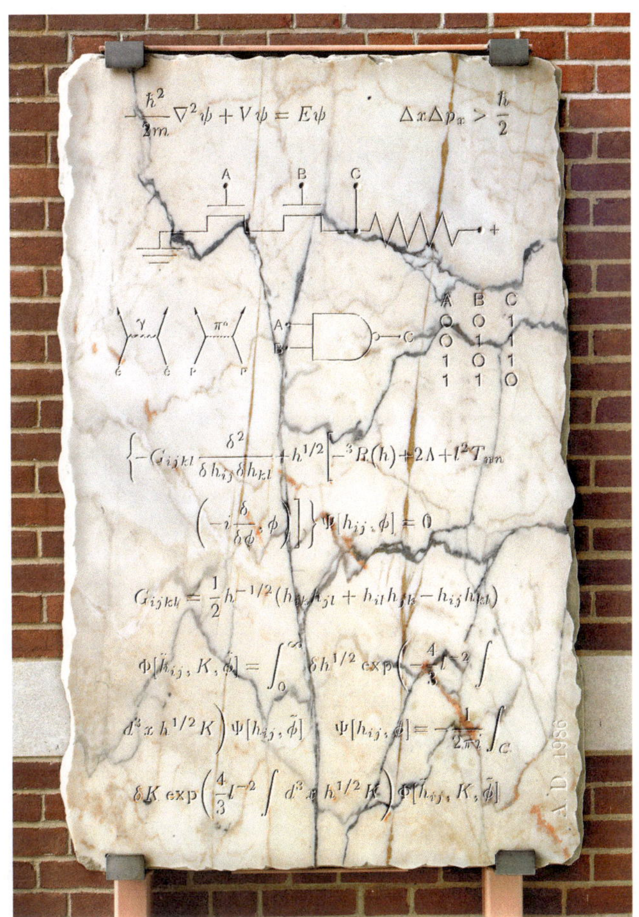

Noah's Ark - A Spaceship, 1982

(Materials: timber, fiberglass, steel, lucite, wire mesh. Roofing: thatched microwave
and radio transceiver, sonar, radar, celestial compass, astro-navigational gear,
computer, 27.4 × 10 × 6.7 m)
Pencil and gouache on vellum

This large ship is a combination of an ancient Viking sea vessel, modern ocean
cruiser, barge, and spaceship. It implies the past and alludes to the future but belongs
to no time except to serve as a metaphor for the present.

The building materials are as diverse and contradictory as its design: old timber,
fiberglass, aluminum, wire mesh, lucite. The huts on the deck are roofed with thatch
grass and lined with animal skin. The interior is lit with florescent lights, while the
hold stores space-age rig and high-tech gear.

Upon one's boarding the vessel, the lights flash, the engines roar; it appears ready
to cast off or fly away. Something is about to happen but nothing does – excitement
gives way to confusion. The rockets seem to suck in air like vacuum cleaners and
throw sparks but cannot ignite. The oars sticking out of its hull are made of lead, its
anchor is balsa wood, and the engine is an intricate and eloquent drawing on the
wall. Assorted astro-gear and computers blink sheepishly. All this equipment seems
pointless unless it was meant for fun. Outfitted with the luxuries and doodads of
a high-tech civilization, the vessel is flashy and impressive yet the overall effect is
one of confusion and futility – a symbol of voyage run aground in twentieth-century
waste, a stranded spaceship with weeds growing around its keel.

The ship is a disturbing blend of contradictions, conflicting aspirations, and confused
objectives. Its exciting, grandiose presence is a salute to human achievement in the
face of prodigality and inefficiency.

(Proposed for Miami International Airport and North Waterfront Park,
a converted dump-site)

© Agnes Denes 1982

Noah's Ark - Proposal for Miami International Airport
and North Waterfront Park, 1982 [fig. 31]

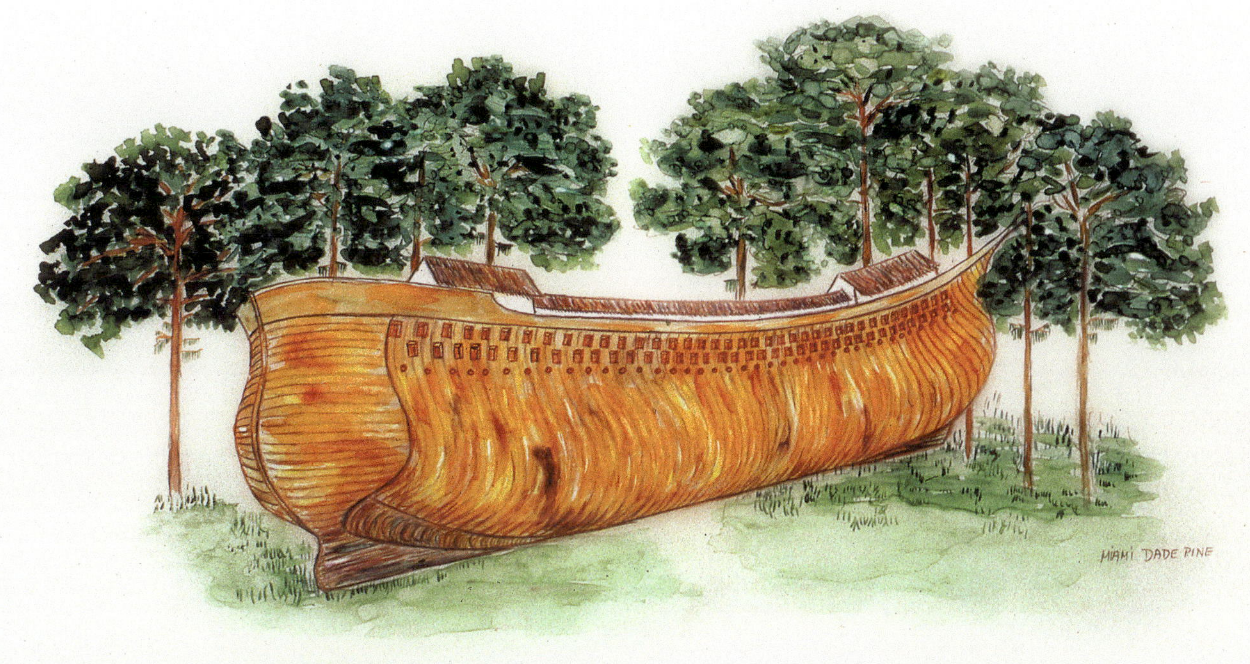

LENGTH : 90 FT

BEAM : 33 FT

HEIGHT : 22 FT

MATERIALS: WOOD, FIBERGLASS, STEEL, ALUMINUM, LUCITE, WIRE MASH, ROPE, SCREWS

HUTS: ROOFING — THATCH GRASS (HYPARHENIA, REEDS, PALM LEAVES, STRAW, RUSHES)

INTERIOR — FLUORESCENT LIGHTS, ANIMAL SKINS

HULL: EQUIPMENT — MICROWAVE AND RADIO TRANSCEIVER, BAROMETER, SONAR, RADAR, CELESTIAL COMPASS, ASTRONAVIGATIONAL GEAR, COMPUTER

North Waterfront Park Master Plan, Berkeley, 1989-1991

Conversion of a 38-hectare landfill (1989–1991)

Art Concept

Today an artist working in public art is called upon to exercise his or her ability to envision vast areas and work on a large scale that goes beyond the traditional parameters of what is usually considered art in this culture. It is also expected that we are equally adept at working with intricate detail and complexity and in a multitude of media.

Public art is a blend of design, landscaping, architecture, urban planning, the social sciences, and philosophy – in addition to being art. Increasingly, artists are recognized by city agencies, developers, and corporations for their ability not only to solve difficult design problems but to come up with unique and creative solutions to all phases of urban planning.

We live in an age of specialization, when disciplines have become progressively alienated from each other, creating communication problems. Unlike other specializations, art is not locked into a single discipline and need not feed upon itself. It is capable of imbibing key elements from other systems and disciplines, unifying them into a unique, coherent vision.

As such, art can become a unifying concept that captures the essence of the site, its purpose and meaning for the community. It sees the past and present and envisions a workable future. Thus the artist emerges as a creative problem solver – sensor and sensitizer – the prophet who is also the carpenter.

North Waterfront Park Masterplan transforms a 97-acre municipal landfill, located along the eastern shore of San Francisco Bay and surrounded by water, into a sustainable natural ecosystem that unites people with nature and each other. It is the first landfill to propose bioremediation programs and a 12-acre wetland/wildlife sanctuary with several art elements, including wildflower and sunflower meadows, wooded hills, petroglyphs carved into earth and stone, lighthouses, an amphitheater and a ship of life.

The art concept goes beyond traditional notions of what a park is by suggesting that it can be an expression of human values and of our sense of responsibility to each other and to the planet. The park – an island made of garbage – becomes an expression of human consciousness.

The overall organization of the park creates a time warp, going from civilization (entrance) to wilderness (end). Walkways and paths crisscross the park, offering changing views as they wind around mounds and trees. A perimeter path circles the park, offering views of and access to water. A wildlife sanctuary establishes the whole park as a life-harboring environment for an increased number of species, and bioremediation programs offer techniques for cleansing landfill pollutants.

The waterfront draws people to the edge and from it to look out at the world. A boardwalk, piers, and jetties offer further accessibility at high and low tides. The water on the site consists of a fresh water lake and brackish marsh, tidal pools with sculptural forms that change with the tides, and water catchments. Brooks and rivulets, like veins and arteries, run across the park, both enhancing its natural beauty and announcing that a manmade environment has come to life.

Note: The Master Plan was approved by the City of Berkeley in 1991. [The project was never realised. – Ed.]

© Agnes Denes 1990

<u>Sound Sculpture for Tidal Pool - North Waterfront Park Plan</u>, 1989 [fig. 32]

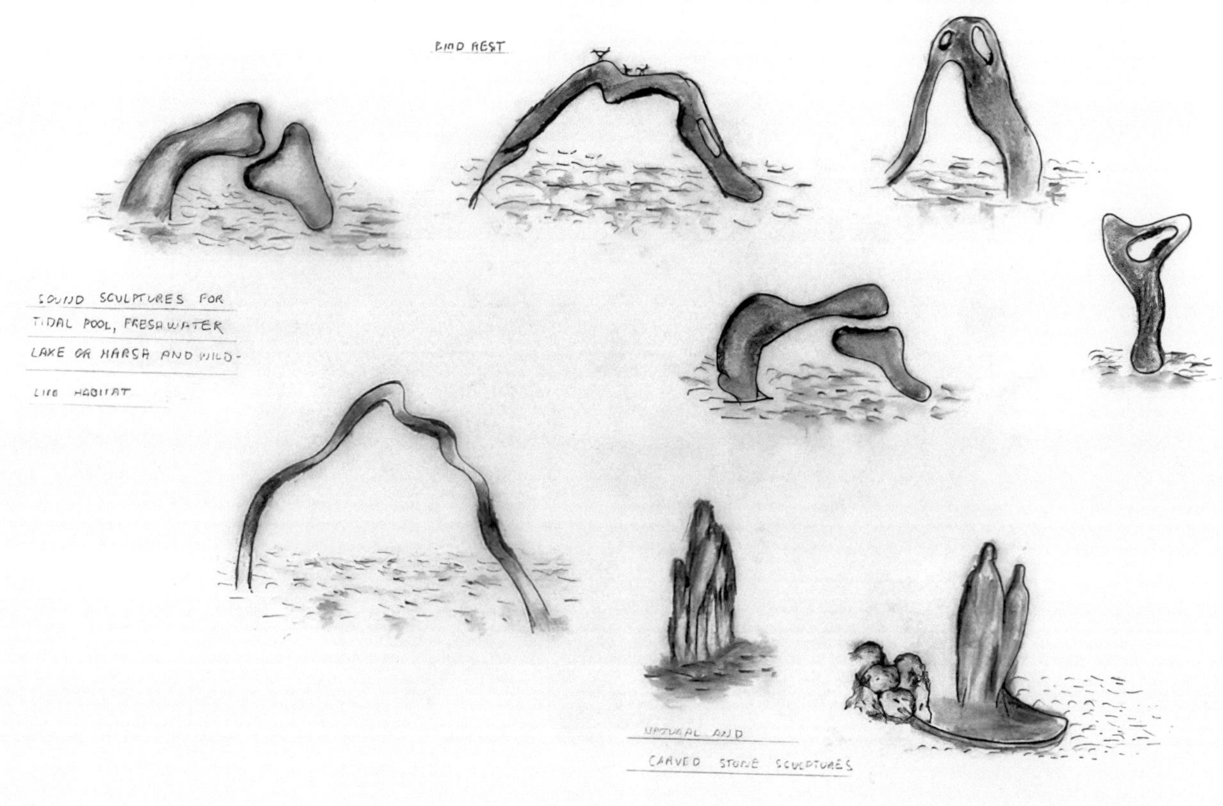

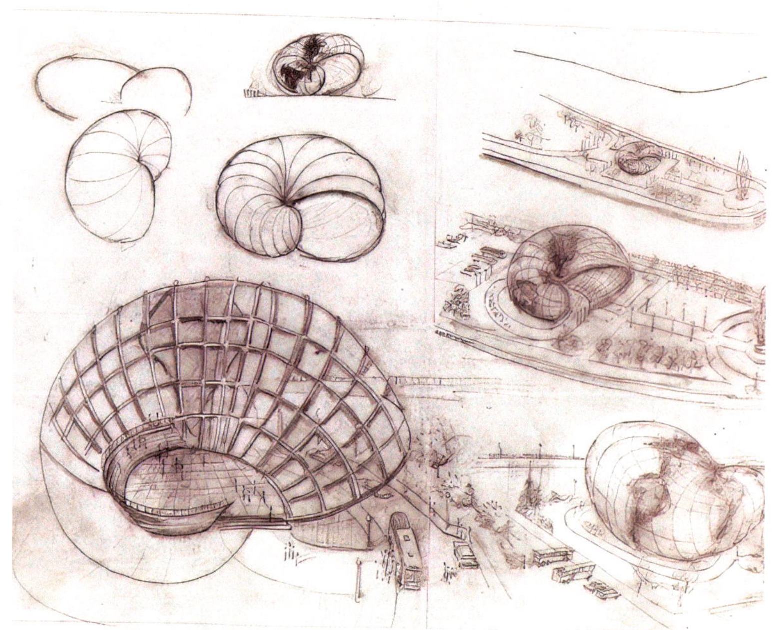

Nautilus Amphitheater - North Waterfront Park Plan, 1990 [fig. 33]
Amphitheaters and Sculpted View Mounds - North Waterfront Park Plan, 1989 [fig. 34]

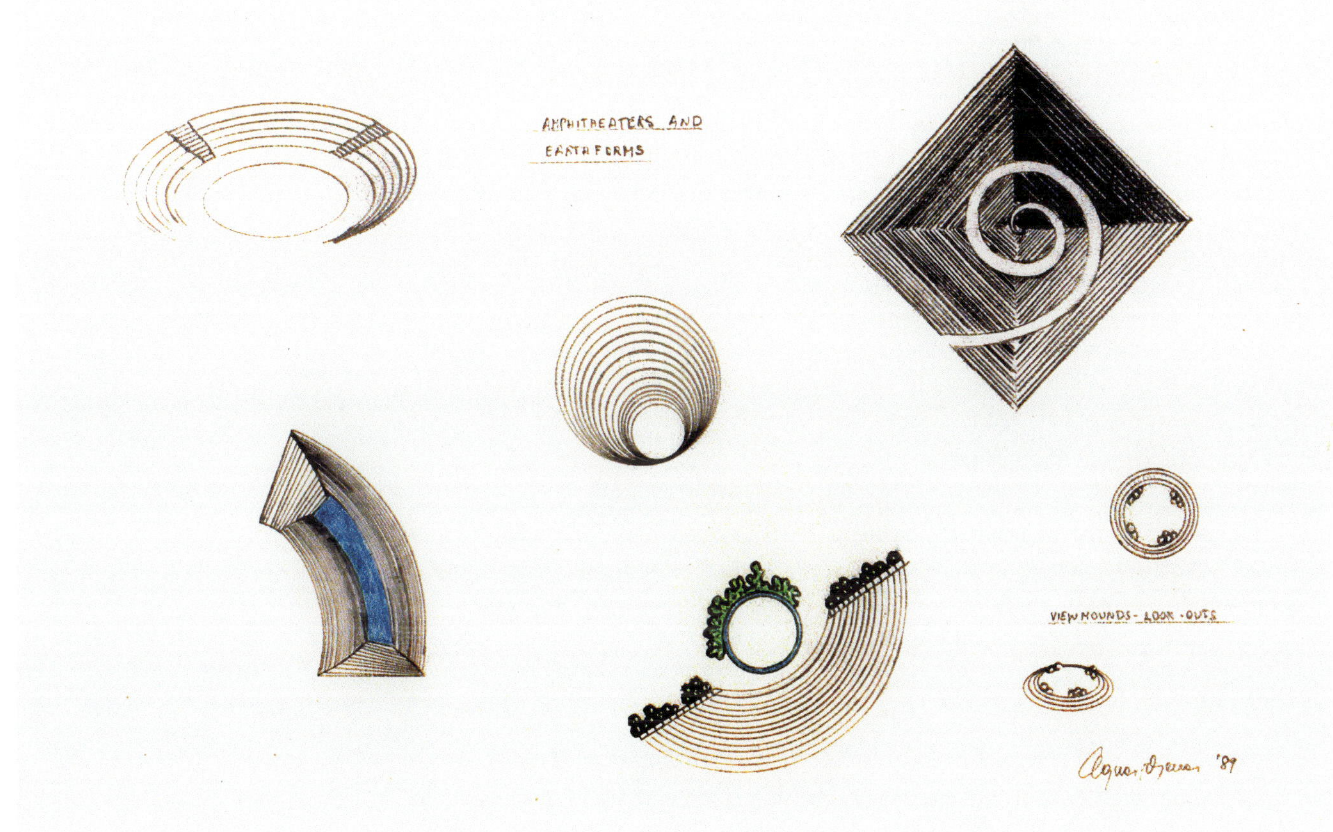

The Wilds, 1992

Envisioning The Wilds as a Work of Art and an Ecological Land
In 1992, I began the first phase of a commission that involves the master plan and
art concepts for a 10,000-acre Wildlife Preserve and Research Center in Columbus,
Ohio – the largest such place in the country. *The Wilds* goes beyond land reclamation
to the actual breeding of wild animals on the endangered species list. The artists
selected to work on this project will interpret and visualize the purpose and mission
of *The Wilds.*

We have stripped the land, and endangered animal species. The mission
of *The Wilds* is to reverse these processes; restore at least this land, and preserve
at least these animals. It must begin somewhere – others will follow.

The Wilds is 10,000 acres of partially reclaimed, surface-mined land, dotted with
over 150 clear lakes. Run by the International Center for the Preservation of Wild
Animals, the mission of *The Wilds* is the preservation of endangered wildlife
and the creation of a bioresearch center.

The goals of the master plan are to heighten appreciation and awareness of natural
systems, land reclamation, endangered species and bioresearch, to reflect the history
of the site, incorporate art into the overall design and individual elements, and provide
community involvement and education.

By inviting artists to create and participate in the conceptual master-planning of this
park, *The Wilds* acknowledges the important contribution that art can make in the
creation of public places. On this scale, art becomes a unifying force that offers
unique, creative and benign solutions to the problems facing our natural and urban
ecosystems. This new art form and philosophical stance

The Wilds enables artists to assume a new role by participating in all phases of
human planning, problem solving and development, including shaping our cities and
replenishing our land. The general concepts proposed involve the entire 10,000 acres
of land and are aimed at transforming *The Wilds* into an exciting and memorable place
while keeping its mission in mind. Strong art concepts based on universal concepts
involve people from all walks of life, not only those initiated in art. The master plan
includes designs for and discussions of the following: circulation/traffic control,
main and secondary roads, footpaths and trails, vegetation, lighting, signage, color
schemes, sculpted view mounds and earthforms, amphitheaters, bad weather
shelters, seating arrangements, transportation, parking lots, picnic areas, information
centers, artworks, and other landmarks.

Circle of Megaliths With Sundial

A group of standing stones is designed to be placed in a wide semicircle at the edge of a small lake into which they cast their reflection. The stones range from 16 to 22 feet in height and are carved from indigenous stone. The images in the reflecting pool create a timeless zone where the past meets the future and time disappears. The stones also cast their shadows on the land, forming different circles each day as the sun passes, and its passage changes with the season.

In the hollow of the stones, on the opposite side of the water, a large sundial is placed, marking celestial phenomena and time more precisely. Thus, on either side of the lake and in the timeless zone of the water, the past meets the future in constant interaction. The stones offer mystery, legend, and a somewhat arbitrary, calendric time-telling, while the Sundial is a precise, state-of-the-art, high-tech machinery.

The Sundial is set for standard local time by making longitudinal corrections appropriate for *The Wilds*. Residual corrections described by the equation of time can be shown as part of the dial furniture, possibly using an analemmatic dial. The Sundial shows a time of day (apparent and real time, direction of the sun, time in other cities and countries), the latitude and longitude of the park and a motto for *The Wilds*. People can interact with the Sundial, learn about celestial motion, and locate themselves geographically. Circle of Megaliths is a ceremonial place – a place for contemplation. It offers The Wilds a larger perspective beyond itself and beyond the moment.

© Agnes Denes 1992

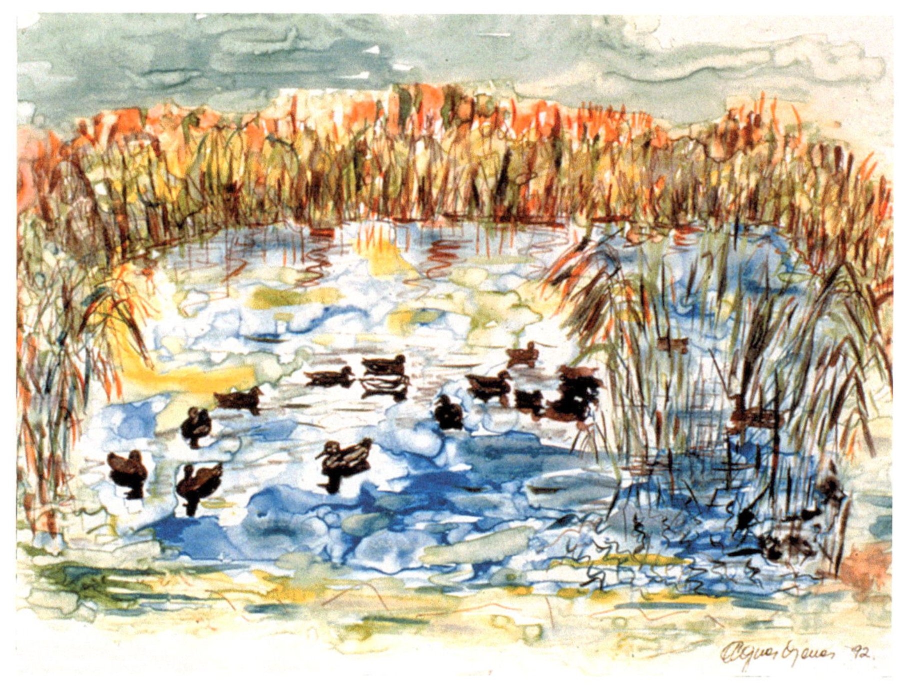

<u>Duckpond</u> - Design for Bioscapes, a Wildlife Preserve
and Research Center, Columbus, Ohio, USA, 1992 [fig. 35]
<u>Circle of Megaliths and Sundial</u> - Design for Bioscapes, a Wildlife
Preserve and Research Center, Columbus, Ohio, USA, 1992 [fig. 36]

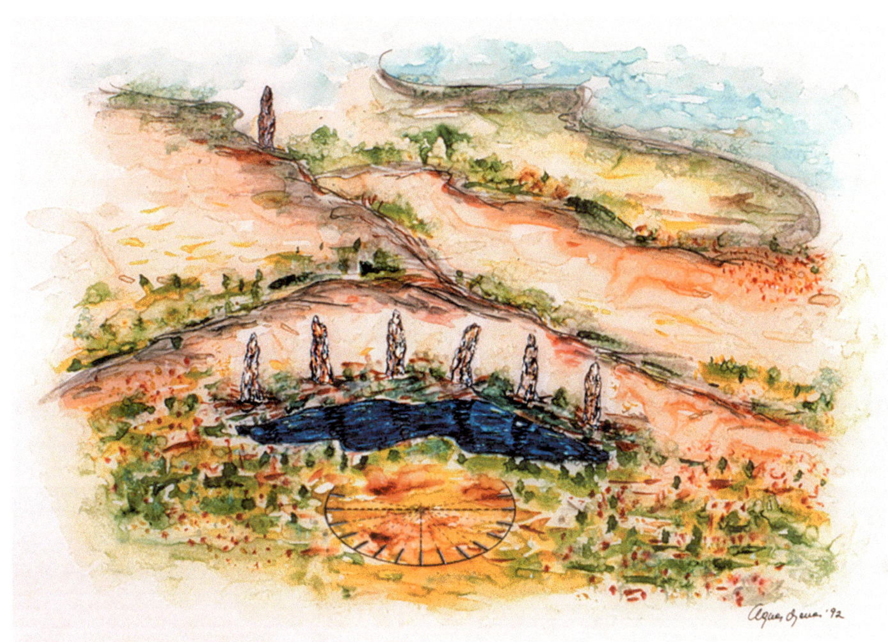

Bird Project - A Visual Investigation of Systems in Motion, 1979

Environmental project – mixed media, photographs

Migratory bird colonies are filmed in the south of Sweden and surrounding islands by flying near and above the flocks to create a unique visual study of bird societies for comparison with human societies in overcrowded situations.

Investigations include social integration, interdependence of societies (flocks), interactive behavior as it affects individuals (birds), inherited traits versus environmental pressures, alienation, and adaptation. One encounters similar issues in large cosmopolitan cities of the world: the problems of coexistence, group mentality, action and reaction, distrust, changing value systems--survival itself in the megacities of the future.

Special photographic techniques will reveal the survival-oriented needs of individual birds versus the integrative tendencies of the flock and shed light on some of the unsolved mysteries of flock behavior: the amazing speed with which they move as one, maneuver to avoid predators or flying into each other, and change directions with stunning fluidity of motion. The study will explore this seemingly intelligent behavior not attributable to individual members, and conversely how simple independent actions can emerge as intelligent flock behavior. Flock response is instantaneous, unconscious, and masterfully coordinated. The study will examine the possibilities of biological radio systems, geomagnetic forces, or thought transference acting on the birds, and other suggested causes for the instant polarization, synchronization, abrupt course changes, and other complicated maneuvers they perform without any wave effects or apparent signals from leaders. The study will record changes in behavioral patterns and rituals and development of mimicry or hostility among flocks, minority groups, and single birds. Some of the footage will be studied by computer analysis, "tagging" the birds for further studies.

This project began when I first saw hundreds of thousands of birds take to the air in Gotland and watched the sky grow dark with the tumult of their fluttering wings. I lived in Sweden in my teens and explored Gotland, Faro, Lilla Karlso, Stora Karlso, Malmo, and many other areas where bird colonies come to breed before flying south for the winter. Wearing earplugs for protection, I followed the synchronized, undulating motion of entire flocks moving as one system, looping around, then seemingly standing still for a fraction of a second, then swooping down and back in virtuosic formation.

In Gotland the many species of birds crowded together struggle for territory while building their nests and tending to their young to prepare them for the "miraculous" journey. As the birds hover over the nests they are forced into each others' airspace, invading the territory of neighboring flocks. The study will investigate how necessity forces them to change habits, coexist, or integrate, reminiscent of similar behavior in large cosmopolitan cities such as New York, Paris, and Tokyo, where varied nationalities share congested city life. Their interactions in the crowded, layered spaces above the nests closely resemble the overcrowded, multicultural interspacing of city existence.

I want to explore how the birds react to this stressful situation: Can they break their own rules or do millions of years of instinctive behavior win over circumstances and pressures? How do they deal with such problems compared to us? How does evolution and the "survival of the fittest" work?

Living organisms rely on instinct, intuition, and intelligence to varying degrees. Humans have gained intelligence and lost some of their instinct and intuition. I am intrigued by these fluctuations and variations, and hope to detect, through comparisons and overlays, some of the secrets of the elusive understructure of behavior.

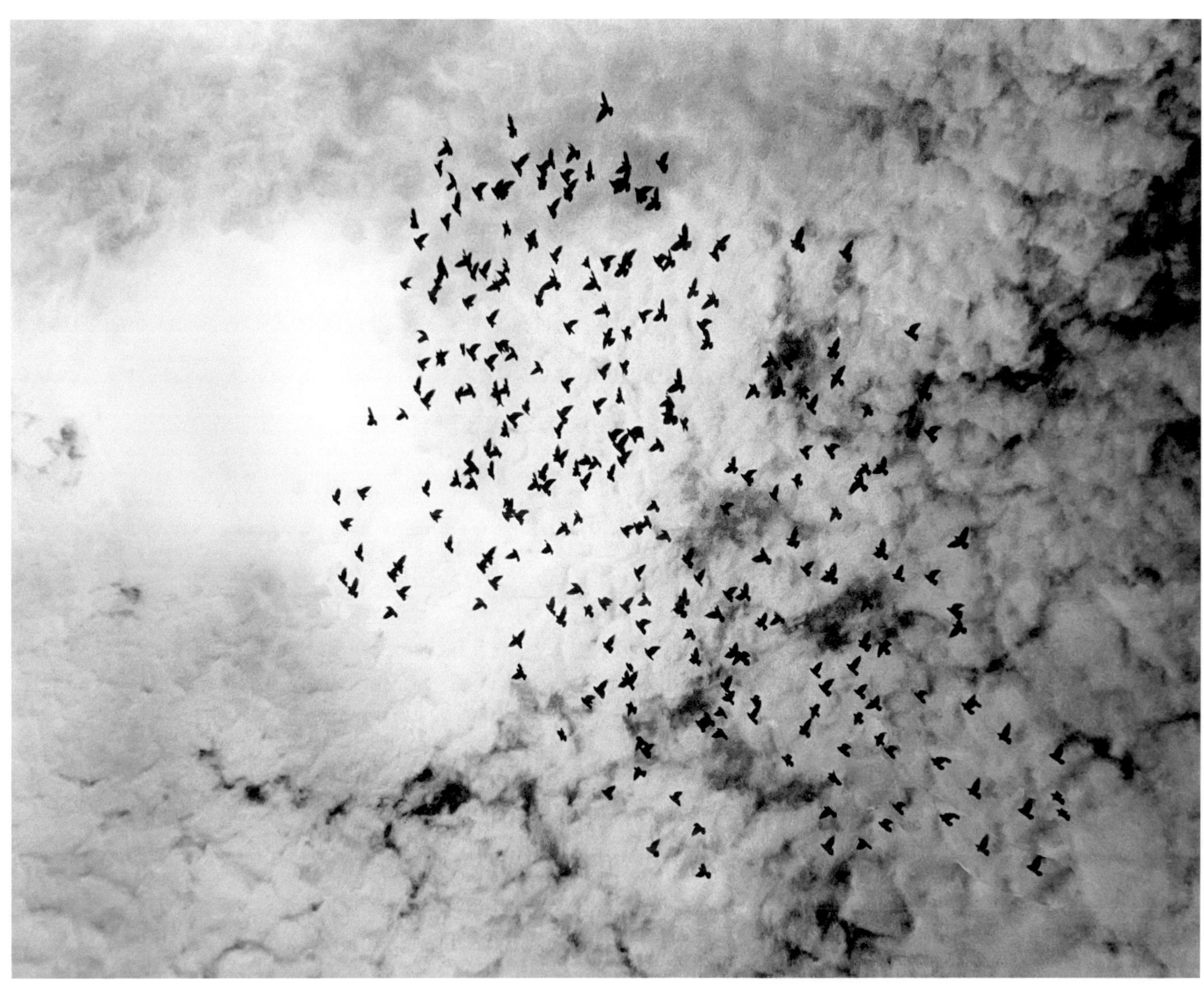

I have chosen a difficult and unusual approach for
this investigation, but one that is expected to yield
extraordinary results on scientific as well as artistic
levels – probing the mysteries of nature while creating
a unique work of art.

This project received a research and development
grant from the American-Scandinavian Foundation
in 1988.

© Agnes Denes 1979

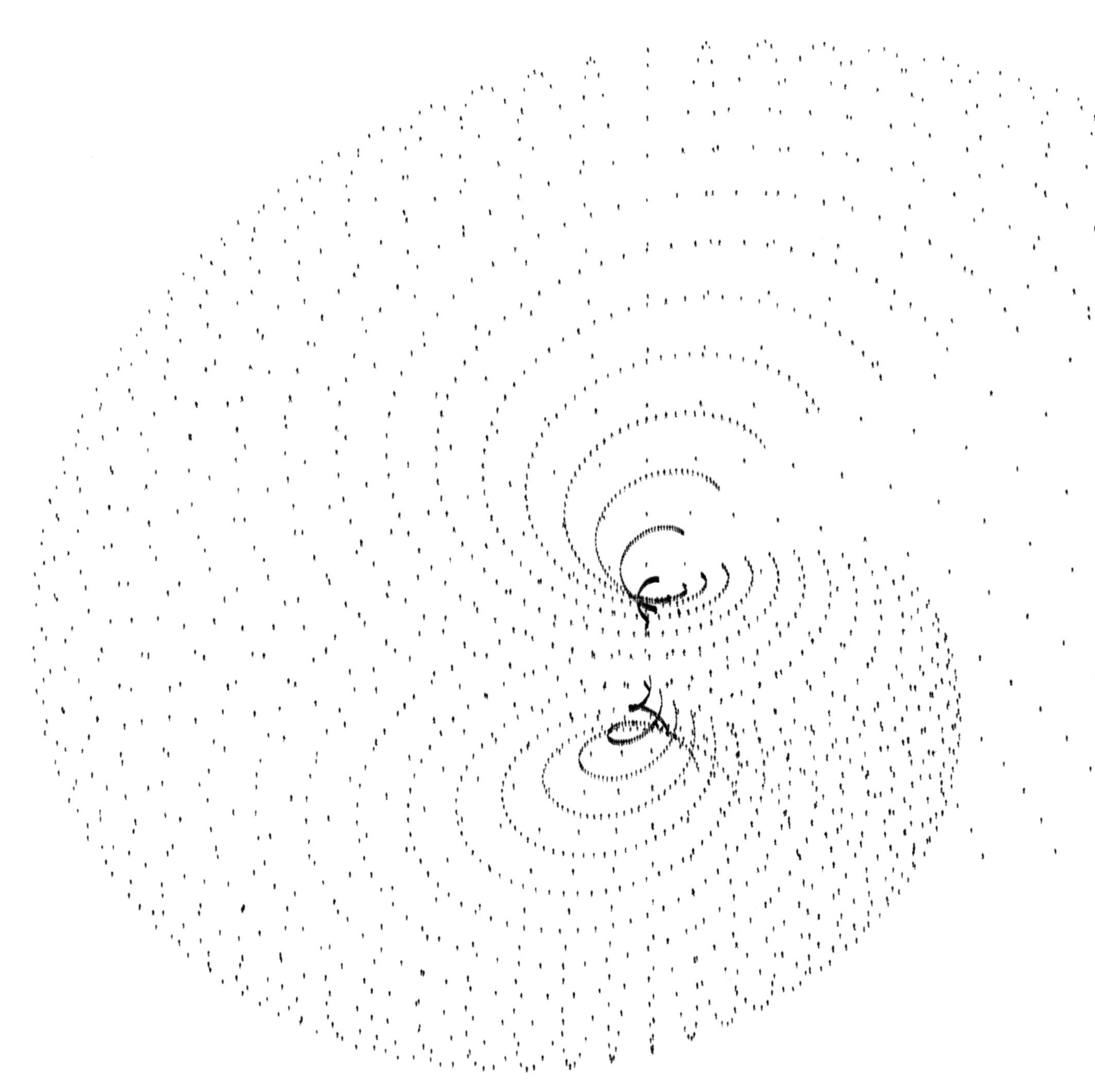

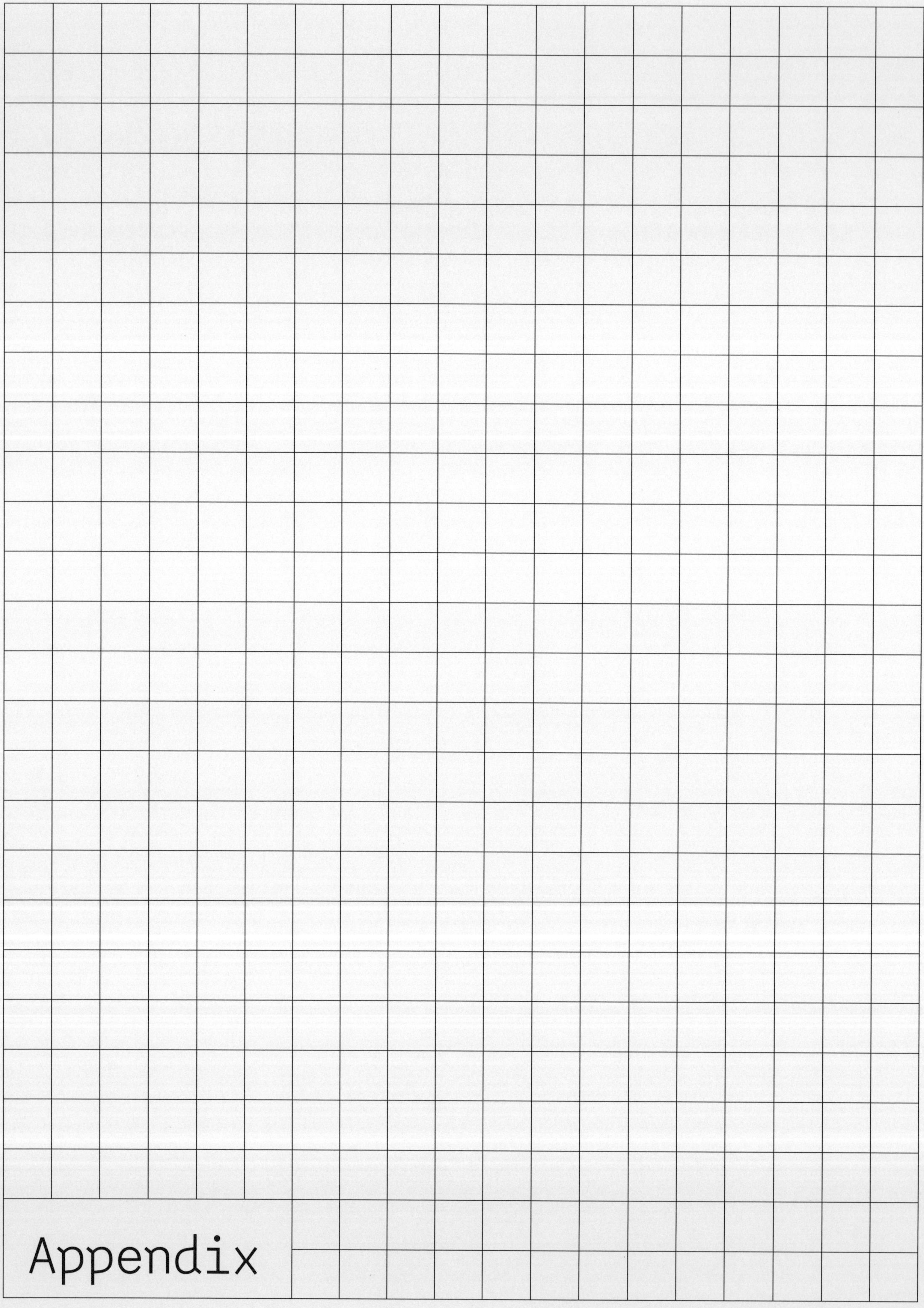

Appendix

Appendix

Biography

AGNES DENES
(1931 Budapest)
Lives and works in New York City

SELECTED SOLO EXHIBITIONS

2024 *Systems of Logic/ Logic of Systems
- the Art and Mind of Agnes Denes*,
Museum of Fine Arts, Budapest, Hungary
_ *Agnes Denes: Exercises in Eco-Logic*,
Lunds konsthall, Lund, Sweden
_ *Agnes Denes: Wheatfield - An Inspiration*,
Tinworks Art, Bozeman, USA
_ *Agnes Denes: Honoring Wheatfield
- A Confrontation*, The Messeplatz Project,
Art Basel 2024, Basel, Switzerland
2023 *Agnes Denes: Early Work, If the Berlin Wind
Blows My Flag. Art and Internationalism
Before the Fall of the Wall*, Galerie im
Körnerpark, Berlin, Germany
_ *Agnes Denes: Philosophy in the Landscape*,
acb Gallery, Budapest, Hungary
2022 *Agnes Denes: The Living Pyramid*, Sakip
Sabanci Museum, Istanbul, Turkey
_ *Agnes Denes: Another Confrontation*,
CIRCA, London, United Kingdom
2020 *Agnes Denes: Photos of the Mind, 1969-
2002*, Leslie Tonkonow Artworks + Projects,
ADAA Member Viewing Rooms, New York, USA
2019 *Agnes Denes: Absolutes and Intermediates*,
The Shed, New York, USA
2018 *Agnes Denes: Works 1969-2018*, acb Gallery,
Budapest, Hungary
2017 *Agnes Denes: Truth Approximations*,
Leslie Tonkonow Artworks + Projects,
New York, USA
2015 *The Living Pyramid*, Socrates Sculpture
Park, Long Island City, USA
_ *In the Realm of Pyramids: The Visual
Philosophy of Agnes Denes*, Leslie Tonkonow
Artworks + Projects, New York, USA
_ *Wheatfield*, Porta Nuova District,
Milan, Italy
2013 *Agnes Denes: Work: 1967-2013*, Firstsite,
Colchester, United Kingdom
2012 *Agnes Denes: Sculpture of the Mind:
1968 to Now*, Leslie Tonkonow Artworks
+ Projects, New York, USA

_ *Agnes Denes: Body Prints, Philosophical
Drawings, and Map Projections: 1969-1978*,
Santa Monica Museum of Art, Santa Monica,
USA (catalogue)
2010 *Agnes Denes: Body Prints and Other Early
Works on Paper*, Leslie Tonkonow Artworks
+ Projects, New York, USA
2009 *Agnes Denes: Philosophy in the Land II*,
Leslie Tonkonow Artworks + Projects,
New York, USA
2008 *Agnes Denes: Art for the Third
Millennium - Creating a New World View:
A Retrospective*, Ludwig Museum, Budapest,
Hungary
2007 *Uprooted & Deified - The Golden Tree*,
BravinLee Programs, New York, USA
2005 *Agnes Denes: Projects for Public Places -
A Retrospective*, Ewing Gallery, University
of Tennessee, Knoxville, USA
2004 *Agnes Denes: Projects for Public Places -
A Retrospective*, Chelsea Museum,
New York, USA
2003 *Agnes Denes: Projects for Public Places
- A Retrospective*, organized by Samek
Gallery, Bucknell University, Lewisburg,
Pa. (catalogue). Travel: Herron Gallery,
Herron School of Art, Indiana University;
Haggerty Museum of Art, Marquette
University, Milkwaukee; Naples Museum
of Art, Naples, USA
1998 *Agnes Denes - Fragmentation*, Gallerie Il
Bulino, Rome, Italy
1997 *Anima/Persona - From the Rice/Tree/Burial
Project*, Joyce Goldstein Gallery, New
York, USA
_ *The Pyramid Suite and Project Drawings*,
View Gallery, New York, USA
1996 *The Visionary Art of Agnes Denes, Gibson
Gallery*, SUNY at Potsdam, New York, USA
1995 *Philosophy in the Land*, Joyce Goldstein
Gallery, New York, USA
1994 *Drawings of Agnes Denes 1969-1994*,
Wynn Kramarsky, New York, USA
1992 *Agnes Denes: A Retrospective*,
Herbert F. Johnson Museum of Art,
Cornell University, Ithaca, USA

1990 *Agnes Denes - Concept into Form,*
Works 1970-1990, Arts Club of Chicago, USA
(catalogue)

_ *Agnes Denes - El Concepto Hecho Forma,*
Obras, 1970-1990, Anselmo Alvarez Galeria
de Arte, Madrid, Spain (catalogue)

1986 Ricardo Barreto Arte Contemporaneo,
Guadalajara, Mexico

1985 University of Hawaii Art Gallery,
Honolulu, USA

_ Northern Illinois University Art Gallery
in Chicago, USA

1982 *Meister der Zeichnung (Master of Drawing)*
Invitational, Kunsthalle, Nurnberg, West
Germany

1981 *Print Retrospective,* Elise Meyer, Inc.,
New York, USA

1980 *Agnes Denes 1968-1980,* Hayden Gallery,
Massachusetts Institute of Technology,
Cambridge, USA

_ *Anima/Persona - The Seed,* Elise Meyer,
Inc., New York, USA

_ *Agnes Denes,* Galleriet, Lund, Sweden

_ Galerie Aronowitsch, Stockholm, Sweden

1979 *Agnes Denes Work: 1968-1978,* Institute of
Contemporary Art, London, United Kingdom

_ Studio d'Arte Cannaviello, Milan, Italy

1978 *Agnes Denes - Philosophical Drawings,*
Amerika Haus, West Berlin, West Germany
(catalogue)

_ *Agnes Denes: Work 1968-78,* Ikon Gallery,
Birmingham, United Kingdom (catalogue)

_ Franklin Furnace, New York, USA

_ *Sculptures of the Mind,* Centre Culturel
Americain, Paris, France

1977 Tyler School of Art, Temple University,
Philadelphia, USA

_ *Animi Pathema - The Emotional Animal,*
112 Greene Street Gallery, New York, USA

1976 Douglass College, Rutgers University,
New Brunswick, USA

_ Newport Harbor Art Museum, Newport
Beach, USA

_ *Sculptures of the Mind,* University
of Akron, USA (catalogue)

1975 Stefanotty Gallery, New York, USA

1974 *Agnes Denes: Perspectives,* Corcoran
Gallery of Art, Washington, D.C., USA
(catalogue)

_ Ohio State University, Columbus, USA

1972 A.I.R. Gallery, New York, USA

1968 Ruth White Gallery, New York, USA

1967 New Masters Gallery, New York, USA

1965 Lewisohn Hall, Columbia University,
New York, USA

SELECTED GROUP EXHIBITIONS

2024 *Shifting Landscapes,* Whitney Museum
of American Art, New York, USA

_ *Save Land. United for Land,* Kunst- und
Ausstellungshalle der Bundesrepublik
Deutschland, Bonn, Germany

_ *Mutual Aid: Art in collaboration with*
Nature, Castello di Rivoli, Torino, Italy

_ *Science/Fiction. A Non-History of Plants,*
Maison Européenne de la Photographie
(MEP), Paris, France

_ *Radical Software: Women, Art & Computing*
1960 -1991, MUDAM, Luxembourg

_ *Abstraction After Modernism: Recent*
Acquisitions, The Menil Collection,
Houston, USA

_ *Artistes et paysans. Battre la campagne,*
Les Abattoirs, Musée - Frac Occitanie;
Toulouse, France

_ *RE/SISTERS,* FOMU Foto Museum, Antwerp,
Netherlands

_ *(Re)Focus: Then and Now,* The Galleries
at Moore, Philadelphia, USA

2023 *Nature Doesn't Know About Us,* Sculpture
Milwaukee, USA

_ *Artists Born Elsewhere: Selections*
from the Museum's Permanent Collection,
University Museum of Contemporary Art,
UMASS, Amherst, USA

_ *The Irreplaceable Human: The Conditions*
of Creativity in the Age of AI, Louisiana
Museum of Art, Humlebæk, Denmark

_ *Extreme Tension: Art between Politics and*
Society 1945-2000, Neue Nationalgalerie,
Berlin, Germany

_ *How is Life? - Designing For Our Earth,*
Toto Museum, Kitkyushu, Japan

– *Our Ecology: Toward a Planetary Living*, Mori Art Museum, Tokyo, Japan
– *Can't See, Sequences Biennial XI*, Icelandic Art Center, Reykjavik, Iceland
– *Agnes Denes: The Debate*, The Armory Show: Platform, New York, USA
– *Coded: Art Enters the Computer Age*, Los Angeles County Museum of Art, USA
– *Schema: World as Diagram*, Marlborough Gallery, New York, USA
– *Pour, Tear, Carve*, The Phillips Collection, Washington, D.C., USA
– *Adaptation: A Re-centered Earth*, Museum of Contemporary Art and Design, Manila
– *The Material Revolution*, E-Werk Luckenwald, Germany
– *Chaleur HumaineTriennale Art & Industrie*, Frac Grand Large - Hauts-de-France, Dunkirk, France
– *Dear Earth: Art in a Time of Crisis*, The Hayward Gallery, London, United Kingdom
– *Groundswell: Women of Land Art*, Nasher Sculpture Center, Dallas, USA
– *RE/SISTERS*, Barbican Art Gallery, London, United Kingdom
2022 *Territories of Waste: On the Return of the Repressed*, Museum Tinguely, Basel, Switzerland
– *How is Life? - Designing for our Earth*, TOTO GALLERY MA, Tokyo, Japan
– *Back to Earth*, Serpentine Gallery, London, United Kingdom
– *The Milk of Dreams*, The 59th International Art Exhibition of La Biennale di Venezia, Italy
– *Chapter 5IVE*, Het HEM, Zaandam, Netherlands
– *Balance: Environment and Society in Swiss Art of the 70s and 80s*, Kunstmuseum Solothurn, Germany
– *Pavilions*, Lisson Gallery, New York, USA
2021 *Land Art: Expanding the Atlas*, Nevada Museum of Art, Reno, USA
– *T Zero*, Ufficio Mostre Palazzo delle Esposizioni, Rome, Italy
– *Autostrada Biennale III*, Prizren, Kosovo, Serbia
– *Dream Monuments: Drawing in the 1960s and 1970s*, The Menil Collection, Houston, USA

– *Climate Care: Reimagining Shared Planetary Futures*, Museum of Applied Arts, Vienna, Austria
– *Tree Story*, Monash University Museum of Art, Caulfield East, Australia
– *Spatial Affairs*, Ludwig Museum, Budapest, Hungary
– *The 18th Tallinn Print Triennial*, Tallinn, Estonia
– *Spatial Affairs*, Museum Ludwig, Köln, Germany
– *I Hate Nature*, Klassik Stiftung Weimar, Germany
– *Nature of Robotics: An Expanded Field*, ArtLab EPFL, Lausanne, Switzerland
2020 *Among Highlights*, Keiselbach Gallery, Budapest, Hungary
– *Apocalypse & World Salvation*, Zeppelin University, Friedrichshafen, Germany
– *Virtual Exhibition: Drawing from the Collection*, Rutgers-Camden Center for the Arts, Camden, USA
– *Redefinition*, acb Gallery, Budapest, Hungary
– *Stayin' Alive*, ANOTHER SPACE, New York, USA
– *In the ever changing world in which we live…*, The Storefront, Bellport, New York, USA
– *Ecofeminism(s)*, Thomas Erben Gallery, New York, USA
– *Down to Earth*, Berliner Festspiele/ Gropius Bau, Berlin, Germany
– *The Penumbral Age - Art in the Time of Planetary Change*, Museum of Modern Art, Warsaw, Poland
– *A Year Without the Southern Sun*, PS120, Berlin, Germany
– *Crear Mundos*, Fundación Proa, Buenos Aires, Argentina
2019 *I Remember Earth*, MAGASIN des horizons - Centre national d'arts et de cultures, Grenoble, France
– *Counter-Landscapes: Performative Actions from the 1970s - Now*, Scottsdale Museum of Contemporary Art, Scottsdale

– *To Light*, Leslie Tonkonow Artworks
+ Projects, New York, USA
– *Pangea United*, Muzeum Sztuki, Łódź,
Poland
– *Line to Form*, Danese/Corey, New York, USA
2018 *Programmed: Rules, Codes, and
Choreographies in Art, 1965-2018*, Whitney
Museum of American Art, New York, USA
– *Territories That Matter: Gender, Art and
Ecology*, Centro De Arte Naturaleza de
Huesca, Huesca, Spain
– *Sense of Humor*, National Gallery of Art,
Washington, D.C. , USA
– *Studio Visit: Selected Gifts from
Agnes Gund*, The Museum of Modern Art,
New York, USA
– *Cosmogonies*, Musée d'art moderne et d'art
contemporain, Nice, France
– *Bending Light: Neon Art 1965 to Now*,
Neuberger Museum of Art, Purchase, USA
2017 *Cosmomorphic Practices and Asian
Environments*, Institut d'art
contemporain, Villeurbanne, France
– *Delirious: Art at the Limits of Reason,
1950 - 1980*, The Met Breuer, New York, USA
– *Thinking Machines: Art and Design in the
Computer Age, 1959 - 1989*, The Museum of
Modern Art, New York, USA
– *The (Partial) Autobiography of an Art
Gallery*, Leslie Tonkonow Artworks +
Projects, New York, USA
– *documenta 14*, Athens, Greece
– *Art in the Open: Fifty Years of Public
Art in New York*, The Museum of the City
of New York, USA
– *The Garden*, ARoS Aarhus Kunstmuseum, Denmark
– *Ecovention Europe*, Museum De Domeinen
in Sittard, Netherlands
– *Urban Planning: Art and the City 1967-
2017*, Contemporary Art Museum,
St. Louis, USA
– *Hybris*, Museo de Arte Contemporaneo
de Castilla y Léon (MUSAC), Spain
– *From Outrage to Action: Proposals for the
Climate, Resources, and the Planet*, The
Gallatin Galleries, New York University,
New York, USA

2016 *Sublime*, Centre Pompidou, Metz, France
– *Drawing Then: Innovation and Influence
in American Drawings of the Sixties*,
Dominique Levy Gallery, New York, USA
– *From Point to Line*, Senior & Shopmaker
Gallery, New York, USA
– *Land, Sea, Air*, The New Art Gallery
Walsall, United Kingdom
– *Land/Sky*, Leslie Tonkonow Artworks
+ Projects, New York, USA
– *City After the City - Urban Orchard*,
La Triennale di Milano, Milan, Italy
– *El mundo fue plano, ahora es redondo
y será un holograma*, Museo de Arte
Zapopan, Zapopan, Mexico
– *Human Interest: Portraits from the
Whitney's Collection*, Whitney Museum
of American Art, New York, USA
2015 *From Drawing to Sign, from Fattori
to LeWitt*, Centro Arte Moderna e
Contemporanea della Spezia,
La Spezia, Italy
– *tout le monde*, Centre d'art contemporain
d'Ivry (Le Crédac), Ivry, France
– *Plastic: Art in the Age of Material
Innovation*, Neuberger Museum, Purchase,
USA
– *Public Works: Artists' Interventions
1970s-Now*, Mills College Museum of Art,
Oakland, USA
– *Counter (Public) Art, Intervention
& Performance in Lower Manhattan from
1978-1993*, organized by the Lower
Manhattan Cultural Council at Arts
Center, Governor's Island, USA
– *The Triumph of Love: Beth Rudin DeWoody
Collects*, Norton Museum of Art,
West Palm Beach, USA
– *The Omnivore's Dilemma: Visualized*,
Contemporary Art Galleries, University
of Connecticut, Storrs, USA
– *Collectibles: Works on Paper*,
Denver Art Museum, Denver, USA
– *Rachael Champion | Agnes Denes | Rachel
Pimm*, Hales Gallery, London, United
Kingdom

–	*(Counter)Public Art, Intervention & Performance in Lower Manhattan from 1978-1993*, Nathan Cummings Foundation, New York, USA

–	*On Paper*, Marsha Mateyka Gallery, Washington D.C. , USA

2014	*PaperWork*, Leslie Tonkonow Artworks + Projects, New York, USA

–	*Art of It's Own Making*, The Pulitzer Foundation for the Arts, St. Louis, USA

–	*Imprints*, Leslie Tonkonow Artworks + Projects, New York, USA

–	*EXPO 1: New York*, Museu de Arte Moderna, Rio de Janeiro, Brazil

–	*As Exciting as We Can Make It: Ikon in the 1980s*, Ikon Gallery, Birmingham, United Kingdom

–	*Beyond Earth Art - Contemporary Artists and the Environment*, Herbert F. Johnson Museum of Art, Ithaca, USA

–	*SITElines: New Perspectives on Art in the Americas - Unsettled Landscapes*, Santa Fe, USA

–	*Frame the Reference: Materials in Time*, The Pulitzer Foundation for the Arts, St. Louis, USA

–	*Painting & Sculpture*, Museum of Modern Art, New York, USA

2013	*Quiet Earth*, Rauschenberg Foundation, New York, USA

–	*EXPO 1: New York*, MoMA PS1, Long Island City, New York, USA

–	*In Cloud Country*, Harewood House, Yorkshire, United Kingdom

–	*Les Immémoriales*, Frac Lorraine, Metz, France

–	*America's Calling*, Syracuse University Art Galleries, Syracuse, USA

–	*Green Acres: Artists Farming Fields, Greenhouses and Abandoned Lots*, American University Museum at the Katzen Center, Washington D.C., USA

–	*A City Shaped*, STUK Arts Centre, Leuven, Belgium

2012	*Materializing "Six Years": Lucy Lippard and the Emergence of Conceptual Art*, Brooklyn Museum, New York, USA

–	*Ends of the Earth: Art of the Land to 1974*, The Museum of Contemporary Art, Los Angeles, USA

–	*Ends of the Earth: Art of the Land to 1974*, Haus der Kunst, Munich, Germany

–	*The Body Argument*, Galerie Emanuel Layr, Vienna, Austria

–	*Erre, variations labyrinthiques*, Centre Pompidou-Metz, France

–	*Green Acres: Artists Farming Fields, Greenhouses and Abandoned Lots*, Contemporary Arts Center, Cincinnati, USA

–	*Carnal Knowledge: Sex + Philosophy*, Leslie Tonkonow Artworks + Projects, New York, USA

2011	*Light Years: Conceptual Art and the Photograph, 1964-1977*, Art Institute of Chicago, Chicago, USA

–	*Contemporary Drawings from the Irving Stenn Jr. Collection*, Art Institute of Chicago, Chicago, USA

–	*Systems, Actions and Process*, PROA Foundation, Buenos Aires, Argentina

–	*Plot : Plan : Process, Works from the 1960s to Now*, Leslie Tonkonow Artworks + Projects, New York, USA

–	*The Last Freedom-From Pioneers of Land-Art of the 1960s to the Cyberspace*, Ludwig Museum, Koblenz, Germany

–	*Erre, (Labyrinths)* Centre Pompidou-Metz, France

–	*Andy Coolquitt, Agnes Denes, Robert Smithson*, Lisa Cooley Gallery, New York, USA

–	*Eco-Art*, Pori Art Museum, Pori, Finland

2010	*Digital 10-Planet Earth*, Art & Science Coll. (ASCI), New York Hall of Science, New York, USA

–	*Agnes Denes: Early Works on Paper*, Leslie Tonkonow Artworks + Projects, New York, USA

–	*Artpark: 1974-1984*, University of Buffalo Art Gallery, Buffalo, USA

–	*Landscape as an Idea: Projects and Projections*, Koldo Mitxelena Kulturunea Cultural Center, San Sebastian, Spain

2009 *Radical Nature: Art & Architecture for
a Changing Planet, 1969 - 2009*, Barbican
Art Gallery, London, United Kingdom
_ *Elles@CentrePompidou: Women Artists in
the Collection of the Centre Pompidou*,
Centre Pompidou, Paris, France
_ *Sites*, Whitney Museum of American Art,
New York, USA
2008 *Drawings on Graph Paper*, Leslie Tonkonow
Artworks + Projects, New York, USA
_ *A.I.R. Gallery Retrospective*, Werkstatte
Gallery, New York, USA
_ *Decoys, Complexes, and Triggers: Feminism
and Land Art in the 1970's*, Sculpture
Center, Long Island City, USA
_ *Genesis - The Art of Creation*, Zentrum
Paul Klee, Bern, Switzerland
_ *Random Utterness*, Hungarian Cultural
Center, New York, USA
_ *To Infinity and Beyond: Mathematics in
Contemporary Art*, Heckscher Museum of
Art, Huntington, New York, USA
_ *Weather Report: Art and Climate Change*,
Boulder Museum of Contemporary Art in
Collaboration with EcoArts, Boulder, USA
2007 *Art in Action: Nature, Creativity and Our
Collective Future*, Natural World Museum,
San Francisco, USA
_ *BIOS 4 - Biotech and Environmental Arts*,
Centro Andaluz de Arte Contemporáneo,
Monasterio de la Cartuja, Sevilla, Spain
_ *Collection Focus I: Recent Work by Women*,
Samek Art Gallery, Bucknell University,
Lewisburg, USA
_ *Devine in-Tent*, The Artists Museum,
The Venice Biennale, Italy
_ *Green Horizons*, Bates College Museum
of Art, Lewiston, USA
_ *Making the Choice: Bringing Forth an
Environmental Renaissance*, City Hall
Gallery Rotunda, San Francisco, USA
(organized by the Natural World Museum)
_ *Weather Report: Art and Climate
Change*, Boulder Museum of Contemporary
Art (in collaboration with EcoArt,
Boulder, USA

2006 *eARTh: The Importance of Environmental
Art*, Herndon Gallery, Antioch College,
Yellow Springs, USA
_ *Women and the Environment: WEAD EAST I*
in conjunction with the KCC ECO-Festival,
Kingsborough Art Gallery, Kingsborough
Community College - CUNY, Brooklyn,
New York, USA
2005 *Area '70*, Studio d'Arte Cannaviello,
Milano, Italy
_ *Building and Breaking the Grid: 1962-2002*,
Whitney Museum of American Art, New York,
USA
_ *Drawings from the Modern*, Museum of
Modern Art, New York, USA
_ *EarthWorksNow*, Internatioal Biennial,
Copper Mountain College, Joshua Tree,
Mojave Desert, USA
_ *Fourth International Artists' Book
Exhibition*, King St. Stephen Museum
and City Gallery, Deak Collection,
Székesfehérvár, Hungary
_ *Poles Apart/Poles Together*, Venice
Biennale, Italy
_ *Treading Water*, (Pyramids of Conscience),
Ballroom Marfa, Texas, USA
_ *Women & The Environment*, Art Gallery,
Kingsborough Community College,
New York, USA
_ *"You Are Here*, Design Museum, London,
United Kingdom
2004 *Contemporary Art and the Mathematical
Instinct*, Stedman Art Gallery, Rutgers
University, Camden, and University
Museums, University of Richmond, USA
_ *Six Centuries of Prints and Drawings:
Recent Acquisitions*, National Gallery
of Art, Washington, D.C. , USA
_ *Tre Incisori Americani*, Galleria Miralli,
Viterbo, Italy
2003 *Contemporary Art and the Mathematical
Instinct*, Tweed Museum of Art, University
of Minnesota, Duluth, USA
_ *Dust*, Dunlop Art Gallery, Regina,
Saskatchewan, Canada
_ *Rhythm of Structure - Math Art
in Harlem*, Fire Patrol No.5 Art Gallery,
New York, USA

2002 *Art and Political Engagement*, House of
DOCS Gallery, Sundance Film Festival,
Park City, USA
– *Ecovention (Current Art to Transform
Ecologies)*, The Contemporary Art Center,
Cincinnati, USA (catalogue)
– *Math/Art - Art/Math*, Selby Gallery,
Ringling School of Art & Design,
Sarasota, USA (catalogue)
– *Second International Art Biennial-Buenos
Aires*, Museo Nacional de Bellas Artes,
Argentina
2001 Curt Marcus Gallery, New York, USA
– *EVO 1*, Gallery L, Moscow, Russia
– Göteborgs Internationalle Konstbiennal,
Göteborg, Sweden (catalogue)
– *Kinds of Drawing*, Herter Gallery,
University of Massachusets, Amherst, USA
(catalogue)
– *Markers*, Construction in Process,
Venice Biennale, Italy (catalogue)
2000 *Art & Mathematics 2000*, Humanities
Gallery & Brooks Design Center, Albert
Nerken School of Engineering, Cooper
Union, New York, USA
– *Collecting Ideas*, (Work from the Polly &
Mark Addison Collection), Vance Kirkland
Close Range Gallery, Denver Art Museum,
Denver, USA
– *Cross-Currents in Modern Art*, (A Tribute
to Peter Selz), Achim Moeller Gallery,
New York, USA (catalogue)
– *Force-fields: Phases of the Kinetic*,
Museu d'Art Contemporani (MACBA),
Barcelona. Travel to Hayward Gallery,
London, United Kingdom (catalogue)
– *Inventional*, Angles Gallery, Santa
Monica, USA
– *Making Choices*, Museum of Modern Art,
New York, USA
– *Muscle - Power of the View*, Boulder
Museum of Contemporary Art, Boulder,
Los Angeles. Travel to: Contemporary Art
Museum, Houston, USA (catalogue)
– *Out/Side/In - Process in Architecture and
Design*, Huntington Gallery, Mass College
of Art, Boston, USA

1999 *Afterimage: Drawing Through Process*,
Museum of Contemporary Art, MOCA,
Los Angeles, USA
– *Recent Acquistions: Prints and Drawings
from 1960s to the Present*, Philadelphia
Museum of Art, Philadelphia, USA
– *Book as Art #II*, The National Museum of
Women in the Arts, Washington, D.C., USA
(catalogue)
1998 *American Academy in Rome - Annual
Exhibition*, Rome, Italy (catalogue)
– *Biennale dei Parchi*, Palazzo delle
Esposizioni, Rome, Italy
– *Into Focus/Art on Science*, Mandeville
Gallery, Nott Memorial, Union College,
Schenectady, USA
– *Light on the New Millennium*,
International Sculpture Symposium & Art
Festival, Pusan Metropolitan Art Museum,
Pusan, Korea
– *Stelle Cadenti*, L'Associazione Culturale
e Il Comune di Bassano in Teverina,
Bassano in Teverina, Italy
– *The Serial Attitude*, Addison Gallery of
American Art, Phillips Academy, Andover.
Travel: Wexner Center for the Arts,
Ohio State University, Columbus, USA
– *Women Artists in the Vogel Collection*,
Simmons Visual Arts Center, Brenau
University, Gainesville, USA (catalogue)
1997 *Artists - Messengers of Peace*, (Art for
Peace Collection), Eretz Israel Museum,
Israel
– *Magie der Zahl in der Kunst des 20.
Jahrhunderts*, Staatsgalerie, Stuttgart,
Germany (catalogue)
– *The Private Eye in Public Art*, La
Salle Partners at Nations Bank Plaza,
Charlotte, USA
– *The Pyramid Suite*, Trans Hudson Gallery,
New York, USA
1996 *Acts of Obsession*, Carla Stellweg
Gallery, New York, USA
– *Neo-Kinetics: Postmodern Technê*,
Eight Floor Gallery, New York, USA
– *Sub Rosa*, Joyce Goldstein Gallery,
New York, USA

- *Sculptor's Drawings*, View Gallery, New York, USA
- *The Nature of Light*, Joyce Goldstein Gallery, New York, USA
- *The Boat: Object and Metaphor*, Pratt Manhattan Gallery. Travel: The Rubelle and Norman Schafler Gallery, Pratt Institute, Brooklyn, New York, USA
- *Women Artists Series: 25th Year Retrospective, 1971-1996*, Rutgers University, New Brunswick, USA

1995 *Adding It Up; Print Acquisitions 1970-1995*, Museum of Modern Art, New York, USA
- *Co-Existence - Construction in Process*, Artists' Museum, Mitzpe Ramon, Israel
- *Giant Earth Projections to Light Up Landmark Buildings* (25th Anniversary of Earth Day), Center for Art and Earth, New York, USA
- *Green Piece*, Castle Gallery, College of New Rochelle, USA
- *In Light of Our Reflection*, Tisch Gallery, Aidekman Arts Center, Tufts University, Medford, USA (catalogue).
- *Mapping: A Response to MOMA*, American Fine Arts Company, New York, USA
- *Prints*, Foundation for Contemporary Performance Art Benefit, Brooke Alexander, New York, USA
- *Sniper's Nest: Art That Has Lived With Lucy R. Lippard*, Center for Curatorial Studies Museum, Bard College, Annandale-on-Hudson, New York, USA (catalogue)

1994 *Blast Art Benefit*, Tz'Art & Co Gallery, New York, USA
- *Blast 4: Bioinformatica*, Sandra Gering, New York, USA
- *Ipotesi sulla Scultura*, Sala Chierici, Venice, Italy (catalogue)
- *Sculpting with the Environment/A Natural Dialogue*, Pratt Manhattan Gallery, New York. Travel: The Rubelle and Norman Schafler Gallery, Pratt Institute, Brooklyn, New York, USA

1993 *Art and Environment*, National Arts Club, New York, USA

- *Art and the Environment*, Bowman, Penelec,Megahan Galleries Allegheny College, Meadville, USA
- *Art on Paper*, Weatherspoon Art Gallery. University of North Carolina, Greensboro, USA
- *Creative Solutions to Ecological Issues*, Council for Creative Projects, New York, and Hofstra Museum, Hempstead. Travel: Dallas Museum of Natural History; Laumeier Sculpture Park and Gallery, St. Louis; Ross Gallery, University of Pennsylvania, Philadelphia; Fullerton Museum Center, Fullerton; Laguna Gloria Art Museum, Austin; Hofstra Museum, Hempstead, USA
- *Différentes Natures - Visions de l'Art Contemporaine.* Galerie Art de la Défense, EPAD, La Défénse, Paris, France. Travel: Barcelona, Spain (catalogue)
- *First Sightings: Recent Modern and Contemporary Acquisitions*, The Denver Art Museum, Denver, USA
- *Le Onde*, San Leonardo of Cannaregio, Venice, Italy
- *Reading Prints*, Museum of Modern Art, New York, USA
- *Women Artist's Books 1969-1979*, Dia Center for the Arts and Printed Matter, New York, USA

1992 *Americas*, Junta de Andalucia for Expo '92, Andalucia Pavilion, Convento de Santa Clara, Moguer, Spain
- *Art About the Environment*, Center for Art & Earth, New York, USA
- *Artists Who Interpret the Earth and Its Systems: Deep Ecology in the Arts, Toward a New Paradigm*, International Sculpture Conference, University of the Arts, Philadelphia, USA
- *Blast Art Benefit*, Blast (X-Art Foundation), New York, USA
- *Completing the Circle: Artists' Books on the Environment*, Minnesota Center for Book Arts, Minneapolis, USA (catalogue)
- *Laboratory Project #7: Atlas*, Art Gallery of Hamilton, Ontario, Canada

– *The Map Is Not the Territory*, Rosenwald-Wolf Gallery, University of the Arts, Philadelphia College of Art and Design, Philadelphia, USA

– *Strata*, Museum of Contemporary Art, Helsinki, and The Art Museum of Tampere, Finland (catalogue)

– Bellas Artes, Santa Fe, USA

1991 *Women Making History - Print Portfolio 1976*, A.I.R. Gallery, New York, USA

– *The Contemporary Drawing: Existence, Passage and the Dream*, Rose Art Museum, Brandeis University, Waltham, USA (catalogue)

– *Visions/Revisions*, Denver Art Museum, Denver, USA (catalogue)

1990 *Artists for Amnesty*, Amnesty International USA,Blum Helman and Germans van Eck galleries, New York, USA (catalogue)

– *Buckminster Fuller, Harmonizing Nature, Humanity and Technology*, Edith C. Blum Art Institute, Bard College, Annandale-on-Hudson, USA

– *Exhibition Diomede*, Institute for Contemporary Art, P.S. 1 Museum,Clocktower, New York. Travel: San Francisco State University Art Gallery, USA

– *Garbage Out Front: A New Era of Public Design*, Municipal Art Society, New York, USA

– *Partnership for the Homeless Auction*, Christie's, New York, USA (catalogue)

– *No Trends*, Nahan Contemporary, New York, USA

1989 *A Garden Walk … A Selection of Photographers' Views of the Garden*, Twining Gallery, New York, USA

– *American Prints*, Sragow Gallery, New York, USA

– *China, June 4, 1989*, Asian American Art Center, New York. Travel: Blum Helman Warehouse, New York, and Institute of Contemporary Art, Long Island City, Buckham Gallery, Flint; Mexie-Arte, Austin, Texas; Cleveland Institute of Art, USA (catalogue)

– *Lines of Vision: Drawings by Contemporary Women*, Hillwood Art Gallery, Long Island University, Brookville. Travel: Blum Helman Warehouse, New York; Grand Rapids Art Museum; University Art Gallery, University of North Texas, Denton; Richard F. Brush Art Gallery, St. Lawrence University, Canton; Murray State University, Murray; University of Oklahoma Museum of Art, Norman, USA (catalogue)

– *Making Their Mark: Women Artists Move into the Mainstream, 1970-85*, Cincinnati Art Museum, Cincinnati. Travel: New Orleans Art Museum, New Orleans; Denver Art Museum, Denver; Pennsylvania Academy of Fine Arts, Philadelphia, USA (catalogue)

– New York Works at Bjorn Olsson Gallery, Stockholm, Sweden

– *Togail Tir - Marking Time*, An Lanntair Gallery, Stornoway, Isle of Lewis, United Kingdom (book)

1988 *Interaction: Science and Art*, quibb Gallery, Princeton, USA (catalogue)

– *Private Works for Public Spaces*, R.C. Erpf Gallery, New York; Mark Twain Gallery, St. Louis, USA

– *A Debate on Abstraction: Systems and Abstraction*, Bertha and Karl Leubsdorf Art Gallery, Hunter College, New York, USA (catalogue)

1987 *Analysis - Textuality - Phenomenology and Visual Arts*, Studentski Kulturni Centar, Belgrade, Yugoslavia

– *Drawing: 1987*, Louise Ross Gallery, New York, USA

– *Down to the Sea*, Snug Harbor Cultural Center, Staten Island, USA

– *Graphica Atlantica*, Kjarvalsstadir, Reykjavík, Iceland

– *Heresies Benefit*, Frank Marino Gallery, New York, USA

– *The International Art Show for the End of World Hunger*, Minnesota Museum of Art, Saint Paul, USA. Travel: Sonja Henie-Neils Onstad Foundation, Hovikodden, and Stavanger Kulturhus, Norway; Göteborgs Kontsmuseum, Göteborg, Sweden;

Kölnischer; Kunstverein, Cologne, West
Germany; Musée des Arts Africains et
Océaniens, Paris, France; Barbican Art
Gallery, London, United Kingdom; Circulo
de Bellas Artes, Madrid, Spain; Arti et
Armiticiae, Amsterdam, The Netherlands;
Salas Nacionales de Exposicion, Buenos
Aires, Argentina; Museu de Arte de São
Paulo, Brazil; Sala Mendoza, Caracas,
Venezuela; Scottsdale Center for the
Arts; Museo de Arte Contemporaneo de
Puerto Rico, San Juan, Puerto Rico;
Schneider Museum of Art, Ashland, USA;
Setagaya Art Museum,Tokyo, Japan;
El Museo de Barrio, New York, USA
   162nd Annual Exhibition, National Academy
of Design, New York, USA
   Very Special Arts, Benefit Art Auction,
Sotheby's, New York, USA

1986 *Archetype: Eastern Cultures - Western Art
of the Twentieth Century*, Ethnographic
Museum, Belgrade, Yugoslavia (catalogue)
   Benefit for Poetry Project, St. Mark's
Church, New York, USA
   Creativity, Santa Maria di Castello,
Genoa, Italy
   V Bienal Americana de Artes Graficas,
Museo de Artes Moderno la Tertulia, Cali,
Colombia (catalogue); Gallery Artists,
Aleman Gallery, Boston
   Letters, The Clocktower, New York, USA
   L'Ideogramma Universale, Galleria e
Liberia Il Segno, Torino, Italy
   Monumental Space Variations, Contemporary
Art at One Penn Plaza, New York, USA
   *1986: A Celebration of the Arts
Apprenticeship Program*, City Gallery,
Department of Cultural Affairs, New York,
USA
   Pay Attention, Brandts Pakhus Galleri,
Copenhagen, Denmark
   Prints by Women, Associated American
Artists, New York, USA
   Prints by Women - Award-Winning Prints,
Print Club, Philadelphia, USA
   Public Visions/Public Monuments,
Soho 20 Gallery, New York, USA

   *State of the Art: An Exhibition
of and about Technology*, Twining Gallery,
New York, USA
   38th Annual Purchase Exhibition,
American Academy and Institute of Arts
and Letters, New York, USA
   Die Wirklichkeit der Bilder, Nürnberg
Kunsthalle, West Germany (catalogue)
   Works on Paper, Rutgers National 85/86,
Stedman Gallery, Rutgers University,
Camden, USA (catalogue)

1985 *American Art: American Women*, Stamford
Museum, Stamford, USA
   *Art, Design, and The Modern Corporation:
The Collection of the Container
Corporation of America, a Gift to the
National Museum of American Art*, National
Museum of American Art, Smithsonian
Institution, Washington, D.C. , USA
(catalogue)
   *Artists and Architects - Challenges
in Collaboration*, Cleveland Center for
Contemporary Art, USA (catalogue)
   The Comet Show, Light Gallery,
New York, USA
   The Drawing Center Show, Elaine Benson
Gallery, Bridgehampton, USA (catalogue)
   KIS '85, Kunsan International Show,
Institute of Contemporary Art, Kunsan
National University, Chonbuk, South Korea
   Large Drawings, Independent Curators,
Inc., New York. Travel: Bass Museum
of Art, Miami Beach, USA; Winnipeg
Art Gallery, Manitoba, and Norman
Mackenzie Art Gallery, University of
Regina, Saskatchewan, Canada; Anchorage
Historical & Fine Arts Museum; Santa
Barbara Museum of Art; Tweed Museum of
Art, University of Minnesota at Duluth,
USA (catalogue)
   Mathematics, Clarity and Thought,
Rosemont College, Rosemont, USA
   Recent Acquisitions, Moderna Museet,
Stockholm, Sweden
   Seeing Anew: Noah and the Ark,
Wilson Arts Center, Rochester, USA

– *37th Annual Purchase Exhibition*, Hassam and Speicher Purchase Award, American Academy and Institute of Arts and Letters, New York, USA

1984 *8 in '84: Franklin Furnace's 8th Anniversary*, Ronald Feldman Fine Arts, New York, USA

– *Exception 2*, Pratt Manhattan Center Gallery, New York, USA (catalogue)

– *Labor Intensive Abstraction*, The Clocktower, New York, USA

– *Land Marks*, Edith C. Blum Art Institute, Milton & Sally Avery Center for the Arts, Bard College, Annandale-on-Hudson, USA (catalogue)

– *New Visions*, Germans van Eck Gallery, New York, USA

– *Projects: World's Fairs, Waterfronts, Parks, and Plazas*, Rhona Hoffman Gallery, Chicago, USA

– *Sculpture: Exploring Three Dimensions*, SITES (Smithsonian Institution Traveling Exhibition Service), Washington, D.C. Travel: West Kentucky University Gallery, Bowling Green; San Antonio Museum Association; Cedar Rapids Museum of Art; Louisville Art Gallery; Dayton Art Institute; Alexandra Art Museum; Woodson Art Museum, Wausau; Santa Fe Community College Art Gallery, Gainesville; Bergstrom-Nahler Museum, Neenah; Museum of Arts and Sciences, Macon; Krasl Art Center, St. Joseph, USA

– *Sculpture in Architecture*, Germans van Eck Gallery, New York, USA; Stockholm Art Fair, Sweden

– *Varieties of Sculptural Ideas*, Max Hutchinson Gallery, New York, USA

1983 *The Examples of Mental and Spiritual Spaces/Works*, Galeria Studentskog, Kulturnog Centar, Belgrade, Yugoslavia (catalogue)

– *Monuments and Landscapes - The New Public Art*, McIntosh/Drysdale Gallery, Houston, USA

– *New York i Linköping*, Östergotlands Länsmuseum, Linköping, Sweden (catalogue)

– *Petit Format de Papier*, Cul-des-Sarts, Ministère de la Communauté Française, Couvin, France. Travel: Namur, La Louvière, Tournai, Bastogne, Loverval, Gerpinnes, Belgium (catalogue)

– *Printed by Women: A National Exhibition of Photographs and Prints*, Port of History Museum at Penn's Landing, Philadelphia, USA (catalogue)

– *World Print Four - An International Survey* and *ContemporaryMasters - The World Print Awards*, World Print Council, San Francisco Museum of Modern Art. Travel: California College of Arts and Crafts, San Francisco; Osaka University of Arts, Japan; Tacoma Art Museum; Anchorage Historical and Fine Arts Museum; Edison Community College Gallery, Fort Myers; University of Southern Mississippi, Hattiesburg; El Paso Museum of Art; Toledo Museum of Art, USA (catalogue)

1982 *The Alternative Image*, John Michael Kohler Art Center, Sheboygan, USA

– *Arte e Scienza per il Disegno del Mondo* (Art & Science for the Representation of the World), Citta di Torino Assessorato per la Cultura, Turin, Italy (catalogue)

– *Books by Printmakers*, Print Club, Philadelphia, USA

– *Copycat Show: An Exhibition of Photocopy Art*, Franklin Furnace, New York, USA

– *The Destroyed Print*, Pratt Manhattan Center Gallery, New York, USA (catalogue)

– *58th Annual International Competition*, Print Club, Philadelphia, USA (catalogue)

– *Nature Transformed*, Anderson Gallery, Virginia Commonwealth University, Richmond, USA

– *157th Annual Exhibition*, National Academy of Design, New York, USA (catalogue)

– *Position 82*, Galleriet, Lund, Sweden

– *Prints America*, Abington Art Center, Jenkintown, Philadelphia, USA (catalogue)

– *Projections*, West Hubbard Gallery, Chicago, USA (catalogue)

– *Sweet Art Sale Benefit for Franklin Furnace*, Ronald Feldman Downtown Gallery, New York, USA

_ *Trycksaker - Printed Matters en Grafikutstallning*, Galleriet, Lund, Sweden
_ *Visual Cataloguing and Mapping*, Visual Studies Workshop, Rochester, USA

1981 *All in Line - An Exhibition of Linear Drawing*, Joe and Emily Lowe Art Gallery, Syracuse University. Travel: Terry Dintenfass Gallery, New York, USA (catalogue)
_ *GLCA Artists Sponsors Exhibition, 1981-1983*, Ohio Wesleyan University, Delaware. Travel: Denison University, Granville, Kenyon College, Gambier, College of Wooster, Antioch College, Yellow Springs; Albion College, Kalamazoo College, Hope College, Holland; DePauw University, Greencastle, Wabash College, Crawfordsville, Earlham College, Richmond, USA
_ *Insights: Small Works from the Past 15 Years*, New Gallery of Contemporary Art, Cleveland, USA (in conjunction with lecture series "Artists in Ellen Johnson Anthology")
_ *Lis '81*, Lisbon International Exhibition of Drawings, Galerie Nacional de Arte Moderna, Lisbon, Portugal (catalogue)
_ *Mapped Art: Charts, Routes, Regions*, Independent Curators Inc., New York. Travel: University of Colorado Art Galleries, Boulder; Arkansas Arts Center, Little Rock; Archer M. Huntington Art Gallery, University of Texas at Austin; Toledo Museum of Art, USA (catalogue)
_ *Messages: Words and Images*, Freedman Gallery, Albright College, Reading. Travel: Ralph Wilson Gallery, Lehigh University, Bethlehem, USA (catalogue)
_ *Musée Modern*, Palais des Beaux Arts, Brussels, Belgium
_ *New Dimensions in Drawing, 1950-1980*, Aldrich Museum of Contemporary Art, Ridgefield, USA (catalogue)
_ *New York City (Donne in Arte - Viaggio a New York)*, Studio Arco d'Alibert, Rome, Italy. Travel: Palazzo Ducale, Genoa, Italy
_ *New York Today*, Galleriet, Lund, Sweden
_ *Petit Format de Papier*, Exposition Internationale, Cul-des-Sarts, Couvin, Belgium (catalogue)
_ *Schemes, A Decade of Installation Drawings*, Elise Meyer, Inc., New York. Travel: Emily Lowe Gallery, Hofstra University, Hempstead; Richard F. Brush Art Gallery, St. Lawrence University, Canton; Rhode Island School of Design, Providence, USA; Musée de l'Art Contemporain, Cité du Havre, Montreal, Quebec, Canada; Leigh University, Bethlehem, USA (catalogue)
_ *Tenth Anniversary Retrospective - The Women Artists Series at Douglass College*, Rutgers University, New Brunswick. Travel: A.I.R. Gallery, New York, USA (catalogue)
_ *Transformations - Women in Art 70's-80's*, New York Coliseum, New York, USA
_ *Vakna! (Wake-Up!)*, Galleriet, Lund, Sweden
_ *Words as Images*, Renaissance Society, University of Chicago, USA (catalogue)

1980 *American Drawing in Black and White*, Brooklyn Museum, New York, USA (catalogue)
_ *American Women Artists 1980*, Museo de Arte Contemporanea da Universidade de São Paulo, Brazil
_ *Apokalypsis*, Nardin Gallery, New York, USA
_ *Cartes et Figures de la Terre*, Musée National d'Art Moderne, Centre Georges Pompidou, Paris, France (catalogue)
_ *cARTography*, John Michael Kohler Arts Center, Sheboygan, USA
_ *Drawings of a Different Nature*, Portland Center for the Visual Arts, USA
_ *Drawings: The Pluralist Decade*, Institute of Contemporary Art, University of Pennsylvania, Philadelphia, USA. Travel: Kunstföreninger Museum, Copenhagen, Denmark; Henie-Onstad Museum, Blommenholm, Norway; Biblioteca Nacional, Madrid, Spain; Gulbenkian Foundation, Lisbon, Portugal (catalogue)
_ *56th International Annual Print*

Competition, Print Club, Philadelphia, USA (catalogue)

_ *The Great Pyramid Show*, Fine Arts Gallery, Wright State University, Dayton. Travel: Midwest Museum of Modern Art, Elkhart; Albright College, Reading; Wesleyan College, Middletown, USA

_ *Pyramidal Influence in Art*, Fine Arts Gallery, Museum of American Art, Elkhart. Travel: Freedman Gallery, Albright College, Reading; Davidson Art Center, Wesleyan University, Middletown, USA (catalogue)

_ *Investigations: Probe, Structure, Analysis*, New Museum, New York, USA (catalogue)

_ *Invitational*, National Academy Galleries, New York, USA

_ *Mail Art*, Centre de Documentation d'Art Actuel, Barcelona, Spain

_ *New York Today*, Galleri Liljan, Varnamo, Sweden

_ *Paesaggio Di Paesaggio*, Amministrazione Communale de Santa Maria C.V., Milan, Italy (catalogue)

_ *The Pluralist Decade*, United States Pavilion, Venice Biennale, Italy

_ *Process Analysis*, Elise Meyer, Inc., New York, USA

_ *Reasoned Space*, Center for Creative Photography, University of Arizona, Tucson, USA Travel: Art Museum and Gallery, California State University, Long Beach, USA (catalogue)

_ *Speaking Volumes: Women Artists' Books*, A.I.R. Gallery, New York, USA

_ *System, Inquiry, Translation*, Touchstone Gallery, New York, USA

_ *Visual Articulation of Ideas*, Visual Studies Workshop Gallery, Rochester. Travel: Millersville State College; James Madison University, Harrisonburg; Everett Community College, USA

1979 *American Art from MOMA*, Kunstmuseum, Berne, Switzerland. Travel: Museum Ludwig, Cologne, West Germany; Gulbenkian Foundation, Lisbon, Portugal; Museo Español de Arte Contemporaneo, Madrid, Spain; Tel Aviv Museum, Israel; Vienna Museum des 20. Jahrhunderts, Vienna, Austria (catalogue)

_ *Drawings About Drawing: New Directions*, Ackland Art Museum, Chapel Hill, USA

_ *A Great Big Drawing Show*, Institute for Art and Urban Resources at P.S. 1, Long Island City, USA

_ *Group Invitational*, Galerie AIX, Stockholm, Sweden

_ *Recent Trends in American Printmaking*, Mitchell Museum, Mitchell Foundation, Mount Vernon, USA

_ Seibu Art Museum, Tokyo, Japan

_ *Time Fuse Attitudes*, Bulderup, Sweden

_ *Word, Object, Image*, Rosa Esman Gallery, New York, USA

1978 *Artists Books*, Franklin Furnace, New York, USA. Travel: Gorett-Brewster, New Plymouth, Auckland City Gallery, National Gallery, Wellington, New Zealand; George Paton Gallery, Melbourne, Experimental Art Foundation, Adelaide, Museum of Contemporary Arts, Brisbane, Australia (catalogue)

_ *Artwords, Bookworks*, Los Angeles Institute of Contemporary Art, USA

_ *Footprint '78*, Davis Gallery, Seattle (catalogue)

_ *Grids*, Pace Gallery, New York. Travel: Akron Art Institute, Akron, USA (catalogue)

_ *Imaginary Worlds*, Rosa Esman Gallery, New York, USA

_ *Materializzazione del Linguaggio*, Venice Biennale, Italy (catalogue)

_ *Numerals 1924-1977*, Yale University Art Gallery, New Haven. Travel: Leo Castelli Gallery, New York; University Art Galleries, University of North Dakota, Grand Fork; Minneapolis College of Art and Design; Fine Arts Gallery, University of California, Irvine; New Gallery of Contemporary Art, Cleveland; Art Museum of South Texas, Corpus Christi; Center for Visual Arts Gallery, Illinois State University, Normal; Center for the Arts, Muhlenberg College, Allentown: Dartmouth

College Museum & Galleries, Hopkins Center, Hanover (catalogue); "Point", Philadelphia College of Art, USA (catalogue)
- Venice Biennale, Italy
- *Women Artists Series Year Five*, Douglass College, Rutgers University, New Brunswick, USA (catalogue)
- *Works from the Collection of Dorothy and Herbert Vogel*, University of Michigan Museum of Art, Ann Arbor, USA

1977 *Art Stories*, Libra Gallery, Claremont Graduate School, USA
- *The City Project 1977*, New Gallery of Contemporary Art, Cleveland State University, USA
- *Computer Genesis: A Vision of the '70's*, Joe and Emily Lowe Art Gallery, Syracuse University, USA (catalogue)
- *Documenta VI*, Kassel, West Germany (catalogue)
- *Drawing Structure*, Rush Rhees Gallery, University of Rochester, USA
- *Maps*, Winter Penthouse Exhibition, Museum of Modern Art, New York, USA
- *Maps: Their Science and Their Art*, Museum of Natural History, New York, USA
- *Oyvind Fahlström: An Exhibition of His Friends*, Galerie Buchholz, Munich, West Germany
- *Space Scapes*, Sid Deutsch Gallery, New York, USA

1976 *Art and World*, Whitney Museum of American Art, Downtown Branch, New York, USA
- *Beyond the Page*, Arts Council, Philadelphia, USA
- *Invitational*, Institute for Art and Urban Resources at P.S. 1, Long Island City, USA
- *New York, Soho Contact '76*, Georgetown College Gallery. Travel: Junior Art Gallery, Louisville and University of New Orleans, USA (catalogue)
- *The 1976 Biennale of Sydney*, Arts Gallery of New South Wales, Sydney, Australia (catalogue)
- *Paper: An Invitational Exhibition*, The Michael C. Rockefeller Arts Center Gallery, State University College at Fredonia, USA (catalogue)

- *Reality Plus - The New Pluralism 1966-76*, James Yu Gallery, New York, USA
- *Thirty Years of American Printmaking and the 20th National Print Exhibition*, Brooklyn Museum, USA (catalogue)
- *Unique Works*, Franklin Furnace, New York, USA (catalogue)

1975 Art Fair, Basel, Switzerland
- *Art in Landscape*, Independent Curators, Inc., New York: Travel: Illinois State University, Normal; University of California, Irvine; University of Montana, Missoula; Earlham College, Richmond; Alberta College of Art, Calgary, Canada; and expanded version subtitled *The City Project* at New Gallery of Contemporary Art, Cleveland, USA
- Associated American Artists, New York, USA
- *Color, Light and Image*, International Women's Year Invitational, Interart Center, New York, USA
- *Language and Structure in North America*, Kensington Arts Association, Toronto, Canada
- *National Drawing Exhibition '75*, Camden College of Arts and Sciences, Rutgers University, New Brunswick, USA
- *Painting, Drawing and Sculpture of the 60's and 70's from the Dorothy and Herbert Vogel Collection*, Institute of Contemporary Art, University of Pennsylvania, Philadelphia, and Clocktower, New York, USA
- *Report from Soho*, Grey Art Gallery, New York University, New York, USA
- *USA Drawings 3*, Stadtisches Museum, Leverkusen, West Germany (catalogue)
- *The Year of the Woman*, Bronx Museum of the Arts, New York, USA

1974 *CACC*, San Francisco Museum of Art, USA
- *Painting and Sculpture Today*, Indianapolis Museum of Art, and Taft Museum, Cincinnati, USA (catalogue)
- *Projekt '74*, Kunsthalle, Cologne, West Germany (catalogue)
- *Women's Work: American Art*, Museum of Philadelphia Civic Center, USA

_ *Word Works*, Mount San Antonio College,
Walnut, USA

1973 *American Drawings 1963-73*, Whitney Museum
of American Art, New York, USA (catalogue)

_ Associated American Artists, New York, USA

_ *C.7,500*, California Institute of the
Arts, Valencia. Travel: Wadsworth
Atheneum, Hartford; Moore College of Art,
Philadelphia; Institute of Contemporary
Art, Boston; Walker Art Center,
Minneapolis; Smith College Museum of Art,
Northampton, USA

_ *Conceptual Art*, Women's Interart Center,
New York, USA

_ *Grafische Techniken*, Neuer Berliner
Kunstverein, West Berlin, West Germany
(catalogue)

_ *Invitational*, Museo Provincial de Bellas
Artes "Emilio A. Caraffa", Cordoba,
Argentina

_ *New Acquisitions*, Museum of Modern Art,
New York, USA

_ *Thought Structure*, Pace College,
New York, USA

_ *Women Choose Women*, New York Cultural
Center, New York, USA (catalogue)

1972 *American Women Artists*, Kunsthaus,
Hamburg, West Germany

_ *18th National Print Show*, Brooklyn
Museum, New York. Travel: California
Palace of the Legion of Honor,
San Francisco, USA

_ New York Institute of Technology,
New York, USA

_ *International Artistic Encounter*,
Pamplona, Colombia

_ *Invitational*, Allen Memorial Art Gallery,
Oberlin College, Oberlin, USA

_ *Kent Invitational*, Kent State University,
Kent, USA

_ *Making Megalopolis Matter*, New York
Cultural Center, New York, USA

_ *National Invitational Print Exhibition*,
Albion College, Albion, USA

_ *Oversize Drawings*, New York University,
New York, USA

1971 *Art Systems*, Museum of Modern Art, Buenos
Aires, Argentina. Travel: Museum of Fine
Arts, Santiago, Chile, and Institute of
Contemporary Art, Lima, Peru

_ *New Acquisitions*, Whitney Museum of
American Art, New York, USA

_ *Oversize Prints*, Whitney Museum of
American Art, New York, USA (catalogue)

_ *Projected Art: Artists at Work*, Finch
College Museum, Finch College, USA

1970 *Invitational*, Hundred Acres Gallery,
New York, USA

_ *Invitational*, National Academy Galleries,
New York, USA

_ *Language IV*, Dwan Gallery, New York, USA

_ *Software*, Jewish Museum, New York, USA
(catalogue)

**COMMISSIONS, ENVIRONMENTAL SCULPTURE
AND INSTALLATIONS**

2025 *The Living Pyramid*, MUDAM, Luxembourg

2024-2025 *The Living Pyramid*, Desert X,
Rancho Mirage, USA

2022- *Art in the Landscape*, Wadi AlFann,
AlUla, Kingdom of Saudi Arabia

2019 "Model for Teardrop-Monument to Being
Earthbound", 1984-2019, The Shed,
New York, USA

_ "Model for Probability Pyramid - Study
for Crystal Pyramid", 1976-2019,
The Shed, New York, USA

_ "Model for A Forest for New York",
2014-2019, The Shed, New York, USA

2017 "The Living Pyramid", 2015/2017,
Documenta 14, Kassel, Germany

_ "Pascal's Perfect Probability
Pyramid & the People Paradox - The
Predicament",1980/2016, The New School,
New York, USA

2015 "Wheatfield", Porta Nuova District,
Milan, Italy

_ "The Living Pyramid", Socrates Sculpture
Park, Long Island City, USA

2011 "Nautilus Amphitheater", Three Rivers
Community College, Norwich, USA

2005 "Indian Bend Wash Public Art Project",
Scottsdale Public Art Program,
Scottsdale, USA (resigned "Poles Apart/
Poles Together", outdoor installation
on the Grand Canal for the 51st Venice
Biennale, the International Artists'
Museum, Museo Storico Navale, Venice,
Italy

2001 "Markers", Venice Biennale, Italy.
Two-meter banner with tree image and
poetry installed above Via Garibaldi
in Venice, Italy

    "Uprooted and Deified - the Golden
Tree" (a fully grown tree unearthed with
roots intact, painted gold and installed
horizontally in midair, Göteborgs
Internationella Konstbiennal, Sweden,
summer/fall)

2000 "Masterplan - Nieuwe Hollandse
Waterlinie", the Fort Asperen Foundation.
25-year Masterplan to bring into
prominence and environmentally sustainable
the 85-km long defense line dotted with
70 forts & fortifications built from
the 16th-19th centuries in the center
region of the Netherlands. The masterplan
includes historical preservation, land
reclamation, water and flood management,
urban planning, landscape architecture,
urban design. An ongoing project.

    "Crystal Fort" - Masterplan-Niewuwe
Hollandse Waterlinie, original design of
a full-scale fortress made of glass, to
be built along the Waterlinie as part
of the overall masterplan and a major
tourist attraction (120' × 120' × 60')

    "The Irish Hunger Memorial", finalist
to create a memorial for a half-acre site
at Battery Park City, New York, USA

    "Poetry Walk - Reflections: Pools of
Thought" (with Time Capsule 2000-3000
A.D.), a permanent installation of 20
granite stones (4 × 5 feet each), carved
with poetry embedded into lawn at
University of Virginia (535 × 60 feet).
A Millennial Project, sponsored by the
University and the University of Virginia
Art Museum, Charlottesville, USA

1998 "A Forest for Australia", six thousand
trees of endangered species with varying
heights at maturity, were planted into
five spirals forming step pyramids for
each spiral when the trees are full
grown, 400 × 80 meters, Altoona Treatment
Plant, Melbourne, Australia

    "Sheep", an installation of live sheep
at the American Academy in Rome, Italy
(while resident there on a Rome Prize
Fellowship)

1992-1996 "Tree Mountain - A Living Time
Capsule", Pinsiö gravel pits, Ylöjärvi,
Finland; co-sponsored by the United
Nations Environment Program and the
Ministry of the Environment, Government
of Finland. 420 × 270 × 28 meters. 11,000
trees planted in an intricate mathematical
pattern by 11,000 people from around the
world, to be preserved for 400 years. One
of the largest reclamation sites in the
world and most complex in its philosophy.
Declared a national forest.

1995 "Art on the Edge", symbols and poetry
carved into edge of Mahtesh Ramon crater;
commissioned by the Artist Museum,
Mitzpe Ramon, Israel

1992 "Hot/Cold Earthship with Heartbeat",
40 ft wooden barge filled with earth,
soundtrack of heartbeat - oars, ancient
anchor, ropes, chains. Also: "Stelae II",
two hand carved granite tablets (1.5
ton each), commissioned by the Museum
of Contemporary Art, Helsinki, and the
Art Museum of Tampere, Finland for the
"Strata" exhibition

1990 "Circle of Megaliths with Sundial".
Commissioned by the International Center
for the Preservation of Wild Animals,
a 10,000 acre wildlife preserve and
research center in Columbus (in process)

1991-1992 "Introspection I - Evolution".
17 ft mural depicts human evolution.
Commissioned by the Harold Washington
Library Center. Winner of Chicago Bar
Assocociation Young Lawyers Public
Art Award. City of Chicago Public Art
Program.

1988-1991 "North Waterfront Park Master Plan".
Art concept, development and design of
97-acre landfill, with 12-acre wildlife
sanctuary, fresh water lake, brackish
marsh, tidal pools, lighthouses and
sunflower/wildflower meadows. Department
of Public Works, City of Berkeley. Master
Plan approved 1991.

1986-1990 "Flying Pyramids for the Twenty-
Second Century", environmental sculpture
with coral rock, wildflowers, and water
features, Miami International Airport,
Metro-Dade County Art in Public Places,
Florida (unrealized)

1988-1989 "Bird Project: Visual Investigation
of Systems in Motion", research and
development grant to produce film on
migratory bird colonies in the south of
Sweden, American-Scandinavian Foundation

1988 "The Human Argument in Steel & Crystal
with Sundial", University City Science
Center, Redevelopment Authority of the
City of Philadelphia (finalist)

1986-1987 "Hypersphere - The Earth in the Shape
of the Universe", five-ton etched glass
suspension ceiling, and complete lobby
design. First National Bank of Chicago's
New York City headquarters at Equitable
Center, New York. Dedicated January 14,
1987

1986 "Stelae - Messages from Another Time -
Discoveries of Minds and People", two
hand-carved marble tablets depict major
scientific breakthroughs, Santa Maria
di Castello, Genoa, Italy. Commissioned
by Department of Cultural Affairs &
Artemesia, Genoa, Italy

1982 "Wheatfield - A Confrontation", two
acres of wheat planted and harvested in
Manhattan's financial district, Battery
Park landfill, downtown Manhattan.
Commissioned by the Public Art Fund,
New York

1980 "Anima/Persona - The Seed in 4-D",
the first 360-degree integral hologram,
a holographic film of the growth
process in motion

1979 "Probability Pyramid - The Crystal
Pyramid and the Seed", commissioned
for the Great Ideas Series, Container
Corporation of America, Chicago

1979 "Time Capsule 1979-2979" (1000 year time
capsule), Artpark, Lewiston, New York

1978 "Time/Fuse/Attitudes", Bulderup, Sweden

1977 "Rice/Tree/Burial", a three-part project
of planting a rice field 200 ft above
the Niagara gorge, chaining the trees
in a sacred Indian forest, burying a
time capsule and filming Niagara Falls
from its edge. Commissioned by Artpark,
Lewiston, New York (catalogue)

1968 "Haiku Poetry Burial, Rice Planting
and Tree Chaining", the first eco/
philosophical work from the "Eco-Logic"
series. Sullivan County, New York, USA.

AWARDS AND PRIZES

2020 Arts Innovation, Impact Honoree, The
Phillips Collection, Washington, DC

_ Albert Nelson Marquis Lifetime
Achievement Award, Marquis Who's Who

2015 Guggenheim Fine Arts Fellowship

2008 Honorary Doctorate of Humane Letters from
Bucknell University, Lewisburg (awarded
for contributions to education, art and
pioneering environmental art)

2007 Anonymous Was a Woman Award

2006 Nomination for the United States Artist
Fellowship

1999 The Watson Award for Transdisciplinary
Achievement in the Arts, Carnegie Mellon
University, Pittsburgh

1997-1998 Rome Prize Fellow (FAAR), American
Academy in Rome

1994 Honorary Doctorate in Fine Arts, Ripon
College, Wisconsin (Environmental
Responsibility)

1993- Studio For Creative Inquiry, Research
Fellow, Carnegie Mellon University,
Pittsburgh

1992 Chicago Bar Association Young Lawyers
Public Art Award, The Harold Washington
Library Art Collection, Chicago
(_Introspection I - Evolution_ - a mural)

_ Herbert F. Johnson Museum of Art purchase
grant; Richard A. Florsheim Art Fund

1990 The Eugene McDermott Achievement Award
"In Recognition of Major Contribution
to the Arts", Massachusetts Institute
of Technology, Council for the Arts,
Cambridge, Ma.

1989 National Endowment for the Arts
Individual Artist Fellowship

1987 The Thord-Gray Memorial Fund Research and
Development Grant, American-Scandinavian
Foundation

1985 American Academy of Arts and Letters
Hassam and Speicher Fund Purchase Award

1984 New York State Council on the Arts,
Visual Artists Program grant toward
the publication of *BOOK OF DUST
- The Beginning and the End of Time
and Thereafter*

1982 The Ann and Donald McPhail Award (first
prize), International Print Competition,
Print Club, Philadelphia

1981 National Endowment for the Arts
Individual Artist Fellowship

1980- Fellow at the Center for Advanced Visual
Studies, M.I.T., Cambridge

1980 Berthe Von Moschzisker Prize,
International Print Competition, Print
Club, Philadelphia

_ New York State Council on the Arts,
Creative Artists Public Service Grant

1978 DAAD Fellowship (Deutscher Akademischer
Austauschdienst), Berlin, Germany

_ Purchase award, Footprint '78,
International Print Competition

1977 Collaboration in Art, Science and
Technology Fellowship (C.A.S.T.), Syracuse
University

1976 Museum of Modern Art Purchase with CAPS
matching grant, New York

1975-1976 International Women's Year Award,
"In Recognition of Outstanding Cultural
Contribution and Education to Women and
Art", International Women's Arts Festival

1975 National Endowment for the Arts
Individual Artist Fellowship

1974 Creative Artists Public Service Grant,
New York State Council on the Arts

_ National Endowment for the Arts
Individual Artist Fellowship

_ Purchase Prize, National Drawing
Competition, Rutgers University,
New Brunswick

1973 Purchase Prize, National Print
Competition, Albion College

1972 Creative Artists Public Service Grant,
New York State Council on the Arts

SELECTED PUBLIC COLLECTIONS HOLDING HER WORKS

Albion College, Albion, Michigan
Allen Memorial Art Museum, Oberlin, Ohio
American Academy in Rome, Rome/New York
Art Institute of Chicago
AT&T Corporation Collection
Bates Museum of Art, Lewiston, Maine
Beijer Collection, Stockholm, Sweden
Boulder Museum of Contemporary Art, Boulder,
     Colorado
Centre Pompidou, Paris
Chase Manhattan Art Collection
Chazen Museum of Art, University of Wisconsin,
     Madison
Corcoran Gallery of Art, Washington, D.C.
Container Corporation of America
Denver Art Museum, Colorado
Des Moines Art Center, Des Moines, Iowa
Ellen H. Johnson Collection, Oberlin, Ohio
Elvehjem Art Museum, University of Wisconsin,
     Madison, Wisconsin
Frac Grand Large - Hauts-de-France, Dunkirk,
     France
FRAC Lorraine, Metz, France
Finch College Museum, New York
First National Bank of Chicago, Illinois
Harvard University Art Museums, Cambridge,
     Massachusets
Hood Museum of Art, Dartmouth College,
     Hanover, New Hampshire
Hirshhorn Museum and Sculpture Garden,
     Washington, D.C.
Honolulu Academy of Arts, Hawaii
Israel Museum, Jerusalem, Israel
Herbert F. Johnson Museum of Art, Cornell
     University, Ithaca, New York

Indianapolis Museum of Art, Indianapolis,
    Indiana
Kunsthalle, Nürnberg, Germany
John D. and Catherine T. MacArthur Foundation
    Collection
Maier Museum of Art, Randolf College,
    Lynchburg, Virginia
The Menil Collection, Houston, Texas
Metro Dade Art in Public Places,
    Miami, Florida
Metropolitan Museum of Art, New York
Middlebury College Museum of Art, Middlebury,
    Vermont
Midwest Museum of American Art, Elkhart,
    Indiana
Moderna Museet, Stockholm, Sweden
Musée de Petit Format, Cul-des-Sarts,
    Couvin, Belgium
The Museum of Modern Art, New York
Museum of Fine Arts, Boston, Massachusetts
Museum of Fine Arts, Budapest
Museum of Fine Arts, Santa Fe, New Mexico
National Air and Space Museum, Smithsonian
    Institution, Washington, D.C.
National Gallery of Art, Washington D.C.
National Museum of American Art,
    Washington, D.C.
Nelson-Atkins Museum of Art, Kansas City,
    Missouri
Nevada Museum of Art, Reno, Nevada
Philadelphia Museum of Art, Pennsylvania
The Phillips Collection, Washington D.C.
Reynolda House, Museum of American Art,
    Winston-Salem, N.C.
Rhode Island School of Design Museum of Art,
    Providence, Rhode Island
Roy R. Neuberger Museum, State University
    of New York at Purchase, New York
Rutgers University Art Collection, New
    Brunswick, New Jersey
San Francisco Museum of Modern Art, California
Smith College Museum of Art, Northampton,
    Massachusets
Smithsonian Institution, Washington, D.C.
Syracuse University Art Collection, New York
University of Kentucky Art Museum, Lexington,
    Kentucky

University of Massachusetts Art Collection,
    Andover
Harold Washington Library Center, Chicago,
    Illinois
Wexner Center for the Arts, Ohio State
    University, Columbus
Whitney Museum of American Art, New York

Compiled by:
Leslie Tonkonow Artworks + Projects

cat. no. 1
*Dialectic Triangulation: A Visual Philosophy
(Including The Human Argument)*, 1968-1983
Hand-pulled lithograph on Japanese blue Moriki
paper, hand-dusted with gold leaf, green-
bronze, and silver-lavender inks; 972 × 647 mm
AELA Collection

cat. no. 2
*Strength Analysis -
A Dictionary of Strength*, 1971/1981
Lithograph on rag paper; 587 × 434 mm
Courtesy of the artist, Leslie Tonkonow
Artworks + Projects, New York,
and acb Gallery, Budapest

cat. no. 3
Matrix of Knowledge, 1970/2017
Type-C print on paper; 723 × 106 mm
Courtesy of the artist, Leslie Tonkonow
Artworks + Projects, New York,
and acb Gallery, Budapest

cat. no. 4
Liberated Sex Machine, 1969-1970/2013
Hand-pulled lithograph on blue Pliké paper;
482 × 618 mm
Courtesy of the artist, Leslie Tonkonow
Artworks + Projects, New York,
and acb Gallery, Budapest

cat. no. 5
Liberated Sex Machine, 1969-1970/2013
Hand-pulled lithograph on purple Pliké paper;
482 × 618 mm
Courtesy of the artist, Leslie Tonkonow
Artworks + Projects, New York,
and acb Gallery, Budapest

cat. no. 6
The Pyramids as They Were, 1994
Lithograph in blue ink with silver metallic
dusting on BFK paper; 639 × 897 mm
Courtesy of the artist, Leslie Tonkonow
Artworks + Projects, New York,
and acb Gallery, Budapest

cat. no. 7
When the Pyramid Awakens, 1994
Lithograph in blue ink with silver metallic
dusting on BFK paper; 639 × 897 mm
Courtesy of the artist, Leslie Tonkonow
Artworks + Projects, New York,
and acb Gallery, Budapest

cat. no. 8
*Fish Pyramid - Noah's Ark
for the New City*, 1994
Lithograph with metallic dusting on BFK paper;
639 × 897 mm
Private Collection

cat. no. 9
Flying Bird Pyramid, 1994
Lithograph in blue ink with silver metallic
dusting on BFK paper; 630 × 905 mm
Courtesy of the artist and
acb Gallery, Budapest

cat. no. 10
Pyramid, 1987
Watercolour and metallic ink on vellum;
432 × 559 mm
Courtesy of the artist and
acb Gallery, Budapest

cat. no. 11
The Reflection, 1981
Lithograph on Japan paper; 838 × 635 mm
Courtesy of the artist, Leslie Tonkonow
Artworks + Projects, New York, and
acb Gallery, Budapest

cat. no. 12
Probability Pyramid, 1978
Lithograph printed in silver ink on paper;
711 × 1011 mm
Courtesy of the artist and
acb Gallery, Budapest

cat. no. 13
Probability Pyramid II, 1981
Lithograph on paper; 749 × 1041 mm
Courtesy of the artist and
acb Gallery, Budapest

cat. no. 14
Half Bird - A Flexible Space Station, 1994
Lithograph in white ink with silver metallic
dusting on black BFK paper; 630 × 905 mm
Courtesy of the artist and acb Gallery, Budapest

cat. no. 15
Flying Fish Pyramid -
A Floating Water Habitat, 1984
White ink with gold dusting on Arches cover
black, hand-pulled lithograph; 863 × 1397 mm
Ludwig Museum, Budapest, inv. no. 2009.19.1

cat. no. 16
Isometric Systems in Isotropic Space -
Map Projections: Pyramidal Projection
(Budapest version), 1973/2018
Archival inkjet print on paper; 943 × 883 mm
Courtesy of the artist and acb Gallery, Budapest

cat. no. 17
Isometric Systems in Isotropic Space -
Map Projections: The Hot Dog, 1976
Four-colour lithograph on Rives BFK paper;
745 × 1041 mm
Courtesy of the artist, Leslie Tonkonow
Artworks + Projects, New York,
and acb Gallery, Budapest

cat. no. 18
Isometric Systems in Isotropic Space -
Map Projections: The Dodecahedron, 1976
Ink and graphite on graph paper
with printed Mylar overlay; 278 × 216 mm
Courtesy of the artist, Leslie Tonkonow
Artworks + Projects, New York,
and acb Gallery, Budapest

cat. no. 19
Isometric Systems in Isotropic Space -
Map Projections: The Snail, 1978
Lithograph on Rives BFK paper; 755 × 922 mm
Courtesy of the artist, Leslie Tonkonow
Artworks + Projects, New York,
and acb Gallery, Budapest

cat. no. 20
Isometric Systems in Isotropic Space -
Map Projections: The Egg, 1976
Four-colour lithograph on Rives BFK paper;
939 × 736 mm
Courtesy of the artist, Leslie Tonkonow
Artworks + Projects, New York,
and acb Gallery, Budapest

cat. no. 21
Map Projections: The Snail, 1974
Coloured pencil on printed paper; 276 × 323 mm
Courtesy of the artist and acb Gallery, Budapest

cat. no. 22
Isometric Systems in Isotropic Space -
Map Projections: The Cube, 1986
Lithograph in three colours on hand-made paper
with metallic dusting and hand-colouring;
922 × 635 mm
AELA Collection

cat. no. 23
Study of Distortions; Isometric Systems
in Isotropic Space - Map Projections:
The Cube, 1975
Watercolour on graph paper with Mylar overlay;
266 × 210 mm
Courtesy of the artist, Leslie Tonkonow
Artworks + Projects, New York,
and acb Gallery, Budapest

cat. no. 24
Isometric Systems in Isotropic Space
- Map Projections: The Doughnut, 1980
India and metallic inks on rag paper
with printed Mylar overlay; 278 × 214 mm
Courtesy of the artist, Leslie Tonkonow
Artworks + Projects, New York,
and acb Gallery, Budapest

cat. no. 25
Rice/Tree/Burial Project (Original Creation
in Sullivan County, New York), 1968/2009
Set of nine archival inkjet prints on paper;
114 × 114 mm each
Courtesy of the artist, Leslie Tonkonow
Artworks + Projects, New York,
and acb Gallery, Budapest

cat. no. 26
Rice/Tree/Burial Project (Original Creation
Artpark Lewiston, New York), 1977–1979/2012
Set of 39 B&W archival photographs on fiber
based paper; 254 × 203 and 203 × 254 mm each
Courtesy of the artist, Leslie Tonkonow
Artworks + Projects, New York,
and acb Gallery, Budapest

cat. no. 27
Wheatfield - A Confrontation:
Battery Park Landfill, Downtown Manhattan -
Before Planting, 1982/2024
Type C-print on paper; 324 × 487 mm
Courtesy of the artist, Leslie Tonkonow
Artworks + Projects, New York,
and acb Gallery, Budapest

cat. no. 28
Wheatfield - A Confrontation:
Battery Park Landfill, Downtown Manhattan -
Aerial View, 1982/2024
Type C-print on paper; 406 × 508 mm
Courtesy of the artist, Leslie Tonkonow
Artworks + Projects, New York,
and acb Gallery, Budapest

cat. no. 29
Wheatfield - A Confrontation:
Battery Park Landfill, Downtown Manhattan -
Green Wheat, 1982/2024
Type C-print on paper; 406 × 508 mm
Courtesy of the artist, Leslie Tonkonow
Artworks + Projects, New York,
and acb Gallery, Budapest

cat. no. 30
Wheatfield - A Confrontation:
Battery Park Landfill, Downtown Manhattan -
Golden Wheat 2, 1982/2024
Type C-print; 406 × 508 mm
Courtesy of the artist, Leslie Tonkonow
Artworks + Projects, New York,
and acb Gallery, Budapest

cat. no. 31
Wheatfield - A Confrontation:
Battery Park Landfill, Downtown Manhattan -
Blue Sky, World Trade Center, 1982/2024
Type C-print on paper; 406 × 508 mm
Courtesy of the artist, Leslie Tonkonow
Artworks + Projects, New York,
and acb Gallery, Budapest

cat. no. 32
Wheatfield - A Confrontation:
Battery Park Landfill, Downtown Manhattan
- With Statue of Liberty Across the Hudson,
1982/2024
Type C-print on paper; 324 × 487 mm
Courtesy of the artist, Leslie Tonkonow
Artworks + Projects, New York,
and acb Gallery, Budapest

cat. no. 33
Wheatfield - A Confrontation:
Battery Park Landfill, Downtown Manhattan -
With New York Financial Center, 1982/2024
Type C-print; 406 × 508 mm
Courtesy of the artist, Leslie Tonkonow
Artworks + Projects, New York,
and acb Gallery, Budapest

cat. no. 34
Wheatfield - A Confrontation:
Battery Park Landfill, Downtown Manhattan
- With Artist Photographing in the Field,
1982/2024
Type C-print; 508 × 406 mm
Courtesy of the artist, Leslie Tonkonow
Artworks + Projects, New York,
and acb Gallery, Budapest

cat. no. 35
Wheatfield - A Confrontation:
Battery Park Landfill, Downtown Manhattan -
Ocean Liner Passing Wheatfield on the
Hudson, 1982/2024
Type C-print on paper; 324 × 487 mm
Courtesy of the artist, Leslie Tonkonow
Artworks + Projects, New York,
and acb Gallery, Budapest

cat. no. 36
Wheatfield - A Confrontation:
Battery Park Landfill, Downtown Manhattan -
Cloudy Sky, 1982/2024
Type C-print; 406 × 508 mm
Courtesy of the artist, Leslie Tonkonow
Artworks + Projects, New York,
and acb Gallery, Budapest

cat. no. 37
Wheatfield - A Confrontation:
Battery Park Landfill, Downtown Manhattan -
With Agnes Denes Standing in the Field, 1982
Type C-print; 406 × 508 mm
Photo: John McGrail
Courtesy of the artist, Leslie Tonkonow
Artworks + Projects, New York,
and acb Gallery, Budapest

cat. no. 38
Wheatfield - A Confrontation:
Battery Park Landfill, Downtown Manhattan -
The Harvest, 1982/2024
Type C-print on paper; 406 × 508 mm
Courtesy of the artist, Leslie Tonkonow
Artworks + Projects, New York,
and acb Gallery, Budapest

cat. no. 39
Wheatfield - A Confrontation:
Battery Park Landfill, Downtown Manhattan -
Harvest with Sailboat, 1982/2024
Type C-print; 406 × 508 mm
Courtesy of the artist, Leslie Tonkonow
Artworks + Projects, New York,
and acb Gallery, Budapest

cat. no. 40
Wheatfield - A Confrontation:
Battery Park Landfill, Downtown Manhattan -
Aerial View 2, 1982/2024
Type C-print; 406 × 508 mm
Courtesy of the artist, Leslie Tonkonow
Artworks + Projects, New York,
and acb Gallery, Budapest

cat. no. 41
Wheatfield - A Confrontation:
Battery Park Landfill, Downtown Manhattan -
Green Wheat Turning Yellow, 1982/2024
Type C-print; 406 × 508 mm
Courtesy of the artist, Leslie Tonkonow
Artworks + Projects, New York,
and acb Gallery, Budapest

cat. no. 42
Tree Mountain - A Living Time Capsule -
11,000 Trees, 11,000 People, 400 Years
(Triptych) 1992-1996, 1992-1996/2013
Type C-print on paper; 914 × 914 mm
Courtesy of the artist, Leslie Tonkonow
Artworks + Projects, New York,
and acb Gallery, Budapest

cat. no. 43
Tree Mountain - A Living Time Capsule -
Ylöjärvi Finland, 1992-1996/2013
Archival inkjet print on resin coated paper;
638 × 914 mm
Private Collection

cat. no. 44
The Future is Fragile, Handle With Care, 2021
Dye sublimation print on polyester with blue
nylon appliqué; 110 × 194 cm
Museum of Fine Arts Budapest, Department
of Art after 1800, inv. no. 2022.1.1.U

cat. no. 45
The Kingdom Series: X-Ray of Roses, 1980
Five-colour hand-printed silkscreen with
metallic inks on paper; 1067 × 749 mm
Courtesy of the artist, Leslie Tonkonow
Artworks + Projects, New York,
and acb Gallery, Budapest

cat. no. 46
The Kingdom Series: X-Ray of Columbine, 1980
Five-colour silkscreen with metallic inks
and hand colouring on paper; 1067 × 749 mm
Courtesy of the artist, Leslie Tonkonow
Artworks + Projects, New York,
and acb Gallery, Budapest

cat. no. 47
The Kingdom Series: X-Ray of Calla Lilies, 1980
Five-colour silkscreen with metallic inks
and hand colouring on paper; 1041 × 743 mm
Courtesy of the artist, Leslie Tonkonow
Artworks + Projects, New York,
and acb Gallery, Budapest

cat. no. 48
The Kingdom Series: X-Ray of Sting Ray, 1980
Four-color silkscreen with metallic ink
on paper; 1041 × 739 mm
Courtesy of the artist, Leslie Tonkonow
Artworks + Projects, New York,
and acb Gallery, Budapest

cat. no. 49
The Kingdom Series: X-Ray of Seahorses, 1980
Four-colour silkscreen with metallic ink
and hand colouring on paper; 1066 × 739 mm
Courtesy of the artist, Leslie Tonkonow
Artworks + Projects, New York,
and acb Gallery, Budapest

cat. no. 50
Anima/Persona - The Seed (white), 1978-1980/2019
Type C-print on paper; 914 × 978 mm
Courtesy of the artist, Leslie Tonkonow
Artworks + Projects, New York,
and acb Gallery, Budapest

cat. no. 51
Anima/Persona - The Seed (black), 1978-1980/2019
Type C-print on paper; 914 × 978 mm
Courtesy of the artist, Leslie Tonkonow
Artworks + Projects, New York,
and acb Gallery, Budapest

cat. no. 52
The Ghost of Nautilus: The Soul of an Image, 2014
Archival inkjet pigment print on rag paper;
291 × 381 cm
Courtesy of the artist and
acb Gallery, Budapest

cat. no. 53
The Artist's Hand, 1971
Ink on paper; 279 × 206 mm
Courtesy of the artist, Leslie Tonkonow
Artworks + Projects, New York,
and acb Gallery, Budapest

cat. no. 54
Hand Color #1, 1971
Ink on paper; 279 × 206 mm
Courtesy of the artist, Leslie Tonkonow
Artworks + Projects, New York,
and acb Gallery, Budapest

cat. no. 55
The Butterfly Effect, 2022
Archival pigment print on Hahnemühle Fine Art
Pearl paper; 742 × 660 mm
Courtesy of the artist, Leslie Tonkonow
Artworks + Projects, New York,
and acb Gallery, Budapest

cat. no. 56
Everything Realized, 2020-2021
Archival inkjet pigment print on rag paper;
215 × 280 mm
Private Collection

cat. no. 57
Purple Rhapsody, 2020-2021
Archival inkjet pigment print on rag paper;
215 × 280 mm
Collection of Erika Kiss and Zsolt Lakatos

cat. no. 58
Butterfly Experiments in Grey, 2015
Archival inkjet print on rag paper;
406 × 485 mm
Courtesy of the artist and acb Gallery, Budapest

cat. no. 59
Butterfly Experiments in Blue, 2015
Archival inkjet print on rag paper;
406 × 508 mm
Courtesy of the artist and acb Gallery, Budapest

cat. no. 60
The Human Argument, 1969/2013
Hand-pulled lithograph on Fabriano cream
or white paper; 622 × 508 mm
Courtesy of the artist, Leslie Tonkonow
Artworks + Projects, New York,
and acb Gallery, Budapest

VIDEOS, ARCHIVE SLIDES, DOCUMENTS

cat. no. 61
Documentation of Tree Mountain -
A Living Time Capsule - 11,000 Trees,
11,000 People, 400 Years
1992-1996, 2019
Single channel digital video; 4'27"
Produced by The Shed, New York
© Agnes Denes, Courtesy Leslie Tonkonow
Artworks + Projects

cat. no. 62
Wheatfield - A Confrontation, 1982 (2023)
Single-channel, digital video; 12'19"
© Agnes Denes, Courtesy Leslie Tonkonow
Artworks + Projects

cat. no. 63
Healing Arts London: "The Future is Fragile,
Handle with Care." Agnes Denes
flag installation
Single channel digital video; 2'58"
© *Produced by CULTURUNNERS and supported*
by Vivobarefoot and Community Jameel

cat. no. 64
Agnes Denes - The Living Pyramid, 2015,
Socrates Sculpture Park, New York
Single channel digital video; 2'06"
© Courtesy of Socrates Sculpture Park, New York

cat. no. 65
Agnes Denes, Selected archival slides
from the DAAD Artists-in-Berlin Archive.
Images with the support of DAAD
Artists-in-Berlin Archive
© DAAD Berliner Künstlerprogramm Archívum
© Agnes Denes, Courtesy Leslie Tonkonow
Artworks + Projects

cat. no. 66
Manifesto
Created by Harvard University for Agnes Denes's
retrospective exhibition at The Shed, New York
City, 2019-2020
Courtesy of the artist and acb Gallery, Budapest

List of Illustrations

fig. 13
*Isometric Systems in Isotropic Space -
Map Projections: The Snail*, 1976
Loloured litograph on paper, 745.2 × 914.4 mm
© Agnes Denes, Courtesy Leslie Tonkonow
Artworks + Projects

fig. 14
Rice/Tree/Burial Project (Rice Planting)
(Original Creation Artpark Lewiston, New York),
1977-1979/2012 [cat. no. 26]
© Agnes Denes, Courtesy Leslie Tonkonow
Artworks + Projects

fig. 15
*Wheatfield - A Confrontation: Battery Park
Landfill*, Downtown Manhattan - With Statue
of Liberty Across the Hudson - 2, 1982
Type C-print on paper, 324 × 487 mm
© Agnes Denes, Courtesy Leslie Tonkonow
Artworks + Projects

fig. 16
Noah's Ark - A Spaceship (Proposal for Miami
International Airport and North Waterfront
Park), 1982
Pencil, watercolor on vellum, 1232 × 895 mm
© Agnes Denes, Courtesy Leslie Tonkonow
Artworks + Projects

fig. 17
The Future is Fragile, Handle With Care, 2021
[cat. no. 44]
© Agnes Denes, Courtesy Leslie Tonkonow
Artworks + Projects

fig. 18
Rice/Tree/Burial Project (Rice Planting)
(Original Creation Artpark Lewiston, New York),
1977-1979/2012 [cat. no. 26]
© Agnes Denes, Courtesy Leslie Tonkonow
Artworks + Projects

fig. 19
*Wheatfield - A Confrontation: Battery Park
Landfill*, Downtown Manhattan - Cloudy Sky,
1982/2024 [cat. no. 36]
© Agnes Denes, Courtesy Leslie Tonkonow
Artworks + Projects

fig. 20
The Living Pyramid, 2015/2017
documenta 14, Kassel, Germany
Wood, paint, soil, grasses, flowers, vegetables
914 × 914 × 914 cm
© Agnes Denes, Courtesy Leslie Tonkonow
Artworks + Projects

fig. 21
*Rice/Tree/Burial Project (Burial of the Time
Capsule)*, (Original Creation Artpark Lewiston,
New York), 1977-1979/2012 [cat. no. 26]
© Agnes Denes, Courtesy Leslie Tonkonow
Artworks + Projects

fig. 22
*Tree Mountain - A Living Time Capsule -
11,000 Trees, 11,000 People, 400 Years -
Winter View*, 1992-1996
Documentary Photograph
© Agnes Denes, Courtesy Leslie Tonkonow
Artworks + Projects

fig. 23
*Tree Mountain - A Living Time Capsule -
11,000 Trees, 11,000 People, 400 Years -
Summer view*, 1992-1996
Documentary Photograph
© Agnes Denes, Courtesy Leslie Tonkonow
Artworks + Projects

fig. 24
Wheatfield - A Confrontation, 1982 (2023)
Single-channel, digital video, 12'19"
(still from the video)
© Agnes Denes, Courtesy Leslie Tonkonow
Artworks + Projects

fig. 25
Antarctic Time Capsules, 1980-1986
Mixed media, 610 × 825 mm
Photo: Agnes Denes
© Agnes Denes, Courtesy Leslie Tonkonow
Artworks + Projects

fig. 26
*Isometric Systems in Isotropic Space - Map
Projections: Pyramidal Projection*, 1973/2018
Archival inkjet prints on board
The Phillips Collection, Washington, D.C., USA
© Agnes Denes, Courtesy Leslie Tonkonow
Artworks + Projects

fig. 27
*Bird Project — A Visual Investigation
of Systems in Motion*, 1948/1979
Environmental project, mixed media
Photo: Agnes Denes
© Agnes Denes, Courtesy Leslie Tonkonow
Artworks + Projects

fig. 28
*Systems of Logic / Logic of Systems:
The Human Argument in Steel & Crystal With
Sundial* — Finalist Drawing for University City
Science Center Philadelphia, 1988
Ink and Metallic ink on Mylar, 609 × 832 mm
© Agnes Denes, Courtesy Leslie Tonkonow
Artworks + Projects

fig. 29
*Systems of Logic / Logic of Systems: Elliptical
Superstructure* — Finalist Drawing for
University City Science Center Philadelphia,
1988
Silver and India ink on Mylar, 569 × 762 mm
© Agnes Denes, Courtesy Leslie Tonkonow
Artworks + Projects

fig. 30
*Stelae — Messages From Another
Time — Discoveries of Minds and People*, 1986
Hand carved white Carrara and pink Portugese
marble, 175.2 × 94 × 15.2 cm;
157.5 × 104.1 × 12.7 cm
Permanent Installation: Bucknell University,
Lewiston, Pennsylvania, USA
© Agnes Denes, Courtesy Leslie Tonkonow
Artworks + Projects

fig. 31
Noah's Ark - Proposal for Miami International
Airport and North Waterfront Park, 1982
Pencil, watercolor on vellum, 1231 × 1153 m
© Agnes Denes, Courtesy Leslie Tonkonow
Artworks + Projects

fig. 32
Sound Sculpture for Tidal Pool
- North Waterfront Park Plan, 1989
Pencil and charcoal on tracing vellum,
305 × 406 mm
© Agnes Denes, Courtesy Leslie Tonkonow
Artworks + Projects

fig. 33
Nautilus Amphitheater
- North Waterfront Park Plan, 1990
Pencil on paper
© Agnes Denes, Courtesy Leslie Tonkonow
Artworks + Projects

fig. 34
Amphitheaters and Sculpted View Mounds
- North Waterfront Park Plan, 1989
Pencil, colored pencil and watercolor
on tracing vellum, 305 × 406 mm
© Agnes Denes, Courtesy Leslie Tonkonow
Artworks + Projects

fig. 35
Duckpond - Design for Wildlife Preserve and
Research Center, Columbus, Ohio, USA, 1992
Pencil, watercolor on vellum, 279 × 355 mm
© Agnes Denes, Courtesy Leslie Tonkonow
Artworks + Projects

**Agnes Denes
Selected Bibliography:
Articles, Books, and Reviews**

2024 "Artists Confronting the Climate Crisis." *Gagosian Quarterly* (Fall 2024): 119.
_ Phaidon Editors. *Great Women Sculptors*. Phaidon Press, 2024, 80.
_ Pofolla, Boris. "Reiche Ernte." *Monopol: Special Issue Art Basel* (2024): 43-43.
_ Riepenhoff, John, ed. *Nature Doesn't Know About Us*. Exhibition catalogue. Sculpture Milwaukee, 4-11.
_ "Messeplatz." *Annabelle* (May 2024): 67.
_ Rosenberg, Douglas. *Staring at the Sky: Essays on Art and Culture*. 1st ed. 2024, Scandinavia
_ Book, 2024, 354, 393, 394.
2023 *Future Is With Us: Our Ecology Toward a Planetary Living Catalogue*. Mori: Mori Art Museum, 2023, 148-61.
_ *How is Life? Designing For Our Earth*. Eds. Yoshiharu Tsukamoto - Manabu Chiba - Seng Kuan - Tsuyoshi Tane. Tokyo: TOTO Publishing, 2023, 315-26.
_ *Enxtreme Tension: Art Between Politics and Society 1945-2000. Collection of the Nationalgalerie*. Eds. Joachim Jäger - Marta Smolińska - Maike Steinkamp. Seemann Henschel GmbH & Co., Leipzig, 2023, 182-87.
_ "Power 100." *ArtReview*,

(December 2023): 71.
_ *Territories of Waste*. Basel: Museum Tinguely, 2022, cover, 40-47.
_ Pardo, Alona. *RE/SISTERS: A Lens on Gender and Ecology*. Barbican Art Gallery. Prestel Publishing, London, 2023, 21, 42, 43.
_ Cassie, Packard. *Art Rules: How Great Artists Think, Create and Work*. London: Frances Lincoln, 2023, 34-35.
_ Liberty, Megan N. *Craft and Conceptual Art*. New York: Center for Book Arts, 2023.
_ Meaker, Abbey. "Entering A World of Concerns, Survival Structures For Humanity." *Autre* no. 16 (2023): 32-33.
2022 Findlay, Michael. *The Value of Art*. National Geographic Books, 2022, 245.
_ Ramade, Bénédicte. *Vers un art anthropocène*. Les Presses du réel, 2022, 171-74.
_ *Balance: 1970-1990: Kunst Gesellschaft, Umwelt*. Kunstmuseum Solothurn. Exhibition catalogue. Solothurn, 2022, 96, 97.
_ Hessel, Katy. *The Story of Art Without Men*. Hutchinson Heinemann, London, 2022. 329, 371-72.
_ Denes, Agnes. "A Manifesto." *Palais de Tokyo Magazine* (2022): 156.
_ "Land Art." *Harper's Bazaar* (Summer 2022): 64.
2019 Saltz, Jerry. "12 Great Things to Do, Through

November 27." *New York Magazine*, November 11-24, 2019.
_ Cotter, Holland. "At 88, Agnes Denes Finally Gets the Retrospective She Deserves." *The New York Times*, November 7, 2019.
_ McCormick-Goodhart, Emma. "If the Earth Were a Hot Dog: A Conversation with Agnes Denes." *Frieze*, October 31, 2019.
_ Midgette, Anne. "Neglected visionary Agnes Denes altered our landscape with her art. At 88, she's finally getting her due." *The Washington Post*, October 24, 2019.
_ Gruenhaeuser, Amber. "Agnes Denes: Ecological Vibrations." *Lodown Magazine* (October-December 2019).
_ Wally, Maxine. "Fifty Years Ago, Agnes Denes Predicted What Climate Change Could Do." *WWD*, October 15, 2019.
_ Minutillo, Josephine. "Expansive Agnes Denes Restrospective Opens at The Shed in New York." *Architectural Record*, October 9, 2019.
_ Cohen, Alina. "Agnes Denes's Manhattan Wheatfield Has Only Grown More Poignant." *Artsy*, October 15, 2019.
_ Richard, Frances. "I Stand in My Place With My Own Day Here: Site-Specific Art at The New School." *The New School* (October 2019).
_ Harvard School of Design. "Pioneering conceptual artist Agnes Denes

addresses the students of the Harvard Graduate School of Design." *Harvard University Graduate School of Design*, April 19, 2019.

_ Haeg, Fritz. "Life with the Land: Fritz Haeg." *Frieze* (September 2019).

_ Block, Annie. "'Agnes Denes: Absolutes and Intermediates' to Open at The Shed." *Interior Design*, September 27, 2019.

_ *Great Women Artists*. Intr. Rebecca Morrill. New York: Phaidon.

_ O'Neill-Butler, Lauren. "Land of the Living." *Artforum* (October 2019).

_ Schwarz, Gabrielle. "Q&A." *Apollo*, September 2019.

_ Dorris, Jesse. "Now is the Time to Get Into Land Art Pioneer Agnes Denes." *Elle*, July 2, 2019.

_ Tarmy, James. "Where to Invest $1 Million in Art Right Now." *Bloomberg*, May 2, 2019.

_ Sandhofer, Margareta. "50 Jahre Land Art." *KunstMagazin Parnass* (March 2019).

_ Sato, Alcira. "Agnes Denes: Agitadora de la naturaleza." *Endemico* (March 2019).

_ Trier Norden, Stine, and Søren Rud. *2030 Now*, Life Publishing, March 2019.

_ Cascone, Sarah. "As Bloomberg Mulls a Presidential Run, His Namesake Art Shed Will Open With an Ambitious - And Decidedly Woke - Lineup." *Artnet News*, January 9, 2019.

2018 *Bookmarks: Revisiting Hungarian Art of the 1960s an 1970s*. Ed. Katalin Székely. London: Koenig Books, 2018.

_ O'Grady, Megan. "Women Land Artists Get Their Day in the Museum." *The New York Times: Style Magazine*, November 21, 2018.

_ Kwong, Lily. "Reap What You Sow." *Cultured Magazine* (October 2018).

_ Steel, Carolyn. "Hungry for Change." *The Architectural Review* (October 2018).

_ Applin, Jo. *Lee Lozano: Not Working*. New Haven: Yale University Press, 2018.

_ Jacobs, Karrie. "The Woman Who Harvested a Wheat Field Off Wall Street." *The New York Times: Style Magazine*, June 14, 2018.

_ Travis, Rebecca. "The Story of Public Art in New York City." *Apollo*, February 20, 2018.

_ Obrist, Hans Ulrich. "Ein Weites Feld." *Das Magazine*, January 27, 2018.

_ Bailey, Stephanie and Woytiuk, Mark. "Remembering What is Not Gone: Towards a Feminist Counter Monument." *The Site Magazine* vol. 38 (May 2018).

_ *All Borders Are Temporary*. Film programme. Curator: Brynjar Bjerkem. Transnational Arts Production, Norway, 2018.

2017 Moll, Sebastian. "Miss Universum." *Monopol* (September 2017).

_ Valentine, Ben. "How Can Ecological Artists Move Beyond Aesthetic Gestures?" *Hyperallergic*, August 27, 2017.

_ Gottesman, Sarah. "10 Female Land Artists You Should Know." *Artsy*, July 18, 2017.

_ Russeth, Andrew. "Flower of the Flock: 'The Living Pyramid' in Kassel." *ArtNews* (June 2017).

_ Forbes, Alexander. "15 Documenta Artists with Staying Power." *Artsy Editorial* (June 2017).

_ *Universe: Exploring the Astronomical World*, Ed. David Malin. Phaidon Press, New York, 2017.

_ Zeunert, Joshua. *Landscape Architecture and Environmental Sustainability: Creating Positive Change Through Design*. Bloomsbury Visual Arts, London, 2017.

_ Kerr, Dylan. "Put a Lid on Creativity: Visionary Eco-Artist Agnes Denes on Her Dauntless Quest to Understand the Universe." *Artspace* (January 2017).

_ Minujin, Marta. "Kasseler Revolte." *Monopol* (July 2017).

2016 Mileaf, Janine. "The Arts Club of Chicago at 100: Art and Culture 1916-2016." *Arts Club Of Chicago* (November 2016).

_ Filippone, Christine. *Science, Technology, and Utopias: Women Artists and Cold War America*. London: Routledge, 2016.

_ Hodge, Susie. *Why is Art Full of Naked People?: And other vital questions about art*. London: Thames & Hudson, 2016.

_ *Art in Unexpected Places II*. Aspen: Aspen Art Press, 2016.

_ *Agnes Denes: Work 1969-2013*. Ed. Florence Derieux. Reims. Milan: Mousse Publishing, 2016.

_ *Art at Work*. Ed. Lisa K. Erf. JPMorgan Chase, 2016.

_ Goodman, Jonathan. "New York: Agnes Denes - Socrates Sculpture Park." *Sculpture* (March 2016).

_ Topaloff, Anna. "Sublime, L'Exposition Écolo." *Le Cahier de Tendances de l'Obs* no. 12 (February 2016).

_ Jenkins, Mark. "In the galleries: Works on paper at Marsha Mateyka Gallery." *The Washington Post*, January 15, 2016.

2015 Gamwell, Lynn. *Mathematics and Art*. Princeton: Princeton University Press, 2015, 120.

_ O'Neill-Butler, Lauren. "Critics' Picks, October 2015." *Artforum* (October 2015).

_ McCoy, Ann. "Agnes Denes *Living Pyramid*." *The Brooklyn Rail*, September 8, 2015.

_ "Agnes Denes, *Living Pyramids* 2015: Socrates Sculptural Park." *Sculpture* vol. 34, no. 6 (July/August 2015).

_ Hoban, Phoebe. "Works In Progress." *The New York Times: Style Magazine*, May 17, 2015.

_ Yablonsky, Linda. "Young at

Art." *W Magazine* (May 2015).

_ Pollack, Maika. "Agnes Denes." *Interview Magazine* (May 2015).

_ Cascone, Sarah. "Agnes Denes to Build Living Pyramid at Socrates Sculpture Park." *artnetnews*, March 17, 2015.

_ Anastasio, Giambattista. "Lo Show A Migalia Contandini Per Un Giorno Sotto I Grattacieli: Che ne sau tu di un campo di grano." *QN Quotidiano Nazionale*, March 1, 2015.

_ Tiziana Lapelosa. "L'iniziativa nel quartiere Porta Nuova: In cinquemila a seminare il grano tra i grattacieli." *LiberoMilano*, March 1, 2015.

_ "In 5 mila per la semina del campo di grano." *Il Giornale Milano*, March 1, 2015.

_ "Milano, firmato Trussardi il grano tra I grattacieli." *L'eco Di Bergamo*, March 20, 2015.

_ "Piccolo Contadini A Milano." *La Gazzetta dello Sport*, March 1, 2015.

_ "Porto Marx alla Biennale perché parla di noi oggi." *La Stampa*, March 1, 2015.

_ "Porta Nuova. In piú di 5mila per la semina di Wheatfield." *Avvenire*, March 1, 2015.

_ "Porta Nuova Parla Catella: presto alter operazioni con il Qatar." *Corriere Della Sera Milano*, March 1, 2015.

_ "Mailander haben Landlust." *Art Investor*

(March 2015).

_ Pappalardo, Dario. "Denes: La mia arte? Tante spighe dentro Milano." *La Republica*, February 23, 2015.

2014 Filippone, Christine. *Science, Technology, and Utopias in the Work of Contemporary Women Artists*. Farnham: Ashgate Press, 2014.

_ Bailey, Stephanie. "Agnes Denes. Firstsite/Colchester." *FlashArt International* (March-April 2014).

_ Homer, Nicola. "Agnes Denes: Interview. A Visionary Artist." *Studio International* (March 2014).

2013 Lescaze, Zoe. "Sandwoman." *The New York Observer*, July 22, 2013.

_ Kozinn, Allan. "Environmental Expo Coming to MoMA PS1." *The New York Times*, March 8, 2013.

_ Swenson, Kristen. "Agnes Denes." *Art in America* (March 2013).

_ Chianese, Robert Louis. "Regeneration on *Tree Mountain*." *American Scientist* (September-October 2013).

_ "Out of the Gallery and Into the Real World." *Flash Art* (July-September 2013).

_ Rawes, Peg. *Relational Architectural Ecologies, Architecture Nature and Subjectivity*. Routledge, 2013.

_ Steadman, Ryan E. "Agnes Denes." *Modern Painters* (March 2013).

_ Davis, Ben. "Agnes Denes's

Sly Eco-Conceptualism Seems More Relevant Than Ever." *ArtInfo*, January 10, 2013.

_ Davis, Ben. "In Defense of Concepts." *9.5 Theses on Art and Class*, Chicago: Haymarket Books, 2013.

_ Stillman, Nick. "Agnes Denes, Santa Monica Museum of Art." *Artforum* (January 2013).

_ Plagens, Peter. "Coloring In Lines of Humanity." *The Wall Street Journal Weekend*, January 5-6, 2013.

_ *Land Art*. Eds. Floriane Herrero - Ambre Viaud. Paris: Editions Palette, 2013.

2012 *From Coneptualism to Feminism: Lucy Lippard's Number Shows 1969-74*. Ed. Cornelia Butler. London: Afterall Books, 2012.

_ Kino, Carol. "Stretching Her Creativity as Far as Possible." *The New York Times*, December, 2, 2012.

_ Johnson, Ken. "Agnes Denes, Sculptures of the Mind: 1968 to Now." *The New York Times*, November 23, 2012.

_ "Exhibit of the Week, Agnes Denes: Sculptures of the Mind - 1968 to Now." *The Week*, December 21, 2012.

_ Selz, Gabrielle. "Agnes Denes: Art Ad Infinitum." *The Huffington Post*, November 27, 2012.

_ Schwendener, Martha. "How Green Was My Alley." *The Village Voice*, June 19, 2012.

_ "Art + Ideology." *The Outlook Magazine* no. 123 (July 2012).

2011 Alonso, Rodrigo. *Sistemas, Acciones y Procesos 1965-1975*, Buenos Aires: Fund. Proa, 2011.

_ Davidson, Margaret. "*Contemporary Drawing - Key Concepts and Techniques*", New York: Watson-Gubtill Publications, 2011, 22-23, 30, 84-85, 88, 90-91.

_ Goldbard, Arlene. "Public Art as a Spiritual Path." *Public Art Review*, "Spirituality and Religion", no. 44 (Spring-Summer 2011): 18, 24, 25.

_ Keehn, Dorka. "*Eco-Amazons: 20 Women Who Are Transforming the World*." Brooklyn, New York: Powerhouse Books, 2011.

_ Knudsen, Palles Ellemann. "Respect the Planet - Everybody is Going Green." *Work Style*, (Spring 2011): 28-29.

2010 Kruk, Liedeke. "Portraits." Amsterdam: Roma Publications, 2010, 16-17.

_ Ole, Bouman - Abhelakh, Anneke - Zoeteman, Martine. "Architecture of Consequence-Dutch Designs of the Future)." Rotterdam: NAi010 Publishers, 2010.

_ Mircan, Mihnea. "History in the Present." *Manifesta Journal*, Journal of Contemporary Curatorship, no. 9. "Art History Interrupted" (2009-2010).

_ Firmin, Sandra Q. *Artpark: 1974-1984*. New York: Princeton Architectural Press, 2010, 35, 39, 98.

_ Barbaux, Sophie. *Jardins Ecologiques: Ecology, Source of Creation*. Paris: ICI Consultants, 2010.

_ Stillman, Nick. "Agnes Denes." (Leslie Tonkonow Artworks + Projects), in *Artforum International* vol. XLVIII, no. 6 (February 2010).

2009 Kuo, Michelle. "The Human Argument: The Writings of Agnes Denes." *Bookforum*, (February-March 2009).

2008 Weiss, Jeffery. "On the Road." *Artforum* (September 2008).

_ Rosenberg, Karen. "This Land is Her Land (and Her Artwork, Too)." *The New York Times*, June 13, 2008.

_ *The Human Argument - The Writings of Agnes Denes*. Ed. Klaus Ottmann. Putnam, Conn: Spring Publications, 2008.

_ Heartney, Eleanor. *Art & Today*. New York: Phaidon Press Ltd. 2008. 403, 406-7.

_ Green Attitude. *Lexus*, no. 37. (Spring 2008): 94.

_ Boettger, Suzaan. "Global Warnings." *Art in America*, no. 6. (June-July 2008): 159-60.

2007 *Art in Action - Nature, Creativity and Our Collective Future*. Eds. Achim Steiner - Randy Jayne Rosenberg. San Rafael, California: Natural Word Museum, United Nations Environment Programme (UNEP), 2007, 154.

_ Japanese Art at Yale. *Yale University Art*

Gallery Bulletin. Ed. Sadako Ohki. New Haven: The Japan Foundation (Agnes Denes: Latitude Lines of the Globe in the Form of a Pyramid, from Fragmentation, 1998), 2007, 221.

_ Wescher, Lawrence. "Fevered Imagination - Artistic Responses to Global Warming." *Special Issue: The Nation*, "Surviving the Climate Crisis, What Must Be Done", May 7, 2007, 38.

_ Gluckstern J. "Weather Report: Art and Climate Change." *Art Papers* (November - December 2007): 54.

_ Margonia, Gege. "Revisione del Tempo che Fara." *Casamica* no. 79 (November 2007).

_ Droitcour, Brian. "Critic's Pick - Decoys, Complexes, and Triggers: Feminism and land Art in the 1970s at Sculpture Center." *Artforum.com*, 2007.

_ Sholis, Brian. "Agnes Denes." *Artforum* (May 2007): 373.

_ "560 Broadway: A New York Drawing Collection at Work, 1991-2006." The Wynn Kramarsky Collection. Ed. Amy Eshoo. New Haven: Yale University Press - Fifth Floor Foundation, 2007. 29, 44-45, 152, 157, 161, 165, 173, 179.

_ Saltz, Jerry. "The Biggest Picture." *Village Voice*, February 1, 2007.

2006 Zuber, David. "Flanerie at Ground Zero: Aesthetic Countermemories in Lower Manhattan." *American Quarterly* vol. 58, no. 2 (June 2006).

_ Smit, Tim. "Imagination Holds the Key." *Resurgence* no. 238 (September - October 2006).

_ Dempsey, Amy. *"Destination Art"*, London: Thames & Hudson, 2006, 156, 157, 159, 264.

_ Selz, Peter. *Art of Engagement - Visual Politics in California and Beyond*. Berkeley and Los Angeles: University of California Press. 2006, 225, 285.

2005 Cook-Romero, Elizabeth. "Framing what cannot be tamed." *The New Mexican* (2005)..

_ Spica, Joyner Heather. "Fruits of Elaborate Vision." *Metro Pulse*, January 20, 2005, 28.

_ Tiberghien, Gilles A. "La nature dans l'art." Paris: Actes Sud, 2005.

_ Julia, Varadi. "Egy nyelv nélküli ember (Interview with Agnes Denes)." *Magyar Narancs*, vol. 17, nos. 50-51, December 15, 2005, 76, 77.

2004 Bentivoglio, Mirella. "Tre Incisori Americani." Viterbo: Galleria Miralli, 2004.

_ Browne, Sarah. "Green Concrete." *Context, Arts and Practice in Ireland*, *The Regeneration Issue* vol. 3, no. 3 (2004): 20-23.

_ Levin, Kim. "Show World." *Village Voice*, September 10, 2004.

_ McEvilley, Thomas. "Philosophy in the Land." *Art in America* vol. 92, no. 10 (November 2004): 158-63.

_ "Milestones." *Sculpture* vol. 23, no. 6 (July-August 2004): 58.

_ Mills, Dan. "Agnes Denes: A Retrospective: Looking Ahead." *New York Arts: Berliner Kunst* vol. 9, nos. 11-12 (November-December 2004): 38.

_ *Society of Fellows News.* Ed. Chaterine Seavitt. New York: American Academy of Rome (Spring 2004): 2, 35. Zoccoli. Franca. "Paesaggi logici con effetti personali." *Il Manifesto*, July 24, 2004.

2003 Berry, S.L. "Public art displays its ambitious scope." *Indystar*, September 19, 2003.

_ Auer, James. "Haggerty looks at an artist by - and of - nature." *Milwaukee Journal Sentinel*, September 29, 2003.

_ Cohen, Mark Daniel. "The Lyricism of Pure Thought: The Unity of Intelligence in the Art of Agnes Denes." *NYArts* (International Edition), vol. 8, no. 5 (May 2003): 63.

_ Heartney, Eleanor. "Cultivating Hope: The Visionary Art of Agnes Denes." In *Agnes Denes: Projects For Public Places-A Retrospective*. Exh. cat. Lewisburg, Pa.: Samek Gallery, Bucknell University, 2003.

_ Fons, Graham. "Art for Earth's Sake." *Shepherd*

Express, September 25-31,
2003.

_ "Land and Eco Art in the
USA." _Landscape and Art_.
Eds. Anne-Katrin Spiess
- Sue Labovie. no. 29
(Summer 2003): 31.

_ "Die Kunst der
Zukunftsfähigkeit." _Agenda-
Transfer_. Ed. Dr. Hildegard
Kurt. 2003, 38-41.

2002 "Cultivos Urbanos (Agnes
Denes: Campo de trigo una
confrontacion)." _Oeste_ vol.
15 (2002): 10-15.

2001 Cohen, Mark Daniel.
"The Reason in the
Art: The Role of the
Rational in the Aesthetic
Imagination." _NY Arts_
(International Edition),
vol. 6, nos. 7-8 (July-
August 2001): 58-59.

_ _Nothing_. Eds. Graham
Gussin - Ele Carpenter.
London,: August and
Northern Gallery for
Contemporary Art, 2001,
84-88.

_ Johnson, Ken. "Listings."
The New York Times, May 18,
2001.

_ McKenzie, Bryan. "Take
a walk among poets..."
in _The Daily Progress_,
Charlottesville, 2001.

2000 Selz, Peter.
"Reviews" (Agnes Denes,
Charlottesville)."
Sculpture vol. 19, no. 10
(2000): 77-78.

_ Buurma, Christine. "Poetry
Walk to display literary
talent." _The Cavalier
Daily_, April 24, 2000.

_ Ford, Jane. "Bringing art
to the surface." _Inside
UVA_, April 28, 2000.

_ Gilbert, Chris. "Hindsight/
Fore-site: Interpreting
Mr. Jefferson." _64_ vol. 1,
no. 7 (2000): 30, 34.

_ Levin, Kim. "Gaining
ground: a retrospective
view of art in nature and
nature in art." In _Trans
Plant: Living Vegetation
in Contemporary Art_. Ed.
Barbara Nemitz. Ostfildern
- Ruit: Hatje Cantz
Publisher, 2000, 13,
16, 42, 43f, 185.

_ Sutton, Beth.
"Environmental Art with
a Social Conscience"
(Agnes Denes, "Poetry
Walk: Reflections - Pools
of Thought", University
of Virginia). _64_ (August
2000): 34.

_ Close, Leslie Rose: "Women
Landscape Designers."
In _Women Designers in the
USA_. Ed. Pat Kirkham.
New Haven and London: Yale
University Press, 2000,
340-41.

1999 Barreto, Ricardo.
"Sculptural Conceptualism:
A New Reading of the Work
of Agnes Denes."
Sculpture vol. 18, no. 4
(May 2000): 16-23.

_ Sabine, Bartelsheim.
"Pflanzenkunstwerke.
Lebende Pflanzen in
der Kunst des 20.
Jahnhunderts." Doctoral
Thesis, Faculty of
Philosophy, University of
Cologne, Munich: Verlag
Silke Schreiber, 1999,
156, 159-62, 185.

_ _Lives and Works: Talks with
Women Artists_. Vol 2. Eds.
Joan Arbeiter - Beryl Smith

- Sally Shearer Swenson.
Lanham Md. & London:
The Scarecrow Press, 1999,
61-76.

_ Uchtrup, von Michael.
"Conjuring New Muses."
Art Papers (January-
February 1999).

_ Wasserman, Krystyna.
"Book as Art XI - Inside
the Artist's Book." _Women
in the Arts_ (Fall 1999):
18-19.

1998 "Agnes Denes." Galleria
Il Bulino, Rome, _Rova/
Roma_.

_ _Land and Environmental
Art_. Eds. Jeffrey Kastner
- Brian Wallis. London:
Phaidon Press, 1998, 160,
161, 261, 262, 289.

_ Mismetti Capua, Carlotta.
"Agnes Denes, Accademia
Americana. Gli orti della
cultura." _Time Out/Roma_
(July-August 1998): 30-32.

_ "Incontro con l'artista
Agnes Denes." (Un
iniziativa de "Stelle
Cadenti", Bassano in
Teverina) _L'Eco Della
Stampa_, no. 111, Milano,
April 24, 1998.

_ Lippard, R. Lucy. "Lure
of the Local: Senses of
Place in a Multicentered
Society." New York:
The New Press. 1998, 192.

_ Zevi, Adachiara. "La
filosofia visiva di Agnes
Denes." _L'Architettura_
no. 516 (October 1998).

1997 Selz, Peter. _Beyond
the Mainstream_. Cambridge,
Mass.: Cambridge University
Press, 1997, 9, 235-49,
308-9, 317.

_ Aberlin, Mary Beth.

"America the Digital." *The Sciences* (May-June 1997): 8.

_ Clark, James. "Fields for Thought: The Art of Agnes Denes." *Public Art Review*, Regarding Land (Spring-Summer 1997): 9-13.

_ Kevles, Bettyann Holtzmann. *Naked to the Bone*. New Brunswick: Rutgers University Press, 1997, 278-81, 279, 315.

1996 "Ahtisaarelle nimikkotaimi Puuvuoreen." *Aamulehti*, June 15, 1996.

_ "Ahtisaari instuttaa Ylöjärven Puuvuoren viimeisen puun tanään." *Aamulehti*, June   14, 1996.

_ "Ahtisaari instutti nimikkotaimensa." *Nokian Uutiset*, June 17, 1996.)

_ "Ahtisaaren kone oikkuili." *Pohjalainen*, June 15, 1996.

_ "Ahtisaaren lentokone lakkoili." *Helsingin Sanomat*, June 16, 1996.

_ "Arvokasta ympäristönhoitoa." *Nokian Uutiset*, June 17, 1996.

_ Hilska, Esko. "Ahtisaari ottaa osaa Ylöjärven ympäristöteokseen." *Keskisuomalainen*, June 13, 1996.

_ Joenniemi, Minna. "Ahtisaari tarjosi takkinsa Suoniolle." *Ilta-Sanomat*, June 15, 1996.

_ "Konevika viivästytti presidenttiä." *Hyvinkään Sanomat*, June 15, 1996.

_ Kuspit, Donald. "Agnes Denes: Joyce Goldstein Gallery." *Artforum International* 6 ("Tree Mountain - A Living Time Capsule"), (February 1996): 82.

_ Kuspit, Donald. *Idiosyncratic Identitites*. Cambridge, Mass.: Cambridge University Press, 1996, 109-20.

_ Kärkkäinen, Anne. "Lahjoja luonnolle ja ihmisille." *Vihreä Lanka*, June 20, 1996.

_ Koskinen, Sirpa. "Pirkanmaa." *Kansan Uutiset*, June 13, 1996.

_ *Le Repértoire Illustré de l'Art Environnemental*. Bruxelles: ISELP, Institut Supérieur pour l'Etude du Langage Plastique, 1996.

_ "Martikainen, Maire - Kalle Parkkinen. "Presidentti Ahtisaari instutti oman puunsa Puuvuoreen." *Iltalehti*, June 15, 1996.

_ "Martti Ahtisaari istutti nimikkopuun." *Uutisvuoksi*, June 16, 1996.

_ "Martti Ahtisaari instutti nimikkopuun." *Salon Seudun Sanomat*, June 15, 1996.

_ "Martti Ahtisaari institti nimikkopuun." *Savon Sanomat*, June 15, 1996.

_ Pitkänen , Ulla. "Puuvuori kaunistaa soramonttua Ylöjärvellä." *Helsingin Sanomat*, June 15, 1996.

_ "Presidentti Ahtisaari kuntavierailulle Ylöjärvelle." *Ylöjärven Sanomat*, June 13, 1996.

_ "Presidentti Ahtisaaren vierailu viivästyi." *Uudenkaupungin Sanomat*, June 15, 1996.

_ "Presidentti jaoutui vaihtamaan konetta." *Itä-Häme*, June 15, 1996.

_ "Presidentti jaoutui vaihtamaan konetta." *Kainuun Sanomat*, June 15, 1996.

_ "Puuta." *Suomen Kuvalehti*, June 14, 1996.

_ "Puuvuori kasvaa perinnöksi." *Aamulehti*, June 15, 1996.

_ "Puuvuori kuin jättiläismäinen muurahaiskeko." *Ylöjärven Sanomat*, June 6, 1996.

_ "Puuvuori muistuttaa ympäristöongelmista." *Kansan Uutiset*, June 18, 1996.

_ "Puuvuori paikkaa ympäristön arpia." *Etelä-Suomen Sanomat*, June 15, 1996.

_ "Puuvuori paikkaa ympäristön arpia." *Kouvolan Sanomat*, June 15, 1996.

_ "Puuvuori paikkaa ympäristön arpia." *Forssan Lehti*, June 15, 1996.

_ "Puuvuori vihitään perjantaina." *Nokian Uutiset*, June 12, 1996.

_ Salo, Seppo. "Puuvuori korjaa ihmisen jäljet." *Kotimaa*, June 20, 1996.

_ Smith, Beryl. *Lives and Works: Talks with Women Artists*. Vol 2. Eds. Joan Arbeiter - Sally Shearer Swenson. Lanham Md. & London: The Scarecrow Press, 1996, 61-76.

_ *Theories and Documents of Contemporary Art: a Sourcebook of Artists Writings*. Eds. Kristine Stiles - Peter Selz.

Berkeley and Los Angeles: University of California Press, 1996, 504, 540-45.
_ *Map*. Ed. Gilane Tawadros. (Agnes Denes: Isometric Systems in Isotropic Space-Map Projections.) London: Institute of International Visual Arts, 1996, 1, 1/24, 2/23, 24, 25, 26.
_ Tikkanen, Elisa Koonnut. "Vuori puusta." *Kodin Kuvalehti*, June 12, 1996.
_ Tuomi, Raimo. "Ahtisaari ei nouse Ylöjärven hiekkavuorelle." *Aamulehti*, June 7, 1996.
_ Vuori, Kristiina. "Vielakin Puuvuoresta." *Ylöjärven Sanomat*, June 13, 1996.
_ Wagner, Monika. "Gras, Steine, Erde. Naturspolien in der Zeitgenössischen Kunst." *Museums Kunde* vol. 61 (September 1996): 26-36.
_ "Ympäristötaideteos Ylöjärvelle." *Kristityn Vastuu*, June 13, 1996.
1995 *New Observations*. Ed. Dickerson, Paul. ("Isometric Systems in Isotropic Space - Map Projection I - Amorphous Continents," 1979), no. 105 (March-April 1995).
_ Kalil, Frederick. "Art: the Technology of Creative Expression." *Tufts Journal* no. 13 (March 1995): 6-7.
_ *Sculpting With the Environment*. Ed. Baile Oakes. New York: Van Nostrand Reinhold, 1995.
_ "The Pyramid Suite, 1993-94." *Print Collector's Newsletter*, no. 26 (May-

June 1995): 64.
_ Robinson, Walter. "Front Page: Tree Mountain in Finland." *Art in America* no. 83 (January 1995): 29.
1994 Bentivoglio, Mirella. "Agnes Denes: Wynn Kramarsky Studio." *Terzio Occhio* no. 20 (September 1995): 62.
_ "Land Art." *Temps El*, January 24, 1995, 92.
_ "L'art de la terra." *Nov Diari (Barna)*, January 21, 1995, 42.
_ *Art and the Public Sphere*. Ed. W. J. T. Mitchell. Chicago: University of Chicago Press, 1994.
1993 "Agnes Denes: A Retrospective." *The American Federation of Arts Exhibitions Program 1993-1994*. New York: The American Federation of Arts, 1994, 9.
_ Chayat, Sherry. "Agnes Denes." *ARTnews* (March 1995): 118.
_ *Contemporary Art*. Catalogue 97, Parts 1-2 (private collections of Robert Pinkus-Witten and Ellen Johnson). Boston: Ars Libri, 1993.
_ Heartney, Eleanor. "Agnes Denes at the Herbert F. Johnson Museum of Art." *Art in America* vol. 81 (April 1993): 135, 136.
_ Konno, Kumi. "Mirror of Memory." *Commercial Photo* (Agnes Denes: Wheatfield - A Confrontation and Tree Mountain), vol 12, no. 363 (1993).
_ Palk, Catherine. "Art, Science, Society With

Agnes Denes." *Cornell Daily Sun*, September 14, 1993.
_ "Introduction: Art and Social Consciousness." Special Issue: *Leonardo*. Ed. Sheila Pinkel. Vol. 26, no. 5 (1993): 365-66.
_ "Public Art with Function." *BT* vol. 76 (1993).
_ Tobia, Blaise - Virginia Maksymowicz: "Confronting New York's Trash. (Defense of Creation)." *The Witness* vol. 76, no. 6 (1993): 22-23.
1992 "Agnes Denes: A Retrospective." *At the Johnson* (Fall-Winter 1992): 5.
_ "Agnes Denes: a Retrospective." *Members' Newsletter* (Spring-Summer 1992): 3.
_ Adams, Barbara. "Denes's Paradox." *The Ithaca Times*, October 8, 1992. 11.
_ "Art and Ecology - Special Issue." *Art Journal*. Ed. Jackie Brookner. (Summer 1992): 11, 22-23.
_ Chayat, Sherry. "Agnes Denes: Herbert F. Johnson Museum of Art, Cornell University." *ARTnews* vol. 92 (March 1992): 118.
_ Chayat, Sherry. "Agnes Denes maps universe in space and time." *Syracuse Herald American*, October 4, 1992, 12.
_ "An Artist's Personal Statement on Spiral and Other Map Projections." In *Spiral Symmetry*. Eds. I. Hargittai - C. A. Pickover. Singapore and London: World Scientific Publishing Co. 1992, 387-391.

_ *Agnes Denes*. Ed. J. Hartz. Ithaca, N.Y.: Herbert F. Johnson Museum of Art, 1992.

_ Grossman, Mary. "New Medium for an Urgent Message." *St. Paul Pioneer Press*, March 1, 1992.

_ Kivirinta, Marja-Terttu. "Strata artist Agnes Denes underlines our responsibility to the earth-The sensitive artist is also a sensitizer." *Helsinkin Sanomat*, January 28, 1992.

_ Kivirinta, Marja-Terttu. "Urgent Demand for the Environmental Art of the 1990's." *Helsingin Sanomat*, March 28, 1992.

_ Paik, Catherine. "Art, Science, Society with Agnes Denes." *The Cornell Daily Sun*, September 14, 1992, 16.

_ Smagula, Howard. *Learning to Draw*. London - U.S.A.: Brown and Benchmark - John Calman & King, 1992.

_ Rosenblatt, Anna. "Agnes Denes: Using Art to Re-connect Humankind and Nature." *Ursus Profile* (Fall 1992): 21-24.

_ Tominen, Marjaana. "Strata Solves Environmental Issues." *Aamulehti*, March 27, 1992, 1, 14.

_ Tuominen, Maila-Katriina. "Nyt Saa Kysan Mita Se Tarkoittaa." *Aamulehti*, May 3, 1992.

_ Tominen, Maila-Katriina. "Trees Planted By Us Will Also Survive Us." *Aamulehti*, February 2, 1992.

_ Wallenstein, Sven-Olov - Erik van der Heeg. "Opposites Attract - An Interview with Agnes Denes." *Material* vol. 6 (1992).

1991 Cembalest, Robin. "The Ecological Art Explosion."*ARTnews* vol. 90 (Summer 1991).

_ Hall, Stephen. "Uncommon Landscapes - Maps in a New Age of Scientific Discovery." *The Sciences* (September-October 1991).

_ Stapen, Nancy. "Drawings at Brandeis ask profound questions." Living Arts Section, *Boston Globe*, March 22, 1991.

1990 Artner, Alan J. "Agnes Denes - Arts Club of Chicago." *Chicago Tribune*, June 22, 1991.

_ Green, Theodora. "Agnes Denes, The Arts Club of Chicago." *New Art Examiner* (September 1991).

_ Hartney, Eleanor. "Landfill Projects." *On View - A Journal of Public Art and Design* vol. 1 (Spring-Summer 1991): 52, 54-55.

_ Merrill, Jennifer. "The Environment by Design--Ecological Art." *ZPG* (Zero Population Growth) *Reporter* (1990): 3.

_ Neff, John. "On Public Art - Daring to Dream." *Critical Inquiry* vol. 16 (Summer 1990): 858.

_ Porges, Maria. "Book review of *Book of Dust*" *Contemporanea* vol. 3 (Summer 1990): 123.

_ "Building the Future." *Orion Nature Quarterly*, ed. George Russell, vol. 9 (Spring 1990): 52-55.

1989 Murray, Jeannette. "Religion, Reality, and Relativity: The Scientific Tradition in Art." *Encyclopedia Britannica: Yearbook of Science and the Future*. Chicago, 1989, 28-29.

_ "Religão, Realidade e Relatividade: A tradicao cientifica na Arte." In *Livro do Ano Ciencia e Futuro 1989, Encyclopaedia Britannica do Brazil*. São Paulo: Publicaciones Ltda., 1989, 89-91.

_ *Contemporary Artists*, 3rd edition, ed. Colin Naylor. London: St. James Press, 1989.

_ Oliver, Cordelia. "Maps and the Artist." In *Togail Tir - Marking Time - The Map of the Western Isles*. Ed. Finlay MacLeod. Isle of Lewis, Scotland: Acair Ltd., 1989, 145-48.

_ Princenthal, Nancy. "Artist's Book Beat." *Print Collector's Newsletter* vol. 20 (November-December 1989): 185.

_ Schwartz, Joyce Pomeroy. "Public Art." In *Encyclopedia of Architecture - Design, Engineering, and Construction*. Vol. 4. Ed. Joseph A. Wilkes. New York: The American Institute of Architects, 1989.

1988 Ahlström, Crispin. "Konst Mot Hunger." *Kultur, Göteborgs-Posten*, February 27, 1988.

"A Londra una grande mostra fino al 2 ottobre." *Il Gazzettino*, September 27, 1988.

"Konstnarer Malar for Svaltande Barn." *Dagens Nyheter*, February 23, 1988.

"Bilder gegen den Hunger." *Der Spiegel*, April 25, 1988.

Boehm, Rachel E. "Prominent Landscaper Hired for Waterfront Park." *Daily Californian*, January 29, 1988, 1-4.

Borgen, Trond. "Art Against Hunger in Solvberget - Food for Thought." *Stavanger Aftenblad*, January 27, 1988.

Cases, Helene. "Les Palettes de la Faim." *Le Quotidien de Paris*, July 18, 1988.

"The Debate - One Million B.C. to One Million A.D." *Evening News*, 1988.

"Gli artisti per la fame nel mondo." *Flash Art* vol. 145 (November 1988).

"Introspection I - Evolution - Art Exhibition." *Trentonian*, October 2, 1988.

Pouchard, Ennio. "Arte Contro Fame." *Il Gazzettino*, September 27, 1988.

Schindler, Jörg. "Kunst gegen Hunger." *Der Spiegel*, April 25, 1988.

Smith, Elisabeth M. "Earth-Shaping Designs." *Savvy* (June 1988): 16-17.

"Squibb celebrates 50th anniversary with exhibition." *Gazette*, September 22, 1988.

Watkins, Eileen. "Art." *Star Ledger*, October 28, 1988.

Wines, James. "Wheatfield - A Confrontation." *De-Architecture* (1988): 172.

1987 Martin, Mary Abbe. "Art Exhibition Aims a Blow at World Hunger." *Star-Tribune*, September 13, 1987.

Schwartzman, Allan. "Public Monuments." *Manhattan, Inc.* (August 1987): 13.

Selz, Peter. "Alternative Aesthetics: Quests for Spiritual Quintessence." *Arts Magazine* (October 1987): 47-49.

Sims, Lowery. "The Envelope, Please . . . The Experts Cast Their Votes." *ARTnews* (November 1987): 170.

1986 *Symmetry - Unifying Human Understanding*. Ed. Istvan Hargittai. London: Pergamon Press, 1986, 835-48.

1985 Castleman, Riva. *American Impressions: Prints Since Pollock*. New York: Alfred A. Knopf, 1985, 136-37.

Haga, Chuck. "Dakota Durum Helped a Bit of the Country Sprout in the City." *Grand Forks Herald*, April 14, 1985, 5a.

Haga, Chuck. "Food Holds Special Magic for City Slickers." *Farm and Home*, April 15, 1985, 44.

Lyon, Christopher. "Strange Hybrids Sprouting." *Chicago Sun-Times*, March 22, 1985, 62.

Selz, Peter. "Agnes Denes: The Visual Presentation of Meaning." In *Art in a Turbulent Era*. Ann Arbor: UMI Research Press, 1985.

1984 "Dialectic Triangulation." *Print Collectors Newsletter* no. 14 (January-February 1984): 213.

1983 Lippard, Lucy R. *Overlay - Contemporary Art and the Art of Prehistory*. New York: Pantheon Books, 1983, 81-82.

1982 "Agnes Denes: A Wheatfield in Manhattan." *The Year in Print*, Public Art Fund, 1982.

Rückblick, Internationale Jugendtriennale und Meister der Zeichnung. Nuremberg: Kunsthalle, 1982.

Cohen, Ronny H. "Agnes Denes: Triumph of the Will." *Print Collector's Newsletter* no. 13 (November-December 1982): 159-61.

Hobbs, Robert. "Earthworks: Past and Present." *Art Journal* no. 42 (Summer 1982): 191-94.

American Artists on Art: From 1940 to 1980. Ed. Ellen Johnson. New York: Harper and Row, 1986, 137-41.

1981 "Art of Maps and Vice Versa." *Milwaukee Journal*, January 11, 1981.

Eleventh Assembling: Pilot Proposals. Eds. David Cole - Richard Kostelanetz. Brooklyn: Assembling Press, 1981.

Cowen, Mary S. "Computers

and the Arts." *Christian Science Monitor*, February 24, 1981.

_ Haglund, Elisabet. "Forvandlingar i Konsten." *Kalejdoskop - Norrsken* no. 5-6 (1981).

_ Kuspit, Donald B. "Agnes Denes: The Ironies of Comprehension." *Arts Magazine* no. 56 (1981): 152-53.

_ Phillips, Deborah C. "Definitely not suitable for framing." *ARTnews* no. 80 (December 1981): 63, 65.

_ Rice, Shelley. "Reviews, New York." *Artforum* no. 19 (February 1981): 81.

_ Selz, Peter. *Art in Our Times - A Pictorial History 1890-1980*. New York: Harry N. Abrams, 1981. 531.

_ Zanetti, Paola Serra. "U.S.A., New York, New York." *Meta: Parole & Immagini* no. 3 (February-March 1981).

1980 Belford, M. - J. Herman. *Time and Space Concepts in Art*. New York: Pleiades Gallery, 1981.

_ Bertsson, Asa. "A New Language of Art." *Sydsvenska Dagbladet Snällposten*, February 26, 1980.

_ "The Space of Communication." In: *Skira Annuel. Art Actuel*. Ed. Jean-Luc Daval. Geneva: Editions d'Art Albert Skira, 1980, 96-97, 156.

_ Eliasson, Karl-Erik. "Truth of Hand and Spirit." *Hellsingborgs Dagblad*, February 20, 1980.

_ "Female Da Vinci Shows at Galleriet." *Lundabladet*, February 11, 1980.

_ Johansson, Hans. "Two Poets of Science." *Arbetet-Kulture*, March 2, 1980.

_ *The List*. New York: Independent Curators, 1980.

_ Lucie-Smith, Edward. *Art in the Seventies*. Ithaca: Cornell University Press, 1980, 31, 123.

_ Nittve, Lars. "Nyavärlds-bilder" *Svenska Dagbladet*, February 29, 1980.

_ Nordgren, Sune. "Dizzying World Images." *Dagens Nyheter*, February 28, 1980.

_ Nyman, Ulla. "Hon Visar Det Osedda - Agnes Denes with Human Dust."*Sydsvenska Dagbladet*, February 9, 1980, 20.

_ Perreault, John. "Old Wine, New Bottles, Bad Year." *Soho News*, June 18, 1980.

_ Rice, Shelley. "Reviews, New York." *Artforum* no. 9 (September 1980): 70.

_ Rickey, Carrie. "Art, Systems, Inquiry, Translation." *Village Voice*, 1980.

1979 *Time and Space Concepts in Art*. Eds. Marilyn Belford - Jerry Herman. New York: Pleiades Gallery, 1979, 129, 133-36.

_ Ferrari, Corinna. "La Bellezza della Logica - Agnes Denes a Milano." *Domus* no. 596 (July 1979): 51.

_ Gonzales, Jose Carlos. "Agnes Denes, el Triangulo y la Piramide Perfecta de Pascal." *Artes Visuales* no. 20 (December-February 1979). Chapultepec, Mexico: Museo de Arte Moderno, 1979.

_ "Isometric Systems in Isotropic Space: Map Projections." *Print Collector's Newsletter* vol. 9 (January-February 1979): 203.

_ Parmesani, Loredama. "Antologia." *Segnoll, Notiziario de Arte Contemporanea* vol. 11 (March 1979): 22.

_ "Probability Pyramid." *Print Collector's Newsletter* no. 9 (January-February 1979): 192.

_ Whelan, Richard. "New Editions." *ARTnews* no. 78 (March 1979): 43

1978 *Skira Annuel. Art Actuel*. Ed. Jean-Luc Daval. Geneva: Editions d'Art Albert Skira, 1978, 111, 152.

_ Hafif, Marcia. "New York - Diversificazione Dell Avanguardia." *D'ars, Periodico D'Arte Contemporanea* vol. 17 (1978): 27-28.

_ Lipman, Jean - Richard Marshall. "Introspection III: Aesthetics." *Art About Art*. New York: E. P. Dutton, 1978, 78.

_ Merz, M. "La Biennale di Venezia." *Domus* no. 586 (September 1978): 46.

1977 Hafström, Jan. "Syner I New York." *Paletten* vol. 2 (1978): 2-4.

_ *The List*. New York: Independent Curators, 1977.

_ Marmer, Nancy. "Art" *New West*, January 3, 1977, PSC-17.

_ *Contemporary Artists*. Eds. Colin Naylor - Gensis P. Orridge. London: St. James Press, 1977, 244-46.

1976 "Agnes Denes, 4,000 Years, If the Mind…" *Print Collector's Newsletter* vol. 7 (November-December 1976): 149.

_ Johnson, Ellen H. *Modern Art and the Object*. London: Thames and Hudson, 1976, 43-47.

_ Lippard, Lucy R. *From the Center*. New York: E. P. Dutton, 1976, 2n, 20, 42, 43.

_ Oliva, Achilee Bonito. *Europe/America - The Different Avant-Gardes*. Milan: Deco Press, 1976, 131.

_ Wortz, Melinda. "Agnes Denes …" *Art Week* vol. 7 (1976): 3.

1975 Boetti, Anne Marie. "Altra Creativita" *Data* (July-August 1975): 54-58.

_ Bourdon, David. "Art." *Village Voice*, March 3, 1975, 92-93.

_ Picard, Lil. "Brief Aus New York." *Kunstforum International* vol. 13 (February-April 1975): 219-23.

_ Popper, Frank. *Le Declin de Objet*. Paris: Chene Publishers, 1975.

_ Selz, Peter. "Agnes Denes: The Visual Presentation of Meaning." *Art in America* vol. 63 (March-April 1975): 72-74.

_ Smith, Phillip. "Dynamic Visual Systems in Process: The Works of Agnes Denes." *Arts Magazine* vol. 50 (December 1975): 77-79.

1974 Reise, Barbara. "Agnes Denes: Analytical Works." *Studio International: Journal of Modern Art* no. 188 (1974): 235-38.

_ Tannous, David. "Quantifying the Unquantifiables." *Washington Star News*, December 13, 1974, E-2.

1973 Lippard, Lucy R. *Six Years: The Dematerialization of the Art Object*. New York: Praeger Publishers, 1973, 107-8.

EXHIBITION CATALOGUES

2023 *Coded: Art Enters the Computer Age, 1952-1982*. Los Angeles: LACMA, 2023, 167, 223. 252.

_ *Dear Earth, Art and Hope In A Time of Crisis*. Ed. Rachel Thomas. London: Hayward Gallery, 2023, 64-75.

2022 *Territories of Waste*. Ed. Sandre Beate Reimann. Basel: Tingueley Museum, 2022, 40. September 14, 2022 - January 8, 2022.

2021 *Spatial Affairs*. Eds. Giulia Bini - Lívia Nolasco-Rózsás. Berlin: Hatje Cantz Vertlag, 2021.

_ *Crear Mundos*. Eds. Adriana Rosenberg - Maria Laura Rosa. Buenos Aires: Fundacion Proa, 2021.

_ *Ich Hasse Die Natur!* Klassik Stiftung Weimar, 2021.

2020 *Blaine De St. Croix: How to Move a Landscape*. MASS MoCA, July 2020.

2019 *Agnes Denes: Absolutes and Intermediates*. Eds. Agnes Denes - Emma Enderby. The Shed, November 2019.

_ *Alicja Kwade*, Eds. Kelly Baum - Sheena Wagstaff. The Metropolitan Museum of Art - Yale University Press, New Haven, 2019.

_ *Coordinates: Maps and Art*. Eds. Emily Prince - David Rumsey. Stanford: David Rumsey Map Center - Stanford Libraries, 2019.

2018 *Virginia Overton: Built, Socrates Sculpture Park*. Eds. Jess Wilcox- Johanna Burton. New York: Henry Luce Foundation, 2018.

_ *Tara Donovan: Fieldwork*. Eds. Nora Burnett Abrams - Jenni Sorkin - Giuliana Bruno. Denver: MCA Denver & Rizzoli Electa, 2018.

_ *Cosmogonies, au gré des elements*. Ed. Hélène Guenin. Nizza: MAMAC, 2018.

_ *Reutilizaciones/ Reutilizations*. Ed. Blanca De la Torre. León: Museo de Arte Contemporaneo de Castilla y Leon, 2018.

2017 *Delirious: Art at the Limits of Reason 1950-1980*. Ed. Kelly Baum. New York: The Metropolitan Museum of Art, 2017.

_ *Ecovention Europe: Art to Transform Ecologies, 1957-2017*. Ed. Sue Spaid. Sittard: Museum De Domijnen Hedendaagse Kunst, 2017.

2016 *Drawing Then: Innovation and Influence in American Drawings of the Sixties*. Eds. Kate Ganz et al.

New York: Dominique Levy Gallery, 2016.

2015 *Public Works: Artists' Interventions 1970s - Now.* Eds. Christian L. Frock - Tanya Zimbardo. Oakland, CA: Mills College Art Museum, 2015.

2014 *Art of its Own Making.* Ed. Gretchen L. Wagner. New York: The Pulitzer Foundation, 2014, 7.

2013 *In Cloud Country: Abstracting from Nature.* Ed. Anna Robinson. Leeds: Harewood House Trust, 2013, 44-45.

_ *Expo 1: New York.* New York: MoMA PS1, 2023, 2.

2012 *Agnes Denes: Body Prints, Philosophical Drawings, and Map Projections: 1969-1978,* Santa Monica Museum of Art, 2012.

_ Cheetham, Mark. "Tense Memory: time, space & the projections in between." In *Conspiracies of Illusion: Projections of Time & Space.* Hamilton, ON, Canada: McMaster Museum of Art, 2012, 9-11.

_ *Civic Action: A Vision for Long Island City.* Elissa Goldstone - Amy Hau. Astoria: The Isamu Noguchi Foundation and Garden Museum and Socrates Sculpture Park, 2012, 100-1.

_ *Light Years: Conceptual Art and the Photograph, 1964-1977.* Ed. Matthew S. Witkovsky. Chicago: Art Institute of Chicago, December 13, 2011. - March 11, 2012.

_ *Green Acres: Artists Farming Fields, Greenhouses and Abandoned Lots.* Ed. Sue Spaid. Cincinnati, OH: Contemporary Arts Center, 2012.

_ *Ends of the Earth: Land Art to 1974.* Eds. Philipp Kaiser - Miwon Kwon. Los Angeles: The Museum of Contemporary Art, 2012.

_ *Hunger City.* Eds. Anne Kersten - Stephane Bauer. Berlin: Kunstraum Kreuzberg / Bethanien, 2012.

2011 Pascale, Mark. *Contemporary Drawings from the Irving Stenn Jr. Collection.* Ed. Mark Pascale. Chicago: Art Institute of Chicago, 2011.

2010 *Elles @ Centrepompidou. Artistes Femmes dans la Collection du Musee National d'Art Moderne.* Paris: Centre de Creation Industrielle, 2010.

_ *Jardins Ecologiques: Ecology, Source of Creation.* Ed. Sophie Barbaux. Paris: ICI Consultants, 2010.

_ *Landscape as an Idea: Projects and Projections 1960-1980.* Ed. Berta Sichel. Donostia-San Sebatian: Koldo Mitxelena Kulturunea, 2008.

_ *Artpark: 1974-1984.* Buffalo, New York: University at Buffalo Art Gallery, 2008.

2007 *Art in Action: Nature, Creativity and Our Collective Future.* Ed. Randy Jane Rosenberg, San Rafael: Natural World Museum, 2007, 154, 175.

_ *Weather Report: Art and Climate Change.* Ed. Lucy R. Lippard. Boulder: Boulder Museum of Contemporary Art, 2007, 42-43, 123.

_ Saltz, Jerry. "The Biggest Picture." *Village Voice,* February 1, 2007.

2006 *Fourth International Artists' Book Exhibition.* Székesfehérvár: St Stephen's Museum, 2006.

2005 *Drawing from the Modern, 1945-1975.* New York: The Museum of Modern Art, 182, 198.

2004 *Contemporary Art and the Mathematical Instinct.* Ed. Peter Spooner. Duluth: Tweed Museum of Art, University of Minnesota, 2004, 59, 82.

2003 *Agnes Denes: Projects For Public Places - A Retrospective.* Lewisburg: Samek Gallery, Bucknell University, 2003.

_ *Biennale de Buenos Aires.* Buenos Aires: Museo Nacional de Bellas Artes, 2003, 2.

_ *Siting Jefferson: Contemporary Artists Interpret Thomas Jefferson's Legacy.* Ed. Jill Hartz. Charlottesville-London: University of Virginia Press, University of Virginia Art Museum, 2003, 22-23.

2002 *Ecovention: Current Art to Transform Ecologies.* Ed. Sue Spaid. Cincinnati, Ohio: Contemporary Arts Center, 2002, 11, 12, 15, 120-24, 139.

2001 *Experience/Dissolution.* Goteborg: Goteborgs Internationella Konsbiennal, 2001, 8, 38-41.

_ *Kinds of Drawing.* Ed. Trevor Richardson. Amherst, Mass.: Herter Art Gallery, University of Mass. 2001, 8, 25.

_ *Markers - Art & Poetry in Venice: Banners by visual artists and poets.* (An Outdoor Banner Event of Artists and Poets for the Venice Biennale) The International Artist's Museum, Tel-Aviv, 2001.

_ *Waterproof.* Kunstenaars Verkennen de Toekoms van de Hollandse Waterlinie. Acquoy: Fort Asperen Foundation, 2001, 27-30.

2000 *Art & Mathematics 2000.* New York: The Cooper Union for the Advancement of Science & Art, Albert Nerken School of Engineering, 2000.

_ *Hindsight/Fore-site: Art for the New Millennium.* Ed. Lyn Bolen Rushton. Bayly Art Museum, University of Virginia, 2000.

_ "Essay Guy Brett: Contingency and Infinity." In *Force fields - Phases of the Kinetic.* Ed. Suzanne Cotter. Barcelona: MACBA, Museu d'Art Contemporani de Barcelona, 2000, 61, 63, 68, 140-41, 129, 133, 219, 221, 304-6. (Book of Dust)

1999 *Afterimage: Drawing Through Process.* Ed. Cornelia H. Butler. Cambridge-London: The Museum of Contemporary Art - MIT Press, 1999, 16, 23, 64, 65, 66, 107, 109, 139, 148.

_ *Book As Art XI.* Washington D.C.: National Museum of Women in the Arts, Library and Research Center, 1999, 1, 2, 9.

1998 *American Academy in Rome, Annual Exhibition.* Rome, 1998.

_ *Into Focus/Art on Science.* Schenectady: Mendeville Gallery, Nott Memorial, Union College, 1998.

_ *Light on the New Millennium - Wind From Extreme Orient.* Metroplitan Art Museum, Pusan International Art Festival - PICAF, Exhibition of Contemporary Art and Sculpture Symposium, Pusan, 1998, 101, 161.

_ *Women Artists in the Vogel Collection.* Gainesville: Brenau University, 1998, 8-9, 28, 52, 58.

_ *Stelle Cadenti.* Bassano in Teverina, L'Associazione Culturale e Il Comunie Di Bassane in Teverina, 1998, 5.

_ *The Serial Attiude.* Columbus: Wexner Center for the Arts, Ohio University, 1998, 5, 9.

1997 *Artists-Messengers of Peace.* Tel-Aviv: Art for Peace Collection, Eretz Israel Museum, 1997.

_ *Magie der Zahl in der Kunst des 20. Jahrhunderts.* Stuttgart: Staatsgalerie, 1997, 201-2, 272, 354.

_ *The Private Eye in Public Art.* Charlotte: La Salle Partners, National Plaza, 1997.

1996 *The Visionary Art of Agnes Denes.* Intr. Dan Mills. Potsdam, N.Y.: Roland Gibson Gallery, New York University, 1996.

_ *Artpartnership.* Intr. Dan Mills. Potsdam, N.Y.: Roland Gibson Gallery, New York, 1996.

_ *Women Artist Series: 25 Years, 1971-1996.* New Brunswick: Rutgers University, 1996, 32. („Flying Pyramid for the Twenty-Second Century - Environmental Sculpture for the Miami Airport")

1995 *In Light of Our Reflection: Visions of Art and Science.* Medford, Mass.: Tufts University Art Gallery, 1995.

1994 *Ipotesi sulla Scultura.* Ed. Virginia Bardel. Rome: M.E.R.C.I. 1994.

1993 *Creative Solutions to Ecological Issues.* New York and Hempstead, N.Y.: Council for Creative Projects and Hofstra University, 1993.

_ *Natures - Visions de l'Art Contemporaine.* EPAD - Ministère de la Culture et de la Francophonie - Délégation aux Arts Plastiques. Paris: La Defénse (FIACRE) 1993, 26, 104., 105, 299.

_ *Le Onde: Scultrici a Venezia.* Ed. Virginia Baradel. Venice: Editrica Eidos, 1993 ("The Human Argument, 1969-71")

1992 *Allocations - Art for a Natural and Artificial*

Environment. Hague: Floriade Den Haag, Zoetermeer, 1992, 190, 191, 193.

_ *Americas*. Expo '92, Junta de Andalucia, Sevilla, 1992, 38, 91, 96.

_ *Completing the Circle: Artists' Books on the Environment*. Minnesota Center for Book Arts, Minnesota, 1992, 4-5.

_ *Fragile Ecologies*. With an essay by Barbara C. Matilsky. Queens Museum, New York, 1992, 50-52, 58.

_ *Strata*. Museum of Contemporary Art, Helsinki, and The Art Museum of Tampere, 1990, 25, 96-107, 169-70, 78-83.

1991 *Atlas: Curatorial Laboratory Project #7*. Intr. Ihor Holubizky. Ontario: Art Gallery of Hamilton, 1991.

_ *Contemporary Drawing: Existence, Passage and the Dream*. Rose Art Museum, Brandeis University, Waltham, Mass. 1991, 4-7, 17-19, 41.

_ *Visions/Revisions*. Denver: Denver Art Museum, 1991.

1990 *Agnes Denes - Concept into Form, Works 1970-1990*. Chicago: Art Club of Chicago, 1990.

_ *Agnes Denes, El Concepto Hecho Forma, Obras, 1970-1990*. Madrid: Anselmo Alvarez Galerie de Arte, 1990.

_ *Artists for Amnesty*. New York: Amnesty International USA, 1990.

1989 *Lines of Vision: Drawings by Contemporary Women*. New York: Hudson Hills Press, 1989, 44, 157.

_ *Making Their Mark - Women Artists Move Into the Mainstream, 1970-1985*. New York: Abbeville Press, 1989, 19, 62, 101, 169, 170-73, 175, 214, 235-36, 244, 286.

_ *25 Jahre Berliner Kunstlerprogramm*. West Berlin: DAAD, 1989, 137, 160.

1988 *A Debate on Abstraction*. New York: Bertha and Karl Leubsdorf Art Gallery, Hunter College, 1988.

_ *Interaction: Science and Art*. Princeton: The Squibb Gallery, 1988.

1987 *Graphica Atlantica*. Reykjavík: Kjarvalsstadir, 1988.

_ *The International Art Show for the End of World Hunger*. New York: Artists to End Hunger and Worldview International Foundation, 1987, 84-87, 103. („Wheatfield - A Confrontation")

1986 *Archetypes: Eastern Cultures - Western Art of the Twentieth Century*. Belgrade: Ethno-graphic Museum, 1986, 138-39. ("4000 Years - If the Mind . . ." and "Evolution I")

_ *Die Wirklichkeit der Bilder - Selected Works from the Collection*. Nuremberg: Kunsthalle, 1986, 10, 19.

_ *V Bienal Americana de Artes Graficas*. Cali, Colombia: Museo de Arte Moderno la Tertulia, 1986.

_ *Works on Paper*. Rutgers National 85/86. Camden, N.J.: Stedman Gallery, Rutgers University, 1986.

1985 *Art, Design and the Modern Corporation (The Collection of the Container Corporation of America, a Gift to the National Museum of American Art)*. Washington, D.C.: National Museum of American Art, Smithsonian Institution, 1985, 72, 87-88.

_ *Artists and Architects - Challenges in Collaboration*. Cleveland: Cleveland Center for Contemporary Arts, 1985, 11, 34.

_ *The Drawing Center Show*. Bridgehamton: Elaine Benson Gallery, 1985.

_ *KIS '85, Kunsan International Show*. Chonbuk, Korea: Institute of Contemporary Art, Kunsan National University, 1985, 85.

_ *Large Drawings*. New York: Independent Curators, 1985.

1984 *Exception 2*. New York: Pratt Manhattan Center Gallery, 1984.

_ *Land Marks*. Annandale-on-Hudson, New York: Edith C. Blum Art Institute, Milton & Sally Avery Center for the Arts, Bard College Center, 1984.

1983 *The Examples of Mental Spiritual Spaces/ Works*. Belgrade: Galeria Studentskog, Kulturnog Centar, 1983.

_ *New York i Linköping*. Essay by Bo Nilsson. Linköping: Östergotlands Länsmuseum,

1983.
_ *Petit Format de Papier*.
Couvin: Cul-des-Sarts,
Ministère de la Communauté
Française, 1983.
_ *Printed by Women - A
National Exhibition of
Photographs and Prints*.
Philadelphia: The Port of
History Museum at Penn's
Landing, 1983.
_ *World Print Four -
International Survey*.
San Francisco: World
Print Council, Fort Mason
Center, 1983, 36.
1982 *Arte e Scienza per
il Disegno del Mondo*.
Torino: Citta di Torino
Assessoratoper la Cultura,
1982.
_ *The Destroyed Print*. New
York: Pratt Manhattan
Center Gallery, 1982.
_ *58th Annual International
Print Competition*.
Philadelphia: Print Club,
1982, 3.
_ *Meister der Zeichnung,
Zeichnung Heute 2*.
Nuremberg: Internationale
Jugendtriennale,
Kunsthalle, 1982, 11-44.
_ *157th Annual Exhibition*.
New York: National Academy
of Design, 1982.
_ *Prints America*.
Philadelphia: Abington Art
Center, 1982.
_ *Projections*. Chicago: West
Hubbard Gallery, 1982.
1981 *Lis '81, Lisbon
International Exhibition
of Drawings* Lisbon:
Galerie Nacional de Arte
Moderna, 1981, 50-51. Note:
Museum burned down before
exhibition opened.

_ *Mapped Art*, *Charts,
Routes, Regions*. Essay
by Peter Frank. Boulder:
University of Colorado Art
Galleries, 1981.
_ *Messages: Words and
Images*. Reading: Freedman
Gallery, Albright College,
1981.
_ *New Dimensions in Drawing
1950-1980*. Ridgefield,:
Aldrich Museum of
Contemporary Art, 1981.
_ *Petit Format de Papier*.
Couvin: Cul-des-Sarts,
Ministère de la Communauté
Française, 1981.
_ *Schemes: A Decade of
Installation Drawings*.
Essay by Shelley Rice. New
York: Elise Meyer, 1981.
_ *Transformations - Women in
Art '70-'80*. New York: Art
Expo, 1981.
_ *Women Artists (Ten Years
of Women Artists at
Douglass College 1971-
1981)*. New Brunswick:
Rutgers University, 1981.
_ "Words as Images."
White Walls, Chicago:
Renaissance Society,
University of Chicago,
1981, 38-45. ("Pascal's
Perfect Probability
Pyramid & the People
Paradox")
1980 *Agnes Denes 1968-1980*.
Cambridge: Hayden Gallery,
M.I.T. 1980.
_ *All in Line - An Exhibition
of Linear Drawing*.
Syracuse, N.Y: Joe and
Emily Lowe Art Gallery,
Syracuse University, 1980.
_ *American Drawing
in Black and White:
1970-1980*. Brooklyn:

Brooklyn Museum, 1980.
_ *American Woman Artists*.
Sao Paulo, Brazil: Museo
de Arte Contemporaneo de
São Paulo, 1980.
_ *Cartes et figures de
la terre*. Paris: Musée
National d'Art Moderne,
Centre Georges Pompidou,
1980.
_ *Drawings: The
Pluralist Decade*.
Philadelphia: Institute
of ContemporaryArt,
University of Pennsylvania,
1980, 80, 89.
_ *56th Annual Print
Competition*. Philadelphia:
Print Club, 1980.
_ *Investigations: Probe,
Structure, Analysis*. New
York: New Museum, 1980,
20-24. (Essay by L. Gumbert
and A. Schwartzman; text
and ills. by A. Denes)
_ *Paesaggio Di Paesaggi*.
Milan: Amministrazione
Communale de Santa Maria
C.V., 1980.
_ *Pyramidal Influences in
Art*. Dayton, Ohio: Fine
Arts Gallery, Wright State
University, 1980.
_ *Reasoned Space*. Tucson:
Center for Creative
Photography, University
of Arizona, 1980, 12-21.
_ *The Women Artist Series
- Tenth Anniversary
Retrospective*. New
Brunswick, N.J.: Douglass
College, Rutgers
University, 1980.
1979 *Biennial of Graphic Art*.
Ljubljana, Yugoslavia:
Moderna Galerija. *Rice/
Tree/Burial Project -
Time Capsule 1979-1979*.

Lewiston, N.Y.: Artpark, 1979.

1978 *Agnes Denes - Work 1968-78*. Birmingham: Ikon Gallery, 1978 (essay by Roy Slade; text and illus. by A. Denes).

_ *Agnes Denes - Sculptures of the Mind - Philosophical Drawings*. West Berlin: Amerika Haus, U.S. Cultural Center, 1978 (essay by Thomas Deecke).

_ *Artists Books*. New York: Franklin Furnace, 1978.

_ *La Biennale Di Venezia: From Nature to Art, from Art to Nature, Nature of Art*. Vol. 3. Ed. J. C. Ammann - A. B. Oliva. Venice: International Commission for the Historic-Critical Exhibition, 1978.

_ *La Biennale Di Venezia: Materializzazione Del Linguaggio*. Cur. M. Bentivoglio. Venice, 1978.

_ *Footprint '78*. Seattle: Northwest International Small Format Print Competition and Exhibition, 1978.

_ *Grids*. New York: Pace Gallery, 1978 (essay by Rosalind Krauss).

_ *Point*. Philadelphia: Philadelphia College of Art, 1978.

1977 "Rice/Tree/Burial Project." *Artpark 1977*. Lewiston: Artpark, Program in Visual Arts, 1977.

_ *Computer Genesis: A Vision of the 70's*. Syracuse: Joe and Emily Lowe Art Gallery, Syracuse University, 1977.

_ *Dokumenta 6 - Book Three. Handzeichnungen, Von Der Landschaft zu Kosmischen Systemen*. Kassel, 1977.

_ *Numerals 1924-1977*. New Haven, Yale University Art Gallery, Yale University, 1977.

_ *Paper*. Philadelphia: Philadelphia College of Art, 1977.

_ *Sculptures of the Mind - Agnes Denes*. Paris: Centre Culturel Americain, 1977.

_ *Sculptures of the Mind (Philosophical Drawings)*. Intr. T. Deecke. West Berlin: Berliner Kunstlerprogram das DAAD und das Amerika Haus, 1977.

1976 *Agnes Denes: Paradox and Essence*. New York: Franklin Furnace Archive, 1976.

_ *Art in Landscape*. New York: Independent Curators, 1976.

_ *Important Post-War and Contemporary Art*. New York: Leo Castelli, Sonnabend Galleries, and Sotheby Parke Bernet, 1976.

_ *Language and Structure in North America*. Toronto: Queen Street Magazine, Kensington Arts Association, 1976.

_ *New York, Soho Contact '76*. Georgetown: Georgetown College Gallery, 1976.

_ *Paper: An Invitational Exhibition*. Fredonia: Michael C. Rockefeller Arts Center Gallery, State University College at Fredonia, 1976.

_ *The 1976 Biennale of Sydney*. Sydney: Arts Gallery of New South Wales, 1976.

_ *Thirty Years of American Printmaking and the 20th National Print Exhibition*. Brooklyn: Brooklyn Museum, 1976.

_ *Unique Works*. New York: Franklin Furnace, 1976 (A. Denes and A. Sondhim).

_ *Women Artists Series Year Five*. Introd. Lucy Lippard. New Brunswick: Douglass College, Rutgers University, 1976.

1975 *National Drawing Exhibition '75*. New Brunswick, N.J.: Camden College of Arts and Sciences, Rutgers University, 1975.

_ *U.S.A. Zeichnungen 3*. Leverkusen: Schloss Morsbroich, Stadtisches Museum, 1975.

_ *The Year of the Woman*. New York: Bronx Museum of the Arts, 1975.

1974 *Agnes Denes: Perspectives*. Washington: Corcoran Gallery of Art, 1974 (essays by L. Alloway, R. Slade, and S. Sollins; text and illus. by A. Denes).

_ *Kunst Bleibt Kunst - Projekt '74*. Cologne: Kunsthalle, 1974.

_ *Painting and Sculpture Today*. Indianapolis-Cincinnati: Contemporary Art Society of the Indianapolis Museum of Art and The Contemporary Art Museum and Taft Museum, 1974.

_ *Die Wiedergefundene Zeit - Projekt '74*. Cologne: Kunsthalle, 1974.

_ *Word Works*. Walnut: Mount San Antonio College, 1974.

1973 *American Drawings 1963-73*. New York: Whitney Museum of American Art, 1973.

_ *Catalogue of the Collection*. New York: Whitney Museum of American Art, 1973.

_ *18th National Print Exhibition*. Brooklyn: Brooklyn Museum, 1973.

_ *Women Choose Women*. New York: New York Cultural Center, 1973.

1971 *Art Systems*. Buenos Aires: Museum of Modern Art, 1972.

_ *Oversize Prints*. Introd. Elke Solomon. New York: Whitney Museum of American Art, 1971.

1970 *Software*. New York: Smithsonian Institution and the Jewish Museum, 1971.

_ *Strength Analysis*. New York: Franklin Furnace, 1971.

PUBLIC ART PUBLICATIONS

1997 "Fifteen Years Ago: Agnes Denes *Wheatfield*." *In Process, Public Art Fund Newsletter* (Spring 1997).

1988 "Flying Pyramids for the Twenty-Second Century, Tamiami Airport, 1986-88." *Metro-Dade Art in Public Places*. Miami: Metro-Dade Center (1988).

1987 "Wheatfield - A Confrontation." *Public Art Fund, Inc., Annual Report - Anniversary Edition* (1987): 38.

1986 "Wheatfield - A Confrontation." *Art in the Environment*. Boca Raton Museum, 1986, 131.

PUBLICATIONS BY THE ARTIST

2011 Agnes Denes. "On Spirituality." *Public Art Review* no. 44 (Spring-Summer 2011): 18, 24, 25.

_ "Interview Dorka Keehn - Agnes Denes restoring the land through art." In *Eco-Amazons: 20 Women Who Are Transforming the World*. Brooklyn: Powerhouse Books, 2011, 58-63.

2009 "Manifesto 1969." In *Radical Nature - Art & Architecture for a Changing Planet 1969-2009*. Exh. cat. London: Barbican Art Gallery, Koenig Books, 2009, 11, 19, 88-94, 238.

2008 *Agnes Denes: Art for the Third Millennium - Creating a New World View*. Exh. cat. Budapest: Ludwig Museum of Contemporary Art, 2008.

_ *The Human Argument - The Writings of Agnes Denes*. Edited with an introduction by Klaus Ottmann. Putnam: Spring Publications, 2008.

2007 "Pyramids of Conscience" 2005 at Ballroom. Marfa, TX. *NY ARTS Magazine* (January-February, 2005).

_ "Manifesto, Mathematics in My Work and Other Essays." *Hyperion: On the Future of Aesthetics* vol. 2, no. 1 (February 2007).

2006 "Notes on a Visual Philosophy." *Hyperion: On the Future of Aesthetics* vol. 1, no. 4 (December 2006).

_ Tim Smit. "Imagination Holds the Key." *Resurgence* no. 238 (September-October 2006): 23.

2005 "Living Murals in the Land - Crossing Boundaries of Time and Space." *Public Art Review* vol. 17, no. 33 (Fall-Winter 2005): 42-47.

_ *Poetry Walk: Reflections - Pools of Thought*. Charlottesville: University of Virginia Art Museum, 2005.

_ "Pyramids of Conscience (Agnes Denes describes her works)." *N Y Arts* vol. 10, nos. 11-12 (2005): 86.

2004 "What Are You Reading? - Artists that make books reveal their current reading interests." *Art on Paper* vol. 8, no. 6 (July-August 2004): 54.

2003 "Healthy Paradoxes." *Land Views - Online Journal of Landscape*, Art and Design (Summer 2003).

_ *Poetry Walk: Reflections - Pools of Thought*, Charlottesville: University of Virginia Art Museum, 2003.

_ "Poetry Walk: Reflections - Pools of Thought." In *Siting Jefferson*. Ed. J. Hartz. Charlottesville and London: University of Virginia Press, 2003, 22-23.

2002 "Tree Mountain - A Living Time Capsule." *Wegway* no. 4 (Fall 2002): 8-11.

1996 "Artistic Vision and

Molecular Genetics." *Art Journal* vol. 55 (Spring 1996): 34-35.

_ "Dialectic Triangulation: A Visual Philosophy and The Kingdom Series - X-ray of Calla Lillies." *Report on Activities*, The John D. and Catherine T. MacArthur Foundation, 1996.

_ "Rice/Tree/Burial (1968-79) and Wheatfield - a Confrontation (1982)." In *Theories and Documents of Contemporary Art: a Sourcebook of Artists' Writings*. Eds. Kristine Stiles - Peter Selz. Berkeley and Los Angeles: University of California Press, 1996, 504, 540-45.

1995 "Pascal's Perfect Probability Pyramid & the People Paradox - The Predicament (1980); Teardrop - Monument To Being Earthbound (1984); Snail People - The Vortex (1989)." *Annual Report: Book Two*. Dun & Bradstreet Corporation, 1995, 10-13.

1993 "Notes on Eco-Logic: Environmental Art Work, Visual Philosophy and Global Perspective." *Leonardo*, Art & Social Consciousness, vol. 26, no. 5 (1993): 367-66, 387-95, 422.

1992 "Introduction: Notes on a Visual Philosophy." In *Completing the Circle: Artists' Books on the Environment*. Ed. Betty Bright. Minneapolis: Minnesota Center for Book Arts, 1992, 4-5.

_ "The Dream." *Art and the Public Sphere* (anthology of *Critical Inquiry* writings). Ed. T. Mitchell. Chicago: University of Chicago Press, 1992, 177-95.

_ "Wheatfield/Tree Mountain." *Art Journal*, Art and Ecology-Special Issue (Summer 1992): 22-23.

1990 "The Dream - Art and the Public Sphere." *Critical Inquiry*, intr. J. Neff, vol. 16 (Summer 1990): 919-39.

1989 *Book of Dust - The Beginning and the End of Time, and Thereafter*. Rochester: Visual Studies Workshop, 1989.

1986 *Mental Space - 3, Community for the Research of Space*. Belgrade: Ethnographic Museum, 1986.

_ "Pascal's Probability Pyramid and the People's Paradox." *1986: Candidate Nominations for Associate Membership*. General Meeting of Academicians and Associations, 1986, 38.

_ "Notes on Visual Philosophy." *Symmetry - Unifying Human Understanding* and in *Computers and Mathematics with Applications*. Ed. I. Hargittai. London: Pergamon Press, 1986.

1983 Lowman, Jr., Paul D. "Faulting Continental Drift." *The Sciences* (July-August 1983): 34, 39.

_ R. Rabinovich. Exh. cat. New York: Center for Inter-American Relations/ Americas Society.

_ "Syzygy." *The Examples of Mental and Spiritual Spaces/Works*. Belgrade: Galeria Studentskog, Kulturnog Centar, 1983.

_ "Pascal's Perfect Probability Pyramid & The People's Paradox - The Predicament." *The Sciences* (November-December 1983): 57.

_ "Wheatfield - A Confrontation." *Reaktion*. Alsbach: Verlaggalerie, 1983.

1982 "Evolution and the Creative Mind." Washington, D.C.: Smithsonian Institution, 1982. (Excerpt from a lecture)

_ *American Artists on Art 1940-1980*. Ed. Ellen Johnson. New York: Harper and Row, 1982.

_ "Hamlet Fragmented." *Shantih* 4 (Winter-Spring 1982): 118-25.

_ "Time/Fuse/Attitudes (Bjerred, Sweden)." *FLUE* 2, vol. 2 (1982).

1981 "Animale, Rationale, Mortale." *Petit Format de Papier, Exposition Internationale*. Couvin: Cul-des-Sarts, 1981.

_ "Pascal's Perfect Probability Pyramid & the People's Paradox." In *White Walls*. Exh. cat. "Words as Images." Chicago: The Renaissance Society - University of Chicago, 1981, 38-45.

_ "Rice/Tree/Burial Project." *ARTextreme* (Fall-Winter 1981-1982).

1980 "The Debate, 1 Million B.C. - 1 Million A.D." *A Critical Assembling*. Ed. Richard Kostelanetz.

Brooklyn: Assembling Press, 1980.

_ "Map Projections - Rice/ Tree/Burial Project." *Skira Annuel. Art Actuel.* Geneva: Editions d'Art Albert Skira, 1980, 96-97, 156.

_ "Organic Notebooks." *Konstnarsbocker - Artists' Books - Kalejdoskop.* Ahus: Kalejdoskop, 1980. 25.

1979 *Isometric Systems in Isotropic Space: Map Projections.* Rochester: Visual Studies Workshop, 1979.

_ "Pyramid Series." *Discovery of the Sources. Skira Annuel. Art Actuel.* Geneva: Editions d'Art Albert Skira, 1980, 73.

1978 "Rice/Tree/Burial Project." *White Walls.* Chicago, 1978. 22-28.

_ "Study of Distortions - The Snail." *The Image of Nature. Skira Annuel. Art Actuel.* Geneva: Editions d'Art Albert Skira, 1978.

1976 *Agnes Denes: Sculptures of the Mind.* Akron, Ohio: University of Akron Press, 1976.

_ "Artists Books." *Art-Rite* vol. 14 (Winter 1976): 7.

_ "Books in Review." *Print Collector's Newsletter* no. 6 (January-February): 171-72.

_ "Dialectic Triangulation: A Visual Philosophy, Study of Distortions: Positions of Meaning, 4,000 Years." *Sun and Moon: A Quarterly of Literature and Art* vol. 1 (Winter 1976): 16-19, 20-26, 27-30.

_ *Paradox and Essence.* Rome:

Tau/ma Press, 1976.

1975 "Anti-Object Art." *Tri-Quarterly* vol. 32 (Winter 1976).

_ "Human Dust Series." *Visual Dialog* no. 1 (1975): 6-7.

1974 "Dialectic Triangulation, Study of Distortions, Studies of Time, Studies of Truth, Study of Human Dust, The Human Argument, Analytical Works." *Studio International* no. 188 (December 1974): 235-38.

1973 "Psychographic." *Duration Piece #8*, Doug Huebler. New York: Castelli and Sperone Gallery, 1973, 40.

BOOKS, EXHIBITION CATALOGUES, AND PERIODICAL COVERS

2019 *Artforum* (October 2019). Cover Image: "The Living Pyramid"

2009 *The Environment and World History.* Eds. Edmund III. Berke - Kenneth Pomeranz. Berkeley: University of California Press, 2009. (Cover Image: Agnes Denes: *Wheatfield - A Confrontation: Battery Park landfill, Downtown Manhattan with New York Financial Center,* 1982.)

2006 *American Quarterly* vol, 58, no. 2 (June 2006). (Cover Image: "Wheatfield - A Confrontation" by Agnes Denes, two-acre wheat field planted and harvested by the artist in Manhattan's financial district, summer 1982. Commissioned by Public

Art Fund, 1982. Art and photography copyright Agnes Denes, 1982.)

1996 Wirth-Nesher, Hana. *City Codes.* Cambridge: Cambridge University Press, 1996. "Wheatfield - A Confrontation."

1993 *Leonardo*, vol. 26 (1993). Cover image: "Isometric Systems in Isotropic Space--Map Projections: The Snail (helical toroid) and the Water Planet"

1992 *Fragile Ecologies.* New York: Queens Museum and Rizzoli International, 1992. ("Wheatfield-- A Confrontation, Battery Park City, 1982")

1990 *Critical Inquiry* vol. 16 (Summer 1990).

_ Reynolds, Frank E. *Beyond the Classics.* Atlanta: Scholars Press, 1990.

1982 Regan, Tom. *All That Dwells Therein.* Berkeley and Los Angeles: University of California Press, 1982.

1981 *ARTextreme* no. 1 (Fall-Winter 1981-1982).

1980 *Cartes et figures de la terre.* Paris: Musée National d'Art Moderne, Centre Georges Pompidou, 1890.

1979 "Natural Science and Mathematics." *The Oberlin College Bulletin* no. 78 (July 1979).

1978 *Glassworks*, 1-3. Metuchen: Scarecrow Press, 1978, 41.

1977 Hafström, Jan. "Syner i New York." *Paletten* 2 (1977).

Systems of Logic / Logic of Systems: The Art and Mind of Agnes Denes
Museum of Fine Arts - Hungarian National Gallery, Budapest
12 December 2024 - 1 June 2025
The exhibition was organised by the Museum of Fine Arts, Budapest in association with acb Gallery, Budapest.

Editor: Mónika Kumin
Authors: Agnes Denes, Róna Kopeczky, Mónika Kumin
Copy editors: Judit Borus, Noémi Böröczki, Zsolt Miklósvölgyi
Translation: Rachel Hideg
Graphic design: Zoltán Szmolka
Prepress: Colorcom Media
Reproduction rights: Franciska Tóth
Editorial coordination: Anikó Petri
Printing: Elektroproduct Nyomdaipari Kft.

On the cover: Agnes Denes, *Snail People - The Vortex*, 1989 © Agnes Denes, Courtesy Leslie Tonkonow Artworks + Projects

© Authors: Agnes Denes, Róna Kopeczky, Mónika Kumin
© Image and reproduction rights: Agnes Denes, Courtesy Leslie Tonkonow Artworks + Projects
© Photo rights: Dávid Tóth
Cat. no. 15, page 63 © Ludwig Museum - Museum of Contemporary Art, photo: József Rosta

The publisher made the most effort to identify the owners of the illustrations in the catalogue; missing data will be added in accordance with the information provided.

ISBN 978-615-6595-55-3

Published by: László BAÁN, General Director
© Museum of Fine Arts - Hungarian National Gallery, Budapest, 2024

Co-operating partner:

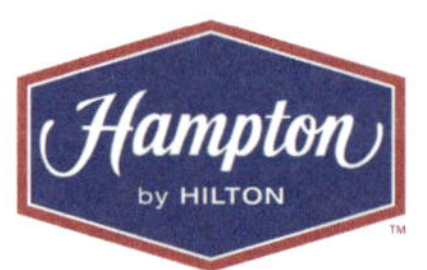

Maintainer of the institution:

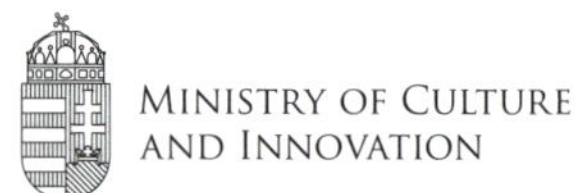

EXHIBITION

Curator: Mónika Kumin
Exhibition consultant:
    Róna Kopeczky
Exhibition organiser:
    Anikó Petri
Registrar: Zsófia Farkas
Exhibition design:
    Lóránt Váradi
Exhibition graphic design:
    Zsuzsanna Brotesser
Technical tasks:
    Beáta Antal-Bali, Zoltán
    Bóka, András Czakó, András
    Ellenbacher, Péter Jakab,
    Csaba Kálmán, Irén Margit
    Kepka, László Ferenc
    Langer, Zulejka László,
    István Litkei, Dénes Rómeo
    Miklós, Szabolcs Molnár,
    Sándor Nagypál, Norbert
    Niederkirchner, István
    Pázmány, Mihály Pozsár,
    Réka Rózsahegyi, Attila
    Sándor, Zoltán Sütő, Dániel
    Szűcsi, Gergő Szilágyi,
    Lajos Tor, Károly Udrea,
    Zoltán Vedres, Martin
    Zoltán Weinberger
Friends of the Museum:
    Krisztina Rébék-Schay,
    Marcell Sztupkai
Security: the Security
    Department of the Museum
    of Fine Arts
Financial tasks: Enikő Cser,
    Szilvia Zalka
Legal tasks: Henriett
    Galambos, Adrienn Gippert,
    Katalin Lapath, János
    Marosi, Ágnes Renfer
Exhibition texts:
    Mónika Kumin
English translation:
    Rachel Hideg
Copy editors: Judit Borus,
    Noémi Böröczki

Communication and marketing:
    Tibor Barcsik, Barbara
    Bergendy, Laura Kund,
    Zsófi László, Zoltán Lévay,
    Boróka Pénzes, Dávid Szabó,
    Anna Vidák-Sarkantyu
Contributors: Anett Mészáros-
    Kecskeméti, Gábor Szolláth,
    Csaba Varga
Communication design:
    Zsuzsanna Brotesser
Visitor services: Anna
    Daróczi, Ágota Nagy,
    Bianka Ney, Ágnes Ruzsits,
    Blanka Csilla Török,
    Erika Zimányi
Museum education: Judit Cser,
    Edina Deme, Zsófia Goda,
    Krisztina Mácsay, Eszter
    Marina, Ágnes Mertus,
    Judit Polner, Viola Varga,
    Szilvia Záray
Art handlers: Zsolt Berta,
    Marcell Budai, Attila
    Csutak, Tamás Kecskés,
    József Mészáros, Tamás
    Pásztor, Gergő Roszoly,
    Csaba Sobotka, Ferenc
    Sóti, Ferenc Tóth
Reproduction rights:
    Franciska Tóth
Corporate partnership:
    Balázs Kégli
The exhibition was organised
    by the Museum of Fine
    Arts, Budapest in
    association with acb
    Gallery, Budapest.
We would like to thank for
    their contribution and
    support: Agnes Denes, Róna
    Kopeczky, Leslie Tonkonow.
We would like to thank the
    technical team of acb
    Gallery for their support:
    Máté Dobokay, Ádám
    Hancsicsák, Ákos Németh,
    Áron Szeghő

Lending institutions:
The Museum of Fine Arts
    Budapest would like
    to thank the following
    institutions and collectors
    who loaned their artworks
    to the exhibition:
acb Gallery, Budapest
AELA Collection
CULTURUNNERS with Vivobarefoot
    and Community Jameel
DAAD Berliner
    Künstlerprogramm
Erika Kiss and Zsolt Lakatos
Leslie Tonkonow Artworks +
    Projects, New York
Ludwig Museum - Museum of
    Contemporary Art, Budapest
Socrates Sculpture Park,
    New York
and to those private
    collectors who wished
    to remain anonymous.